BUSINESS AND GENERAL REFERENCE BOOK SERIES FROM IDG

Basketball For Dummies

Cheat Sheet

Finding Your Way Around the Court

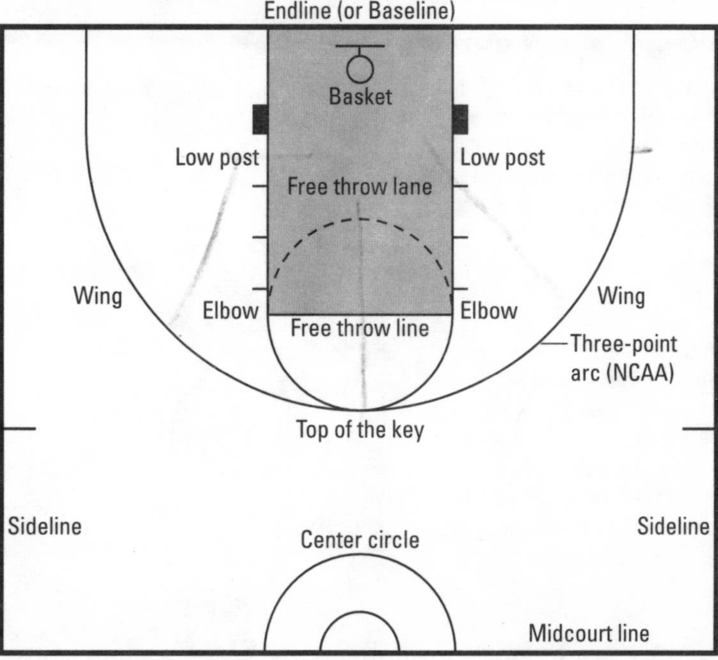

How to Sound Like a Pro On or Off the Court

boards: Rebounds.

brick or **clank:** An especially ugly, misfired shot that clanks hard off the rim.

bucket: A good multipurpose word that can mean the basket itself or a made basket; also can be used as an adjective for an especially good shooter, as in "That guy is bucket."

bury a jumper: To make an especially pretty jumpshot.

charity stripe: The free throw line.

deuce: A made field goal, worth two points.

downtown: A long way from the basket, as in, "He just hit that shot from downtown!"

in the paint: In the free throw lane.

nothin' but net: A shot that goes through the rim without touching the rim or any other part of the basket.

take it to the hole: To drive toward the basket in an attempt to score.

trey: A made field goal from behind the three-point arc, worth three points.

triple double: Racking up ten or more points, rebounds, assists, steals, or blocked shots in three or more categories — for example, 21 points, 11 rebounds, and 10 assists.

walk: To travel.

Cheat Sheet $2.95 value. Item 5042-X.
For more information about IDG Books, call 1-800-762-2974.

...For Dummies: Bestselling Book Series for Beginners

BUSINESS AND GENERAL REFERENCE BOOK SERIES FROM IDG

Basketball For Dummies™

Cheat Sheet

Understanding Player Positions

Point Guard: Usually the shortest player on the team. Should be the team's best passer and ball handler; not primarily a shooter. Traditional role is to push the ball upcourt and start the offensive wheels turning. Should either take the ball to the basket or remain near the top of the key, ready to retreat on defense. Prototype: Magic Johnson.

Shooting Guard: Generally taller than a point guard but shorter than a small forward. Not necessarily a great ball handler, but normally the team's best perimeter shooter. A good shooting guard (or *two guard*) comes off screens set by taller teammates prepared to shoot, pass, or drive to the basket. Also tries to grab rebounds on offense. Prototype: Michael Jordan.

Small Forward: The all-purpose player on offense: aggressive and strong; tall enough to mix it up inside but agile enough to handle the ball and shoot well. Must be able to score both from the perimeter and from inside. Prototype: Scottie Pippen.

Power Forward: Has muscles or at least a little bulk. Must be able to catch passes and hit shots near the basket. A good, rugged rebounder, but athletic enough to move with some quickness around the lane on offense and defense. Expected to score when given the opportunity on the baseline, much like a center, but usually has a range of up to 15 feet, all around the basket. Prototype: Karl Malone.

Center: Usually the tallest player on the team. Should be able to post up offensively — that is, receive the ball with his back to the basket and use pivot moves to hit a variety of short jumpers, hook shots, and dunks. Also must know how to find the open player in the paint and grab offensive rebounds. Prototype: Kareem Abdul-Jabbar.

Deciphering Common Referee Signals

Jump Ball

Shot Clock Violation

3-Second Violation

Traveling

Illegal Dribble

Foul

Player Control Foul

Technical Foul or Time-out

Blocking

Holding

Pushing or Charging

Praise For Basketball For Dummies

"Great reading from a man who knows basketball."

— Charles Barkley, Houston Rockets

"To put in Vitalese, this book is simply Awesome, Baby!"

— Dick Vitale, ESPN/ABC Basketball Analyst

"*Basketball For Dummies* is written by one of the greatest coaches and personalities in the game. I loved it and will refer to it often."

— Frank Layden, President of the Utah Jazz and Former NBA Coach of the Year

"A must-have book for all basketball coaches and fans! A proven winner on the hardwood, Digger brings the basketball knowledge and experiences that made him a great coach right into your hands."

— Jeff Nix, Assistant Coach, New York Knicks

"Having played for and coached against Digger Phelps, I know firsthand that there is no dummy better qualified to write this book. Digger's knowledge and expertise make *Basketball For Dummies* a fun, easy-to-follow, and informative read for every level of basketball fan."

— P. J. Carlesimo, Head Coach, Golden State Warriors, Fordham University '71

"I have known Digger a long time, and his basketball experience and knowledge are exceptional. *Basketball For Dummies* makes for some great reading, and I highly recommend it."

— Bobby Cremins, Head Men's Basketball Coach, Georgia Tech University

"One of the best teachers in the game, Digger Phelps, will give all 'Dummies' readers terrific insight into the most popular sport of our times."

— Matt Kilcullen, Jr., Head Men's Basketball Coach, Western Kentucky University

"Basketball is the fastest growing sport in the world. Unfortunately, most people only know the sport on the surface. After reading *Basketball For Dummies,* the reader will have the insight and knowledge to better understand and appreciate the greatest sport in the world.

"One of Digger's favorite expressions is 'G.I.D.' — 'Get It Done.' *Basketball For Dummies* gets it done for everyone!"

— Frank McLaughlin, Director of Athletics, Fordham University

"*Basketball For Dummies* is a useful combination of broad advice and specific tips that should be invaluable to both basketball beginners and veterans. Digger is an excellent coach!"

— Chris Fowler, ESPN College Sports Studio Host

"I have been involved with basketball for the last 25 years, be it playing, coaching, or broadcasting. While some might argue that Digger wrote this book especially for me, I sometimes take for granted that everyone knows everything about the great game of basketball. *Basketball For Dummies* is a great tool to learn more about the game, not only for novices but also for those who fancy themselves as basketball experts. Digger Phelps is a great basketball mind with a clever wit, which makes *Basketball For Dummies* an enjoyable, informative book."

— Nancy Lieberman-Cline, TV Analyst and Player for the Phoenix Mercury of the WNBA

"During the four years I was starting point guard for Digger's teams at Notre Dame (a 77 percent winning percentage), no one in the country worked harder than Digger at preparing teams offensively and defensively for winning basketball. This book does an excellent job of communicating those battle-tested winning principles!"

— Rich Branning, Vice President, The Staubach Company

"Exciting, Excellent, Elevating, Entertaining, Energizing . . . A great way to learn more about self-improvement drills, as well as the rules and regulations of the game. My teammates would also love to see you come out with *Officiating For Dummies*!"

— Patrick Featherston, 7th Grade Student and Avid Basketball Player, Berkely Heights, NJ

"Yes . . . and it counts! One of the all-time best 'upset' coaches in NCAA history has finally scripted all of his proven X's and O's and last-minute, game-winning plays into a book that only he could write. Consider this your ultimate playbook, whether you are a first-time coach or hoop junkie like myself. Digger, I am still mad that you left Fordham for Notre Dame, but you delivered a great read, baby. Thanks!"

— John Kilcullen, Head Dummy

"Digger has hit a game-winning trey with *Basketball For Dummies.* I plan to put my new hoop knowledge to good use and win a few NCAA tournament pools in the future."

— Colleen Burke, Supervisor, Shaklee Corporation, Brookfield, Connecticut

"Digger the motivator: I asked a teammate, 'Why is the basketball coach speaking at the biggest football pep rally of the year?' Then I heard Digger speak. He had the place rocking!"

— Tim Koegel, International Communication Consultant and Owner of The Koegel Group

"Whether you are a basketball junkie, a coach, or a fan, *Basketball For Dummies* is not only enjoyable reading but informative, too."

— Al Seibert, Assistant Men's Basketball Coach, Western Kentucky University

BUSINESS AND GENERAL REFERENCE BOOK SERIES FROM IDG

References for the Rest of Us!™

Do you find that traditional reference books are overloaded with technical details and advice you'll never use? Do you postpone important life decisions because you just don't want to deal with them? Then our *...For Dummies*™ business and general reference book series is for you.

...For Dummies business and general reference books are written for those frustrated and hard-working souls who know they aren't dumb, but find that the myriad of personal and business issues and the accompanying horror stories make them feel helpless. *...For Dummies* books use a lighthearted approach, a down-to-earth style, and even cartoons and humorous icons to diffuse fears and build confidence. Lighthearted but not lightweight, these books are perfect survival guides to solve your everyday personal and business problems.

"More than a publishing phenomenon, 'Dummies' is a sign of the times."
— The New York Times

"...you won't go wrong buying them."
— Walter Mossberg, Wall Street Journal, on IDG's ...For Dummies™ books

"A world of detailed and authoritative information is packed into them..."
— U.S. News and World Report

Already, millions of satisfied readers agree. They have made *...For Dummies* the #1 introductory level computer book series and a best-selling business book series. They have written asking for more. So, if you're looking for the best and easiest way to learn about business and other general reference topics, look to *...For Dummies* to give you a helping hand.

5/97

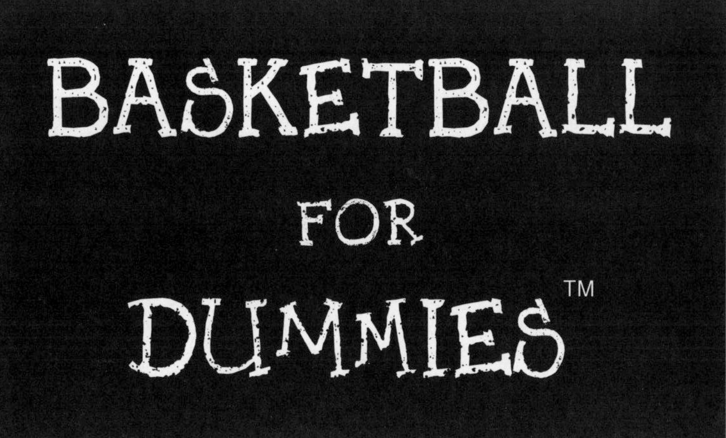

by Richard "Digger" Phelps
with John Walters

Foreword by Dick Vitale

IDG Books Worldwide, Inc.
An International Data Group Company

Foster City, CA ♦ Chicago, IL ♦ Indianapolis, IN ♦ Southlake, TX

Basketball For Dummies™

Published by
IDG Books Worldwide, Inc.
An International Data Group Company
919 E. Hillsdale Blvd.
Suite 400
Foster City, CA 94404
www.idgbooks.com (IDG Books Worldwide Web site)
www.dummies.com (Dummies Press Web site)

Library of Congress Catalog Card No.: 97-80304

ISBN: 0-7645-5042-X

Printed in the United States of America

10 9 8 7 6 5 4 3 2

1E/SR/RR/ZX/IN

Distributed in the United States by IDG Books Worldwide, Inc.

Distributed by Macmillan Canada for Canada; by Transworld Publishers Limited in the United Kingdom; by IDG Norge Books for Norway; by IDG Sweden Books for Sweden; by Woodslane Pty. Ltd. for Australia; by Woodslane Enterprises Ltd. for New Zealand; by Longman Singapore Publishers Ltd. for Singapore, Malaysia, Thailand, and Indonesia; by Simron Pty. Ltd. for South Africa; by Toppan Company Ltd. for Japan; by Distribuidora Cuspide for Argentina; by Livraria Cultura for Brazil; by Ediciencia S.A. for Ecuador; by Addison-Wesley Publishing Company for Korea; by Ediciones ZETA S.C.R. Ltda. for Peru; by WS Computer Publishing Corporation, Inc., for the Philippines; by Unalis Corporation for Taiwan; by Contemporanea de Ediciones for Venezuela; by Computer Book & Magazine Store for Puerto Rico; by Express Computer Distributors for the Caribbean and West Indies. Authorized Sales Agent: Anthony Rudkin Associates for the Middle East and North Africa.

For general information on IDG Books Worldwide's books in the U.S., please call our Consumer Customer Service department at 800-762-2974. For reseller information, including discounts and premium sales, please call our Reseller Customer Service department at 800-434-3422.

For information on where to purchase IDG Books Worldwide's books outside the U.S., please contact our International Sales department at 415-655-3200 or fax 415-655-3295.

For information on foreign language translations, please contact our Foreign & Subsidiary Rights department at 415-655-3021 or fax 415-655-3281.

For sales inquiries and special prices for bulk quantities, please contact our Sales department at 415-655-3200 or write to the address above.

For information on using IDG Books Worldwide's books in the classroom or for ordering examination copies, please contact our Educational Sales department at 800-434-2086 or fax 817-251-8174.

For press review copies, author interviews, or other publicity information, please contact our Public Relations department at 415-655-3000 or fax 415-655-3299.

For authorization to photocopy items for corporate, personal, or educational use, please contact Copyright Clearance Center, 222 Rosewood Drive, Danvers, MA 01923, or fax 508-750-4470.

Cover photo of Digger Phelps courtesy of ESPN, Inc.

About the Authors

Richard "Digger" Phelps (center) is the renowned basketball coach from Notre Dame, where he won more games than any coach in the school's history. He is now a college basketball analyst for ESPN, and he served as basketball analyst for CBS Sports during the 1992 and 1993 NCAA tournaments. In 1984, he was a commentator for ABC Sports' coverage at the Summer Olympics in Los Angeles.

John Walters (left) has been writing and reporting on basketball, football, and general interest topics for *Sports Illustrated* for the past eight years.

Special contributor **Tim Bourret** (right) is the Sports Information Director at Clemson University in South Carolina. He is in his 20th year at the school and has won over 80 national and regional awards for his publications, including a dozen dealing with basketball. He is also the color commentator on the Clemson Basketball Radio Network. Bourret, a Double Domer (1977 and '78), has followed Digger Phelps' career since 1974, when he was one of the 11,000 Notre Dame fans who stormed the court after the Fighting Irish ended UCLA's 88-game winning streak.

ABOUT IDG BOOKS WORLDWIDE

Welcome to the world of IDG Books Worldwide.

IDG Books Worldwide, Inc., is a subsidiary of International Data Group, the world's largest publisher of computer-related information and the leading global provider of information services on information technology. IDG was founded more than 25 years ago and now employs more than 8,500 people worldwide. IDG publishes more than 275 computer publications in over 75 countries (see listing below). More than 60 million people read one or more IDG publications each month.

Launched in 1990, IDG Books Worldwide is today the #1 publisher of best-selling computer books in the United States. We are proud to have received eight awards from the Computer Press Association in recognition of editorial excellence and three from *Computer Currents*' First Annual Readers' Choice Awards. Our best-selling *...For Dummies*® series has more than 30 million copies in print with translations in 30 languages. IDG Books Worldwide, through a joint venture with IDG's Hi-Tech Beijing, became the first U.S. publisher to publish a computer book in the People's Republic of China. In record time, IDG Books Worldwide has become the first choice for millions of readers around the world who want to learn how to better manage their businesses.

Our mission is simple: Every one of our books is designed to bring extra value and skill-building instructions to the reader. Our books are written by experts who understand and care about our readers. The knowledge base of our editorial staff comes from years of experience in publishing, education, and journalism — experience we use to produce books for the '90s. In short, we care about books, so we attract the best people. We devote special attention to details such as audience, interior design, use of icons, and illustrations. And because we use an efficient process of authoring, editing, and desktop publishing our books electronically, we can spend more time ensuring superior content and spend less time on the technicalities of making books.

You can count on our commitment to deliver high-quality books at competitive prices on topics you want to read about. At IDG Books Worldwide, we continue in the IDG tradition of delivering quality for more than 25 years. You'll find no better book on a subject than one from IDG Books Worldwide.

John Kilcullen
CEO
IDG Books Worldwide, Inc.

Steven Berkowitz
President and Publisher
IDG Books Worldwide, Inc.

Eighth Annual Computer Press Awards 1992

Ninth Annual Computer Press Awards 1993

Tenth Annual Computer Press Awards 1994

Eleventh Annual Computer Press Awards 1995

IDG Books Worldwide, Inc., is a subsidiary of International Data Group, the world's largest publisher of computer-related information and the leading global provider of information services on information technology. International Data Group publishes over 275 computer publications in over 75 countries. Sixty million people read one or more International Data Group publications each month. International Data Group's publications include: **ARGENTINA:** Buyer's Guide, Computerworld Argentina, PC World Argentina; **AUSTRALIA:** Australian Macworld, Australian PC World, Australian Reseller News, Computerworld, IT Casebook, Network World, Publish, Webmaster; **AUSTRIA:** Computerwelt Osterreich, Networks Austria, PC Tip Austria; **BANGLADESH:** PC World Bangladesh; **BELARUS:** PC World Belarus; **BELGIUM:** Data News; **BRAZIL:** Annuário de Informática, Computerworld, Connections, Macworld, PC Player, PC World, Publish, Reseller News, Supergamepower; **BULGARIA:** Computerworld Bulgaria, Network World Bulgaria, PC & MacWorld Bulgaria; **CANADA:** CIO Canada, Client/Server World, ComputerWorld Canada, InfoWorld Canada, NetworkWorld Canada, WebWorld; **CHILE:** Computerworld Chile, PC World Chile; **COLOMBIA:** Computerworld Colombia, PC World Colombia; **COSTA RICA:** PC World Centro America; **THE CZECH AND SLOVAK REPUBLICS:** Computerworld Czechoslovakia, Macworld Czech Republic, PC World Czechoslovakia; **DENMARK:** Communications World Danmark, Computerworld Danmark, Macworld Danmark, PC World Danmark, Techworld Denmark; **DOMINICAN REPUBLIC:** PC World Republica Dominicana; **ECUADOR:** PC World Ecuador; **EGYPT:** Computerworld Middle East, PC World Middle East; **EL SALVADOR:** PC World Centro America; **FINLAND:** MikroPC, Tietoverkko, Tietoviikko; **FRANCE:** Distributique, Hebdo, Info PC, Le Monde Informatique, Macworld, Reseaux & Telecoms, WebMaster France; **GERMANY:** Computer Partner, Computerwoche, Computerwoche Extra, Computerwoche FOCUS, Global Online, Macwelt, PC Welt; **GREECE:** Amiga Computing, GamePro Greece, Multimedia World; **GUATEMALA:** PC World Centro America; **HONDURAS:** PC World Centro America; **HONG KONG:** Computerworld Hong Kong, PC World Hong Kong, Publish in Asia; **HUNGARY:** ABCD CD-ROM, Computerworld Szamitastechnika, Internetto online Magazine, PC World Hungary, PC-X Magazin Hungary; **ICELAND:** Tolvuheimur PC World Island; **INDIA:** Information Communications World, Information Systems Computerworld, PC World India, Publish in Asia; **INDONESIA:** InfoKomputer PC World, Komputek Computerworld, Publish in Asia; **IRELAND:** ComputerScope, PC Live!; **ISRAEL:** Macworld Israel, People & Computers/Computerworld; **ITALY:** Computerworld Italia, Macworld Italia, Networking Italia, PC World Italia; **JAPAN:** DTP World, Macworld Japan, Nikkei Personal Computing, OS/2 World Japan, SunWorld Japan, Windows NT World, Windows World Japan; **KENYA:** PC World East African; **KOREA:** Hi-Tech Information, Macworld Korea, PC World Korea; **MACEDONIA:** PC World Macedonia; **MALAYSIA:** Computerworld Malaysia, PC World Malaysia, Publish in Asia; **MALTA:** PC World Malta; **MEXICO:** Computerworld Mexico, PC World Mexico; **MYANMAR:** PC World Myanmar; **NETHERLANDS:** Computer! Totaal, LAN Internetworking Magazine, LAN World Buyers Guide, Macworld Netherlands, Net, WebWereld; **NEW ZEALAND:** Absolute Beginners Guide and Plain & Simple Series, Computer Buyer, Computer Industry Directory, Computerworld New Zealand, MTB, Network World, PC World New Zealand; **NICARAGUA:** PC World Centro America; **NORWAY:** Computerworld Norge, CW Rapport, Datamagasinet, Financial Rapport, Kursguide Norge, Macworld Norge, Multimediaworld Norge, PC World Ekspress Norge, PC World Nettverk, PC World Norge, PC World ProduktGuide Norge; **PAKISTAN:** Computerworld Pakistan; **PANAMA:** PC World Panama; **PEOPLE'S REPUBLIC OF CHINA:** China Computer Users, China Computerworld, China InfoWorld, China Telecom World Weekly, Computer & Communication, Electronic Design China, Electronics Today, Electronics Weekly, Game Software, PC World China, Popular Computer Week, Software Weekly, Software World, Telecom World; **PERU:** Computerworld Peru, PC World Profesional Peru, PC World SoHo Peru; **PHILIPPINES:** Click!, Computerworld Philippines, PC World Philippines, Publish in Asia; **POLAND:** Computerworld Poland, Computerworld Special Report Poland, Cyber, Macworld Poland, Networld Poland, PC World Komputer; **PORTUGAL:** Cerebro/PC World, Computerworld/Correio Informático, Dealer World Portugal, Mac*In/PC*In Portugal, Multimedia World; **PUERTO RICO:** PC World Puerto Rico; **ROMANIA:** Computerworld Romania, PC World Romania, Telecom Romania; **RUSSIA:** Computerworld Russia, Mir PK, Publish, Seti; **SINGAPORE:** Computerworld Singapore, PC World Singapore, Publish in Asia; **SLOVENIA:** Monitor; **SOUTH AFRICA:** Computing SA, Network World SA, Software World SA; **SPAIN:** Communicaciones World España, Computerworld España, Dealer World España, Macworld España, PC World España; **SRI LANKA:** Infolink PC World; **SWEDEN:** CAP&Design, Computer Sweden, Corporate Computing Sweden, Internetworld Sweden, it.branschen, Macworld Sweden, MaxiData Sweden, MikroDatorn, Nätverk & Kommunikation, PC World Sweden, PCaktiv, Windows World Sweden; **SWITZERLAND:** Computerworld Schweiz, Macworld Schweiz, PCtip; **TAIWAN:** Computerworld Taiwan, Macworld Taiwan, NEW ViSiON/Publish, PC World Taiwan, Windows World Taiwan; **THAILAND:** Publish in Asia, Thai Computerworld; **TURKEY:** Computerworld Turkiye, Macworld Turkiye, Network World Turkiye, PC World Turkiye; **UKRAINE:** Computerworld Kiev, Multimedia World Ukraine, PC World Ukraine; **UNITED KINGDOM:** Acorn User UK, Amiga Action UK, Amiga Computing UK, Apple Talk UK, Computing, Macworld, Parents and Computers UK, PC Advisor, PC Home, PSX Pro, The WEB; **UNITED STATES:** Cable in the Classroom, CIO Magazine, Computerworld, DOS World, Federal Computer Week, GamePro Magazine, InfoWorld, I-Way, Macworld, Network World, PC Games, PC World, Publish, Video Event, THE WEB Magazine, and WebMaster; online webzines: JavaWorld, NetscapeWorld, and SunWorld Online; **URUGUAY:** InfoWorld Uruguay; **VENEZUELA:** Computerworld Venezuela, PC World Venezuela; and **VIETNAM:** PC World Vietnam. 3/24/97

Dedication

To those who have been a part of my basketball life.

—Richard "Digger" Phelps

Authors' Acknowledgments

From Digger Phelps: To John Walters, Tim Bourret, and Rose Pietrzak, the writing team, as well as Team IDG, for all your efforts to make this book become a reality. This book is all about teams and how they work together, and our South Bend-Chicago-Indianapolis team proved that the team concept really works!

From John Walters: Thanks my managing editor Bill Colson and the rest of the editors at *Sports Illustrated* for their patience during the last year (not to mention the previous seven), and to my parents, William and Phyllis, for never telling me not to play ball in the house.

From Tim Bourret: To my proofreading parents, Chuck and Irene Bourret. To my good friend (Saint) Rose Pietrzak, who transcribed endless conversations between myself and Digger. Rose is now an expert on Notre Dame basketball of the 1970s and 1980s. To Bob Bradley, my Clemson mentor, who provided many an interesting college basketball anecdote from his over 40 years in college athletics. To Dan Ahearn, Rick Barnes, Dennis Felton, Craig Miller, Steve Nelson, Reno Wilson, and Todd Wright for providing input for various chapters of this book. To Matt Cashore and Bob Waldrop for taking the photos in this book, and Merl Code, Gene Brtalik, R. C. Deer, Justin Dunn, Mike Empey, Chris Hogan, Ben Murphy, Willie MacKey, Stephen Tessier, and Gabe Thompson for being in the photos. To Mike Danch, Mike Enright, and John Heisler for helping to set up the photo shoot at Notre Dame. And to my army of assistants in the Clemson Sports Information Office who spent "off hours" typing and researching: Bert Berg, Sam Blackman, Adair Clairy, Brian Hennessey, Jeff Martin, Meredith Merritt, Amy Moore, Will Peeler, Brenda Rabon, Emily Rabon, and Brett Sowell.

Publisher's Acknowledgments

We're proud of this book; please register your comments through our IDG Books Worldwide Online Registration Form located at `http://my2cents.dummies.com`.

Some of the people who helped bring this book to market include the following:

Acquisitions, Development, and Editorial

Senior Project Editor: Pamela Mourouzis

Acquisitions Editor: Stacy S. Collins

Copy Editor: Suzanne Thomas

General Reviewer and Fact-Checker: B. J. Schechter

Editorial Manager: Leah P. Cameron

Editorial Coordinator: Ann Miller

Production

Project Coordinator: E. Shawn Aylsworth

Layout and Graphics: Cameron Booker, Linda M. Boyer, Angela F. Hunckler, Todd Klemme, Brent Savage

Proofreaders: Betty Kish, Christine Berman, Joel K. Draper, Nancy Price, Rebecca Senninger, Robert Springer, Janet M. Withers

Indexer: Ty Koontz

Special Help

Jeff Cox; Nickole J. Harris, Acquistions Coordinator; Sarah Kennedy, Executive Editor; Kyle Looper, Project Editor; Darren Meiss, Editorial Assistant

Special Art

Matt Cashore, Photographer; Bob Waldrop, Photographer

General and Administrative

IDG Books Worldwide, Inc.: John Kilcullen, CEO; Steven Berkowitz, President and Publisher

IDG Books Technology Publishing: Brenda McLaughlin, Senior Vice President and Group Publisher

Dummies Technology Press and Dummies Editorial: Diane Graves Steele, Vice President and Associate Publisher; Mary Bednarek, Acquisitions and Product Development Director; Kristin A. Cocks, Editorial Director

Dummies Trade Press: Kathleen A. Welton, Vice President and Publisher; Kevin Thornton, Acquisitions Manager; Maureen F. Kelly, Editorial Coordinator

IDG Books Production for Dummies Press: Beth Jenkins, Production Director; Cindy L. Phipps, Manager of Project Coordination, Production Proofreading, and Indexing; Kathie S. Schutte, Supervisor of Page Layout; Shelley Lea, Supervisor of Graphics and Design; Debbie J. Gates, Production Systems Specialist; Robert Springer, Supervisor of Proofreading; Debbie Stailey, Special Projects Coordinator; Tony Augsburger, Supervisor of Reprints and Bluelines; Leslie Popplewell, Media Archive Coordinator

Dummies Packaging and Book Design: Patti Crane, Packaging Specialist; Lance Kayser, Packaging Assistant; Kavish + Kavish, Cover Design

♦

The publisher would like to give special thanks to Patrick J. McGovern, without whom this book would not have been possible.

♦

Contents at a Glance

Cartoons at a Glance

By Rich Tennant

page 5

page 61

"JUST HOW MUCH DO YOU THINK YOU CAN EMBARRASS ME? IF YOU THINK I'M GOING TO THE BASKETBALL GAME WITH YOU WEARING THOSE RIDICULOUS SOCKS, YOU'RE SADLY MISTAKEN!"

page 181

"IT FIGURES YOU'D MAKE A BIG STINK OVER THIS, BUT HAS ANYONE BOTHERED TO NOTICE HOW MANY MORE BASKETS WE'RE MAKING FROM THE THREE-POINT LINE SINCE WE STARTED PRACTICING WITH BOWLING BALLS?"

page 303

"WHAT DID I TELL YOU?! WHAT DID I TELL YOU?! YOU WANT TO BE LIKE DENNIS RODMAN?! THEN EXPECT TO GET YOUR NOSE RING CAUGHT IN THE NET!"

page 363

Fax: 508-546-7747 • E-mail: the5wave@tiac.net

Table of Contents

Part II: The Fundamentals of Basketball 61

Foreword

If you have a passion and love for basketball as much as I do, it is a must to get this book by Digger Phelps and John Walters. It covers every phase of the game with an exciting style. All the terminology is broken down in simple terms to make it easy for any basketball fan.

Digger demonstrates in the text his keen knowledge about the game that has meant so much to him in his career as a coach and broadcaster. John utilizes his expertise in writing, and together they make basketball music. You will have a keen appreciation for the game that I love, after reading *Basketball For Dummies*. To put it in Vitalese, "This book is simply Awesome, Baby!"

— Dick Vitale, ESPN/ABC Basketball Analyst

Key to Diagrams in This Book

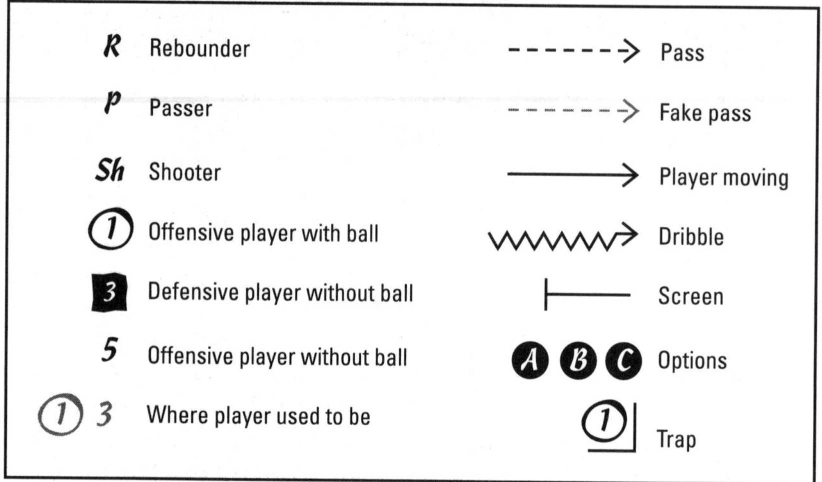

Prologue

Digger the Player, to Digger the Coach, to Digger the Fan

I played college basketball at Rider College (my roommate was Nick Valvano, brother of the late, widely loved coach of North Carolina State, Jimmy Valvano) in New Jersey. When I graduated in 1963, I had no intention of pursuing the sport any further than recreationally. I had planned to enter the Simmons School of Embalming that summer, because that was the family business (hence my nickname). But I was born to coach the American game. Heck, I was born on the 4th of July in 1941.

At the time, Tom Winterbottom was a high school coach in Beacon, New York. The previous winter, Tom had taken Beacon High to a 20-0 record, and now he wanted to start a summer league. He knew that I had played for Rider, and he asked me to coach one of his teams. Thus my career in embalming was forever sidetracked.

The Early Years

Obviously, that summer changed my life: I returned to Rider for graduate school and volunteered as an assistant coach. (Today, those positions are more coveted on college campuses than long-distance calling cards.) I knew that I would need a master's degree in education as an entree into coaching.

As a graduate assistant coach at Rider that first year, my job was to scout upcoming opponents. The New York University Violets were a hoops power at the time and an away game for us that season. NYU had not lost a home game since 1938 and, perhaps because he sensed that our plight was hopeless, Bob Greenwood, the Rider head coach, allowed me to devise a game plan.

We won 66-63. I thought to myself: I can do this.

I got my start as a head coach, as most people do, at the bottom. St. Gabriel's High School in Hazleton, Pennsylvania, took a chance on me in 1964. The team was winless the year before. In my second year as head coach, though, we won the Class C state title.

Shortly before that season began, one day late in October, I sat down and wrote a presumptuous letter, the type of letter that only a 23-year-old with outlandish dreams can write. Seldom, if ever, do these dreams come true. On that day, I wrote a letter to Ara Parseghian, the head *football* coach at the University of Notre Dame in South Bend, Indiana. In the letter, I explained that my big dream was to coach at Notre Dame. (I assume Ara realized that I was not after *his* job.) Then I affixed my 5-cent postage to the envelope and spent the next six years pursuing that dream.

In those days, I had tunnel vision: I applied for ten assistant coaching jobs at the college level and was turned down ten times. I even wrote a letter to Dean Smith, the head coach at the University of North Carolina. He replied that he was going to hire one of his former players — a guy named Larry Brown. All Larry did was take two different schools — UCLA and Kansas — to the NCAA (National Collegiate Athletic Association) title game in the 1980s, winning once. Today, he coaches the Philadelphia 76ers. Obviously, Dean had no eye for talent.

In 1966, I landed a position as the freshman coach at the University of Pennsylvania, an Ivy League school. One of my duties was to recruit, and I found that a few players did not know the difference between Penn and Penn State, the football powerhouse. "Are you going to a bowl?" they'd ask. Who was I to tell them no?

For two years, we were horrible. In Philadelphia, there are five area Division I colleges — LaSalle, Penn, St. Joe's, Temple, and Villanova — who form an unofficial league known as the Big Five. One night, I noticed a sign hanging in our gym, the Palestra, that read, "The Big Four and Penn."

But I managed to develop as a recruiter. ("Of course we're going to a bowl!") In my third season, the freshman team went undefeated. It was time to move on.

The next stop, in 1970, was Fordham, which is located in The Bronx. We were a small team that pressed and ran and kept the heat on for 40 minutes. At a time when New York City was all abuzz with the Miracle Mets, Joe Namath of the Jets, and the Knicks — a hat trick of pro sports championships within a 16-month period — we took our own bite out of the Big Apple by going 26-3. The highlight of the season was when our little Catholic school from The Bronx stole into Madison Square Garden and defeated mighty Notre Dame. Three weeks earlier, the Fighting Irish had handed eventual national champion UCLA their only loss of the season.

Little did I know at the time that I would be coaching Notre Dame the next season.

Tunnel Vision: Notre Dame

In 1968, I was in Illinois recruiting for Penn when I decided to drive over the state line into Indiana and see Notre Dame for myself. Notre Dame, especially for a Catholic kid raised on its football games via the radio, never seemed to be bound by such a trivial thing as geography. Notre Dame had always seemed to exist more so in my mind, sort of like Oz.

Even though basketball is my passion, when I arrived at Notre Dame that day, I proceeded directly to the football stadium. As I entered the stadium tunnel, with the light from the field gleaming in, I started to cry. This was where I wanted to be.

I understand that many a cynic is eager to dismiss the aura of the school, but I never have questioned the effect that it had on me. Besides, Notre Dame had just built a new basketball arena — the Athletic & Convocation Center (ACC) — and Austin Carr was the National Player of the Year. And, as anyone who ever survived a winter in South Bend will tell you, students need someone to cheer for in January and February, when football begins its hibernation.

To this day, the serendipity of my 20s boggles my mind. I wrote a letter to Ara Parseghian when I was 23, and six years later, my dream came to pass. As Bob Costas once said regarding his own meteoric rise to the top, "I would have been happy to pay my dues, but nobody ever made me."

Building a Program

You don't get tougher by picking fights with your little brother; you toughen up by taking on your *big* brother. (Although it helps if you and your little brother team up against big bro, but now I'm in the realm of child psychology.) So when I arrived at Notre Dame, I resolved to build one of the nation's premier basketball programs. To do so, I believed that we needed to challenge the best.

At that time, the best was spelled U-C-L-A.

We scheduled a home-and-home series with the Bruins so that each year we played them twice (once at Notre Dame, once at UCLA). I'll not deny that Notre Dame's football reputation allowed us to make such a series attractive to UCLA. Besides, I knew that John Wooden, UCLA's coach, grew up in South Bend and would look forward to an annual homecoming. Finally, it never hurt recruiting to have a game in sunny LA on the schedule.

A rivalry blossomed between Wooden, the game's reserved elder statesman, and myself. This rivalry was good for the game and definitely good for our program. The first year (1971) we played UCLA, the Bruins beat us by 58 points. Wooden still had his defense pressing us with four minutes remaining. During the 1973 season, UCLA entered the ACC with an NCAA-record 88-game winning streak. We ended it. That one game did more for our program than any 20-win season could have.

Digger the Fan

After more than 20 years in coaching, I am now simply a fan of basketball. When I left Notre Dame in 1991, I figured that basketball was behind me. I went to work for then-President George Bush, helping to apprise him on issues such as drugs and education in inner cities. Had Bush been reelected the following November, I thought that I may possibly become the Drug Czar. From Notre Dame to the White House. Some alums of that school would consider this a demotion.

My first year away from the game, I doubted that I would become a big fan. I've always enjoyed other interests, such as painting, and believed that I'd devote myself to these pursuits. But then, even in my coaching days, I had moonlighted as a broadcaster.

In December 1973, UCLA met Indiana. This game, at the time, was a dream matchup, and I was given the opportunity to be a part of the broadcast. (Of course, Notre Dame was not playing that day.) Ten years later, I shared the microphone with Marv Albert for the National Invitational Tournament (NIT) in New York. Tulsa was playing Syracuse, and I made an innocent observation — which was true, I might add — that probably caused a few beer cans to be tossed at TV sets back in Oklahoma.

The game was a tight one. In the final moments, a Tulsa player went to the free throw line to shoot a one-and-one. In a *one-and-one* situation, the player must make the first free throw in order to attempt a second. If the player misses the first shot, the ball is in play. Noting that the Tulsa player's body language suggested a lack of confidence, I said, "He's not going to make the shot." And he didn't. Their fans thought that I was rooting for Syracuse. I wasn't.

In April 1994, Jimmy Valvano, the charismatic former North Carolina State coach who won the 1983 NCAA title and who worked for the last few years as an ESPN commentator, died of cancer. I knew Jimmy very well and, like all basketball fans, was saddened by his loss. After Valvano died, ESPN offered me the position that he had held. I've had the job ever since, and I love it. It's a college hoops fan's paradise.

Introduction

Welcome to *Line Dancing For Dummies!* Before I show you that first two-step, I'd like to — gotcha! Don't worry; you're in the right book. This is *Basketball For Dummies,* and I'm glad to have you on board.

Basketball is the most popular participatory sport in the United States (more popular even than Yahtzee). I've got the numbers and stuff to prove that, but I'll spare you the boring figures. Trust me; you're in with the popular crowd.

I'm biased, of course, but I believe that basketball is the best sport ever invented. It combines physical prowess, intelligence, grace, and coordination. Although more than 46 million Americans play basketball (okay, so I won't spare you the boring figures), the game is flexible enough to enable each player to develop his or her own style.

I've devoted my entire adult life to basketball. As simple as the game often seems — throw the ball through the hoop — I discover new nuances of the sport each day. I've learned a lot since I first decided to abandon my chosen career path as a mortician (seriously!) to pursue my real love. I'm only too happy to share what I know with you.

Oh, about line dancing. According to Weight Watchers, an hour of line dancing burns off just as many calories as an hour of basketball. The choice is yours.

Foolish Assumptions

You notice that in basketball, the basket is the same height (10 feet above the ground) for everybody — young and old, tall and short, male and female. I want this book to be that 10-foot basket. No matter who you are and how much or how little you know about the game, this book should provide the information you're looking for.

I am a coach. For more than a quarter of a century, I pursued that career at Catholic schools, so I'm used to preaching to the converted. And isn't that what any author of *Basketball For Dummies* would be doing? The game is more popular than oxygen, or so it seems. But you bought this book for a reason, right?

Maybe you have an unquenchable thirst to find out more about the game. Or you know all there is to know about playing the game, but none of the history. Or vice versa. Perhaps you are completely unfamiliar with basketball and are curious as to what all the fuss is about. Or you want to improve your own game. No matter what your craving, this book should satisfy.

How to Use This Book

Well, of course, if I were you I would read it. The paper is entirely too small for you to use it to, say, wrap fish in. I mean, if I caught a fish that small, I'd toss it back. Read the book the way you might read *People* magazine's "Most Beautiful People" issue: Pick your favorite spots. There's no need to read the chapters in numerical order.

It might not hurt to have a basketball and a basketball hoop nearby while you're reading. You may happen upon the chapter that talks about shooting and want to put some of my advice to use right away. Go ahead; put the book down and head for the basket. The whole idea of this book is to get you better acquainted with the game, anyway. Go ahead, stop and shoot! You won't hurt my feelings.

How This Book Is Organized

This book is divided into sections called, cleverly enough, parts. Here's what you can find in each part.

Part I: Basketball 101

If you have no idea what's going on when you see the players running up and down the court bouncing that round orange thing, this part is a good place to start. First I take some time to explain why basketball is the greatest game on earth (as if I need to tell you that!), and then I talk about what you need to play the game. Chapters 3 and 4 talk about the all-important rules of basketball and explain how to keep and interpret the statistics.

Part II: The Fundamentals of Basketball

Now comes the fun part: picking up a ball and playing the game yourself! The chapters in this part take you through the techniques of shooting, playing offense, playing defense, and rebounding. Chapter 9 talks about setting up special plays and strategies for specific situations.

Part III: The Fanfare of Basketball

You don't have to play on a formal team to enjoy the sport of basketball. This part talks about being a fan at every level of the game: high school, college, professional, and international. I also talk about playing pickup basketball — from the driveway to the playground to the neighborhood gym. Finally, I give you some tips for following the NCAA tournament and taking top honors in your office or family pool.

Part IV: Coaching Teams and Yourself

I can't help myself — I have to throw in my two cents about coaching. These chapters talk about forming your own coaching philosophy, motivating your players, and special considerations when coaching kids. I also talk about getting yourself or your team in top physical shape for basketball.

Part V: The Part of Tens

If you have only a few moments to spare (maybe you're between halves of a game), this is the part for you. Here you can find lists of history-making basketball games and NBA greats. If tourism is your thing, I also list ten terrific places to watch a game. And if you've always wondered what coaches are yelling from the sidelines, you can find that information here, too.

Appendixes

At the end of the book, you can find two quick appendixes: a glossary of basketball terms both serious and fun, and a listing of World Wide Web sites that you can visit when you're craving even more information about hoops.

Icons Used in This Book

Are you tired of struggling to figure out what Dickie V. and all the other hoops broadcasters are talking about? This icon demystifies those bizarre languages of basketball-speak and sportscaster-ese.

The record books of basketball are full of fascinating stories and fantastic players. This icon points to true stories of basketball stars past and present.

What can I say? Coaches are never at a loss for words. When you see this icon, you can look forward to an anecdote from my coaching career or my opinion on a controversial basketball issue.

This icon steers you toward helpful advice for players of the game.

With 25 years of coaching under my belt, I have plenty of advice for coaches, too. This icon helps you find those words of wisdom.

Watching hoops in person or on TV is much more enjoyable when you know a little bit about what's going on. This icon highlights information that can help you become a more educated viewer of the game.

If you're a parent who's coaching your kids in basketball — or you're just cheering them on from the stands — look to this icon for tips for making the experience fun for both of you.

This icon points out important techniques and truisms that you shouldn't forget.

Where to Go from Here

If you're just getting started in basketball — as a player, as a coach, or as a fan — you may want to start at the beginning of the book to find out about how the game is played. If you're an experienced hoopster, you may want to jump into Part II to work on your fundamentals and pick up a few new tricks, too. Coaches may want to head to Part IV, and fans to Part III.

In this book, I give you timeless information that can help you build a solid foundation of basketball knowledge. If you're interested in finding out more about what's going on in basketball *right now* — whether you're watching the first games of the NCAA season, following March Madness, or watching the NBA or WNBA playoffs — check out the Dummies Web site, which you can find at `www.dummies.com`, and use the search tool for "basketball." There, I give tips on which teams are hot, which teams are not, which players you should be watching, and much more.

Part I
Basketball 101

In this part . . .

This part gives you an overview of basketball basics. I tell you how the game originated and why basketball is such a great sport — whether you're a player, a coach, or a fan.

Here, you can find out what you need to wear whether you play in your driveway or for the WNBA. You can't play without proper equipment, either, so I also give you the scoop on balls, backboards, rims, and nets. I provide some hints on great places to play ball, too, from a local church parking lot to a playground.

Of course, you can't really play basketball unless you know how. This part answers all your questions about the different elements of the court, rules of the game, fouls, and violations. Finally, I provide a nonintimidating explanation of the statistics of the game — points scored, assists, rebounds, turnovers, and so on — which help you determine which team outplays another.

Chapter 1

Bare-Bones Basketball

In This Chapter

- Man-eating sharks! (Okay, not really)
- This game's for everyone
- Whither to play, coach, or cheer?

Outside death, basketball may be the most nondiscriminating exercise known to humanity. The Chicago Bulls team that won an NBA-record 72 games during the 1995–96 season featured among its top six players three black athletes and three white athletes from three different continents: Australia, Europe, and North America. (I take the liberty of assuming that Dennis Rodman is from this planet.) And basketball is even *less* discriminating when you're tall. The following season, the 29-team league boasted 16 players at the center position — the tallest people play center — who hailed from 15 countries on four different continents.

What other sport is this accessible? You can always play basketball. You can play indoors or outdoors. By yourself or with a friend (or a few). Half-court or full-court. Winter, spring, summer, or fall.

You need a basket. And a ball. (You're beginning to understand the etymology here, eh?) But that's all you need. No mitt, racquet, shoulder pads, or five-iron required. No ice, no pitcher's mound, and no tee time.

We're Having a Ball

Basketball is an American game — invented by a Canadian (Dr. James Naismith) — that has gained worldwide popularity. Sort of like Levi's. Or *Baywatch.* Why? Because basketball, also known as *hoops, roundball,* and so on, is fun to watch, play, and even — unlike most other sports — practice. When was the last time you witnessed a football offensive lineman working on his blocking technique in the park?

You can practice alone: just you, the ball, and the basket. Practicing alone is a great way to meditate. Or you can grab a friend. Shooting hoops is one of the most fail-safe means of bonding (male or female) around — see the sidebar titled "Male-female bonding" at the end of this section if you don't believe me. Nothing is better than just standing around a basket with a pal, shooting the ball and the breeze, getting to know one another better as you work on your jump shot. Such a scene often appears on the hit television show *ER:* Just outside the emergency room, not more than a bounce pass away from the defibrillators and operating tables, is a back-alley basketball hoop.

Here's how the game evolves: You shoot alone long enough, and eventually someone will amble over and ask if she can shoot with you. You say yes — having someone rebound your misses saves energy. Competitive juices soon begin to flow, and the two of you find yourselves playing one-on-one. The game attracts a crowd, and now you have enough players, ideally six, to stage a half-court contest, in which both teams shoot at one basket. Such spirited action attracts more interest, and now you have a bona fide full-court, two-basket game. Just add uniforms, referees, 18,000-seat arenas, and a 7-foot center or two dozen and — *voilà!* — you have the National Basketball Association (NBA).

Male-female bonding

Steve Alford, the former All-America guard who led the Indiana University Hoosiers to the 1987 National Collegiate Athletic Association (NCAA) championship, used to love shooting baskets by himself. For hours upon hours, during summer vacations and on weekends, Alford practiced his outside shot. Eventually, Alford's girlfriend, Tanya Frost, realized that if she wanted to spend some quality time with her beau, she'd have to visit the gym.

Frost was the ideal partner for Alford at these shooting sessions. She rebounded for him, and on those occasions when he "hung the net" (meaning that his shot had swished through so cleanly that the bottom of the net had lapped up and become entangled in the rim), as deft shooters often do, Frost located a stepladder and untangled it for Alford. In basketball-mad Indiana, Frost was nothing less than a dream girl.

Alford realized this. One afternoon in the summer of 1986, he arrived at the gym early and hung the net. When Frost appeared, Alford behaved as if he had just hung the net moments earlier. Without a word, she grabbed a ladder and began climbing — and then noticed a tiny box perched on the back of the rim.

Inside the box? An engagement ring. (She said yes.)

The Object of the Game, Simplified

Basketball is a simple game, though it may not seem so simple to everyone. At an interview session with Dream Team III prior to the 1996 Olympics, a Finnish journalist timidly approached NBA forward Karl Malone and said, "Excuse me, I'm not very familiar with this game. Why do you get *two* points for a basket?"

Malone laughed, but that was a good question. I answer that and similar questions — like, what's that white square on the backboard for? — later, in Chapter 3. For now, I can tell you the simple object of the game: *to put the ball in your basket and try to prevent your opponents from putting the ball in theirs.*

Digger's Ten Reasons to Like Basketball

Like basketball? Maybe I should say *love.* This section lists a few reasons why Cindy Crawford, Billy Crystal, Spike Lee, and I love this game — and why I think you should, too.

Basketball is ballet

The 94-x-50-foot stage (or 91'10"x 49'25" in international basketball) holds ten performers (the players) and two maestros (the coaches). Seeing the grace and finesse of the performers is like watching the ballet *Swan Lake.* The performers run, leap, and even pirouette in the air to perform a dunk; it's pure Baryshnikov.

The NBA's clever marketing arm often sets promotional highlights to classical pieces of music. It's a perfect fit. No other team game flows so freely and allows its performers such freedom of expression.

Basketball is a simple game

Put the ball in the basket. Keep your opponent from doing the same. Do I need to review?

Okay, coaches can make the game sound complicated. You may hear nonsense like, "Double down on the center in the low post after he puts the ball on the floor, and watch the skip pass to the three man beyond the arc." But making baskets and keeping your opponent from scoring is the gist of it.

Very little equipment is required

What are you wearing right now? Chances are you can play basketball in it. Shorts, a shirt, and sneakers are the only outfit you need to play the game. And if you're playing a pickup game (see Chapter 11), one side is probably skins anyway, so you may not even need the shirt. True, you wear less in surfing, but then not everyone lives near an ocean or owns a board.

Not everyone owns a basket, either, but you can find a court in practically every gym or playground. If you can't find a court, you can improvise by using a milk crate with the bottom punched out; that's almost exactly what founder James Naismith used. If a peach basket was good enough for him, it's good enough for anyone. But don't forget a ball — playing hoops isn't much fun without one.

You don't even need a net to play hoops; you can get by with just the rim and a backboard. Many an outdoor court at a school or playground is net-free — but it's a shame. If I were elected president, one of my first initiatives would be "No rims without nets." Every good shooter lives for the satisfying swish.

You don't need anyone else to play

One of my neighbors in South Bend has had a hoop over his garage for ten years. Just about every weekend or after school, he is out in his driveway shooting jumpshots.

You can play basketball by yourself like my neighbor, or you can play the game with any number of players. If you have an even number, divide by two and play a half-court or full-court game, depending on the number. (If you're in good shape, four-on-four is a good full-court run.) If you have 15 people, split up into three five-person teams and play a revolving format, with the loser going out each game. If you have 637 people, I'd suggest ordering out for pizza instead.

Don't forget your helmet

I can find only one report of a basketball player wearing a helmet onto the court, at least for pregame warm-ups. In the early 1960s, Clemson's Fike Fieldhouse had a reputation for being a poorly lit facility.

Duke coach Vic Bubas had complained in the newspapers about this prior to a game against the Clemson Tigers. One of Bubas's players, Bobby Joe Belmont, lodged a silent protest. During pregame warm-ups, he ran onto the court wearing a lighted miner's helmet. Everyone got a big kick out of that, but Clemson still didn't spring for new lights.

You're watching people, not uniforms

Whether you attend a game in person or view it on TV, basketball is intimate theater. You can see the faces of the players because they're not hidden by caps or helmets. Plus, the dimensions of the court allow less distance between the fan and the athlete. As a result, you experience the emotion up close. You see the players' emotions when they go up for a rebound or dive after a loose ball. By the time you're done watching a game, you feel as if you've glimpsed the character of at least a few players.

One of the reasons that NBA stars Michael Jordan and Charles Barkley are so marketable is that everyone can see their expressions on the court. Michael with his tongue sticking out is pure determination. Charles's wicked smile lets you know that he has another trick up his sleeve.

You're home by supper

You don't need all day to play hoops. You set your own time limit, by virtue of how many points you're playing to in a pickup game. If you have time to play to 21 baskets, do it. If it's getting dark outside, or if Mom said that you had to be home for dinner (it's lasagna night), shorten the game to 15 points. You're still playing the same game.

Watching hoops can be another story, however. College games usually take about two hours, and pro games are just slightly longer. But coaches — and I was as guilty of this as anyone — milk the clock at all levels. Coaches seem to have an endless reserve of time-outs at the end of a game. (Don't you hate that?) I tried to save all my time-outs for the end of the game to help set up the defense after a scored basket in case my team was behind. I'm sure that many of my cohorts can make the same argument. (If you were late for Saturday night mass or a date because of all those time-outs, I'm sorry.)

Ironically, in the greatest comeback Notre Dame ever made (UCLA in 1974), we made up an 11-point deficit in the final 3 minutes and 22 seconds without taking a time-out. Hmm.

The game flows

Basketball is constant action. As an experiment, I invite you to videotape a baseball game, a basketball game, and a football game. Now break down each tape into the amount of minutes of live action, and divide this number by the total time that it took to tape the game. You'll find that basketball is your best action-per-game deal around.

The momentum of hoops is one of its greatest entertainment assets. Say that Desmond Howard, formerly of the Green Bay Packers, runs back a punt for a touchdown in the Super Bowl as he did in Super Bowl XXXI. The arena is jumping. But by the time the extra point is kicked, the network goes to three minutes of commercials, and then the ball is kicked off . . . well, do you even remember how I began this sentence? Exactly my point.

Basketball, however, moves a lot faster. In the 1997 NCAA Final Four, North Carolina's Vince Carter delivered a thunderous slam dunk against Arizona, and before announcer Jim Nantz had finished describing it, University of Arizona guard Mike Bibby had already drained a three. How can you top that?

Weather or not, you can play

Rain, sleet, or snow — it's not just the mail that will go. Your scheduled basketball game will go on because you can play inside.

A baseball game can be rained out. A football game can't, but at times, excessive heat or cold may make you wish that you'd taken up bowling instead.

Unlike baseball or football, hoops can be played just as easily indoors as outdoors. If it's a beautiful summer day and you want to hoop it up outside, you can take your shirt off (if you're male) and bask in the sun. On a snowy New Year's Day, you can still play; just move the game indoors.

Basketball's all-season accessibility may explain why the college and pro seasons usually run from November to April or later, but as an Olympic sport, it's played in the summer.

March Madness

Upsets. Cinderella stories. Miracle buzzer-beater shots. 64 teams, 63 games. Nothing in sports matches the 19-day spectacle that is the NCAA tournament. The single-elimination format means that everyone has a chance. Unlike the NBA playoffs, you have to be sharp every game, or it's *hasta la vista.*

Above all, the single-elimination format of the tournament is what makes everything so dramatic. During the 1997 tournament, for example, Kansas was the favorite to win the tourney. The Jayhawks were ranked number one and had a 34-1 record heading into its third-round contest versus Arizona. Kansas lost. In a best-of-seven series, Kansas probably would have atoned for its errors, but that would hardly be as exciting. The fact that Kansas lost may seem cruel, but watching the upset as it occurred was terribly exciting, you have to admit. (See Chapter 13 for more information about the NCAA tournament.)

The Final Four

How interwoven into the American psyche has the Final Four weekend become? Consider: The term *Final Four* is copyrighted. President Bill Clinton appeared on the cover of *Sports Illustrated* in an Arkansas warm-up jacket, holding a basketball on the week that his home-state Razorbacks advanced to the Final Four in 1994 (the Hogs won the title, obliterating the theory about the *SI* cover jinx).

Fun for boys and girls everywhere

Although basketball is not the only team sport that offers men and women opportunities to play professionally (volleyball comes to mind), it is the most visible. Presently, there are two female pro leagues (the ABL and the WNBA) in the United States. Pro leagues for both sexes also exist overseas. Someday, who knows when, a female will have the goods to play in the NBA.

Coaching a Team

Basketball is the best team sport to coach. Every player must be able to play both offense and defense (unlike football) and must be ready to switch from one to the other at any moment (unlike baseball). If you enjoy teaching, these are two huge plusses, the former because any lesson you teach applies to all your students, and the latter because you must teach those students to make split-second decisions on their own.

Soccer is similar to basketball in this respect, but soccer games last more than twice as long — and soccer fans have been known, on occasion, to kill one another. That puts a little undue pressure on a coach.

Intimacy is another attractive facet of coaching this sport. A basketball court is tiny compared to a football field or a baseball diamond, and you have fewer athletes to manage. When you conduct a basketball practice, you don't feel as if you're Louis Gossett, Jr., in *An Officer and a Gentleman;* you feel as if you're Professor Kingsfield in *The Paper Chase* . . . although you may bark like Louis Gossett, Jr.: "I am a basketball coach. The court is my classroom. Class is never canceled on account of lightning."

Another thrill that a basketball coach has is proximity to the opposing team's coach. Unlike football, for example, you share the same sideline, and you are usually no more than 40 feet apart — almost within spitting distance and, yes, definitely within shouting distance. Coaches are competitive, after all. Being that close to your nemesis is much more exhilarating. See the sidebar "Facing the master" for one of my favorite coaching run-in tales.

Facing the master

In my second season at Notre Dame, we played UCLA. The Bruins were quite the juggernaut in those days, winning 10 national titles in 12 years. All those championships came under the guidance of coach John Wooden, a.k.a. "The Wizard of Westwood." Never a belligerent coach, Wooden was nevertheless an intimidating presence, simply because of his awesome success.

So here I was, a young Turk just barely past my 30th birthday. I had read Wooden's books on coaching and watched him at coaching clinics when I was pacing the sidelines at St. Gabriel's in the early days of my career. And now I found myself coaching against him. The whole experience was like being in a bake-off against Betty Crocker.

The game was physical. My center, John Shumate, was muscling up against the Bruins' outstanding center, Bill Walton, one of the most gifted big men ever to play the college game. The Wizard of Westwood went wild. Storming down the sideline toward me, he threatened that if I didn't tell Shumate to ease off on Walton, he would send in his burly Norwegian 7-footer, Swen Nater, to bully Shumate. I was awestruck. But not for long. "Go right ahead," I said. "I've got three Notre Dame football players on my bench, and they'll take on your whole team!"

Don't Become a Tunnel-Vision Fan

Unlike many other sports, basketball can be as fun to watch as it is to play. But hoops is more than just the score and Michael Jordan, believe it or not. As a fan, you can watch the game being played away from the ball, something easier done when you attend a game in person. Observe how Houston Rocket forward Charles Barkley, though short for his position at 6'6", uses his ample posterior to position himself for the many rebounds he grabs. Keep an eye on Utah Jazz guard John Stockton, who, despite his choirboy features, has been known to toss an elbow when setting a pick for a teammate.

Hopefully, after you read this book, you'll be able to spot a double down on defense or a pick and roll on offense. But in order to truly understand the game, you'll need to take that last step: Play. You can memorize notes and chords, but unless you pick up a guitar and strum, you don't really understand music. The same rule applies here.

So grab a ball and shoot. It'll make you a better player *and* a better fan. Making two free throws in a row isn't as easy as it looks on TV, is it?

Chapter 2

The Wear and Where of Basketball

In This Chapter

- Knowing what to wear
- Choosing the correct equipment
- Finding a game

A big advantage of hoops is that very little is required in the way of equipment. This chapter tells you exactly what you need to be able to play — and how to find a game after you're all geared up.

The Wear of Basketball

No shoes, no shorts, no game. That's the etiquette of basketball, pure and simple. While most dining establishments insist that you wear a shirt (although their "No shoes, no shirt, no service" signs make no mention of pants), basketball doesn't even require that much — if you're male. All you need are some rubber-soled shoes, cotton socks, and a pair of gym shorts or sweats. I recommend a shirt, too, in case you have big social plans after the game.

Sneakers

The sneaker craze all started in the 1950s. The Chuck Taylor Converse All-Star was the first shoe that anyone really bothered to market. It was a simple canvas shoe with a rubber sole and — for the high-top version — a round patch on the ankle that bore the sneaker's name. The white Chuck Taylor, the most popular color, had red and blue stripes along the side of the sole, providing an all-American touch.

Clyde: The first sneaker contract

The first pro basketball player to be paid to wear a certain type of basketball shoe was Walt Frazier of the New York Knicks. Frazier, far and away the most stylish player of his era (he played from 1967–1980), even earned his nickname, "Clyde," because of his flair for fashion. Folks thought that he dressed like a gangster, as in "Bonnie and Clyde." Frazier, who also happened to be a future Hall of Famer who helped the Knicks win two championships, was paid $5,000 by Puma to wear a low-cut suede sneaker, known as "the Clyde," in the 1970s. At the time, other NBA players were receiving free shoes, but nobody was being *paid* to wear them.

If you keep something (with regard to fashion) long enough, it comes back in style. (Just look at my ties!) The Chuck Taylor went out of style in the mid-1970s as players switched to leather shoes that, to be fair, offer far more ankle support. But today, you can see that hoops icon of the early 1970s, Julius Erving, promoting a modern version of the Chuck Taylor Converse All-Star shoe. This shoe is extremely popular with kids, almost all of whom wear it as a street shoe instead of using it for hoops.

High or low?

In the early years of sneakerdom, all players wore high-tops. Then John Havlicek of the Boston Celtics began wearing low-cuts in the 1960s because he felt that a lighter shoe made him quicker. When you're as gifted a player as "Hondo," people begin to imitate you — low-tops became a fad. Soon, players who didn't even rely on their quickness were wearing them. Havlicek's Hall of Fame partner on the Celtics, center Bill Russell, wore them, too.

If you play forward or center and are thus less reliant on speed than a guard, I'd suggest a high-top sneaker or at least the three-quarter-cut shoe that is out on the market today. This type of shoe extends to cover the ankle but doesn't go as high as a normal high-top. I advise the three-quarter-cut for guards as well. It's a very popular style in college and pro hoops.

Purchasing a sneaker

A good fit is critical for basketball shoes — you can acquire some serious blisters if your feet slide around inside your shoes. Do the following when you're shopping for sneakers to make sure that you get the best fit:

- Shop late in the day when your feet are swollen, because your feet swell while you're playing hoops, too.
- Measure your feet before you buy, even if you're an adult.
- When trying on a pair of sneakers, wear socks of the same thickness, and the same number of pairs, that you'll be wearing when you play.
- Don't be satisfied with the first pair you put on, no matter how good they look or how comfy they feel. Try a few different brands.
- Walk around in the shoes. Jog in the store if you so desire. Make quick starts and stops. Just don't ask the salesperson if you can dunk on the store's hoop.
- Lace up the sneakers tightly (as if you were playing) to make sure that they get snug everywhere.
- Check out the big toe in each foot. Is the big toe separated from the toe of the shoe by about the length of your thumbnail? It should be.
- Sizes can vary according to brand and product line. Always try on the shoe that you're considering buying.
- Pick up the shoe and try to bend it in half. If it flexes at the arch, you don't want it. If it bends at the ball of the foot, it deserves to remain in the running.

Socks

Also in the 1950s, the University of North Carolina players started a fad by wearing powder blue socks (with white stripes) to match their powder blue jersey and trunks. These socks went all the way up to the player's knees. Fortunately, the socks were only a fad and did not become an institution.

The 1960s are remembered in sock circles, if indeed such things exist, for Pete Maravich's floppy socks. "Pistol Pete" wore socks that drooped around his ankles. The socks had a strategic importance: Maravich used them to dry his hands before shooting free throws. With all the time Maravich handled the ball, he went to the foul line often.

Socks have realized a lot of fads in recent years. As shorts have gotten longer, socks have grown shorter. Ankle socks, like those worn by tennis players, are in vogue today. A few years ago, Michael Jordan began wearing *black* socks, and NBA players and high school kids alike copied that fashion statement. When you're wearing black sneakers, as Jordan does, the black sock is a good look.

Some players feel comfortable wearing two pairs of socks. Others prefer one thick pair of cotton socks. Listen to your feet and choose what works for you.

A mouthpiece

Many players, most visibly the NBA's Charles Barkley, wear a mouthpiece during games. If your position has you crashing the boards for rebounds quite often, then a mouthpiece — available at most sporting goods stores — is a good idea. Elbows have a way of displacing teeth from gums. Getting used to breathing with a mouthpiece in your mouth takes a little time. But getting used to root canal surgery takes even longer. Wear your 'piece.

Accessories

Keep accessories simple when playing hoops. Leave the bracelets, rings, tiaras, and other finery back in your jewelry drawer. The NCAA and most state high school athletic associations actually have rules against wearing jewelry on the court because of the potential for injury to other players.

The NCAA rule book outlaws "any equipment that is unnatural and designed to increase a player's height or reach, or to gain an advantage." In other words, if you own a pair of platform shoes or clogs, save them for the next "Retro Seventies" party you attend. Otherwise, use common sense. If your ancillary gear serves a protective purpose, such as a knee pad, and has no sharp or hard edges, wearing it in a game is okay. If the gear does not meet those two requirements, it doesn't belong on the court.

Uniforms

The basic uniform resembles a men's underwear ad: shorts and a tank top. Of course, you can pay as much as $150 for an official NBA team jersey — *sans* shorts — which is about the same price as a year's supply of undergarments for some people. But if you're just looking to play in a pickup game and the weather is nice, here's all you need:

- A loose-fitting pair of gym shorts
- A T-shirt or tank top

Remember these Hoops Fashion Don'ts:

- *Don't* play hoops in blue jeans, cycling shorts, or a bathing suit. (You need to be as comfortable as you can to really get into the game, so avoid tight clothing.)
- *Don't* play hoops in shirts that have buttons. (Other players may get caught on your buttons and hurt themselves — or your shirt.)

- *Don't* wear your watch. (It will inevitably scrape someone.)
- *Don't* wear a baseball cap. (The bill of a baseball cap may injure someone, and it will definitely impair your vision.) However, a 'do rag — that is, a handkerchief wrapped around your head — is acceptable in pickup games.)

Of all the equipment used in basketball, uniforms change the most. In the old days of basketball, uniforms were made of wool. Players wore tape on their chests because the jerseys irritated that part of their body. Later, the switch to cotton was made, and the game moved forward in a rash-free manner.

The most noticeable change in uniform style this decade has been the universal switch to baggy shorts, spearheaded by Michael Jordan. He wore them first, after he entered the NBA. Then the University of Michigan's Fab Five (including Juwan Howard, Jalen Rose, and Chris Webber, who started together and advanced to the NCAA championship game as freshmen) took the hem to even lower levels.

But unlike so many fashion revolutions, the baggy trunk has a practical purpose. When players are fatigued, they've always found that a good way to catch their breath is to bend over while free throws are being shot. But where would they rest their hands — on their thighs? Their thighs were sweaty, and their hands would slip. Baggy trunks allow players to grab the hem of their shorts, and make bending over much more comfortable.

Equipment

Any Generation X'er is familiar with the mantra: "Mom always says, 'Don't play ball in the house.'" This piece of sage advice was delivered on an episode of *The Brady Bunch* after Peter, the middle boy, broke a vase with a basketball. Peter had been playing hoops in his bedroom when his ill-advised (not to mention ill-fated) toss missed its target, a trash can, flew into the hallway, hit a wall, bounced down the stairs, and crushed said pottery. Sadly, thanks to syndication, this may be one of the most recognized shots in television history.

Although no bats (baseball), blades (hockey), or teeth (boxing) are used in basketball, hoops equipment is not intended for domestic use. Play outside or at a gym. Mom knows what she's talking about.

The ball

As far as game equipment, all you need are a basketball and a basket complete with rim and net. The ball part isn't too complicated: A basketball is spherical and orange and has eight panels. The old American Basketball

Association (ABA) used a red, white, and blue ball (the colors alternated on each panel), and the new Women's NBA (WNBA) uses an orange and white ball.

A regulation men's basketball is 9 inches in diameter. A slightly smaller ball is available for women; women's teams at most levels play with this ball.

The numbers game

A uniform number can make a statement. Athletes are more superstitious than the average Joe, and once they find a number they like, they don't want to part with it. When baseball pitcher Roger Clemens moved from the Boston Red Sox to the Toronto Bluejays in 1997, he gave new teammate Carlos Delgado a $20,000 Rolex watch in gratitude for Delgado's yielding his number 21 to Clemens, who had always worn that number. Clemens promptly went out and began the year with a 10-0 record.

Following is a list of some of the more recognized numbers in hoops and the reasons behind why the players chose them:

- **Michael Jordan, Chicago Bulls: 23**

  Jordan's older brother, Larry, played on the same team as Michael when the two were youths. Larry wore number 45, so Michael decided that he wanted to be half that number. The number 22½ was unavailable, so Michael simply rounded up to 23.

  When Jordan returned to the NBA in 1995 after a nearly two-season sabbatical — he had been playing minor-league baseball — he chose to wear 45 in the playoffs against the Orlando Magic. His 23 had already been ceremonially retired by the Bulls and hung in the rafters of the Bulls arena. But the Bulls were beaten by the Magic in what was probably Jordan's worst postseason series ever. In the third game of that series, Jordan, clearly ill at ease, switched back to wearing 23. The league fined the Bulls $50,000, but nevertheless, Jordan's 45 went the way of the vinyl 45 record: extinct.

- **Chamique Holdsclaw, University of Tennessee: 23**

  Chamique, the finest player in women's college basketball today, is a Jordan fan but did not choose wear 23 in his honor. She wears number 23 in praise of the 23rd Psalm: "The Lord is my Shepherd."

- **Gheorge Muresan, Washington Wizards: 77**

  Big George, the tallest player in NBA history, is 7'7". 'Nuff said.

- **Dennis Rodman, Chicago Bulls: 91**

  Rodman wanted to wear number 10 with the Bulls, which he had worn throughout his NBA career. But the Bulls had already retired number 10 in honor of Bob Love. Rodman chose 91 because 9 + 1 =10.

- **Randy Brown, Chicago Bulls: 1**

  Randy Brown used to wear number 0. When Robert Parrish joined the Bulls prior to the 1996–97 season, he wanted to continue to wear 00. The NBA allows teams to have a 0 or a 00, but not both. So Brown switched to 1.

- **Orlando Woolridge, Chicago Bulls, Los Angeles Lakers, 4 other NBA teams: 0**

  Woolridge's nickname is "O."

If you play outdoors on concrete or blacktop often, invest in an outdoor or indoor/outdoor ball. An outdoor ball is made of rubber as opposed to leather, which is the material used for indoor balls. You'll play outdoors 80 percent of the time and outdoor balls can be used indoors, too. If you do own a leather ball, *never* use it outdoors. Concrete or blacktop will scuff it, and rain will ruin it.

The backboard

The backboard is a rectangular mount upon which a rim is hung. Regulation backboards measure 6 feet x $3^1/_2$ feet and are made of transparent Plexiglas. Backboards have been known to shatter due to the excessive force of some dunks, which cause the rim to shake. The resulting tremor shatters the Plexiglas. A shattered backboard requires a good half-hour to replace. The thrill of witnessing a backboard-breaking slam is not worth the wait, believe me.

Darryl Dawkins, who played in the NBA in the 1970s and '80s, was the first famous backboard shatterer. Shaquille O'Neal, who has shattered two backboards thus far in the NBA, presently poses the greatest threat to backboards. All NBA backboards are now fitted with *breakaway rims,* which are supposed to come unhinged from the backboard when too much force is placed upon them, thus sparing the backboard. (See the "Breakaway rims" sidebar.)

Fan-shaped backboards were an experiment in the early days of basketball. I don't mean fans like the ones who sit in the seats — you know, the other kind. Fan-shaped backboards are still prevalent at many parks and, until a few years ago, were all the rage at Illinois high schools. The major detriment to these backboards is that they make shooting a bankshot more difficult. A shooter doesn't have as much room to work with.

Breakaway rims

The breakaway rim operates on a total force system. When enough force is exerted on the basket, the rim releases from the lip and folds down. The rim takes only a few seconds to spring back up. Without a breakaway rim, extreme force would pull it away from the backboard and hence shatter the backboard. A shattered backboard makes for an electrifying photo or piece of video footage, but nobody likes to wait for a new backboard to be installed.

Breakaway rims were introduced after dunking became chic. Between 1967–68 and 1975–76, dunking was illegal in college hoops, and folks saw no real need for breakaway rims. When dunking was legalized, the breakaway rim made its debut. Dunking has always been legal in pro basketball. Now it's simply cliché.

The rim

The rim is attached to the backboard and is suspended 10 feet above the floor. That's the way the rim was 100 years ago, and that's the way the rim is today, even though humans on average are much taller today. NBA center Shawn Bradley, who stands 7'6", can touch the rim with his middle finger when he stands on his tiptoes.

The inside of the rim is 18 inches in diameter, exactly twice the diameter of a men's basketball.

The net

The net, which is composed of nylon mesh cord, hangs down from the rim approximately 15 to 18 inches. The net hooks onto the rim at eight different rungs located around the rim's bottom. Ostensibly, the net's function is to slow the path of the ball as it passes through the basket and help you tell whether the ball actually went through the hoop, as well as to provide depth perception for the shooter. (See the sidebar "The net effect.")

The net effect

Nets can have a significant impact on a game. For example, when John Wooden coached at UCLA, his teams employed an effective full-court zone trap press. The key to the press's success was having the defenders in position as soon as the other team in-bounded the ball.

One way to ensure that the Bruins always had enough time to set up a press was to make the nets tight. When the net was tight, the ball was momentarily trapped inside it. The net was never so tight as to restrict the ball's passage, but rather just tight enough to slow the ball's momentum. After UCLA made a shot, therefore, you'd have to wait for the ball to drop from the net as if a hen were laying an egg. By the time you were set to in-bound the ball, the Bruins were already in their press positions.

Coach Paul Westhead's Loyola Marymount teams of the late '80s used the exact opposite tactic. Westhead wanted to accelerate the action, to run, run, run until the opponent was gasping for air. So Westhead put loose nets on his rims. Loose nets, which let the ball pass through the cylinder with negligible loss of speed, allowed the Lions to retrieve the ball quicker and charge upcourt before the opponent was able to catch its breath.

Too bad Wooden and Westhead, whose schools are located not far from one another in Los Angeles, coached in different eras. I would have liked to see their teams play one another to see what the "net" effect would have been.

Here are two interesting bits of trivia concerning nets:

- When you watch players cut nets down in celebration after a big victory, understand that *cutting* the net is not necessary. They could just as easily unclasp the net from the rungs on the rim. However, they take turns snipping the net — one player per rung — so that everyone receives a strand of the net.
- The net is the only piece of equipment after which an NBA team (the New Jersey Nets) is named.

My beef: baskets with no nets. You see this a lot in inner-city courts. People steal nets or hang from them — if the nets aren't chain-linked, which are tough on the fingers — and that causes them to fray. Nets are a shooter's dessert. Please, I implore you: If your playground or school yard hoop has a net, don't steal or abuse it.

The Where of Basketball

Although astronauts don't play basketball on the moon — the low force of gravity there *would* make for a fun game — hoops is played almost everywhere else. In prison yards. On ships. Chevy Chase's Fletch character in the movie *Fletch* — ignoring the wisdom of *The Brady Bunch* — used his living room as a court.

You really need little more than a flat surface roughly the size of a classroom and at least 20 feet of vertical space.

Your own driveway

The fact that basketball and the automobile were invented within 15 years of one another is indeed serendipitous. For the advent of the auto meant the arrival of the driveway, which can serve a dual role as a basketball court. And the garage has long been an ideal place upon which to mount a backboard and rim.

Putting up a hoop in the driveway or backyard

Installing your own basketball hoop in or near your driveway can cost anywhere from $50 to $250, the high-end hoops being mobile units mounted upon dollies that require nearly no assembly. Before you decide to install a court at your home, first decide whether your driveway or other concrete or asphalt surface is level. If it's relatively level, the next step is to choose whether to purchase a pole that you will plant in the ground, and upon which the backboard and rim will be mounted; or to simply mount the backboard and rim on or above a preexisting structure, such as a garage, a sloped roof, or a barn. (A common good-natured taunt when your shot is off is, "You couldn't hit the broad side of a barn!" Well, now you can.)

Neither option is better than the other. Simply assess your own property. If you select a pole, be sure to plant it at least 24 to 36 inches in the ground and support it by fixing it into the ground in a bed of cement. Allow the cement to set for 48 hours before mounting the backboard on the pole.

Mounting a hoop on the garage

From a cost point of view, the less expensive approach is a universal mounting bracket, which costs about $20. This bracket allows you to mount the backboard to a garage wall with the hoop at the desired level. The advantage of a universal bracket is that you can mount it on a sloping roof, a side wall, or a pole. To that, you attach the backboard, which should already have a rim attached. You can buy a quality backboard and attached rim for about $20.

Schoolyards or playgrounds

Schoolyard and playground hoops offer full-court game possibilities and so much more. It's where you meet new people — hopefully upstanding types (the only junkies I ever want to see at a schoolyard are basketball junkies). You also face better levels of competition. (The driveway court is fun, but face it; Uncle Leo can't drive to his left.)

Literally taking matters into your own hands

The Bookstore Courts at Notre Dame are located just 200 yards from Sacred Heart Church. On Sundays, the courts are used for parking. (Doesn't anybody walk anymore?) In 1976, when the school's Bookstore Basketball tournament field was expanded to 256 teams, some games had to be played on Sunday.

Tournament commissioner Tim Bourret, a contributor to this book (and the real brains behind it), was aware of the dual usage of the Bookstore Courts on Sunday mornings. However, Bourret figured that the crowd from the 10:45 a.m. mass would already have dispersed by the start of the first game, at noon.

He was right... with one exception. At noon, a 1973 Volkswagen was still parked in the foul lane of one of the courts. At 12:15, something had to be done. Fortunately, Bourret had scheduled a game at this time in which four Notre Dame football players were competing. Taking a page from Moses, Bourret commanded that the VW be moved. The gridders complied. Game on.

An hour later, players and fans alike watched with delight when the owner of the car returned. For a moment, he looked befuddled. Had he witnessed a miracle? Then he simply stepped into his car and drove away.

The schoolyard is also where children learn to be grownups in a positive sense. They learn how to fit in with a group, settle disputes ("Call the foul before the shot misses the basket!"), and stand up for themselves.

Youngsters should always be accompanied — if not by an adult, then at least by an older sibling — when going to shoot at a schoolyard. Also, no matter how badly you get beaten on the court, don't ever take your basketball and go home as a retort. Crybabies are not welcome at the schoolyard.

See Chapter 11 for more information about pickup basketball.

Churches

Your local church may have a court, indoor or outdoor. A church usually doesn't have an indoor facility, however, unless it is affiliated with an adjacent school.

One big problem with outdoor church courts: parking. At a Catholic church, for example, your court is likely to double as a parking lot on Saturday night and Sunday morning. When I see people parking on basketball courts, I pray to God for their enlightenment.

Community centers

When the Village People sang, "You can hang out with all the boys," in the classic hit "YMCA," I don't think that they had basketball in mind. But hoops facilities at community centers such as the YMCA and YWCA have existed for many years and are a step up, in terms of supervision and organization, from the schoolyard.

Most community center facilities are indoor and have someone in charge. These facilities have house rules — such as "winners remain on the court, losers must sit out" — that lend order to the scene. These facilities are also prime arenas for the older generation, players 25 to 35, who are looking for a weekly workout. Warning to those under 25: Once the legs go, players hack (foul) more often. Also, they seem to remember themselves being better shots than they actually were.

Wheelchair basketball

In Chapter 1, I mention that basketball does not discriminate. Nowhere is this point better made than in the various leagues that exist for the mentally and/or physically disabled. Wheelchair basketball leagues, for example, including the National Wheelchair Basketball Association (NWBA), exist all over the United States. If you don't think that the game is as competitive as what you see in the NBA, I invite you to attend a game. These guys may take the game even *more* seriously.

Wheelchair basketball games are played on regulation courts, and the league has its own rulebook. Most of the same rules apply, with certain exceptions. (For example, the rulebook doesn't say anything about penalizing a player who hangs on the rim too long after a dunk.)

A sampling of wheelchair basketball rules:

1. To execute a dribble, a player may

   a. Wheel the chair by two pushes on the wheels (one hand or two hands, in either direction) of the chair followed by one or more taps of the ball to the floor, after which she may start pushing again.

   b. Wheel the chair and bounce the ball simultaneously (just as a player may run and bounce the ball simultaneously in regular basketball).

   Taking more than two pushes in succession constitutes a traveling violation, and the ball is awarded to the other team.

2. The location of the player is determined by where any part of the chair is touching the floor. This theory is used when determining whether or not a player is inbounds.

3. All rules that relate to a three-second violation in regular basketball apply, except wheelchair basketball uses a four-second violation.

4. A team loses possession when a player leans either forward or backward to the extent that the chair tilts and the foot rest makes contact with the floor.

Basketball Hotbeds: Where the Best Players Come From

When I was recruiting during the 1960s at Penn and in the 1970s and 1980s at Notre Dame, basketball was a city game. My best players in the 1970s were from the New York and Washington, D.C., areas. When Notre Dame defeated UCLA in 1971, the only loss the Bruins suffered that year, three of the Fighting Irish starters were natives of Washington, D.C. When we ended UCLA's 88-game winning streak three years later, my starting five consisted of three New York metro players and a D.C. player.

New York was the hotbed then. Chicago, D.C., Detroit, and Los Angeles were not far behind. Today, that situation has changed; you find outstanding hoops players not only all over the country but also all over the world. (See Chapter 15 for more information about international basketball.)

Consider for a moment some of the NBA MVPs (most valuable players) of the past two decades. Sure, Kareem Abdul-Jabbar was a native New Yorker, but look further. Larry Bird? From French Lick, Indiana. Michael Jordan? From Wilmington, North Carolina. Karl Malone of the Utah Jazz? From Summerfield, Louisiana. True, Houston Rocket center Hakeem Olajuwon is from a big city, Lagos. But that's in Nigeria.

For many years, though, New York was the epicenter of basketball talent. Table 2-1 shows the top ten states of high schools attended by All-America college players. The majority of those from New York state hailed from the Big Apple.

Table 2-1 State of High School Attended by Division I Consensus All-Americans, 1928–1997

Rank	*State*	*Number of Players*
1.	New York	29
2.	Indiana	27
3.	Pennsylvania	25
4.	California	22
5.	Illinois	19
6.	Ohio	13
7.	North Carolina	11
7.	Kentucky	11
9.	Texas	8
9.	New Jersey	8

Source: Mike Douchant, *Inside Sports College Basketball* (1997).

Note: Three Division I Consensus All-Americans were indeed not United States citizens but hailed from foreign countries. And 15 states have never produced a Division I Consensus All-American.

Check out Table 2-2 for a list of the NBA's 50 greatest players by home state or country. Home state is based on where the player played high school basketball.

Table 2-2 The NBA's 50 Greatest Players by Home State/Country

Home State	*Number*	*Players*
New York	7	Kareem Abdul-Jabbar, Nate Archibald, Bob Cousy, Billy Cunningham, Julius Erving, Dolph Schayes, Lenny Wilkins
North Carolina	5	Sam Jones, Michael Jordan, Pete Maravich, Earl Monroe, James Worthy
Louisiana	5	Robert Parrish, Bob Petit, Willis Reed, Karl Malone, Elvin Hayes
Ohio	3	John Havlicek, Jerry Lucas, Nate Thurmond
California	3	Bill Russell, Bill Sharman, Bill Walton
Michigan	3	Dave DeBusschere, George Gervin, Magic Johnson
Pennsylvania	2	Paul Arizin, Wilt Chamberlain
Washington, D.C.	2	Elgin Baylor, Dave Bing
Indiana	2	Larry Bird, Oscar Robertson
Illinois	2	Isiah Thomas, George Mikan
West Virginia	2	Hal Greer, Jerry West
Virginia	2	Moses Malone, David Robinson
Kentucky	2	Wes Unseld, Dave Cowens
Texas	2	Clyde Drexler, Shaquille O'Neal
Alabama	1	Charles Barkley
Arkansas	1	Scottie Pippen
Georgia	1	Walt Frazier
Massachusetts	1	Patrick Ewing
Minnesota	1	Kevin McHale
New Jersey	1	Rick Barry
Washington	1	John Stockton
Nigeria	1	Hakeem Olajuwon

Chapter 3

The Rules

In This Chapter

- Getting around the court
- Playing a game
- Understanding fouls and violations

In December of 1891, James Naismith introduced his gymnastics class at the Springfield (Massachusetts) YMCA to his yet-unnamed invention. Naismith, a physical education teacher, nailed peach baskets to the lower rail of the balcony at both ends of the gym, and then grabbed a soccer ball. Finally, he tacked a list of 13 rules, which would govern this new game, to a bulletin board. Soon after the first game was played, the rules were stolen. (I guess "Do not steal the rules" was not one of the original 13 rules.)

A few days later, one of Naismith's students, Frank Mahon, 'fessed up to the crime. "I took them," Mahon told his teacher. "I knew that this game would be a success, and I took them as a souvenir. But I think now that you should have them."

Mahon later atoned for his crime by suggesting a name for the infant sport. Having had his first idea *(Naismith Ball)* rejected by Naismith himself, Mahon asked, "How about *basketball?*"

"We have a basket and a ball," said Naismith. "It seems to me that would be a good name for it."

Those were simpler times.

Naismith's Original 13 Rules

In less than one hour, James Naismith, sitting at a desk in his office at the YMCA, framed the 13 rules that would govern basketball. (Compare that to today, when it takes rules *committees* months to make a decision about a single rule.) Here's how the father of the game envisioned it:

1. The ball may be thrown in any direction with one or both hands.
2. The ball may be batted in any direction with one or both hands (but never with a fist).
3. A player cannot run with the ball. The player must throw it from the spot on which he catches it; allowance to be made for a man who catches the ball when running at a good speed.
4. The ball must be held in or between the hands; the arms or body must not be used for holding it.
5. No shouldering, holding, pushing, tripping, or striking in any way the person of an opponent shall be allowed. The first infringement of this rule by any person shall count as a foul; the second shall disqualify him until the next goal is made, or, if there was evident intent to injure the person for the whole of the game, no substitute allowed.
6. A foul is striking at the ball with the fist, violation of Rules 3, 4, and such as described in Rule 5.
7. If either side makes three consecutive fouls, it shall count as a goal for the opponents. (*Consecutive* means without the opponent in the meantime making a foul.)
8. A goal shall be made when the ball is thrown or batted from the grounds into the basket and stays there, providing that those defending the goal do not touch or disturb the goal. If the ball rests on the edge and the opponent moves the basket, it shall count as a goal.
9. When the ball goes out of bounds, it shall be thrown into the field and played by the person first touching it. In case of a dispute, the umpire shall throw it straight into the field. The thrower-in is allowed five seconds. If he holds it longer, it shall go to the opponent. If any side persists in delaying the game, the umpire shall call a foul on them.
10. The umpire shall be the judge of the men and shall note the fouls and notify the referee when three consecutive fouls have been made. He shall have power to disqualify men according to Rule 5.
11. The referee shall be judge of the ball and decide when the ball is in play, in bounds, and to which side it belongs, and shall keep the time. He shall decide when a goal has been made, and keep account of the goals, with any other duties that are usually performed by a referee.
12. The time shall be two 15-minute halves, with 5 minutes rest between.
13. The side making the most goals in that time shall be declared the winners. In case of a draw, the game may, by agreement of the captains, be continued until another goal is made.

You may notice a few discrepancies between Naismith's rules and those adhered to today. For one, they're shorter — the NBA's illegal defense rule alone is more verbose than Naismith's entire set of rules. Another difference: The game, as originally conceived, doesn't account for dribbling.

The Court

A basketball court has symmetry; one half of the court is a mirror image of the other. The entire court, as shown in Figure 3-1, is 90 feet x 54 feet. On each half-court, painted lines show the *free throw lane* and *circle,* as well as the *three-point arc,* whose distance from the basket varies according to the level of hoops being played. (For example, the men's pro line is farther from the basket than the college line by 4 feet.)

Indoor basketball courts are almost always made of hardwood. Outdoor courts are most commonly composed of asphalt.

The borders of the court have their own commonsense names:

- Along the length of the court, the borders are known as the *sidelines.*
- Along the ends, the borders are called the *endlines,* or *baselines.*
- Separating both halves of the court is a *midcourt line.*
- In the very center of the midcourt line is the *center circle* (12 feet in diameter), where the *center toss* takes place to begin the game. (See the section "To begin" later in this chapter, for more information about the center toss — also known as a jump ball or tipoff.)

The free throw lane and free throw line

The *free throw lane* is the hub of the action, the Times Square, in each half-court. This rectangle is 12 feet in width — 16 feet at the men's pro level. Its length, as measured from the basket to the *free throw line,* is 15 feet at all levels. An offensive player may not stand inside the lane for more than three seconds unless the ball is being shot. A defensive player may remain inside the lane for as long as she desires.

A player who is fouled (see the "Fouls" section later in this chapter for a list of common fouls) is awarded *free throws* (also known as *foul shots*). These shots (they aren't really "throws") are taken from the free throw line at the end of the lane — 15 feet from the basket. The shots are "free" because the shooter is not guarded by a defender while shooting. When a player shoots a free throw, his feet may not cross the free throw line as he is taking the shot, or the shot is nullified.

The remaining players line up alongside the free throw lane (or behind the shooter) and cannot interfere with the shot. The fans behind the basket, however, usually scream, jump up and down, and wave their hands to try to distract an opposing team's shooter during free throws.

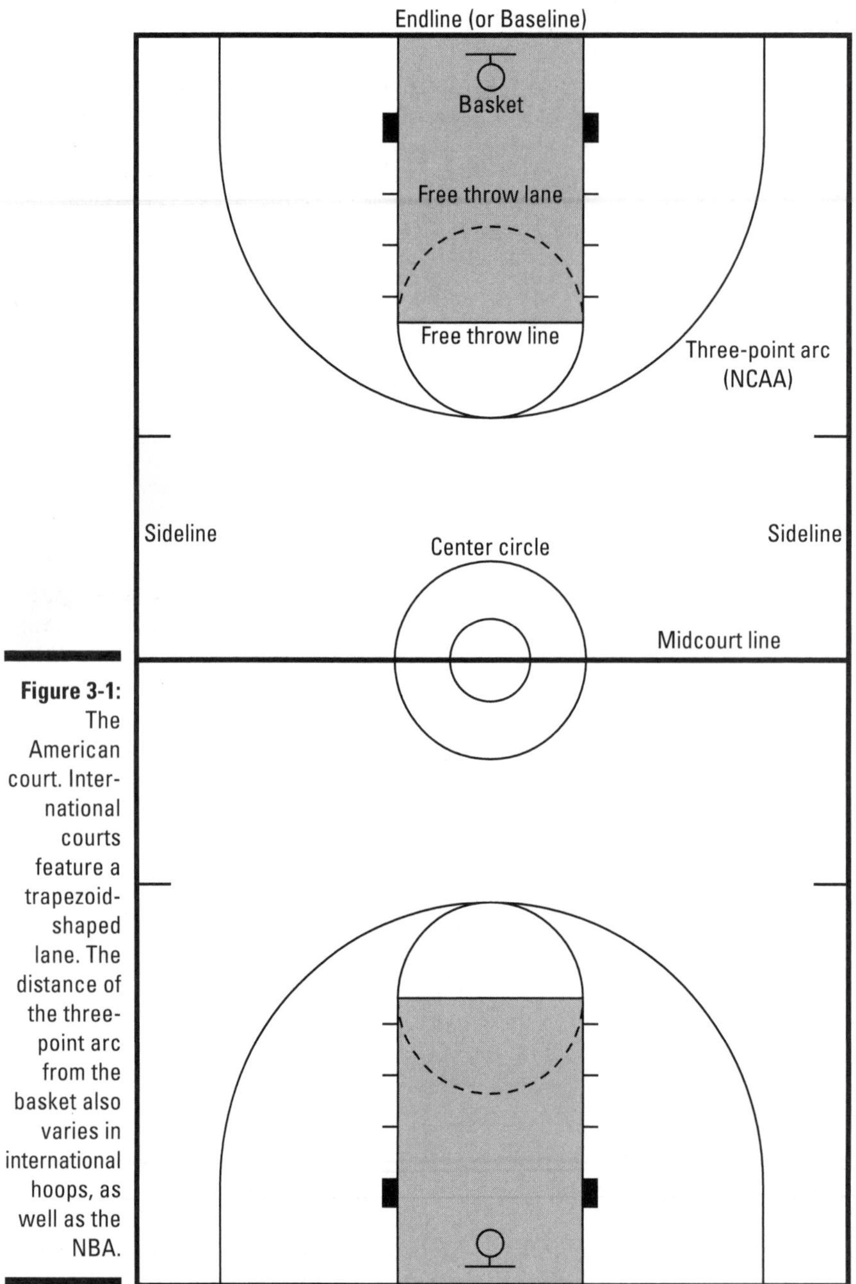

Figure 3-1: The American court. International courts feature a trapezoid-shaped lane. The distance of the three-point arc from the basket also varies in international hoops, as well as the NBA.

The three-point arc

The *three-point arc* is the other important marked feature of the court. The arc extends around the basket in a near semicircle, and its distance from the basket differs according to the level of play. Even at one level, the distance has been known to change as rules committees grapple with what is the best distance for the good of the sport. The NBA has changed the three-point distance on two different occasions since first adopting the *trey,* as it's called, in the 1979–80 season. The three point distance has been moved back to its original 23' 9" for the 1997-98 season.

Any shot made from beyond this arc — even a desperation half-court shot at the buzzer — is worth three points. A three-point shooter must have both feet behind the arc as he launches this shot, but either foot is allowed to *land* on the other side of the arc.

The backcourt and frontcourt

Thinking of the entire court as two half-courts, divide it into frontcourt and backcourt. The *frontcourt* is the half of the court where the offense's basket is located. The *backcourt* is the other half. Thus one team's backcourt is the other team's frontcourt.

The Players

At every level of organized basketball, five players per team are on the court at one time. The usual division of players by position is two *guards,* two *forwards,* and one *center.* (See Chapter 6 for information about what players at each position do.)

Most basketball teams consist of 12 players. In the NBA, 12 players is the rule. High school and college teams may have a few more or less. Each player wears a uniform that, in most cases, consists of trunks and a tank top.

One player may be substituted for another only during a stoppage in play. The player or players intending to enter the game approach the *scorer's table,* which is located at midcourt along one sideline. The scorer's table is where the game's official scorer and timer sit. When play stops for whatever reason, the referee acknowledges the player's presence at the table — although he doesn't shake his hand or hug him or anything that friendly — and waves him into the game (at which time the player being substitued for leaves the game).

The Game

The objective in basketball is simple: to score more points than your opponent. This is accomplished by making baskets on *offense* (when your team has the ball) and preventing your opponent from scoring baskets while you're playing *defense* (when your opponent has the ball).

Unlike football, in basketball, the same players remain in the game to play both offense and defense. In rhythm and in the roles of its players, basketball is more closely related to soccer or hockey, where the transition from offense to defense can occur in the blink of an eye. You can find out much more about what the offense and defense do specifically in Chapters 6 and 7, respectively.

To begin

Each game begins with a *tipoff,* or *center toss,* at the center circle. The referee stands in the center of the circle and tosses the basketball directly upward. Each team's center then leaps and attempts to tap the ball (you are not allowed to grab the ball) to one of her teammates, who must position themselves outside the 12-foot-diameter circle. Any player may be involved in the tipoff, but the center — usually the tallest player — almost always does the honors. (Height is very helpful in this case.)

Time-in, time-out

Think of the game in two parts: time-in, when the clock is moving and the action is taking place; and time-out, when play (and therefore the clock) is stopped. "How much time is in a game?" may be your first question. Well, that varies from level to level:

- An NBA or ABL (American Basketball League, a women's pro league) contest has four 12-minute quarters.
- WNBA (Women's NBA, another women's pro league), international, and college basketball games are divided into two 20-minute halves.
- High school basketball games have four 8-minute quarters or two 16-minute halves.

The shot clock

The offense must shoot the basketball within a certain amount of time, kept by the shot clock, or forfeit the ball to the defense. The reason for this shot clock rule is to provide the game with more offense and to reward the defense for a job well done. In the NBA, the shot clock is 24 seconds. In men's college hoops, the shot clock is 35 seconds, and in women's pro and college, 30 seconds is the agreed-upon time.

The shot clock was invented in 1954 by Danny Biasone, a bowling alley proprietor and owner of the Syracuse Nationals, an original NBA franchise. The shot clock may have saved the pro game. The college game, which has featured games with scores as low as 1-0, did not adopt the shot clock until 1985-86.

Ten seconds

After a team makes a basket, the opposing team takes the ball out of bounds under the basket at which the points were just scored. The team with the ball must in-bound it within five seconds of touching it and then advance it toward their own basket and past the midcourt line within ten seconds of *in-bounding* the ball. (This rule does not apply in women's college basketball.) Failure to do either results in a loss of the ball.

Once the offensive team advances the ball past midcourt, the ball — or the player possessing it — may not retreat behind the center line (in other words, to his team's backcourt), although an offensive player not in possession of the ball may stand there. Obviously, though, that player is of no help to his team.

Time-out

Time stands still for no one — except a referee. The game clock in basketball can stop for the following reasons:

- A coach on either team calls a time-out to discuss matters with her players.
- The referee blows his whistle to signal a violation.
- The ball goes out of bounds.
- A quarter or period ends.
- A basket is made inside the last minute of a game in college, and the last two minutes in the NBA.

A coach or player may call time-out only during a stoppage in play or if his team has the ball. In other words, a defensive player may never request a time-out while the clock is running. Each team is allotted a specific number of time-outs per half; if the teams exceed that number, they are penalized with a technical foul (see the sidebar "Bending the rules" for a famous example of this).

Bending the rules

More than a few hoops fans consider Game 5 of the 1976 NBA Finals to be the most exciting NBA game ever played. The upstart Phoenix Suns took the Boston Celtics, the vanguard of the league, to three overtimes at Boston Garden before losing 128-126. The game may never have extended beyond the second overtime, though, were it not for the chicanery of Suns guard Paul Westphal — who, oddly enough, had spent the previous three seasons of his career playing for the Celtics.

With one second remaining in the second overtime, Celtics forward John Havlicek banked in an off-balance shot on the run to give Boston a one-point lead, 111-110. The mob at the Garden, ecstatic that their Celtics had won (and perhaps a tad delirious due to the lack of air-conditioning), rushed onto the court to celebrate. But Westphal, a heady player, knew that one second remained, and considered his team's options in the ensuing chaos.

In the NBA, a team that calls time-out in the final two minutes of the game is allowed to in-bound the ball at half-court. But the Suns were out of time-outs, meaning that they would have to in-bound the ball from their own endline. Westphal realized that in-bounding the ball from so far away from the basket would give Phoenix a long shot — both figuratively and literally — at victory. But what choice did the Suns have?

Westphal pondered the crisis. Then he realized that, if he called time-out, the Suns would be whistled for a technical foul — and Boston would be awarded one free throw — but that the Suns would receive a time-out and get the ball at midcourt. Westphal called time-out.

All went according to plan. Jo Jo White of the Celtics made the free-throw, giving Boston a 112-110 lead. The ball was then in-bounded from midcourt to Suns forward Garfield Heard, who calmly sank a jumper from beyond 25 feet (today that shot would be worth three points, giving Phoenix the win) as the buzzer sounded. Triple overtime.

In Hollywood, the Suns would have ridden that emotional high to victory, but in Boston Garden, the Celtics won. The league later changed the rules so that a repeat of Westphal's trickery would not occur. A technical foul now results in two free throws plus automatic loss of possession.

Overtime

A basketball game cannot end in a tie. When a regulation game ends with the score tied, the teams play an extra period, five minutes in length. This rule applies at all levels. Each player retains his personal fouls; you often see one or more players foul out during this extra session. No matter how large a lead one team may build during overtime, the game doesn't end until all five minutes are played. If the score is still tied at the end of the five-minute overtime, the game goes into another overtime period — ad nauseum, until one team comes out victorious.

Fouls

A *personal foul* is a violation that occurs when, in the official's opinion, a player has engaged in illegal contact with an opponent. Both defensive and offensive players can commit fouls, although defensive fouls are much more common. (You can read about the more common fouls later in this chapter.) Though a certain amount of contact in the game is both permissible and inevitable, you can think of a foul as physical contact that disrupts the normal flow of a game.

You often hear announcers say that the referees (there are three for most games) are calling the game *close* or *loose.* If they're calling it close, that means even minor contact is resulting in a foul call. A loosely called game, or "letting the players play," resembles a playground or pickup game: More physical play is allowed.

Fouling out

If players could foul with impunity, nobody would be able to launch a shot without being fouled — or *hacked,* in basketball parlance. Thus, rules limit the number of fouls a player is allowed. In pro basketball, players are allowed six fouls; at all other levels, they are allowed five. Upon committing a sixth (if she plays in the pros) or fifth foul, the player *fouls out* and must leave the game. She may be replaced by another player, but she may not reenter the game.

Fouling out plays a tremendous role in the strategy of a game. Most coaches live by the credo that no player should pick up more than three fouls (in pro ball) or two fouls (at other levels) before halftime. If a player exceeds this limit, the coach usually sits him down until the second half begins to try to lessen the possibility that he'll foul out.

What happens when a foul is whistled? First, play stops and the referee signals to the scorer's table the number of the player who committed the foul. If an offensive player commits the foul, the penalty is loss of the ball. If a defensive player commits the foul, the penalty depends on who was fouled:

- If the defensive player fouls the player with the ball *while she is attempting a shot,* the shooter is rewarded with two free throws if the shot misses, and one if the shot is good.
- In all other situations, the offense simply takes the ball out of bounds, and the shot clock (in pro and college) is reset — that is, unless the team that committed the foul is over the limit.

Over the limit

Just as a player is allowed to commit only a limited number of personal fouls (there are no such things as impersonal fouls, no matter how aloof the guilty party is) during a game, his team as a whole is also limited in the number of fouls it may commit during a quarter or half. This limit is known as the *team foul limit.*

Each team is allowed six fouls, either in a quarter or — in college, international, and WNBA games — in one half. Any more fouls, and the team is *over the limit.* Once a team is over the limit in the pros, the fouled offensive player is awarded two free throws. In college ball, the fouled offensive player is awarded a one-and-one. In a *one-and-one situation,* the player goes to the free throw line and shoots one free throw. If that shot goes in, she gets a second free throw. However, if that shot misses, the rebound is *live* — that is, the shot is treated like a missed shot during regular play. (A second free throw, then, is not awarded.)

On the tenth and subsequent team fouls in college ball, the one-and-one is no longer in effect, and the fouled player gets two free throws for every foul. This rule was designed to discourage teams who are trailing in the closing minutes of a game from fouling constantly. It is unofficially known as the Valvano Rule, after the late North Carolina State coach whose Wolfpack won the 1983 NCAA title by employing this strategy.

Offensive fouls

The three most commonly called offensive fouls are

- **Charging:** When the player with the ball moves into a defender who has already established his stationary defensive position.
- **Moving pick:** When the player setting a pick for his teammate moves to block the path of the defender. (See Chapter 6 for more on picks.)
- **Over the back:** When an offensive player who is boxed out while attempting to grab a rebound tries to jump over the defender and makes excessive contact with the defender. (See Chapter 8 for a description of boxing out.)

An offensive personal foul, like a defensive personal foul, counts as one foul against the player who committed it.

Technical fouls

Technical fouls (which someday may be redubbed "Rodmans") may be whistled against either a coach or a player. A referee whistles a technical foul against someone who has either spoken or behaved in an extremely unsportsmanlike fashion. Dennis Rodman of the Chicago Bulls, whose dossier includes kicking a courtside photographer and headbutting a referee, was called for one technical foul in each of the Bulls first 11 playoff games in 1997. Two technical fouls equal an automatic ejection.

A technical foul does not count against a player's personal fouls in the pros, but it does in college. Thus if Rodman had five personal fouls and was then whistled for a technical foul, he would remain in the game.

Nonfoul Violations

Because most nonfoul violations are whistled against the offensive team, I'll discuss the defensive nonfoul violations first:

- **Goaltending:** Goaltending is called when a defensive player illegally interferes with a shot. If he touches the ball as it makes its downward path to the basket, touches the ball while it is on the rim, or touches the rim or net itself as the ball is being shot, goaltending is called, and the offensive team is awarded the basket.
- **Kicking:** The defensive player is not allowed to kick the ball as a means of deflecting a pass. On any kicked ball violation, the offense retains possession of the ball, but the shot clock is not reset. Most, if not all, coaches encourage this defensive tactic even though it's against the rules, because it forces the opponent to reset its offense.
- **Illegal defense:** In the NBA, *zone defenses* — defenses where players defend an area, or zone, instead of a specific player — are not allowed (although well-disguised zones are all anyone seems to play). The first time a team is whistled for illegal defense, the team receives a warning. On all subsequent illegal defense calls during the game, the team is assessed a technical foul and the offense is awarded one free throw, retaining possession of the ball.

Offensive nonfoul violations result in a loss of possession. Such a violation is listed as a *turnover,* and almost all are concerned with the player mishandling the ball. For that reason, most coaches put a premium on having a reliable point guard who commits as few of these violations as possible. The team that turns over the ball the most usually loses. These are the mistakes that cause coaches' hair to turn gray. A few of the more grating offenses:

- **Traveling:** Anytime a player possessing the ball is not dribbling, he must keep one foot (known as his *pivot foot*) planted on the floor. He may move the other foot in any direction and as many times as he desires. Once a player establishes a pivot foot, he may not move it, or he is whistled for traveling.

- **Double dribbling:** A double dribble occurs when a player either dribbles the ball with two hands at the same time or dribbles the ball, stops, and then resumes his dribble (known as *picking up his dribble*).
- **Carrying** or **palming:** A player dribbling the ball is not allowed to bring her palm under the ball when it reaches its apex off the dribble. Always keep your palms facing the floor when dribbling the ball.
- **Up and down:** A player in possession of the ball may not jump and then land while still in possession of the ball. Technically, he has traveled. In moving both feet, he has lifted his pivot foot.
- **Three seconds:** No part of an offensive player may remain in the free throw lane for more than three consecutive seconds unless the ball is being shot. If the shot hits the rim, the player standing in the lane gets a new three seconds. Thus if you happen to be camping out in the lane for two seconds and the shot hits the rim, you may remain in the lane for another three seconds.

  Once a player steps out of the lane, the count resets, and she can re-enter the lane for another three seconds. A player can go in and out of the lane as often as she likes.

  For your own sake, treat the three-second lane as if you were swimming in the ocean: When you feel as if you may have ventured too far off-shore, you probably have. Swim back to shore. (That is, jump out of the lane — quick!)

- **Lane violation:** This rule applies to both offense and defense. When a free throw is being attempted, none of the players lined up along the free throw lane may enter the lane until the ball leaves the shooter's hands. If a defensive player jumps into the lane early, the shooter receives another shot if his shot misses. If an offensive player enters too early, the shot is nullified if it is made.

And finally, not a violation but a good rule to know:

- **Out of bounds:** When the ball touches the floor outside the borders of the court (or on the borders themselves), it is awarded to the team that did *not* touch the ball last. What constitutes out of bounds is not the plane of the borders (sideline and endline), but rather the ground itself. Thus if the ball is flying out of bounds and a player jumps from in bounds and tosses it back in bounds before any part of his body touches the out-of-bounds floor, the ball is still live.

  Just be careful — as Dennis Rodman learned by sailing into a photographer — where you hurtle yourself. The landing is not always soft.

Chapter 4

Statistics

In This Chapter

- Keeping scoring-related stats
- Understanding what official scorekeepers do
- Following other important stats

If a basketball game were decided as if it were a trial — in court — then statistics would be the evidence that each side would use to make its case. Points scored, of course, is the single most important piece of evidence, but other statistics, or *stats,* such as assists, rebounds, and turnovers, usually offer convincing proof as to which team outplayed the other — and won the game.

At halftime of pro, college, and often even high school games, you may spot coaches studying the stat sheet before addressing their respective teams. The stat sheet provides all the incriminating evidence that the coach needs to see: who's being outplayed, who's got the hot hand from three-point range, and so on. Stats quantify the game. They never tell the *whole* story, but they don't lie, either.

Scoring: King of Stats

You may win every other statistical battle in the game, but if you fail to outscore your opponent, then you've lost the war. You score more points than your opponent, you win; assists and all other such self-gratifying stats don't matter. It's that simple.

Of course, all other stats are simply tributaries feeding this big river called Scoring. For example, if you grab more offensive rebounds, you take more shots and hopefully score more points. That's why stats mean so much.

Scoring: One, two, three

Each free throw that is *converted* (that is, made) is worth one point. Field goals converted from within the three-point line, or with at least one foot touching that line when the shooter takes the shot, are worth two points. Field goals made from beyond the three-point line are worth three points.

Scoring was not always this way. Before 1896, all shots — field goals and free throws alike — were worth three points. Prior to the 1979–80 NBA season, the three-point line did not exist, so all field goal attempts were worth two points. The college game did not adopt the "trey" (three-point goal) until the 1986–87 season. Keep all that in mind when evaluating individual players' scoring averages over different eras. Table 4-1 lists scoring records for college men, college women, and the NBA, respectively.

Table 4-1 Single Game Individual Scoring Records

NCAA Men				
Points	***Name***	***Team***	***Opponent***	***Date***
113	Clarence "Bevo" Francis	Rio Grande	Hillsdale	2/2/54
100	Frank Selvy	Furman	Newberry	2/13/54
85	Paul Arizin	Villanova	Philadelphia NAMC	2/12/49
81	Freeman Williams	Portland State	Rocky Mountain	2/3/78
73	Bill Mlkvy	Temple	Wilkes	3/3/51
72	Kevin Bradshaw	U.S. International	Loyola Marymount	1/5/91
69	Pete Maravich	Louisiana State	Alabama	2/7/70
68	Calvin Murphy	Niagara	Syracuse	2/7/68
NCAA Women				
Points	***Name***	***Team***	***Opponent***	***Date***
67	Jackie Givens	Fort Valley	Knoxville	2/22/91

(continued)

Points	Name	Team	Opponent	Date
NCAA Women				
64	Kim Brewington	Johnson Smith	Livingston	1/6/90
63	Jackie Givens	Fort Valley	LeMoyne-Owen	2/2/91
61	Ann Gilbert	Oberlin	Allegheny	2/6/91
60	Cindy Brown	Long Beach State	San Jose State	2/16/87

Points	Name	Team	Opponent	Date
NBA				
100	Wilt Chamberlain	Philadelphia	New York Knicks	3/2/62
78	Wilt Chamberlain	Philadelphia	Los Angeles Lakers (3 overtimes)	12/8/61
73	Wilt Chamberlain	Philadelphia	Chicago Bulls	1/13/62
73	Wilt Chamberlain	San Francisco	New York Knicks	11/16/62
73	David Thompson	Denver	Detroit Pistons	4/9/78
72	Wilt Chamberlain	San Francisco	Los Angeles Lakers	11/3/62
71	Elgin Baylor	L os Angeles	New York Knicks	11/15/60
71	David Robinson	San Antonio	Los Angeles Clippers	4/24/94

Free throws

Anytime a player is fouled while in the act of shooting, no matter how poorly she shot the ball or how unlikely it was to drop, that player is awarded free throws. (The shot attempt does not count against her FGA, or *field goal attempts,* total.) If she was fouled on an attempt from inside the three-point arc, she gets two free throws. If she was fouled while attempting a three-point shot, she gets three free throws — and the player who fouled her usually gets a hurricane of verbal abuse from her coach.

Frank Selvy's 100-point game

The all-time collegiate record for points scored by an individual in a Division I college basketball game is 100 by Frank Selvy on February 13, 1954. Although Selvy is the only person listed for the accomplishment, 500 names really can be added to the record.

Selvy must give partial credit to his hometown of Corbin, Kentucky, for this record that has stood for over 40 years. He was in his senior year at Furman, where he had a celebrated career laced with All-America honors and records. When Newberry College visited on that February evening, Selvy was averaging more than 40 points a game, then a national record. In appreciation of their hometown hero, the folks from Corbin assembled a large caravan of cars and made the 300-mile trek to watch him play one of his last college games.

The sellout crowd of 4,000 was not disappointed on that rainy night, as Selvy scored 24 points in the first quarter. At halftime, he had 37, and it looked as if the only player on the court capable of stopping Selvy from scoring was sophomore teammate Darrell Floyd, who had 25 points at the half. Favoring his senior, and perhaps listening to the Corbin contingent in the stands, Coach Les Alley benched Floyd for the entire second half.

With Floyd on the bench, Selvy kept firing away. He had 94 points with 30 seconds remaining. He then hit a pair of quick jumpers. With 2 seconds showing on the clock, the ball was put into Selvy's hands one last time. Standing near midcourt, with everyone yelling for him to shoot, Selvy fired away just before the buzzer sounded. Swish.

Selvy accomplished his 100-point game by shooting 41-66 from the field and 18-22 from the foul line. He scored 63 points in the second half, 37 of those coming in the final quarter.

Keep an eye on Charles Barkley, one of the wiliest players ever to bounce a ball. "Sir Charles" has perfected the art of throwing the ball toward the hoop the moment he hears a whistle. Often Barkley has no intention of taking a shot but is fouled while moving, so he heaves up a prayer at the shrill of the whistle, hoping to be awarded two free throws. Barkley is so talented, however, that sometimes the heave actually goes in.

You cannot shoot a free throw unless you are fouled. But not every foul results in a pair of (or even three) free throws. Each level of basketball allows a defensive team a certain number of nonshooting, or *common* fouls, before that team shoots free throws. (See Chapter 3 for more information.)

Why do people love free throw stats? Because free throw shooting is the lone statistic that can be compared across all levels; it's the only aspect of the game that remains static regardless of the level of competition. Every player — man or woman, NBA, college, or high school — shoots the ball from 15 feet away at a basket that's 10 feet above the floor. You can compare, say, Joe Dumars's free throw shooting percentage for the Detroit Pistons with your son's at the junior high level. Table 4-2 lists the players with the greatest free throw shooting percentages of all-time.

Table 4-2 Greatest Individual Free Throw Shooting Seasons in History

Player	*M/F*	*Level*	*Team*	*Year*	*FT-FTA*	*Percentage*
Paul Cluxton	Male	College	Northern Kentucky	96-97	94-94	1.000
Daryl Moreau	Male	High school	De LaSalle (Lousiana)	78-79	119-122	.975
Craig Collins	Male	College	Penn State	84-85	94-98	.959
Calvin Murphy	Male	NBA	Houston Rockets	80-81	206-215	.958
Mahmoud Abdul Rauf	Male	NBA	Denver Nuggets	93-94	219-229	.956
Thomas Rinkus	Male	College	Pace	96-97	65-68	.956
Valerie Kepfer	Female	College	Baldwin-Wallace	88-89	63-66	.955
Samual Jones	Male	High school	St. Mary's (West Virginia)	90-91	125-131	.954
Andy Enfield	Male	College	Johns Hopkins	90-91	123-128	.953
Chris Carideo	Male	College	Eureka	91-92	80-84	.952
Yudl Teichman	Male	College	Yeshiva	88-89	119-125	.952
Keith Wagner	Male	High school	Primghar (Iowa)	86-87	113-119	.950
Rod Foster	Male	College	UCLA	81-82	95-100	.950
Ginny Doyle	Female	College	Richmond	91-92	96-101	.950

Although I cover free throw shooting in depth in Chapter 5, I want to stress the importance of free throw shooting in this chapter, too. The free throw is the highest-percentage shot available to a team (meaning that it's the easiest shot to make). A good squad converts at least 70 percent of its free throws. (The national average for college men last season was 68 percent; the NBA average was 74 percent; and some teams average 80 percent.) Compare that with field goal percentages, which seldom eclipse 50 percent.

Field goals

Field goals can be scored from anywhere on the court. They are worth two or three points, depending on the point of departure of the shooting player's feet. (See "Scoring: One, two, three" earlier in this chapter.)

A field goal attempt must come from within the boundaries of the court. Any in-bounds pass that happens to go in the basket without being touched first by a player in bounds is disallowed and results in a turnover.

The three-pointer

Three-point goals, which have revolutionized basketball by affecting offensive positioning and, ergo, defensive positioning, were introduced in the 1967–68 season via the now-defunct American Basketball Association (ABA).

Before the 1975–76 season, the NBA, wise to the cult-like popularity of the ABA and covetous of its cache of offensive showstoppers (open-floor artists such as Julius Erving, George Gervin, and David Thompson), offered a merger. Four ABA teams (the Denver Nuggets, Indiana Pacers, New Jersey Nets, and San Antonio Spurs, none of which have since advanced to the NBA Finals) joined the fold, and the remainder of the league went under.

Maybe the establishment league was too proud to admit that some facets of the ABA, such as the three-pointer, which nowadays might be termed "intellectual property" of the ABA, would improve the NBA. That might explain why the NBA dragged its feet before adopting the rule four years later — to overwhelming support, even from traditionalists.

Suddenly, the guard, who had been forgotten in the late '70s while giants such as Kareem Abdul-Jabbar and Bill Walton were terrorizing the league, was a threat again. Nowadays, the trey is so much more than a gimmick, especially in the college game (where I believe it is too simple a shot). Today, 30 percent of all shots in college and 33 percent of all shots in the NBA are three-point shots.

For a shot to count as a three, both of the shooter's feet must be entirely behind the arc as the ball leaves his hands. The player can land on the line or over the line, but when he leaves his feet, no part of his feet can be on that line. Officials may tell you that this judgment call is most difficult when a player's sneakers are the same color as the painted line.

The greatest shot I ever saw

The greatest shot I ever saw did not count. In 1977, Notre Dame was playing Pittsburgh at Notre Dame. Seconds before halftime, we were in-bounding the ball from beneath our defensive basket. Billy Paterno attempted a full-court lob pass to Toby Knight, who leapt futilely skyward as the ball sailed over his head . . . and into the basket: a dead swish on the fly from more than 90 feet away. The crowd went nuts — heck, I went nuts — but it went down in the books as nothing more than a turnover for the Fighting Irish.

Perhaps the most unusual application of this rule took place on January 27, 1997, when Villanova freshman Tim Thomas attempted a pass over a Georgetown defender. The Hoya defender deflected the ball while his own feet were outside the three-point line. The ball caromed high in the air and banked into the basket. The officials huddled and awarded three points to Villanova, crediting them to Thomas. Had his defender been standing inside the three-point line, Thomas would have received two points for his "shot."

Three versus two

The three-pointer has transformed coaches into mathematicians and probability specialists. Smart coaches (not an oxymoron, I swear) understand that a 33 percent shooter from three-point range can score as many points as a 50 percent shooter from two-point range.

At the college level in 1995–96, the national average for three-point goals was just 34.3 percent. The national average for two-point field goal shooting was 44 percent. Ask yourself, "Would I prefer a 34 percent three-point shooter or a 44 percent two-point shooter?" Of course, you take other factors into account when rating a player, but in terms of pure shooting, you can examine the products.

The formula is simple. Say that Rebecca Lobo makes 34 of 100 shots from three-point land. How many points did she score? The answer is 102 (34×3). If Kate Starbird makes 44 of 100 two-point attempts, how many points did she score? 88 (44×2). There's no contest; Lobo wins 102-88.

A more realistic means of evaluating the production of a three-point shooter is to convert her three-point performance on a two-point basis. Here's the formula:

1. **Take the total of a player's three-point conversions and multiply that number by 3.**

   For example, if Lobo made 34 treys, multiply by 3. The answer is 102.

2. **Divide that number by 2.**

   $102 \div 2 = 51$.

3. **Divide that quotient by the number of field goals the player attempted.**

   Sticking with Lobo, who had 100 attempts, the figure is .51. That figure is the three-point shooter's *effective yield* (in this case, 51 percent).

This statistic puts things in perspective. Folks have a tendency to think that a skilled college three-point shooter converts roughly 40 percent of her shots. But even if she is only a 33 percent shooter from outside the arc, that's equivalent to being a 50 percent shot from two-point range. Hoopsters, as you've no doubt discovered, are skilled in their multiplication tables. (See Table 4-3.)

Table 4-3 Three-Point Shooting Yield Chart

Three-Point Shooting	*Percentage*	*Points*	*Two-Point Shooting Field Goal Percentage*
1-10	.100	3	.150
2-10	.200	6	.300
3-10	.300	9	.450
4-10	.400	12	.600
5-10	.500	15	.750
6-10	.600	18	.900
7-10	.700	21	1.050
8-10	.800	24	1.250
9-10	.900	27	1.400
10-10	1.000	30	1.500

Finding a 50 percent three-point shooter is like uncovering a 75 percent marksman from inside the arc: No starter at any level has ever shot 75 percent from the field. You can find a few 50 percent three-point shooters in college today, but you won't see 75 percent field goal shooters.

To foul or not to foul?

The three-point shot has created another dilemma for coaches: to foul or not to foul. Here's the scenario: Your team leads by three with little time remaining — say, less than ten seconds. The opposition is on offense. Do you foul them before they can attempt a three, thereby putting one of their shooters on the free throw line to shoot just *two* free throws? Or, in hopes that your opponent misses the three, do you adopt the more traditional, pre-three-point era strategy of playing tough defense?

As a coach in this situation, you must compare your team's ability to defend the three-point goal versus its prowess in rebounding a missed foul shot. It's a potential darned-if-you-do, darned-if-you-don't situation. Play straight-up D and you'll be second-guessed. Foul someone and you can be sure that the opposition will intentionally miss the second free throw (provided that they make the first), resulting in chaos under the hoop — and possibly an offensive rebound or a careless foul by your defense.

Most coaches choose not to force the action — they attempt to defend the three-point shooter. If you spread out your defense and get a defender's hand in the face of the shooter, the three-point shot is difficult to make. The worst that can happen is that your defender will allow the three-pointer *and* foul the shooter: You were up three a second ago, and now you lose by one, assuming that the shooter makes the free throw.

Three- and four-point plays

The *four-point play* already exists — although, like polyester, it does not occur naturally. The four-point play (the *quad?*), the rarest of scores, occurs when a player makes a three-point goal and is fouled in the process. Some players, usually poorer shooters, attempt to draw this foul by intentionally taking a dive after minimal contact with a defender. This action is akin to a punter in football summoning his thespian skills to draw a Roughing the Kicker penalty.

A *three-point play* is registered when a player scores a two-point field goal and is fouled in the act of shooting. If she converts the free throw, her team accumulates a total of three points.

Keeping Score

Keeping score at a basketball game is a demanding job because the action moves so swiftly. However, keeping score is fun. This job keeps you involved in the game and keeps you attuned to which individuals are shooting well and which are shooting poorly.

Here are two methods, one simple and one slightly more advanced, for keeping score:

- **Running score:** This method entails keeping track of the total points that each team scores. You can do so by folding a piece of paper vertically in two. Each team occupies a side. When team A scores a field goal, write down 2. If the team scores another field goal before team B scores, go down to the next line and write 4. If team B scores a three-pointer next, skip down to the next line and, this time, on B's side, write 3. You get the idea.
- **Individual scoring:** Another basic way to keep score, one that you might teach to a statistically precocious youngster, involves a horizontal piece of paper. Divide the paper in half and put the names and numbers of the individuals at the top of the page, the home team on the left and the visiting team on the right. As the game progresses, keep a running score of the individual point totals. Across the bottom of the page, in a horizontal fashion, keep a running score for each team.

Go to a game someday (one in which you do not have a rooting interest for either team), buy a game program, and try keeping score. Most programs have a scoresheet in the middle where you can monitor points and fouls.

The official scorer

The duties of the *official scorer* in a game make air-traffic control work seem like a cinch. This person is responsible for tabulating field goals made, free throws made and missed, and a running summary of the points scored as well. In addition, the scorer must record the personal and technical fouls whistled against each player and must notify the official immediately when a player fouls out (five fouls in college, six in the NBA).

The scorer also records time-outs taken by each team and keeps track of the possession arrow in high school and college hoops, which alternates with each held ball situation. The scorebook of the home team is the official book. If discrepancies arise between the home team's book and that of the visitor, the home book assumes priority.

Each team's scorer is obligated to enter the complete roster in the scorebook before the game, matching numbers with the players' names.

Statistical genius: The box score

The ultimate statistician keeps all the elements of the *box score.* In addition to field goals, free throws, points, and fouls, an official box score contains assists, turnovers, blocked shots, steals, field goal attempts, three-point goals and attempts, and playing time. In all college and pro games, an official statistician keeps tabs on the following items for each player in the box score:

- Field goals made (FG) and attempted (FGA)
- Three-point goals made (FG) and attempted (FGA)
- Free throws made (FT) and attempted (FTA)
- Rebounds: offensive (Off.), defensive (Def.), and total (Tot.)
- Personal fouls (PF)
- Total points scored (TP)
- Assists (A)
- Turnovers (TO)
- Blocked shots (BLK)
- Steals (S)
- Minutes played (MIN)

A stat crew keeps the other items on the box score, such as turnovers, blocked shots, and steals.

For one person to monitor all these items is nearly impossible. *Do not try this at home,* especially because you are unable to see the clock in order to monitor each player's minutes played. Keeping every stat may be possible if you are watching a slow-down tempo team, such as Princeton. But doing so while watching an up-tempo team, such as the Los Angeles Lakers, is out of the question unless you've been doing so for years.

The more stats you try to keep, the less accurate you're going to be. Start out slowly when it comes to keeping stats. Keep a few items like scoring and fouls first, and master the process before you move on.

Other Statistics Worth Watching

Some ratio stats that are not found in the box score have tremendous appeal to both coaches and fans. Again, the more you understand about the game, the greater meaning these stats have. They reveal why one team consistently plays better (or worse) than its foes.

Assists

An *assist* is a pass that leads directly to a basket. And I do mean directly. Assists are not credited when a player receives a pass, dribbles the ball many times, double-pumps, and then scores. Perhaps the best way to think of an assist is as a pass without which the receiver would not have been able to score.

The assist is the most discretionary of all stats. The definition reads that an assist may be credited when a player, "in the judgment of the statistician," makes the principal pass contributing directly to a field goal. The distance of the pass or the distance from where the player who receives the pass shoots is irrelevant. Here are two examples:

- **March 28, 1992:** Duke trails Kentucky 103-102 in the East Regional final of the NCAA tourney. Only two seconds remain, and the Blue Devils must in-bound the ball from their own baseline. Grant Hill tosses a 60-foot pass to teammate Christian Laettner, who fakes to his right, dribbles, and then spins left to shoot. Assist to Hill? You can argue that Hill's pass led directly to Laettner's field goal — and what a superb pass it was. Then again, you can argue that Laettner was not in a scoring position when he received the pass and that he could never have made the shot without faking to his right and then spinning.
- **May 26, 1987:** Detroit is playing Boston at Boston during Game Five of the NBA Eastern Conference Finals. The Pistons lead the Celtics 107-106 in the waning seconds when the Celtics' Larry Bird steals the ball in Detroit's backcourt. Bird dishes to teammate Dennis Johnson, who

> catches it to the left of the free throw lane, dribbles once, and then scores the winning lay-up. Assist? Yes. Although "DJ" did not score from the point at which he caught the ball, Bird's pass led directly to his basket.

I feel that two aspects of the assist should be changed. First, I have always felt that you should be able to give two assists — like in hockey — on one play. Many times, a point guard gives a great pass, and another player makes a pass that leads to the basket. That first pass should get some credit because it can be more important than the second pass.

Second, at present, a great pass that leads to the shooter being fouled is not credited as an assist, and it should be. How many times have you seen a player on a fast break make the extra pass to a teammate, leaving the defender no choice but to either foul the receiver of that pass or surrender an easy deuce? Shouldn't the player who made that pass be rewarded with an assist if his teammate makes both — or even one — of the subsequent free throws? As the rule reads now, you may only give an assist on a made field goal.

A decent assist total for a college point guard is about five per game; for his counterpart in the NBA, where games are eight minutes longer and the shot clock is six seconds shorter, I'd consider seven assists per game to be a good average. An average of ten assists per game usually leads the NBA or is at least among the leading averages, and it usually is among the best in the nation at the college level.

Team figures vary dramatically when it comes to assists. You cannot determine the best passing team simply by which one leads the league in assists. Assist totals fail to take into account a team's preferred tempo (the Cleveland Cavaliers are a good passing club that prefers a low-scoring game, thus they have fewer assists) or its proficiency at grabbing offensive boards. Remember, baskets scored on offensive rebounds are usually accomplished without assists.

Turnovers (not the cherry kind)

A *turnover* occurs when the offense loses possession of the ball by a means other than a missed shot. An offense, or offensive player, that's prone to turnovers is usually considered sloppy, not very smart, poorly coached, or all of the above. Defenses that force a lot of turnovers usually win. After all, an opponent can't score if they don't shoot or have possession of the ball.

Turnovers are far more important in football, where fewer possessions occur per game. However, in hoops, turnovers can be huge in terms of building or losing momentum. And just because a team is skilled at forcing turnovers does not mean that it knows how to avoid turnovers on offense.

During the 1995–96 NBA season, for example, Seattle SuperSonics guard Gary Payton led the league in forcing turnovers (231), but his teammate, forward Shawn Kemp, was second in the NBA in committing turnovers (315).

Following are the common causes of turnovers:

- **Violations:** Offensive violations that result in loss of possession include traveling, double dribbling, palming, standing in the free throw lane for more than three seconds, stepping out of bounds while in possession of the ball, and offensive goaltending.
- **Offensive fouls:** When your team has possession of the ball and you are called for a *charging foul* (you have the ball, and you initiate contact with the defender) an *illegal screen* (a teammate has the ball, and you block off a defender illegally), you lose possession of the ball and are thus charged with a turnover. An offensive foul called during a rebounding situation is not considered a turnover as long as the shot was attempted before the foul was whistled.
- **Steals:** A steal is a stat in itself (see "Steals" later in this chapter), but it is also a turnover. When a defender intercepts a pass or simply takes possession of the ball away from the offensive player controlling it, a turnover is charged against the last offensive player who had possession of the ball before the steal.
- **Technical fouls:** If your team is in possession of the ball and you mouth off at the referee or perform another such reckless act (such as kicking an opponent), a technical foul is called. Your team loses possession of the ball, and you are charged with a turnover.
- **Special situations:** There are all kinds of special examples when it comes to the turnover statistics. For example, what happens when a defender forces an offensive player into a *held ball* (a.k.a. *jump ball*) situation? If you have possession of the ball and a held ball situation arises, you establish the next possession in two ways. In the NBA, the two players involved participate in a jump ball: The ref tosses up the ball, and the players attempt to tap it to their teammates. In college, players use an alternating possession arrow.

  Stat rule: If your team loses possession of the ball as the result of a held ball, a turnover must be charged. The turnover is charged to the person who last had possession of the ball. That could be the person involved in the tug of war, but not always. If Player A has the ball knocked loose by Player B, for example, and Players C and D are involved in a held ball situation, the turnover is charged to Player A, not Player C or D. Player A is the one who made the mistake that led to the held ball. On the other hand, if Player A happens to be simply holding the ball and Player B (a defender) grabs it, resulting in a jump ball, then Player A is charged with the turnover.

Blocked shots

Blocked shots are credited only to defensive players. When, in the opinion of the head statistician, a defender alters the shot by making contact with the ball and the shot fails to go in, a blocked shot is credited to that player.

According to the NCAA rule book, under blocked shots, the ball "must leave the shooter's hand." I think that phrase has to go — quite frankly, most statisticians don't pay any attention to it. Former Wake Forest center Tim Duncan, for example, was a maestro at stuffing a shot before it even left the shooter's hand. Why should he wait?

No other stat in hoops is so closely associated with a player's height. Taller players not only stand above their opponents, but they almost always have longer arms, too. More often than not, leading shot blockers are 7-footers (for women, players who are taller the 6'5"), such as NBA center Shawn Bradley (who stands 7'7"). The best shot blockers are those who understand that swatting a shot is only half the job. Swatting it to another defensive player, or at least keeping it in bounds so that a teammate may grab it, is ice cream with your cake.

Steals

A *steal* is credited to a player who makes a positive, aggressive action that causes the opponent to turn over the ball. This may be accomplished by

- Taking the ball away from an opponent who had control.
- Instigating a held ball situation, leading to the defender's team gaining possession. If the defender's team does not gain possession, it is not a steal.
- Batting a ball off an opponent to a defensive teammate, who then gains possession.
- Batting a ball off an opponent out of bounds, leading to the defense gaining possession.
- Intercepting an opponent's pass.

In case you're wondering, the first and the last items in the preceding list are the most common types of steals, as well as the biggest crowd-pleasers. Players who lead the NBA in steals, such as Seattle's Gary Payton or Phoenix's Kevin Johnson, are generally quick, smart players who are able to anticipate an offensive player's actions.

Minutes

Playing time is the easiest of all statistics with which a player may be credited: Just get into the game.

Statistically, playing time is kept to the nearest minute. If a player sees action for 27 minutes and 15 seconds, his playing time appears in the box score, under MIN, as "27". If he plays for 27 minutes and 35 seconds, it appears as "28".

A player can appear in a game — even score a basket — and yet have a playing time figure of 0. This occurs when a player participates for less than 30 seconds. On the stat sheet, her minutes figure is recorded as "0+".

Playing time is an important statistic because it allows you to compile ratios from raw data. With these ratios, you can compare performance of players whose length of participation varies dramatically.

Ratios

Ratios measure the relationship between two pieces of data. Speed, for example, is a ratio of distance to time. Hoops junkies use ratios to measure the relationship between two statistical units that are related to one another (such as offensive rebounds and second-shot baskets) or that are in direct contradiction to each other (such as assists and turnovers). These ratios enable hoops junkies to measure a player's worth. (Fear not: None of the following information will be on the final exam.)

Assist/turnover ratio

There's more to a great point guard than just assists. If she averages ten assists per game but just as many turnovers, her coach may want to advise her to play more conservatively.

An assist/turnover ratio, which is most often used to compare point guards, measures a player's effectiveness as a passer. It is a more revealing stat than assists alone because each pass that is stolen negates an assist. Would you rather have a player with 100 assists and 50 turnovers, or a player with 80 assists and 20 turnovers? Obviously, you want the latter because you get 30 more shots at the basket with the second player.

A good assist/turnover ratio is 2 to 1 or better at the college level and 3 to 1 or better at the NBA level. Why the difference? The NBA is more liberal with assists, plus each team has more possessions in an NBA game, leading to more scoring and more opportunities for an assist.

Thievery: Pros and cons

If you want to measure a team's defensive aggressiveness, look at its steal total.

Defensive aggression does not, however, always translate into defensive greatness. Some poor defensive teams average a high number of steals because they gamble, overplaying passing lanes or lunging at a dribbler when there's little hope of robbing him of the ball. In the late 1980s, Loyola Marymount was famous for this. That team seemed to surrender as many baskets while going for steals as they ever garnered from the steals they actually made.

You calculate an assist-to-turnover ratio like this: Say that Player A collects 12 assists in a game but turns over the ball four times. You find his assist-to-turnover ratio by dividing:

Assists ÷ Turnovers = 12 ÷ 4 = 3, or a 3:1 assist-to-turnover ratio

Per-minute statistics

You can have only five players on the floor at one time, which invariably leads to some players seeing more action than others. As a coach or fan, how can you measure the contributions of players who play less and thus have fewer points, rebounds, and so on, than the starters?

Use the per-minute stat to measure a player's value in terms of any other raw data stat. Say that Sue Wicks of the WNBA's New York Liberty scores eight points in a game. However, Wicks plays only eight minutes. Her per-minute scoring average is one point per minute, which, extrapolated to a 40-minute game, would be 40 points per game. Nobody in the WNBA — or the NBA, for that matter — averages 40 points per game. Suddenly, Wicks's eight points looks more impressive.

Although coaches find the per-minute stat helpful in evaluating players, and this stat makes for great arguments among fans, it has its limitations. Obviously, Shaq plays three times as many minutes as Knight for a reason: He's a better center. Also, shorter time periods may yield misleading stats. Imagine that Knight had buried a three-pointer in his first minute of play and then sat out the rest of the game. Does anyone truly believe that he would've scored 144 points (3 × 48 minutes) in that game had he played its entirety?

Per-game statistics

Per-game statistics are for fans and the media, and per-minute statistics are for coaches. Per-minute stats are a little more technical because the raw numbers don't look meaningful. Comparing 0.5 points per minute to 0.67 points per minute just doesn't have a ring to it.

However, you do see scoring averages of 12.5 or 16.0 per game, and these are meaningful. Per-game statistics enable fans to make comparisons between players, especially when comparing a player who's been injured and missed a few games to someone who's been healthy all year.

More tellingly, per-game stats are the basis for determining who is recognized as the league leader in a statistical category. For example, if Michael Jordan played only 70 games in a season (all these numbers are hypothetical) and scored 2,100 points, and David Robinson played all 82 games and scored 2,378 points, Jordan would be recognized as the league scoring leader for having a higher per-game average (30 points per game to Robinson's 29 points per game).

Here's where the per-game stat becomes even kookier. Imagine that Jordan played 40 minutes per game, whereas Robinson played 30. ***(Remember:*** *None of this is on the final. Relax.)* Multiply each player's total games played by his average minutes per game to find his total minutes (Jordan 2,800, Robinson 2,460). Now divide total points by total minutes to find each player's points per minute. Jordan's average would be .75 points per minute, and Robinson's average would be .96.

Hence Robinson could score more total points *and* average more points per minute (the more valid stat), but on the basis of points per game, Jordan would win the scoring title. "Life isn't always fair" is one lesson to be gleaned from that example. Another is "Michael Jordan always wins."

Bench scoring

To calculate bench scoring, you add up the points scored by players who did not start the contest.

What's so important about bench scoring? A team that consistently receives a lot of scoring from its bench is able to substitute more freely, hence all the players are fresher at game's end. Also, the impact of a starter fouling out is less.

The duel of 1978

The closest race for scoring leader in the NBA's 50-year history occurred in 1978, when George Gervin of the San Antonio Spurs edged out David Thompson of the Denver Nuggets by .07 points per game. Gervin, "The Iceman," averaged 27.22 points per game, while Thompson, who, like Gervin, was a guard who had gotten his start in the ABA, ended the season with a 27.15 average.

Gervin needed every last minute to outscore Thompson, and their duel culminated in one of the wildest final regular-season days that the NBA has ever witnessed. The date was April 9. The Nuggets, who, like the Spurs, were playoff-bound, had a meaningless afternoon game at home against the Detroit Pistons. The Spurs played seven hours later on the road in a similar play-out-the-string contest against the New Orleans Jazz. When Gervin and Thompson awoke that morning, The Iceman was averaging 26.7 points per game; his Nugget counterpart had a 26.5 average.

Thompson made no attempt to hide his desire to wrest the scoring crown away from Gervin, scoring 53 first-half points on 20-23 shooting, meaning that he attempted 23 shots and made 20 of them. (Remember, this was in the pre-three-point-shot NBA era.) Thompson cooled off in the second half, though, shooting 8-15 to finish with 73 points.

Thompson set the bar awfully high for Gervin. No other player before or since (with the exception of Wilt Chamberlain) has scored that many points in a game. But Gervin scored 33 of the Spurs' 36 first-quarter points that night and equaled Thompson's 53 first-half points. Needing 11 more points to secure the scoring title, Gervin scored 16 in the third quarter, and didn't even have to play the last quarter.

Eighteen years later, Gervin and Thompson were linked again. In May 1996, both players were inducted into the Basketball Hall of Fame.

This stat has more relevance at the college level. Most players who advance to the NBA are capable of scoring 20 points a game at least once a season. However, many a winning college team gets exposed in the NCAA for its lack of depth. In the 1996 championship game, for example, Kentucky's bench outscored Syracuse's 26-0. Not surprisingly, in the final ten minutes, Kentucky pulled away from the valiant Orangemen, who by that time were out of juice.

Second-chance points

Second-chance points are points scored on offensive rebounds. In the 1995 NCAA championship game between UCLA and Arkansas, for example, UCLA got 21 offensive rebounds and scored 27 points off those offensive rebounds — or second-chance points.

Note: Getting an offensive rebound by itself is not enough; you have to score off the offensive rebound.

Points off turnovers

Points off turnovers are very similar to second-chance points. Forcing turnovers is great, but you have to score points when you get those extra chances.

Triple doubles

Triple double may sound like a figure skating term, or perhaps two very productive at-bats in baseball. But in fact, this basketball term was coined by former Los Angeles Lakers public relations director Bruce Joelsch in the early '80s. Joelsch, ever the dedicated PR flak, was in search of a pithy way to describe the all-around contributions of Laker point guard Earvin "Magic" Johnson.

Magic was above all other things a master passer, arguably the best that the game has ever seen, but at 6'9", he was also a point guard who could use his height advantage to outscore and outrebound opponents. Magic rarely led the NBA in those other two categories, though, so Joelsch invented the triple double. Every time Magic reached double digits (that is, at least ten) in assists, points, and rebounds, Joelsch credited him with a triple double. Joelsch's gimmick stuck; it's now recognized, though not in the box score, as a legitimate stat.

Oscar Robertson

Magic Johnson recorded 82 triple doubles in his 13-year career. For that reason, his name is most closely associated with the feat. But had the triple double existed 35 years earlier, we'd be giving that honor to former Cincinnati Royal/Milwaukee Buck guard Oscar Robertson. "The Big O" is the only player in NBA history to *average* a triple double over the course of an entire season, which he did in 1961–62. That season, Robinson's second in the NBA, he averaged 30.8 points, 12.5 rebounds (his career high), and 11.4 assists per game in 79 games.

Perhaps even more phenomenal, Robertson almost averaged a triple double his rookie year, but his 9.7 assist average was just a bit short. In his fourth year, he averaged 31.4 points per game, 11.0 assists, and 9.9 rebounds. Had he picked up just seven more rebounds that year, he would have averaged a triple double.

A triple double may be any troika of positive double-digit stats. Points-assists-rebounds are the most conventional means of achieving a triple double, but a point guard may achieve a points-assists-steals triple double, or a center may achieve a points-rebounds-blocked shots triple double.

While traveling back in time to record triple doubles, such as those of Oscar Robertson, is possible, you cannot tabulate triple doubles for players who may have done so via blocked shots. The blocked shot stat was not introduced in the NBA until the 1973–74 season. By then, noted sultans of swat, such as Bill Russell, had retired. In fact, Wilt Chamberlain actually led the NBA in assists (8.6) in 1967–68, in addition to leading the league in rebounding (23.8) and finishing third in scoring (24.3). I'm sure that he had many triple doubles, and probably a few quadruple doubles, that season if you factor in blocked shots.

Quadruple doubles

A *quadruple double* is the same as a triple double, except that it involves one more category of ten or better. Only four quadruple doubles have occurred in NBA history. (I have not uncovered any in college.) Table 4-4 lists the quad squad of centers who have achieved this feat.

Table 4-4 All-Time NBA Quadruple Doubles

Player	*Team*	*Date*	*Points*	*Rebounds*	*Assists*	*Blocked Shots*	*Steals*
Nate Thurmond	Chicago Bulls	10/18/74	22	14	13	12	0
Alvin Robertson	San Antonio Spurs	2/18/86	20	11	10	0	10
Hakeem Olajuwon	Houston Rockets	3/29/80	18	16	10	11	0
David Robinson	San Antonio Spurs	2/17/94	34	10	10	10	0

On December 8, 1996, the fledgling American Basketball League (ABL) was host to the first distaff quadruple double. Colorado Xplosion point guard Debbie Black — who was, coincidentally, the league's shortest player at 5'3", had the following line beside her name in the box score: 10 points, 14 rebounds, 12 assists, and 10 steals. Black's excellent effort lifted Colorado to a 91-75 win against the Atlanta Glory.

Part II
The Fundamentals of Basketball

In this part . . .

Chock-full of information, this part gives you the lowdown on basketball fundamentals like shooting, playing offense and defense, rebounding, and setting up plays. For your added reading pleasure, I sprinkle in my personal anecdotes from my coaching career to help illustrate my points.

Whether you are a coach, a fan, or a player, you can't help but benefit from the information here. One chapter is devoted to each fundamental element, so just read whichever chapters interest you (or read about the element you need help with!).

Chapter 5

Shooting

In This Chapter

- Shooting free throws
- Shooting from the five sweet spots on the floor
- Dunking, shooting three-pointers, and other fancy stuff
- Shooting drills
- Great shooters in basketball history

This chapter talks about that all-important aspect of basketball, shooting. Simply put, *shooting* is the act of tossing the ball toward the basket in an attempt to *score,* which happens when the ball goes through the basket. If you don't shoot, you don't score. And if you don't score, you can't win.

Every player in the game may shoot.

Understanding the Difference between Shooters and Scorers

Note: Odd as it sounds, being a great *shooter* is not the same as being a great *scorer.* Wilt Chamberlain is the NBA's second most prolific scorer behind Kareem Abdul-Jabbar. In 1962, he scored 100 points in a game versus the Knicks (during which some of his Philadelphia Warriors teammates were heard to utter, "Hey, Wilt, I'm open!") — a record that still stands — yet no one ever ranks him as one of basketball's great shots.

There are shooters and there are nonshooters. You may improve a player's form and hence his shooting percentage, but some players simply do not have the touch.

Why not? They lack the proper mechanics and, more important, they lack confidence. It's like being a gunslinger: You can buy John Wayne in the role, but not Woody Allen. Two of the NBA's current more prolific scorers, Charles Barkley and Michael Jordan, are the last guys you'd ever find reading *I'm OK,*

You're OK. Dan Majerle of the Miami Heat routinely wins pregame bets with teammates by draining half-court shots — while facing the opposite basket. He just has confidence.

Putting a 9-Inch Ball through an 18-Inch Hoop

The first step in confidence-building is to recognize how easy it is to toss a basketball through that gaping hole 10 feet above. I recently visited UCLA and worked with Bruins forward Kris Johnson, whose dad, Marques, was a scoring machine for the Milwaukee Bucks, LA Clippers, and Golden State Warriors in the NBA for a total of 11 years. That afternoon, I asked a student manager to lower the basket so that the rim was at eye level. Then I grabbed two basketballs, which are 9 inches in diameter, and showed Kris that both balls can fit simultaneously within the 18-inch diameter rim. (See Figure 5-1.) He was shocked! "I never thought of it that way," he said.

If you ever wonder why making a shot at one of those booths at a county fair seems so impossible, it isn't because you're trying too hard to impress your girlfriend or boyfriend. The rim diameter is much smaller.

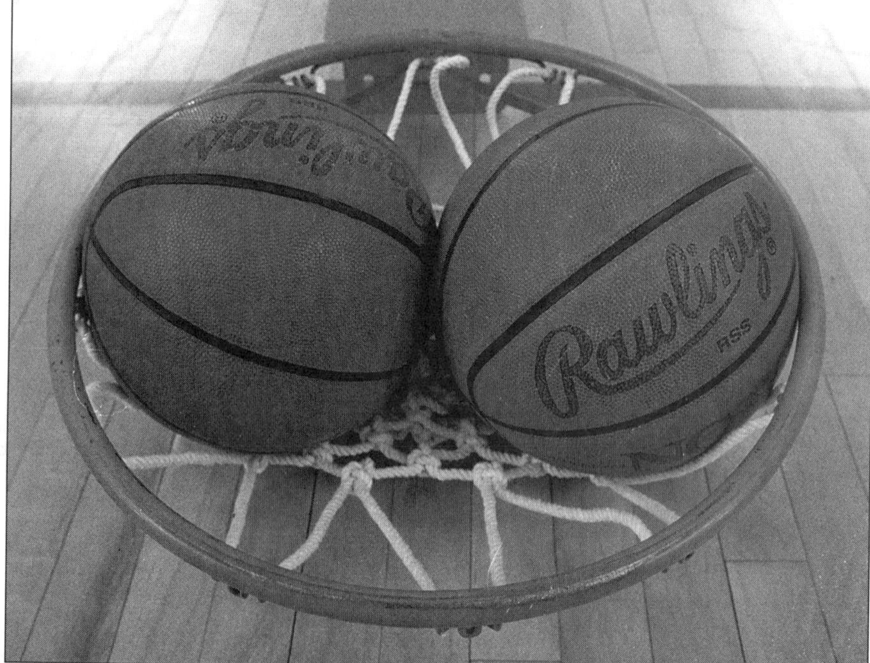

Figure 5-1: Shooting seems much easier when you keep in mind that two basketballs fit through the hoop at once.

Making the Shot You Miss

Keep in mind that *shooting* is an anagram of *soothing,* which is how a shot should feel: soft, with a light touch. Play word-association for a moment. Former Los Angeles Laker forward Jamaal Wilkes, a deadly shooter, was nicknamed “Silk.” The onomatopoetic term *swish,* which describes the feathery sound of a basketball sailing through the net without hitting the rim, conjures images of softness. On the other hand, poorly shot balls are commonly known as *bricks,* and players who shoot them, such as Laker center Shaquille O’Neal, earn nicknames such as “Clank-fu.” Not very soothing.

If you have a soft touch, you can make the shot you missed. Sure, Larry Bird used to swish many a shot, but he also scored a lot of buckets with shots that rattled around the rim or ricocheted off the backboard beforehand. Proper mechanics allow you to take advantage of the rim’s diameter — commentators refer to this as “getting the kind bounce” — so even if you don’t shoot the ball with a marksman’s precision, the ball has a chance to fall through the basket. Remember, shooting baskets is more like pitching horseshoes than firing darts.

The Free Throw: The Most Important Shot

The *free throw* is the most important shot in basketball. Shoot it poorly, and it becomes an Achilles heel that defenses will exploit; shoot it well, and it becomes the most potent weapon in your offensive arsenal. (See Chapter 3 for more information about free throw situations.) It should also be the easiest shot. You stand 15 feet from the rim, perpendicular to the backboard, and, most important, nobody is covering you. You even have plenty of time — ten seconds — to relax. Your only opposition when you attempt a free throw is yourself, so you need to find a way to get yourself on your side.

The free throw is the shooter’s shot because it’s all about proper mechanics. If basketball has an equivalent to figure skating’s compulsory figures, it’s the free throw. Of course you want to soar like Air Jordan, but first you must make your free throws. And nowhere does it say that you must be a pro to shoot free throws well. The man who owns the world record for consecutive free throw shooting, Tom Amberry of Rossmoor, California, is a podiatrist. In 1993, at age 70, Amberry made 2,750 free throws in a row.

Note: The mechanics are the same for all types of shooting, so everything I discuss in shooting free throws carries over to shooting in a live offense. If I can get you shooting foul shots at 75 percent like the pros do (which is about 30 percentage points higher than for shots attempted during live action, known as *field goals*), then I can get you to shoot a 12-foot jumper.

Shaq and his free throw percentage

Why is there so much talk about Shaquille O'Neal and his inability to hit free throws? O'Neal, at 7'1" and 300 pounds, is a beast when he's near the basket. Shaq is the most agile player — and perhaps the strongest — at his size in the history of hoops. But foul Shaq as he leaps for a dunk and force him to earn his two points from the free throw line, which opposing defenses do to him each game, and suddenly he's is no better than a high school player.

The more Shaq misses from the foul line, the more his confidence wanes. It's a downward spiral. O'Neal's Achilles Heel has in the past cost his team games and will continue to do so until he improves from what is known as the "charity stripe." During the 1995–96 season, when Shaq played for the Orlando Magic, he shot 48.7 percent (249-511) from the free throw line. The league average was 70 percent. Shaq averaged 9.46 foul shots per game. Had he shot the league average, not only would he have improved his own scoring by two points per game but, based on the final scores, the Magic also would have had five more victories.

Shaq's Free Throw Shooting Stats

Year	*Games*	*Team*	*FTM-FTA*	*%*
1992–93	81	Orlando Magic	427-721	.592
1993–94	81	Orlando Magic	471-850	.554
1994–95	79	Orlando Magic	455-854	.533
1995–96	54	Orlando Magic	249-511	.487
1996–97	51	Los Angles Lakers	232-479	.484

Actually, you shouldn't be satisfied with 75 percent success on free throws. Look at it as, "Why should I give up 25 percent at the foul line?" Don't be satisfied to give up 25 percent of your scoring ability. Why let that rim beat you 25 percent of the time?

Digger's Five Keys to Shooting

San Antonio Spurs forward Chuck Person, a terrific free throw shooter, is known as "The Rifleman." The comparison between shooting a basketball and shooting a rifle is worth making. Your feet are the butt of the rifle; your arm is the barrel of the rifle; and your hand is the nose of the barrel. Everything between your feet and your shooting hand must move in one fluid motion toward the target: the rim. Ready. Aim. Fire!

This section talks about the five main points that you should concentrate on when working on your shooting form.

Balance yourself

One day, Kris Johnson and I were practicing free throws on a side basket at the UCLA gym. After he shot a free throw, I pushed one finger on his chest and he teetered off balance. "That's your problem," I told him.

So we worked on having him balance his body as he came out of a shot, just as a baseball pitcher should have both feet facing home plate, ready to field his position, after hurling a pitch. "Spread your feet the width of your shoulders," I said. Kris did so and then shot again. This time, when I nudged him with my finger, Kris was a sequoia. (See Figure 5-2.)

Figure 5-2: At left, the shooter's feet are too close, resulting in no balance after the shot. At right, the shooter's feet are spread to shoulder width to give him balance.

You should be in balance after every shot, even when you follow the shot in case it misses and you're in quest of the rebound. (See Chapter 8 for more on offensive rebounding.) You can become a better shooter if you're in balance with your lower and upper body. Having your upper body in balance and square to the target (facing the basket) is more important.

Shoot with your knees

Then I said to Kris, "Let's talk about your knees." The knees and associated leg muscles needed to propel the basketball are the booster rockets for the body, the spark of flint igniting with gunpowder that provides thrust. Have you noticed that most deft three-point shooters, such as Joe Dumars of the Detroit Pistons or John Stockton of the Utah Jazz, are not big guys? They heave the ball up from 22 feet away, however, better than players who can probably bench press 100 more pounds than they do. That's because they shoot with their knees. (See Figure 5-3.)

Figure 5-3: Flex your knees to get maximum power from your shot.

Your legs are much stronger than your arms. Your arms, all the way down to the tips of your fingers, are involved in aiming the ball toward the rim. The less power your arms exert, the more precision you get. Guitarists wear shoulder straps for the same reason.

By bending your knees and thrusting upward, you provide all the thrust that the ball needs to reach the basket. Let your arms be the guidance system.

Grab the rim

The majority of missed shots are not too short or too long, but rather off a little to the right or left. This happens when you fail to extend your arm straight. You turn your hand, and that's how you miss half the shots. When you do that, you reduce your ability to make the one you miss. If you shoot it straight and are a little short or long, the ball still has a chance to go in.

When Kris and I analyzed his shot with the rim at eye level, I had him stand close enough to the rim so that he could grab it with his fingertips on the follow-through. When he grabbed the rim, his hand didn't turn. It was straight and parallel to the ground. If you grab the rim straight on, you are in balance and have a straight follow-through. That's what you should visualize. (See Figure 5-4.)

During a game, the rim is never that low, but you still should visualize your hand grabbing the rim during the follow-through of every shot. Doing so accomplishes two goals:

- It lines up the shot as straight as it can be.
- It gives the ball a backward rotation, the result being the softest shot possible.

Watch any good shooter and you notice that his arm looks like the neck of a swan on his follow-through, and that the ball spins heavily backward. When you see a good shooter swish a shot, the twine of the net often jumps up onto the rim. I'm no physicist, but I do know that the backward rotation of the ball is responsible for that. A net entangled in the rim is the sign of a shooter who "grabs the rim."

Figure 5-4: Visualize grabbing the rim when you shoot a free throw.

Think 18 inches for a 9-inch ball

Look at all that room: 18 inches for just a 9-inch ball! Knowing that as you do now, don't you have just a little more confidence than you did before you picked up this book? Just get that shot up there, keep it soft, and let gravity do the rest.

Control the ball with your fingertips

Quarterbacks grip a football by the seams for control. You should do the same when shooting a basketball. The best shooters give their shots a high arc, which starts with having good fingertip control on the seams. Try this one-hand shooting drill:

Lay the ball in the palm of your hand. Grab the seams with your fingertips and pretend that you're going to shoot, only shoot the ball straight up in the air, just a few feet above your head. Concentrate on your fingertips giving the ball backspin, using the seams to initiate the spin.

Only your middle three fingers are on the seams. The middle finger should rest a little bit higher on the seam, and your ring and index fingers rest in the seam. The thumb plays more of a support role, and the pinkie, as in so many situations, does best by just staying out of the way.

Taking the Shot: The System Beats the Pressure

You have your feet in balance, at shoulder width and parallel to each other. You know that your knees are going to provide the thrust and that you grab the rim after you shoot, and you're visualizing how big that hoop is: twice as big as the ball. You can add your own routine at the beginning: dribble one, two, or three times, talk to the ball, anything.

Adrian Dantley, who was an All-American while playing for me at Notre Dame, had a distinct preshot ritual. Massaging the ball close to his chest, Adrian would repeat the following mantra: "Over the rim, backspin, follow through." That little reminder helped Dantley shoot 81.8 percent from the line for his 15 years in the NBA.

No matter what your system of dribbles before a free throw (Kris takes three), take a deep breath. Suck it in and let it out. This relaxes your body, a requisite when 20,000 lunatics are screaming at you and the folks behind the backboard are waving balloons in an attempt to distract you.

If you relax your shooting arm, you have a better chance of making the shot. If you shoot like a stiff board, you're going to catapult the shot, not shoot it.

Now simply aim for the top of the front of the rim. *Just get it over the rim,* that's what you should be thinking — along with how big that rim is. You don't necessarily look at the square on the backboard, although doing so helps you keep your arm straight and have that all-important accuracy. But look over the rim; get it on top of the rim.

The ball rests loosely in your hand. Your palm does not touch it; your fingertips control the shot. Hold the ball at waist level with both hands, take your deep breath, and then lift it up, aim, and shoot. (See Figure 5-5.)

Only Two at a Time

Nobody shoots more than two, and on rare occasions three, free throws in a row during a game. Neither should you. When shooting free throws for practice, shoot two straight and then step off the line. Too many young players can make nine of ten without moving their feet from the same spot because their body gets into a rhythm. This instills a false sense of accomplishment. Instead, back off and reset after every two free throws.

Be realistic in everything you do in practice. After all, that's what practice is: preparation for a real game.

Free Throw Shooting Drills

To keep free throw practice fun, I try to make it competitive. The following games add a little pressure to free throw practice, which only makes sense. So much of it is, after all, nerves.

80 percent from everyone . . . or no training table

At the end of a tough practice, break up the team into groups (divide by number of available baskets) and have every player shoot ten free throws. Remember, step off the line after each set of two. Those not shooting should stand along the free throw lane, just like in a game.

Stay in the gym until every player makes eight out of ten during a set. This somewhat Draconian method is quite effective: Once the stomach starts rumbling, motivation and concentration *increase,* not decrease.

A

B

C

D

Figure 5-5: Taking the shot.

Don't psyche out a tyke

If you're teaching your 7-year-old to shoot free throws, the best way to ruin him is to have him shoot from the regulation free throw line with a regulation-sized ball on a 10-foot basket. He'll have to fling it slingshot-style just to reach the rim. Innocent bystanders will be bonked in the head, and your nascent Penny Hardaway won't develop any real skills. He'll soon become bored because this sport seems too difficult, and he'll want to take up another sport, such as stock car racing.

Use a 7-foot basket if you can find one. Have the child shoot from 8 feet away, not 15. If you have a smaller basketball, such as a women's ball, use that. Then go over the system beginning with nudging your child in the chest to show the importance of balance.

First team to 21

Divide your squad in two and direct them to different baskets. Players line up and take turns shooting one free throw at a time until one side makes 21. Whoever loses runs sprints.

Ten straight one-and-ones

The *one-and-one* situation, in which the shooter must convert his first free throw attempt in order to receive a second, exists in high school and college play. It must have been invented by a coach, because it directly rewards good free throw shooting and punishes bad. As if free throws weren't stressful enough.

A good drill to simulate the one-and-one situation is vital. At the end of practice, have the team line up on the baseline. Then randomly call on players to step to the foul line to shoot both ends (you hope) of a one-and-one. If the player misses his first shot, call another player. Oh, but first have the team sprint down to the other baseline and back. The drill ends only after ten players in a row make both ends of the one-and-one.

Free throw practice and conditioning are two of the less popular aspects of practice. You may as well combine them.

Situations in a scrimmage

Be realistic. When someone is fouled during a scrimmage, stop play and have the fouled player shoot free throws. But make every free throw situation a one-and-one. I cannot overemphasize how important one-and-ones are. These are bonus points that you're giving away when you miss.

Team shooting

Assemble your top five players who are likely to be on the court during crunch time. Put them on the foul line one at a time, with the challenge being for them to make seven shots in a row. That means that two players shoot more than once. Have those two be your guards, because in the waning moments of a game, especially if you're in the lead, they'll be the ones you'll want handling the ball the most — and therefore the ones the opponent will be forced to foul and put on the free throw line.

Save free throw drills until the end of practice, when your players are pooped. Why? Because the most critical free throws are attempted at the ends of games, when fatigue begins to addle a player's concentration. Practice should mirror a real game situation.

The Five Areas of Shooting

Now that you know how to shoot, where do you shoot from? Trigger-happy shooters such as Dan Majerle of the Miami Heat would answer, "From wherever you're open." For us mortals, this section talks about five sweet spots on the floor. Jump back to Chapter 3 if you need a refresher on the areas of the court.

Everyone sooner or later finds a favorite spot on the floor. Center Patrick Ewing of the New York Knicks prefers the baseline. Another center, retired Detroit Piston Bill Laimbeer, craved the 15-footer from the free throw line.

Under the basket (the lay-up or dunk)

Lay-ups and dunks are easy shots if no defenders are nearby. Use the square on the backboard instead of aiming for the top of the rim. Expect to extract a defender or two from your tonsils; defenses don't surrender the lay-up — or dunk, for that matter — gladly.

If you're tall or springy enough to dunk the ball, be my guest. In a bygone era, the dunk was seen as a showboat play; now coaches and players see it for what it is: the game's highest-percentage shot.

The square is your friend

Behind every missed lay-up is a tale of the square neglected. When shooting a lay-up, you need not even look at the rim. Focus on the square painted on the backboard. Lay the ball there — again, softly, no matter how speedily you race down the court to beat your defender.

When you become more advanced with the lay-up, learn to use the rim as your friend, too. Go up and under the rim — a reverse lay-up — so that the rim wards off a defender's outstretched arm.

Why is someone like Charles Barkley, who stands only 6'6", such an effective scorer down low? Because he understands the terrain. He uses his ample gluteus maximus to create space for himself and then the rim and backboard as shields. And he always lays it in off the square if the dunk is not available. Sir Charles realizes that if Shaq is between him and the basket, he'd better figure out a way to get the basket between himself and Shaq unless he wants his shot blocked.

Use the correct foot

Lay-ups start at the bottom; that is, at your feet. Beginners must learn to shoot lay-ups off the proper foot. A right-handed lay-up requires your left foot as the spring (the right foot is in the air first). The left-handed lay-up uses the right foot.

If you can teach a youngster to shoot lay-ups with either hand, you give her a tremendous advantage over her peers. Lay-ups from the right side of the bucket should always be shot with the right hand, and those from the left with the left hand. Why? A righty who shoots a lay-up from the left side with her right hand is going to discover that the rim (and the defense) blocks a lot of her shots. It's never too early to teach a youngster to be ambidextrous, at least when it comes to lay-ups. And remember, when using the opposite hand, she also must use the other foot as her launcher. (See Chapter 18 for detials about teaching the lay-up to kids.)

Footstep drill

Player A receives the ball at half-court and takes it in for a lay-up as if it is a fast break. Player B begins from 5 feet behind and act as a chasing defender. Will the offensive player blow the lay-up because he hears footsteps?

Player A should *not* look behind him or take his eye off the square on the backboard. What he *should* be thinking about:

- Beating the defender downcourt.
- Jumping off the correct foot.
- Putting the ball in the square.

The top of the key

Think of the top of the key as the free throw line extended toward midcourt. This is the best spot from which to launch a three-pointer because you have the opportunity to make the one you miss. If the shot falls short, the ball may bounce off the front of the rim and climb into the basket; long, and there's always the hope that it will carom off the backboard. At every level in the U.S. below the pros, the top of the key corresponds to the three-point arc, which is located 19'9" from the rim. So again, this is a free throw with a little more *oomph* required.

The elbows

Elbow is a term for the two spots on the floor that mark the theoretical intersection of the foul line extended and the circle at the head of the lane. Why do they call it the elbow? Face the basket and extend your arms to mimic the three-point arc. Your elbow is the court's elbow. (Your Adam's apple is sort of the top of the key, but I doubt that anyone has ever called it that.)

The right or left wing

Former U.S. Senator Bill Bradley (who won two NBA titles as a forward with the Knicks) is a moderate, but he was definitely a right wing and left wing proponent during his playing days. Located between the elbow and baseline, the wing is the best place on the floor for those shooters who prefer bankshots. Scottie Pippen of the Chicago Bulls, who, like Bradley, is a forward (this is usually where at least one forward places himself on offense), will tell you that this is his favorite spot.

The right or left corner

So you want to make it a little tough on yourself, eh? From the corner, also known as the *baseline shot,* the backboard cannot be your ally. It's not in your sight line to provide depth perception, nor is the square visible. You shoot most of your blush-inducing airballs from here.

That said, many a pure shooter, especially those who love the feel of a swished shot, swear by the corner shot.

The Bankshot

The bankshot is one of the lost arts of basketball. When you know the angle, the target is easy to hit. Legendary UCLA coach John Wooden, who directed the Bruins to ten NCAA titles in the 1960s and '70s, had his teams practice this shot all day. Watch some old films — I suggest any that include UCLA's undefeated 1972–73 team that won the championship. Notice how many times center Bill Walton and forward Keith (later "Jamaal," of Silk fame) Wilkes banked in shots.

A good exercise is to play an entire pickup game, or a game of H-O-R-S-E (see Chapter 11), shooting nothing but bankshots.

Use the square as your target on the bankshot, though you learn via practice that from different spots on the court you have to aim for different areas of the square. Why is the bankshot so successful? One reason: It compels you to give your shot a higher arc to hit the square, and high-arcing shots always necessitate proper mechanics.

The Baby Jumper

Who says that you have to shoot from far outside or directly under the hoop? Give me the guy who can shoot the 8- to 12-foot jumpshot, the *baby jumper.* I can teach him how to pivot with his back to the basket to create room for himself.

The skills required to shoot the baby jumper are the same as those needed to make free throws. The big difference between the two is that with the baby jumper, you often are shooting off-balance because your body is twisting in midair. But remember this: Only your lower body is off-balance. The upper body is square to the rim. Watch any pure shooter and note this (Michael Jordan, as with so many basketball skills, is your best example). No matter how he twists, wriggles, or soars to give himself an opening, by the time he shoots his upper body is facing the basket and in control. The elbow is inside the hip to act as the barrel of the rifle.

Always look for the location of your defender's hands. Does the man guarding you have his hands down at his sides? If so, you're golden. Shoot, baby!

Baby Jumper Drill: Place your player, with his back to the basket, about 12 feet from the bucket. Pass the ball to him — the bounce pass or high lob are the two most likely passes in a real game — and have him square up and shoot. Do so repeatedly for 30 seconds and keep track of how many he makes. Do this every day, and when his improvement begins to plateau, place a defender on him — just to stand there as an obstruction — to give him a new challenge.

Believe it or not, you catch the ball with your eyes, not your hands. Look the ball into your hands before you try to do anything else with it. What else do you have to look at? The fans? Sharon Stone attends Laker games, and chances are you're not a Laker.

The Three-Point Shot

The three-point shot, which was introduced into the NBA in 1979–80 and in college seven years later, has provided the biggest revolution in the game since the shot clock. The NBA actually stole this idea from the now-defunct American Basketball Association (ABA) with the intent to open up the floor offensively.

Although the three-pointer (or, in sportscaster-ese, the *trey*) has greatly benefited the crowded NBA court, it has gained too large a role in the college game, where it is too easy a shot to convert. We need to strike a balance, to move the arc back a few feet, say to 20 feet, 6 inches, the international distance. The three would still be an option, but the inside post game would not be compromised as it currently is. Teams are hoisting up 30 three-point shots a game, and have forgotten the post offense. (See Chapter 6 for details about a post offense.)

The best teams are those who have a fine complement of the two offensive styles, sort of like an entree with vegetables. Wake Forest's 1996–97 squad best exemplified this. The team's All-American center, Tim Duncan, was such an offensive force not only because he could hit the baby jumper, but also because his passing ability opened up the Demon Deacons' three-point game.

Shoot with your legs

Leg strength is the most important thing when shooting the three. You still follow the basic mechanics, but you must have the natural strength to get the ball to the hoop with your legs. Always start in close and then move out to three-point land.

Choose the right spot

There are hot spots on the floor when it comes to shooting the three. Like other shots, a straightaway shot has the best chance of going in, making the one you missed. But shots from the wings are open, and the bankshot is still there, although players today who bank it in usually smile as they head down court to play defense because they were going for a swish.

To live and die by the three

When trying to come back from a huge deficit, teams that rely too much on the three-pointer usually get burned. Down by five with a minute remaining? Still too soon. Give me the easy two baskets instead of the three. Plus, I might get fouled. I've seen teams lose NCAA tourney games because they resorted to the three too soon. Kentucky did that in a regional final loss to North Carolina in the 1995 NCAA tournament, when the Wildcats shot a pathetic 7 of 36 from beyond the arc.

About eight years ago, a World University Games final pitted the USSR against Yugoslavia. The game was televised stateside and, judging by the way games are coached today, it seems as if every coach in the U.S. watched it. The Soviets, trailing by nine with 30 seconds left in the game, nailed down a trio of three-pointers to extend the contest into overtime, where they won. Since then, everyone has been chucking threes. But that outcome was the exception.

Watch some game tapes of the pre-three-point days of college basketball, and you'll see some pretty amazing comebacks. On March 2, 1974, North Carolina once found itself trailing Duke by eight points with 17 seconds left. The Tar Heels tied the game and won it in overtime. The three-point-goal rule was still 13 years away for the college game. How did they do it? By forcing turnovers and with good, solid shooting.

Shooting Drills

Scientists have yet to find a basketball player who prefers defense drills to shooting drills. You'll never have a problem motivating your players for this phase of practice. Still, shooting drills should have a purpose: Relate the exercise to actual game conditions so that it has meaning for the players, and they'll derive more from it.

Drills without a defender

The following drills are great for improving your or your players' shooting skills (if only real games were this simple). Chapter 11 talks about another perennial favorite defenderless shooting drill: H-O-R-S-E.

30-second spot shooting

Three players participate in this drill: One (Sh) shoots, and the second (R) rebounds and passes the ball to the third (P), who then passes to the shooter. (See Figure 5-6.) Use two balls to keep the drill fast-paced. After 30 seconds, all three rotate roles so that, after 90 seconds, everyone has had a turn as the shooter.

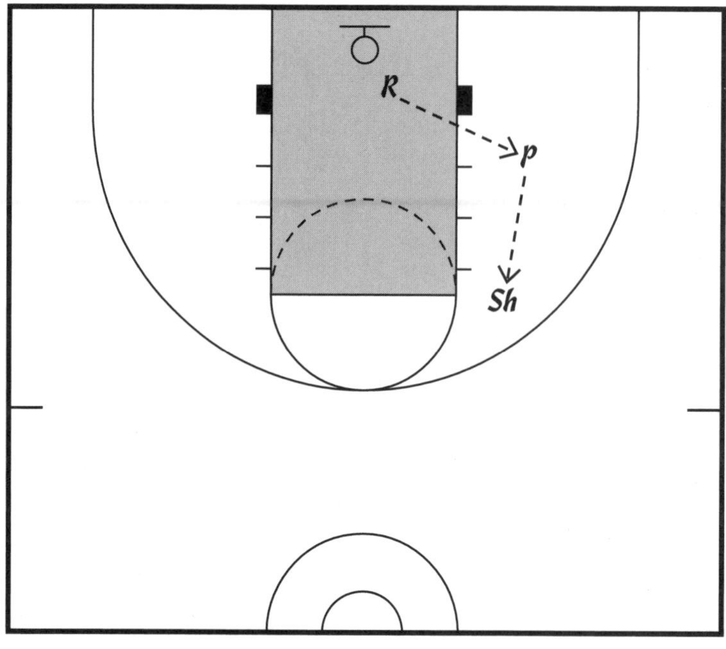

Figure 5-6: The 30-second shooting drill.

Work different spots on the floor during each 90-second rotation. Start, for example, at the left corner, and then the left wing, left elbow, top of the key, right elbow, and so on. It only takes 13 minutes and 30 seconds for each player to cover all the key spots on the floor.

Have a manager or an assistant coach chart the number of shots each player attempts and makes in this drill. Players need something to shoot for — besides the hoop — and charting their progress on a daily basis accomplishes this. That said, impress upon your players not to fire up as many shots as possible in their allotted time. Make each shot a good shot. Shooting as quickly as you possibly can does not simulate actual game conditions . . . unless you play for Paul Westhead (former Loyola Marymount coach whose teams were known for their high scoring averages).

Benefits: The shooter gets needed repetition of shots and takes shots off a pass, which is how most game shots are taken.

Come off a chair

The chair acts as your teammate setting a screen for you (student managers espouse the traditional folding chair as opposed to, say, a Barca-lounger).

Catch the ball coming around the chair just as if your teammate is setting a screen for you. Plant your lead foot, catch the ball (with your eyes), and face up to the hoop. Come around the chair, catch, turn, and face up. Your trail foot can help you square up and balance before you shoot. You want to catch and turn off the lead foot simultaneously. (See Figure 5-7.)

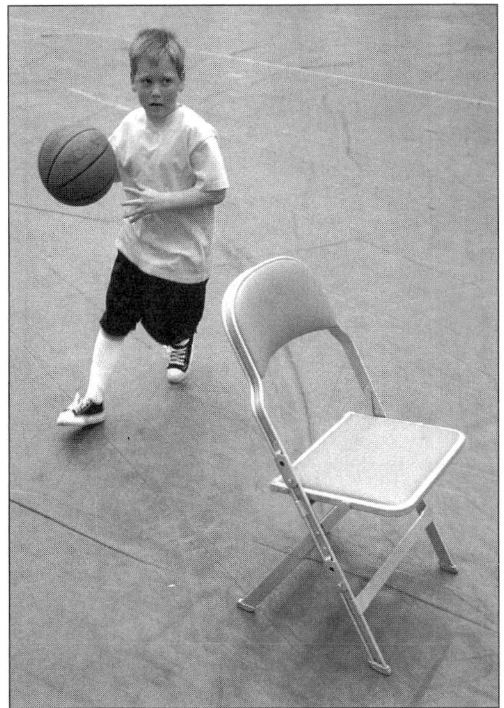

Figure 5-7: The "come off a chair" drill.

This drill can be done on multiple baskets at the same time. Just pair up two players so that while one player is doing a shooting drill, her partner is actually working on her passing. Sneaky, eh?

Benefits: Shooting after working to get yourself open. The game moves quickly; this drill echoes that pace.

Fifty shots, three balls

Place three groups of three players at three of the five shooting areas of the court. For example, start with three players in the left corner, three in the right corner, and three at the top of the key. (See Figure 5-8.)

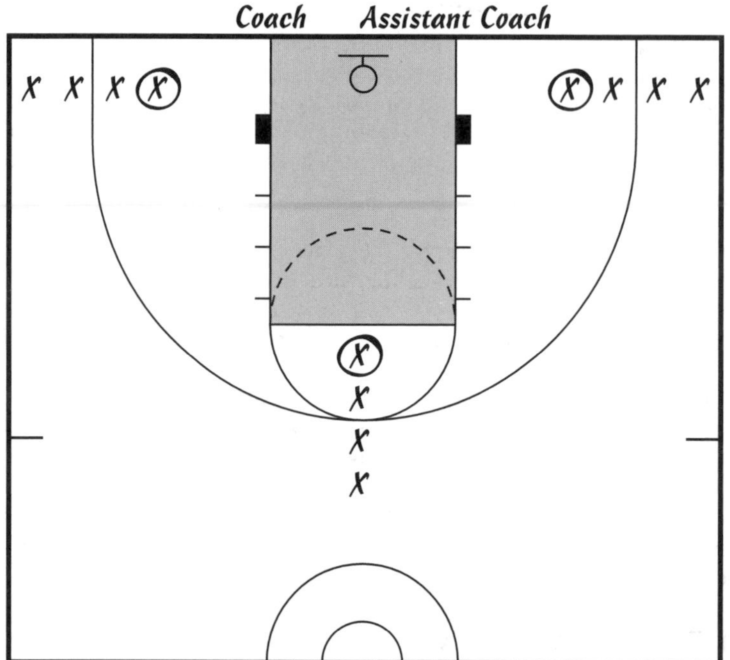

Figure 5-8: The 50-shot, three-ball drill.

Each group gets one ball and, with managers or other teammates rebounding, takes 50 shots. With three balls soaring toward one hoop, you occasionally have some interference, but that's okay: Shooters must learn to live with distractions. Managers or teammates count the shots as the groups proceed. After one rotation, double the number of shots each group made; that number is their shooting percentage. Rotate the groups from spot to spot so that the drill has a total of three rotations.

Benefits: Repetition builds confidence. Competition keeps it interesting.

From the elbow

There are two elbow areas per half-court, so split up your squad into four groups and place each group at an elbow. Managers or teammates feed players the ball, and players shoot one at a time. Vary the drill: Sometimes make it a catch-and-shoot situation, and other times a stutter-step with a single dribble to get open.

Benefit: This is the Spago of three-point shooting in game situations. Have your players get accustomed to this popular, trendy spot.

Fast-break shooting drill

Form three lines at the baseline, with your guards (1) in the middle. The guard penetrates up the middle of the court with a player on either side (2 and 3) filling the fast-break lanes. (See Figure 5-9.) By the time the guard reaches the far free throw line, he should either pass the ball to one of his wings, who pulls up for a jumper or take the jumper himself (making him a somewhat unpopular guy with his teammates).

When the point guard gets to that spot where he's going to either pass or shoot, he needs to correct his forward momentum and get under control. He should jump stop (plant both feet) so that he doesn't draw a charging foul if a defender is standing right in front of him. Now he can pass or shoot.

Variation: As the three players race upcourt, have the player in the middle alternate passes from one wing to the other — no dribbling allowed until the middle player receives the ball beyond midcourt.

Benefits: Conditioning, teamwork, and simulating game situations. Chart each player's percentage from each wing if you can to find out who's stronger from which side.

DeBusschere bad pass drill

Named for former Knicks forward Dave DeBusschere (a recent selectee to the NBA's Fifty Greatest Players list), who was not a bad passer. Rather, he had an innate ability to pick up a loose ball, set his feet, square up, and shoot. DeBusschere was a great outside shooter for a big guy, perhaps the best among players who were 6'6" or taller.

In the drill, a coach stands near midcourt. The player stands at the baseline and throws a half-court pass to the coach. Then the player sprints to the frontcourt, where the coach leads him with a bad pass tossed into the corner. The player chases down the ball (cursing the coach under his breath), sets himself, squares to the hoop, and shoots. The player then rebounds his own shot and runs back to the baseline of origin.

Benefits: Conditioning. Players learn to react quickly to bad situations and maintain focus.

Skip pass shooting drill

The term *skip pass* refers to a pass that does the job of two passes. In a half-court offense, if a player has the ball on the right wing, for example, and the play is designed to get the ball to the left wing, normally the ball would first be passed to the top of the key and then to the other wing. A skip pass, which is riskier because it must travel cross-court, goes directly from one wing to the other. It's like buying wholesale: You cut out the middleman.

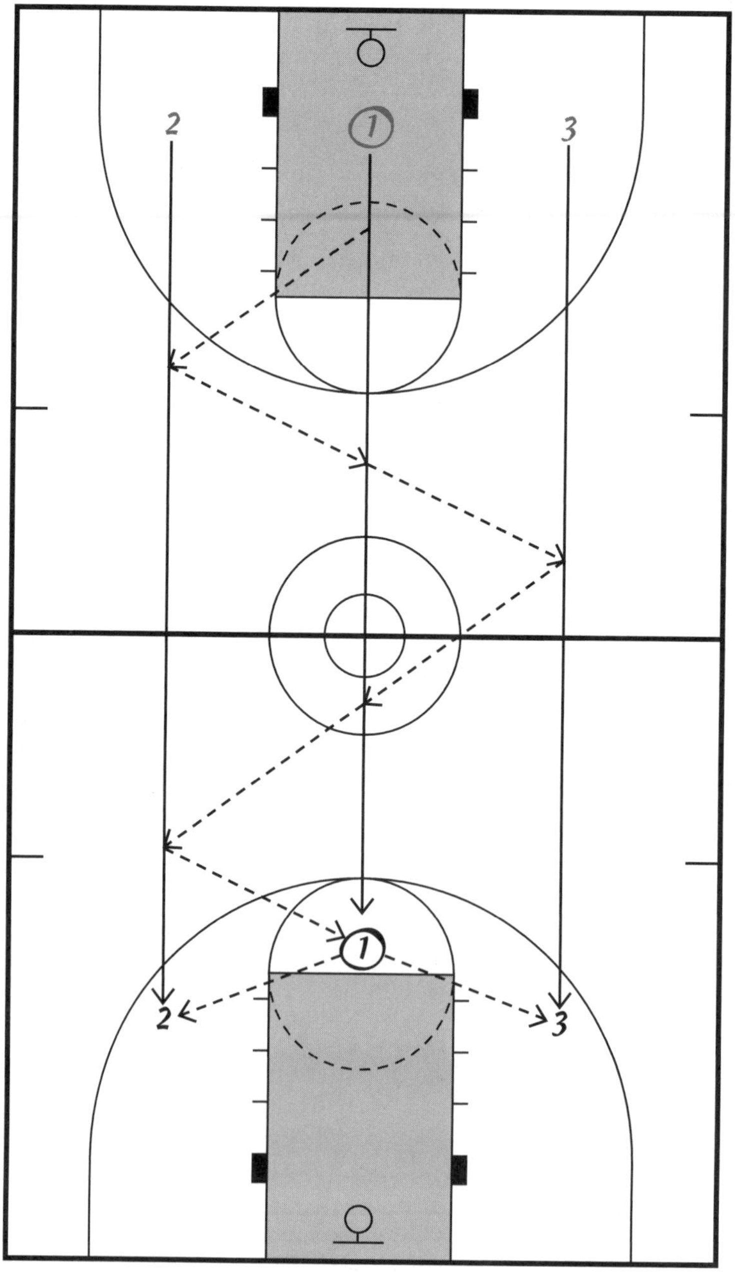

Figure 5-9: The fast-break drill.

In this drill, have one player at the top of the key pass the ball to either wing. The player at that wing then skip passes to the opposite wing, who shoots. You can even add this drill as a variation to the fast-break drill listed earlier.

Benefits: Simulates actual game passes. Players learn to catch and shoot longer passes.

Drills with a defender

Fly at the shooter

This drill uses two balls and three players. Player 1 shoots the ball while Player 2 *flies,* or lunges, at him from a few feet away, as a defender would do in a zone defense. Player 1 follows his shot and rebounds the ball. Player 2 turns and becomes Player 1; that is, becomes the shooter. Player 3, who has the second ball, passes the ball to Player 2 and lunges at him. Player 2 rebounds, Player 3 becomes Player 2, and 1 becomes 3. Player 1 then flies at 3 as he attempts his shot. Lather, rinse, repeat, you get the idea. (See Figure 5-10.) Have the shooter stand at different spots on the floor for this drill.

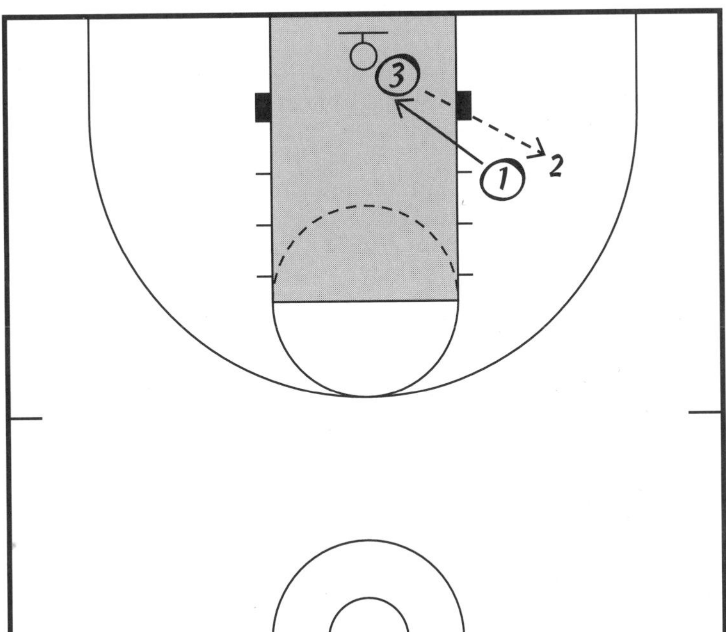

Figure 5-10: The fly at the shooter drill.

With the advent of the trey, this drill takes on even greater importance. Division I college teams attempt on average 16 to 18 three-point shots per game. When the defense plays a zone, that number is even greater. Often, defenders find themselves in the middle of the floor playing a helping-style defense (see Chapter 7) and have no chance to block a three-point attempt. Instead, they charge at the shooter in an attempt to distract him.

Benefits: The shooter learns to focus on the shot, not the defense. Good three-point practice. Mild conditioning.

It's okay for the defender in this drill to clap his hands together or yell or sing if he feels the urge — anything to distract the shooter, who should use this drill as a means to hone his focus. As you're shooting, remember that the defender isn't going to run into you — that's football — so don't concern yourself with him. And if he does, and you bury the trey, you're looking at that rarest of offensive conquests: the four-point play.

Post-feed kickout

This is another shooting drill that has very practical application to the basics of the game whether you're playing against a zone defense or man-to-man. Three people and one ball are required.

The shooter, who's the off-guard (in hoops numerology, the 2 man), has the ball on the wing and is guarded by a defender (D2). The post player on offense (5) starts from the baseline, flashes to the middle of the lane, and moves to a position between the high and low posts. You, 2, pass him the ball. Your defender then *doubles down;* that is, leaves you to guard the 5-man, because this five player is someone who will draw a double team from the wing.

After you, 2, pass the ball into the post, move to the corner. Don't stay in the same spot after you make that pass, because if you do, it will be easy for D2 to find you (the same technique applies for avoiding the boss at holiday parties). If you make him take the time to look for you, you enhance your chances of having an open shot. Player 5 then passes the ball to you in the corner. Shoot quickly, before D2 can reach you. (See Figure 5-11.)

Benefits: Involves two offensive players working together. Incorporates fly-at-the-shooter techniques. Teaches the shooter to move without the ball.

To make this a defensive drill, order that no shot be taken until five passes have been made. In other words, when Player 2 receives the ball back from Player 5, he returns it and moves back to another spot along the three-point arc. Do this a few times. It's good practice for guards playing defense who also have double-down responsibilities.

Great Shooters: Players to Emulate

For help in visualizing the proper mechanics of shooting, track down videos or even still photos of the following shooting virtuosos. As you watch, notice that although they all have distinctive styles, every one of them launches a shot that has good backspin and "grabs the rim" with his shooting hand during the follow-through.

Figure 5-11: The post-feed kickout drill.

Elgin Baylor (1958–72, Minneapolis/Los Angeles Lakers): Elgin Baylor typifies what I say about looking as if you're shooting off-balance but having your upper body under control. Baylor, who many an old-timer will tell you was the progenitor of Michael Jordan, went through some Houdini contortions to get open on the baseline, but he always had the top of his body square to the basket. Sometimes you hear about a player who is a scorer, not a shooter. Elgin Baylor was both.

John Havlicek (1962–78, Boston Celtics): A maestro of the clutch shot, Hondo always seemed to put daggers into other team's heart at the end of a playoff game. One of those players who seemed to shoot better when off-balance, witness his game-tying bankshot against the Suns in the '76 Finals that led to Boston's triple overtime victory.

Sam Jones (1957–69, Boston Celtics): Sam Jones was the master of the bankshot. This 1983 Hall of Fame selection was one of more graceful and professional players the game has known. In 1968, he won an NBA finals contest with a bankshot from about 25 feet from the right side. Jones came off a screen at the top of the key as if he were doing a chair drill, squared up, and drilled it. Ball game.

Pete Maravich (1970–80, Atlanta Hawks, New Orleans/Utah Jazz, Boston Celtics): Did he like to shoot? Heck, his nickname was Pistol Pete. Maravich was a showman and a revolutionary as well. Nobody took as many crazy shots as this former Louisiana State star. In many ways, especially to folks in the South, he is to basketball what Elvis is to rock 'n' roll.

Despite playing only three seasons at LSU in the late 1960s, Maravich is still the number-one scorer in college history (3,667 points, 44.2 points per game). That record is even more remarkable when you consider that one of the game's all-time long-range bombers compiled those stats before the advent of the three-point shot.

Rick Mount (1970–75, four different ABA teams): Mount, who found his greatest success on the hardwood at Purdue, was the master of squaring up. In the 1969 NCAA quarterfinals versus Marquette, Mount won a game for the Boilermakers with an amazing shot. With one second remaining and his back to the hoop, Mount caught a pass, leapt and turned 180 degrees, squared up, and hit the 25-foot jumper to send Purdue to the Final Four.

Someone at Purdue recently reviewed a 1970 game in which Mount scored a school-record 27 field goals and determined that 18 of them would have been three-point goals had the trey been in existence at the time.

Calvin Murphy (1970–83, San Diego/Houston Rockets): Murphy stood only 5'9", but he could jump out of the gym. He attributed his superb eye-hand-ball coordination to his favorite hobby, baton twirling. The concentration and coordination needed to twirl the baton made its presence felt on the free throw line, where Calvin distinguished himself as one of the best ever. In the 1980–81 season, when Murphy made a record 95.8 percent of his foul shots, he hit 78 in a row over one stretch. A smart player as well, he rarely had a shot blocked despite his size.

Oscar Robertson (1960–74, Cincinnati Royals, Milwaukee Bucks): The only player to average a triple double (at least ten points, rebounds, and assists per game) for an entire season (1961–62), Robertson used all five areas of the floor as a shooter. He often shot the ball with one arm, neglecting to use his left arm for support. Still, the Big O had a textbook follow-through.

Dennis Scott (1990–present, Orlando Magic): I have reviewed a lot of players from the 1960s and '70s. But if you look around the NBA today, Dennis Scott is as pure a shooter as you can find. The former Georgia Tech forward is among the leaders in college history in three-point goals and, in 1995–96, set an NBA single-season record by making 267 treys.

Jerry West (1960–74, Los Angeles Lakers): I may have saved the best for last. A natural athlete who had all the elements of a great shooter, West rarely had his shot blocked because he always released it from the top of his jump. Sounds natural, I know, but too many players shoot as they're still ascending. West, whose form in every facet of the game was so flawless that he literally became the model for the NBA logo (a silhouetted player dribbling), may have possessed the most seamless jumper in hoops history.

"Mr. Clutch" could score from anywhere at any time. In Game 3 of the 1970 NBA Finals against the Knicks, for example, he hit a last-second shot to tie the game — from 74 feet away. (They won in overtime but lost the series.)

Chapter 6
Offense

In This Chapter

- Understanding what guards, forwards, and centers do
- Playing to your team's strengths
- Passing, screening, and other offensive moves
- Playing offense against a man-to-man defense, a zone defense, or a press

The objective on offense is simple: to put the ball in the basket. But how do you go about doing so?

Offense is equal parts choreography and improvisation. Coaches can design offensive schemes and have players run through them for hours. But this is not chess, a game in which position means everything — (Sean) Rooks-4 to (Brevin) Knight-6. No, each offensive possession allows for a multitude of options, which is one of the reasons why the game is always captivating. So remember that when watching or teaching offense, positioning players correctly is only half the battle.

Offense is actually dictated by the defense. If the defense plays man-to-man — that is, each defensive player is assigned to one offensive player, following him wherever he goes — the offensive scheme usually follows suit. (Chapter 7 explains the major types of defenses and the differences between them.)

Note: Zone defense is illegal in the NBA, so nobody plays it (ahem) in that league. Thus all offense at the NBA level is (theoretically) man-to-man.

Establishing Your Position

Every player on the court has a position, and with the position comes a job description. Don't ever send a player into the game without her being aware of her job description. If you do, you're setting her up to fail. This section gives a typical résumé for each position.

Point guard (alias: "Ball Handler")

Prototypes: Bob Cousy (Boston Celtics), Earvin "Magic" Johnson (LA Lakers), John Stockton (Utah Jazz)

Flavor of the Day: Terrell Brandon (Cleveland Cavaliers), Damon Stoudamire (Toronto Raptors), Jamila Wideman (LA Sparks)

Physique/Skills: Usually the shortest player on the team (Stoudamire is 5'10"), though exceptions exist (Johnson was 6'9"). Should be team's best passer and ball handler.

Tell-All Stat: Assist-to-turnover ratio

Job Description: The quarterback on offense, the point guard's traditional role is to push the ball upcourt and start the offensive wheels turning, either by dribble penetration into the lane or by passing. Though not primarily a shooter, he can be. The point guard, like a quarterback, is the coach on the floor; his job is to correct teammates if they forget their responsibilities. He should be the most level-headed player, if not the one who's most respected by his teammates. Unless he takes it to the basket himself, he should remain near the top of the key, ready to retreat on defense.

At the NBA level especially, teams must have a great point guard. NBA playoff contests are slower and more half-court-oriented than their regular-season precursors. Teams need a point guard who is a brilliant creator on the floor because, in tense situations, offensive players have a bad habit of standing around.

The point guard stands tall for several reasons:

- **A good point guard can dribble through a full-court press all by himself.** (Watch Allen Iverson of the Philadelphia 76ers, for example.) Not only does this demoralize the defense, but it also creates four-on-three or three-on-two situations (which give the offense an advantage) and easy baskets.
- **The point guard is a double threat; he can pass or shoot.** If he beats his defender one-on-one, he penetrates to score until another defender helps out, which means that someone else is open.
- **The point guard runs the fast break off a rebound or steal, or by beating the press.** Fast-break baskets are easy baskets; you want as many of those as possible. Magic Johnson attempted to make every offensive possession a fast break. On turnover violations, for example, Magic scooted to the sideline and tried to hurry the official into handing him the ball. Then he pushed the ball upcourt while the other team was still hanging its head about the turnover. Magic was very smart on the court; great point guards have to be.

The Guards Must Be Crazy

The point guard/shooting guard tandem is known as the *backcourt*. With rare exceptions, the backcourt dictates a team's personality and success. While the great Boston Celtics teams of the 1980s were best known for their Hall of Fame frontcourt of Larry Bird-Kevin McHale-Robert Parish, hoops fans by and large find great backcourt duos as easy to remember as Lennon and McCartney (you know . . . of the Beatles).

A brief quiz: Match the tandem with the appropriate championship team (point guard is listed first).

1. Walt Frazier-Earl Monroe	A. Los Angeles Lakers
2. Gus Williams-Dennis Johnson	B. Boston Celtics
3. Isiah Thomas-Joe Dumars	C. New York Knicks
4. Magic Johnson-Byron Scott	D. Seattle SuperSonics
5. B.J. Armstrong-Michael Jordan	E. Detroit Pistons
6. Jo Jo White-Don Chaney	F. Chicago Bulls

Answers: 1-C, 2-D, 3-E, 4-A, 5-F, 6-B

Shooting guard (alias: "Two-Guard")

Prototypes: Jerry West (LA Lakers), Michael Jordan (Chicago Bulls)

Flavor of the Day: Jordan, Joe Dumars (Detroit Pistons)

Physique/Skills: Anywhere from 6'4" to 6'7" for men, or 5'9" to 6'1" for women, seems to be the current ideal height. Must display a willingness to shoot game-winning shots, have a quick release on the jumper, and be a good three-point shooter.

Tell-All Stat: Points per game

Job Description: The shooting guard, known in NBA lingo as a *two-guard*, is not necessarily a great ball handler. She is, however, normally the team's best perimeter shooter. The shooting guard frees herself up for shots by working off screens set by larger teammates. The best two-guards come off screens prepared to react to the defense: shoot, pass, or drive. The two-guard tries to crash the boards while the point guard stays back and defends the fast break. The principal beneficiaries of the three-point line, shooting guards are as prominent as they've ever been.

The two-guard is often number one for these reasons:

- **The three-pointer:** A shooting guard can single-handedly destroy the opponent by scoring three-pointers in the clutch moments of a game.
- **Jordan:** More people pattern their games after Michael than they do after Hakeem or Shaq. Simply put, the majority of people fall into the two-guard height range as opposed to the center height range (respective to their level of play). If you have mostly bricks, you build brick houses. If you mostly have two-guard players, they dominate your offense.

Small forward (alias: "Swingman")

Prototypes: Elgin Baylor (LA Lakers), Julius Erving (Philadelphia 76ers), Larry Bird (Boston Celtics)

Flavor of the Day: Grant Hill (Detroit Pistons), Reggie Miller (Indiana Pacers), Sheryl Swoopes (Houston Comets)

Physique/Skills: The decathlete of hoops: 6'4" to 6'8" for men, or 5'11" to 6'3" for women, aggressive, and strong; tall enough to mix it up inside, but agile enough to handle the ball and shoot well.

Tell-All Stat: Triple doubles

Job Description: Small forwards must be able to score from both the perimeter and the inside. They're all-purpose players on offense and should be too tall, physical, or tenacious for a defense's two-guard to handle.

Adrian Dantley was the best small forward I ever coached. After playing at Notre Dame, he went on to many years of success in the NBA and is still one of the top ten scorers in the history of the league. He could score inside and hit the 15-foot jumper. He would have to increase his range today to include the three-point shot, but he was the best I've seen at getting fouled and going to the line, where he was an 83 percent free throw shooter.

Power forward (alias: "The Enforcer" or "Four Spot")

Prototype: Bob Pettit (St. Louis Hawks), Karl Malone (Utah Jazz)

Flavor of the Day: Dennis Rodman (Chicago Bulls), Rebecca Lobo (New York Liberty)

Proof in the stats

The proof of the worth of the shortest players (the guards) in a big man's game is in the following table. Look how often the MVP of the NBA Finals has been a guard (indicated in bold), especially in recent years.

NBA Finals MVPs

Year	*Player*	*Team*	*Position*
1969	**Jerry West**	**Los Angeles Lakers**	**G**
1970	Willis Reed	New York Knicks	C
1971	Kareem Abdul-Jabbar	Milwaukee Bucks	C
1972	Wilt Chamberlain	Los Angeles	C
1973	Willis Reed	New York Knicks	C
1974	John Havlicek	Boston Celtics	F
1975	Rick Barry	Golden State Warriors	F
1976	**JoJo White**	**Boston Celtics**	**G**
1977	Bill Walton	Portland Trail Blazers	C
1978	Wes Unseld	Washington Bullets	C
1979	**Dennis Johnson**	**Seattle SuperSonics**	**G**
1980	**Magic Johnson**	**Los Angeles Lakers**	**G**
1981	Cedric Maxwell	Boston Celtics	F
1982	**Magic Johnson**	**Los Angeles Lakers**	**G**
1983	Moses Malone	Philadelphia 76ers	C
1984	Larry Bird	Boston Celtics	F
1985	Kareem Abdul-Jabbar	Los Angeles Lakers	C
1986	Larry Bird	Boston Celtics	F
1987	**Magic Johnson**	**Los Angeles Lakers**	**G**
1988	James Worthy	Los Angeles Lakers	F
1989	**Joe Dumars**	**Detroit Pistons**	**G**
1990	**Isiah Thomas**	**Detroit Pistons**	**G**
1991	**Michael Jordan**	**Chicago Bulls**	**G**
1992	**Michael Jordan**	**Chicago Bulls**	**G**
1993	**Michael Jordan**	**Chicago Bulls**	**G**
1994	Hakeem Olajuwon	Houston Rockets	C
1995	Hakeem Olajuwon	Houston Rockets	C
1996	**Michael Jordan**	**Chicago Bulls**	**G**
1997	**Michael Jordan**	**Chicago Bulls**	**G**

Physique/Skills: A Mack truck (appropriately enough, Malone moonlights as the driver of his own 18-wheeler); anywhere from 6'7" to 6'11" (for men) or 6'1" to 6'4" (for women) with muscles or at least a little bulk. Must be a good rebounder and able to handle passes and hit shots near the basket.

Tell-All Stat: Rebounds

Job Description: The power forward, known in NBA lingo as a *four spot,* is a rugged rebounder, but athletic enough to move with some degree of quickness around the painted area (the free throw lane) offensively and defensively. She is expected to score when given the opportunity at the baseline, much like a center; but she usually has a range of up to 15 feet, 180 degrees around the basket. The prototype power forward scores from the baseline, in front of the basket, and can bank it in from close range.

Twenty years ago, not much difference existed between a power forward and a center. But today, power forwards run the floor well and move farther out from the basket.

Watch Christian Laettner of the Atlanta Hawks, for example. At 6'11", Laettner was forced to play center his first four years in the NBA, and he never resembled the college player who led Duke to a pair of NCAA titles. When Laettner squared off against then-Orlando Magic center Shaquille O'Neal in the 1996 Eastern Conference playoffs, he was so physically outmanned that one Hawks assistant coach said, "Christian's not a center; he just plays one on TV." Then last year, center Dikembe Mutombo joined the Hawks. Laettner moved to power forward, where he was able to face the basket. Voilà! He made the All-Star team.

Center (alias: "The Big Man")

Prototype: Wilt Chamberlain (LA Lakers), Kareem Abdul-Jabbar (LA Lakers)

Flavors of the Day: Hakeem Olajuwon (Houston Rockets), Shaquille O'Neal (LA Lakers); Lisa Leslie (Los Angeles Sparks)

Physique/Skills: Typically the tallest player on the team, the center should be able to post up offensively — that is, receive the ball with his back to the basket and use pivot moves to hit a variety of short jumpers, hook shots, and dunks. Great centers — presently, this separates Olajuwon from O'Neal — are also able to pass from the pivot.

Job Description: Consider NBA newcomer Tim Duncan, who played four years for Wake Forest. Duncan is the best of *all* worlds because he's also a point guard in the paint. He can shoot the jumper, face the basket, and because of the length of his arms, go over the top of his opponents to get offensive rebounds. He can power in for the dunk, make the baseline move for a little jumper, and even score from the outside, even three-point range. But most important, in the paint, he knows how to find the open man. He ranked first in assists on Wake Forest's team his senior year.

The center may not be as important on offense as he is on defense. This fact may surprise people who historically think of centers Wilt Chamberlain and Kareem Abdul-Jabbar as the greatest scorers in NBA history. But these two are the exception. More often than not, centers are on the court to clog the middle, block shots, and grab rebounds.

Especially in the college game, passing ability is an increasingly important asset for a center. Watch a center receive the ball in the post: If the center has any scoring ability, a defensive guard will *double down* on him (in other words, leave the player he's guarding to double team the center). When this happens, the center must locate the open teammate with a soft pass. No longer can the center be a "black hole" (passing the ball to a center used to be like throwing it into a black hole — you didn't see it again, at least not on that possession, because the center always took a shot).

Playing to Your Strength

As a coach, your first move in setting up an offense is to evaluate the talents of your players. The bottom line is that you need to score. It would be nice if the five players who hustled the most were also your five best shooters, but that's almost never the case. Take what's available — that is, understand the makeup of your team and develop your offense around it. Learn each of your players' offensive capabilities as shooters, passers, and even *dribble penetrators* (guards who are able to drive into the lane), and position them in your offense accordingly. For example:

- Two years ago, the best player for Oklahoma State was a plodding 7-footer with a soft shot — his name, Bryant Reeves. To exploit Reeves's offensive skills, Cowboys coach Eddie Sutton had his team play a *half-court game*, slowing down the offense so that the action took place on the offensive half of the court.
- The Arizona Wildcats' top scorers this decade are undersized point guards (Khalid Reeves, Damon Stoudamire, and Mike Bibby) who are excellent shooters and penetrators, so Wildcat coach Lute Olson builds his offense around their points potential.

The best teams have offensive balance: an inside scorer, good perimeter shooting, and a penetrating guard. But the majority of teams are deficient in one of those areas or, at the very least, lack balance. Know your strengths and play to them.

If you watched Tim Duncan in college, for example, you saw that Wake Forest coach Dave Odom made him the fulcrum of the offense. He'd position one teammate on the wing and one on the point to create a triangle with his All-America center (this is the choreography part of playing offense). The object was to get the ball to Duncan and then see whether the double down came from the defender guarding the point or the defender guarding the wing. Duncan would either hit the open man, shoot, or pass to the weakside (this is the improvisation part). The point is, Duncan dictated the offense.

Offensive Plays and Maneuvers

The best-known plays and maneuvers involve just two offensive players. (But don't interpret that to mean that their three teammates are simply standing around.) A single offensive possession may use one or more of the plays/maneuvers that I discuss in this section.

If one offensive credo is universally espoused, it is that you must space out your five offensive players on the floor. If you cluster two players together, one defender can effectively guard them both. Watch any good offense and notice how, next to scoring, the priority is to keep the five players as far away from one another as possible.

The pass

A *pass* involves one player throwing the ball to a teammate, either through the air or by bouncing it off the floor. As simple as a pass is, it's the first step in playing great offense.

A great one-on-one offensive player may score 40 points every once in a while, but usually to the detriment of his team. Playground legends such as Pete Maravich, George Gervin, and Bob McAdoo (around whom the offense was centered) never played for NBA teams that even made it into the NBA Finals. The LA Lakers, on the other hand, won five titles in the 1980s largely on the strength of Magic Johnson's ability to find the open teammate. A fine pass that leads to a lay-up is more demoralizing to a defense than an 18-foot jumper.

What about Michael Jordan, you ask? Jordan is a scorer, yes, but he also knows how to find the open teammate. In a March 1995 game, Jordan — recently returned from baseball's Birmingham Barons — torched the New York Knicks for 55 points. With the game tied in the final seconds, Jordan took the ball to the hoop. As three Knicks converged on him, he dished it to center Bill Wennington for the easy, winning bucket.

Unselfish teams — that is, *passing* teams — play the best offense.

The screen

A screen frees up a dribbler or an intended receiver. To set a screen, an offensive player without the ball uses her body as a shield to ward off a defender who is trying to follow an offensive player. For a screen to be legal, the screener must remain stationary for at least a full second and must have her arms in toward her torso. Otherwise, the screener is charged with an illegal screen foul.

To see an offense that knows the value of screening, watch Bob Knight's Indiana Hoosiers. On every single half-court possession, IU's offense runs at least two screens. Often, IU sets up three screens on one play just to free one shooter. If you can't set a screen, you can't play for the "General."

The give-and-go

A play that every schoolyard hoopster knows, the give-and-go burns the lazy defender. As shown in Figure 6-1, Player 1 on offense passes to Player 3 and then cuts sharply to the basket. Player 3 returns the ball to Player 1 — because Player 1 is moving quickly, Player 3 should use a bounce pass — who has beaten the defender who made the mistake of relaxing after his man passed the ball.

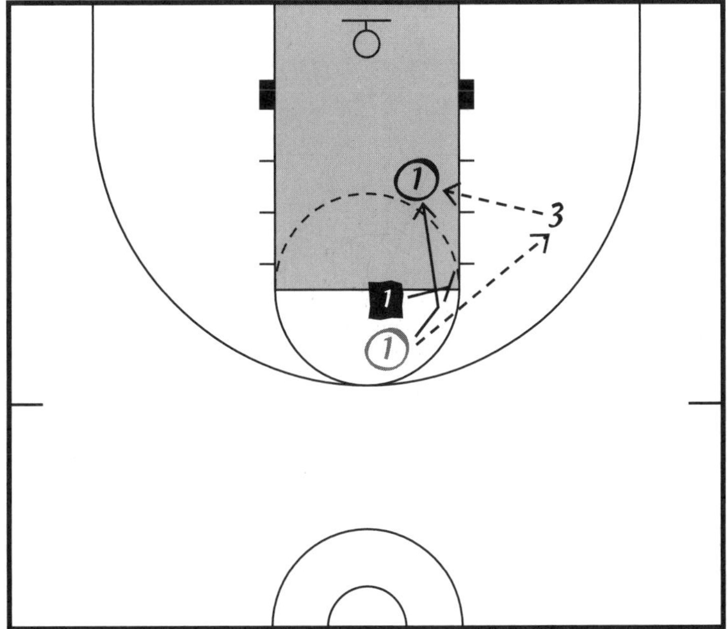

Figure 6-1: The give-and-go.

Pass and screen away

Okay, you've passed the ball. Now what do you do? You can stay where you are, but that makes you easy to defend. You can move toward the player you passed to with the idea of setting a pick. You can try the give-and-go. Or as Figure 6-2 shows, you (1) can move *away* from where you passed it (3), toward another teammate (4), and set a pick (or screen) — also known as the pass and screen away play. Player 4 then receives a pass from 3.

An effective offense always has movement, but with the idea of creating space for each player.

The pick and roll

A *pick* is simply a screen for the player with the ball. The pick and roll play is nearly as old as Dr. Naismith's peach baskets (see Chapter 3), but it's still very much in use today. The Utah Jazz, specifically point guard John Stockton and power forward Karl Malone, have been running the pick and roll for more than a decade, and no one's figured out how to stop them yet.

To execute a pick and roll (as shown in Figure 6-3), one offensive player (5) sets a pick for the player with the ball (1, who's almost always dribbling it at the time) and then rolls away from the pick, usually toward the basket. Why is such a simple play so difficult to defend? Because this play creates chaos on defense.

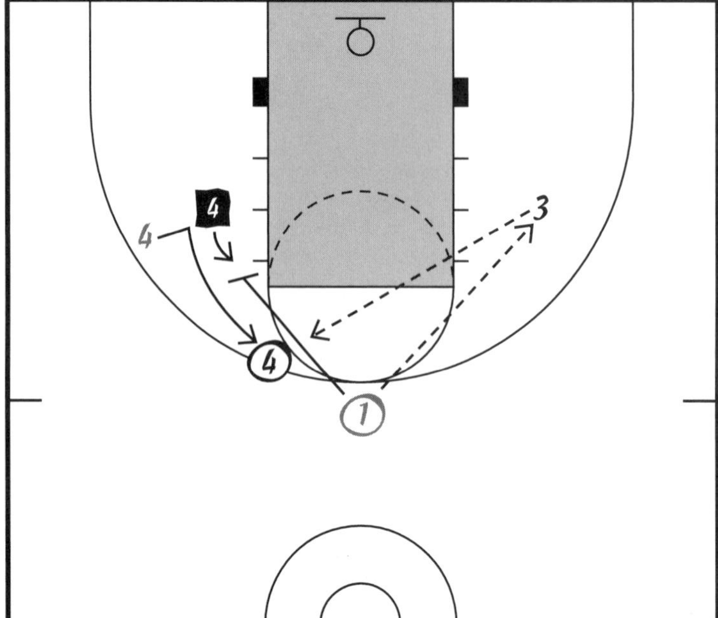

Figure 6-2: The pass and screen away play.

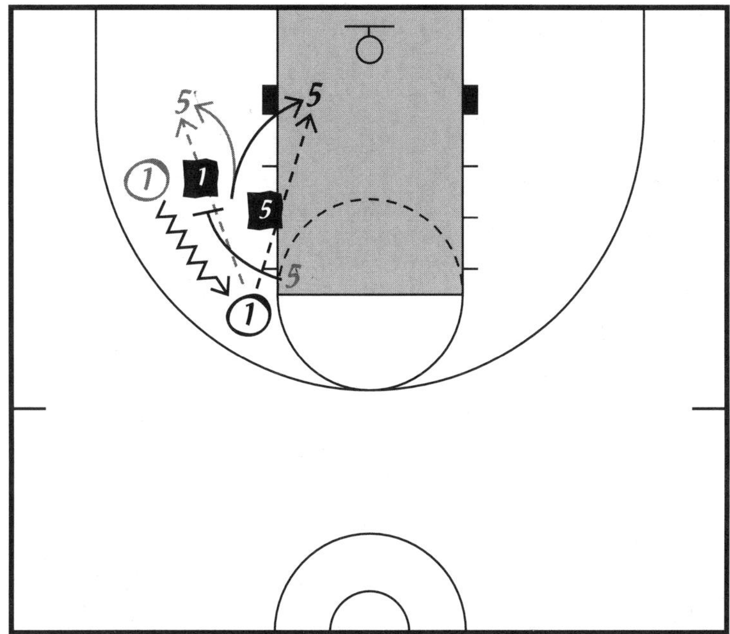

Figure 6-3: The pick and roll.

When Malone sets a pick on a smaller defender, he creates an area for Stockton. If Malone's defender jumps out to stop Stockton, Malone rolls away, leaving the smaller guard to defend Malone. Stockton, meanwhile, attempts to drive the lane and draw both defenders to him as Malone rolls to the basket. In this example, you usually see one of three outcomes of the pick and roll:

- Stockton beats his man off the screen and drives for a lay-up or short jumper.
- Stockton creates a mismatch, whereby he passes to Malone as he rolls toward the hoop.
- Both defenders follow Stockton, who again passes to Malone for an easy lay-up.

The back door

If your offense is slow, you have to be smart. The back door is used against an aggressive defense that overplays passing lanes.

As Figure 6-4 shows, a player on the wing (3) is usually the receiver of the pass in the back door play. If the receiver's defender is attempting to deny her the pass, the receiver takes a step higher up on the wing as if she's going toward the dribbler. When the defender moves to deny that pass, the

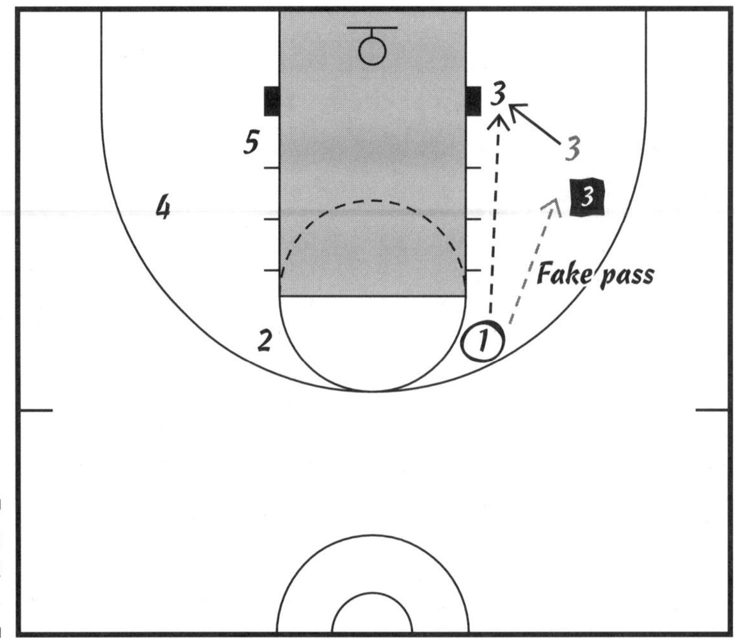

Figure 6-4: The back door play.

receiver reverses direction toward the basket. Then the receiver catches the pass and makes an easy lay-up.

As a defender, you have no excuse for allowing this play. The fundamental concept of man-to-man defense is to keep yourself between your man and the bucket. If the back door play works, the defender took a risk — going for a steal — and the offense duly burned her.

In the 1996 NCAA tournament, the most surprising first-round upset culminated in a back door lay-up. Defending national champ UCLA met Ivy League champ Princeton, a team that employs a disciplined passing offense and very few one-on-one maneuvers. The score was tied late in the game, and the Princeton Tigers had the ball. Tiger center Steve Goodrich, who had the ball on the high post, found teammate Gabe Lewullis on a simple back door pass that led to the lay-up that knocked out the UCLA Bruins.

Backscreen to alley-oop

This play, not often seen below the college level, involves three players. This play is part screen and part back door. Player A has the ball near the top of the key; Player B is on a wing, and Player C is in the low post on the same side as B. Player C cuts toward B to screen his man, and B then moves toward the bucket. If B's and C's defenders do not switch in time, then B is free to receive an alley-oop pass from A, who often is on the opposite wing.

Scottie Pippen, in the role of Player B, loves this play.

Being Alert (The World Needs Lerts) on Offense

Although a successful offense usually involves a skilled set of players, as well as a well-crafted strategy, the players' alertness can make a huge difference in whether an offensive possession results in a bucket. A few things that smart offensive players look for:

- While the defenders switch off a screen, the player who set the pick should be open, at least momentarily.
- When catching a pass that requires them to leave the floor, post players land on both feet simultaneously. I'm not telling you this for safety reasons. By landing with both feet on the floor, you leave yourself open to establish either foot as your pivot foot and move in either direction.
- If you're being double teamed, someone else is open. Pass the ball!

Setting the Tempo

Talent precedes tempo. Most up-tempo teams are better offensive teams — and are certainly more athletic — than slow-down teams. If you sense that your team is in better shape or is more athletically gifted than your opponent, push the pace. (We rarely had such a team at Notre Dame, so I preferred to play more of a half-court game.)

Watch a gifted team like Kentucky, for example. On the rare occasions that the Wildcats lose, the score is usually in the 50s or 60s for both teams. When they can push the pace so that they score above 70, they can say goodnight.

Whether or not to push the pace is a common question for coaches when evaluating their offense. In 1987, my Notre Dame team prepared to play top-ranked North Carolina, who was leading the country in scoring. I knew that we didn't have 90 points in our lineup. (Heck, we didn't have 70 points in our lineup!) But if we could hold our opponent's score in the 50s, we could win.

We controlled the tempo in the second half, and it bothered North Carolina because they liked to run. We won 60-58, thanks in part to our controlling the tempo with David Rivers. This example shows the importance of the point guard (which I documented in the first part of this chapter).

LSU versus Kentucky, 1994

When you have a potent offense, as former Kentucky coach Rick Pitino knows, you're never out of the game. On February 15, 1994, Pitino's 11th-ranked Wildcats traveled to Baton Rouge to play Louisiana State. These were the weary days of the tough SEC schedule, late in the regular season, and Kentucky came out flat.

Down 48-32 at halftime, the Wildcats surrendered 18 straight points early in the second half to trail 68-37. Only one other team in NCAA history (Duke in 1950) had recovered from a 31-point deficit to win a game. Pitino called a time-out.

He told his team to show their character. He also told them to shoot three-pointers and nothing but. Kentucky attempted 23 treys in the second half, making 12 of them. A 24-4 run cut the lead to eight points with more than six minutes left, and the Wildcats eventually won 99-95 to tie Duke for the greatest comeback in NCAA history.

Teams control tempo offensively and defensively. We controlled the tempo by playing zone defense in that game. We also controlled the tempo offensively; even when we broke the press, we didn't take it to the basket quickly, which is what they wanted us to do. Instead, we broke the press, put the ball in David Rivers' hands, and ran our offense, which frustrated North Carolina.

Man-to-Man Offense

As I mentioned at the beginning of this chapter, teams run a man-to-man offense when the defense is playing them man-to-man. Man-to-man offense involves a lot of cutting and screening, give-and-goes, and pick and rolls, because the offensive players have to work to lose their defenders and get open.

Famous man-to-man offenses include the following:

- **UCLA's high post:** UCLA's glory teams of the 1960s and 1970s always had a great center. From Lew Alcindor (who later took the Muslim name Kareem Abdul-Jabbar) to Bill Walton, coach John Wooden took advantage of having the game's most dominant center by playing the high post offense.
- **James Madison's five-man passing game:** James Madison University turned more than a few heads with an inventive, all-inclusive approach during the 1982 NCAAs. It was called the flex offense, always remaining in a 2-3 set (2 out, 3 in). Coach Lou Campanelli's team met North

Carolina in the first round and nearly upset a Tar Heel squad that boasted Michael Jordan, Sam Perkins, and James Worthy — a squad who escaped with a two-point victory and then won the national title.

- **Bulls' triangle offense:** Bulls assistant coach Tex Winter learned the triangle offense (also known as the triple post) from coach Sam Barry as a guard at Southern Cal in the 1940s. He installed this offense in Chicago in 1989 when Phil Jackson took over as head coach. The Bulls have won five NBA championships since converting to Winter's offense.

  The triangle offense assumes that all players are versatile and can play any position on the court — which makes it an ideal situation for the Bulls. The triangle formation balances the court and allows for a variety of movements that are difficult to defend.

- **Notre Dame's stack:** Before I arrived at Notre Dame, coach Johnny Dee recruited Austin Carr, the greatest player in Notre Dame history. Carr, 6'4", was swift and strong, but what I remember most about him was that he could shoot well from many areas of the floor.

  Gene Sullivan, one of Dee's assistants, devised an offense that set double screens for Carr at different areas of the court — but on the baseline in particular. The bread and butter of the offense was a double screen on the baseline that always seemed to free up Carr. The point guard, Jackie Meehan, remained up top as the other four players, Carr included, formed a box on the low post. Stationed low, Carr could then break high for the ball and then either shoot or drive to the basket.

- **North Carolina's high post passing game (four corners):** One of the most devastating offenses ever was created with the intent *not* to score. When run by superb point guard Phil Ford back in the mid-1970s, North Carolina's four corner offense, which was nothing more than a form of keep-away, was almost impossible to stop. Or should I say start?

  The Tar Heels simply spread the floor, putting one player in each of the four corners and Ford in the middle. Ford dribbled around the court like a waterbug until a second defender left his man to trap Ford. When that happened, Ford passed to the player left open in the corner. The corner player held on to the ball until someone approached him; then he dribbled into the middle, and Ford assumed his corner spot. The idea, though, was to have the ball in Ford's hands as much as possible. UNC was not looking to score, but rather take time off the clock. If UNC had the lead and the ball with four minutes left, the game was over.

  Perhaps the only thing capable of stopping the four corners was itself. This offense was so effective that it hastened the end of the no-shot-clock era. Fans were left bored, and opposing coaches were frustrated.

Teams often run more than one offense in the course of a game. If you happen to have nosebleed seats high up in the stands, use your high vantage point to observe how the offense develops; watch which players are setting screens, who is moving toward the ball and who away, and who runs the baseline. Do you detect an alignment — for example, the triangle — toward which the offense is constantly moving? Bring a notepad and pen and diagram an offensive formation that you see being repeated.

If you happen to be sitting at court level, look at the game through the offensive players' eyes. What passing lanes are open? Should a player have cut high up on the wing to receive the ball, or should she have gone back door? Should she have shot the ball, dribbled it, or made the pass?

Zone Offense

Zone defenses force an offense to alter its style. Why would an opponent play a zone against you?

- They don't believe that your perimeter shooting is accurate enough to beat the zone. (Shooting over the zone normally forces the zone to come apart because the defense has to come out and get right up on the shooters.)
- You have a terrific scorer in the post who cannot be stopped by just one defender. In a zone, your opponent can surround him with three players.

How the zone bothers the offense

Screens, back doors, and pick and roll plays are virtually negated against a disciplined zone defense because individual defenders are guarding areas, not people. Instead, the offense must work the ball around, find openings in the defense, and penetrate to the basket.

How the offense can bother the zone

Zone defense works best when the ball is on the perimeter. So if you can get the ball inside to your post player (the center), you force the defense to converge on him, which creates new passing lanes and open teammates. This is why Wake Forest's Tim Duncan was such a valuable college player: A big target inside, he was also a deft passer against a zone.

A zone defense, be it a 1-3-1 or a 2-3 (which I explain in Chapter 7), is always trying to maintain its arrangement. If you dribble or hesitate between receiving the ball and passing it, you allow the zone time to react. Quick passes catch the zone off-guard, and eventually someone will overcommit or fail to recover in time. Six quick passes before a shot are not too many — you want to keep the defense moving.

A passed basketball moves faster than you do when dribbling it. A passed ball also moves faster than a defender. *Passes* beat the zone, not dribbles.

Another tactic to try: Start draining three-pointers. You'll force the zone to come out and play you. That, in turn, opens things up inside, not only for post players but also for *dribble-drive penetration* (dribbling in the lane and going to the basket to create shots and passing lanes).

Playing against a 2-3 zone

The 2-3 zone is the most common zone that teams face. Against a 2-3 zone, most offenses often use a 1-3-1 alignment. As Figure 6-5 shows, the point guard (1) up top may throw to either a wing (2 or 3) or a post player (4). (So in the 1-3-1 alignment, you have the point guard representing "1" and the two wings and one post player representing "3.") If the wing receives the pass, she can either look for the player running the baseline (5, who is the other "1" in the 1-3-1 alignment) or throw the ball to the post (4).

On the pass from point guard to wing, the high post player dives to the low post on the side of the ball, and the other post player/baseline player takes her place. It's like an X move, low to high and high to low.

If the wing passes back to the point, the point may want to consider penetrating. A talented point guard — Allen Iverson did this well at Georgetown — forces the zone to collapse or overcommit. That means that someone else is open.

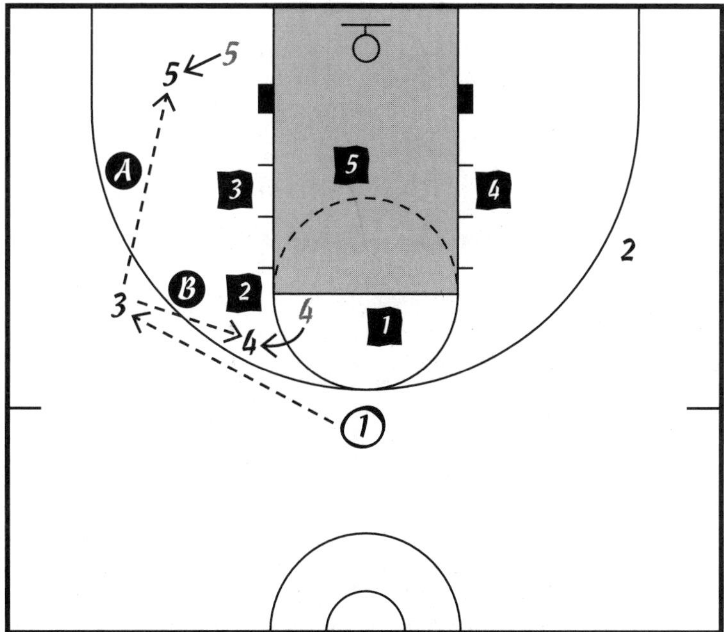

Figure 6-5: The 1-3-1 set versus a 2-3 zone defense.

Playing against a 1-3-1 (point) zone

Coaches usually run two players (preferably two guards) out on the perimeter and keep three on the baseline (two big players and maybe one shooter — like Minnesota with Sam Jacobson) — a 2-1-2 set or 2-3 set. Some teams keep the low post player low; some teams also run a double low post with two out (two guards out), lock the two post players and the 4 and 5 spot players, and have the shooter going from baseline to baseline.

Playing against a matchup zone

In a matchup zone defense, the defense tries to switch, slide, or trade players to stay matched to cutters so that they are still playing man-to-man. But they end up playing a sagging man-to-man instead. Most of the matchups come out of a 2-3 zone.

The key is to beat the matchup: Run your man-to-man offense. The more movement, the more screening you have. Look to screen and release. The screener is open against a matchup. Try to get the ball inside with a bounce pass.

Because you're playing the zone, the bounce pass is the toughest to defend — especially when you screen on the weakside against a matchup zone (or any zone, for that matter). Another option is to screen on the weakside on the baseline, like a downscreen. Then the screener is open, or the baseline player gets a jumpshot because he just got a screen off the player down low.

In its heyday, North Carolina was very good at running *inside screens* (screen in the post) and throwing a lob against the zone. You may think that getting a lob pass for a dunk against a zone is impossible, but this amazing team did it — a lot.

Getting the ball inside against a zone

Some teams send a cutter through but screen off the defender near your big player so that he can loop around to the post and go get the ball. In a 1-3-1 zone (because the zone makes certain slides) or a 1-2-2 zone, the middle is open. When you get a skip pass and the zone slides, the center sees the gap in the post, goes to that gap, and looks for the ball.

Take a look at what happens after the skip pass. The ball leaves the fingertips of the passer and goes to the opposite wing. The center follows the pass. Before the receiver catches the ball, the center is already at the opposite wing. Essentially, the center follows the pass, reads the passer, knows that the ball is going opposite, looks for a gap in the zone, and gets to the spot. As a result, the pass is almost a touch pass.

The receiver throws the ball into the post. The post player must work to get open. Sometimes he must step out of the lane to get the ball high, and at other times, he must step out low to get the ball low. He can't lock himself in; otherwise, defending him is too easy.

Paul Westhead and Loyola Marymount's offense

When Paul Westhead was coaching at Loyola Marymount (LMU), he imposed a rule on his players: When playing offense, they had to move the ball past half-court in three seconds and shoot it within seven.

Preseason camp at LMU resembled Parris Island, as Westhead threw all sorts of conditioning drills at his players to mold them into top shape for the running (and gunning) they'd be doing. One drill involved players running with small parachutes on their backs to maximize wind resistance, a tactic that many other college and pro teams have since stolen.

From the opening tip-off, LMU did nothing but fast breaks and three-pointers. Westhead recruited players who could run and shoot the outside jumper. In 1989–90, his third year at the Los Angeles school, he had his athletes in place. Against Louisiana State that season, LMU won 148-141 (Westhead's sprinters gave up a load of points as well). That game was temporarily stopped when the play-by-play typewriter broke, apparently from exhaustion.

That LMU team averaged 122.4 points per game that season. A glance at the record books reveals LMU's impact on the game during Westhead's grand experiment. While he was coach there (1987 to 1991), Loyola notched five of the ten highest-scoring games in NCAA history. Each of its four seasons are included among the top ten highest-scoring seasons in NCAA history as well, as the following table shows.

Highest-Scoring Teams in NCAA History, Single Season

Team	*Year*	*Games Played*	*Points*	*Average*
Loyola Marymount	1989–90	32	3,918	122.4
Loyola Marymount	1988–89	31	3,486	112.5
UNLV	1975–76	31	3,426	110.5
Loyola Marymount	1987–88	32	3,528	110.3
UNLV	1976–77	32	3,426	107.1
Oral Roberts	1971–72	28	2,943	105.1
Southern Univ.	1990–91	28	2,924	104.4
Loyola Marymount	1990–91	31	3,211	103.6
Oklahoma	1987–88	39	4,012	102.9
Oklahoma	1988–89	36	3,680	102.2

Centers must move and work to get open, but the perimeter passers must be patient and read and wait. One of the weaknesses of the zone offense, no matter whether it's against a 2-3 or a point zone defense, is that the wing players don't look into the baseline or to the foul line area before they reverse the ball. Remember, any post feed bothers a zone. A post feed is the toughest thing for a zone to defend; someone will be open, either on the baseline opposite, or the wing opposite, or the post can even toss the ball back to the point.

Fast Break Offense

To *fast break* means simply to push the ball upcourt before the defense has a chance to set up. The key to running an effective fast break is to get the ball to the middle of the floor (that is, away from the sidelines). The defense then must play one of three options: a pass to the left, a pass to the right, or the player with the ball keeping it.

The player with the ball must decide what to do by the time she reaches the foul line: pass it, continue driving, or stop and shoot. Don't force a shot on a fast break if it's not there. Good teams transfer right into their set offense.

When Sonny Allen was coaching at Old Dominion, he numbered certain spots on the floor and assigned individual players to run to each spot — such as a corner or wing — on the fast break. Even after allowing a score, Sonny had his players do this. This drill gave new meaning to the phrase, "See Spot run."

Why the fast break works

The offense usually outnumbers the defense, whether it's three on two, three on one, or two on one. The job of the ball handler on the fast break, especially in the latter two scenarios, is to force the defender to commit, and then to hit the open teammate.

The three-man weave drill

No dribbling is involved in this drill. Three players, spaced about 15 feet apart, start out on the baseline. The player in the middle passes to a wing and then runs toward that player and *behind* him. The player who caught the pass throws it across to the third player, running toward and behind him as well. And so on. Do this until the player who catches the ball is just above the far foul line, and then treat the situation like a fast break: The receiver passes to one of his two teammates on the wing (a bounce pass, I say) or keeps it and shoots or drives.

Benefit: Players learn to pass on the run and understand the concept of filling the lanes on the fast break.

The three-on-two, two-on-one drill

Position two defenders at the far end of the court — one at the foul line and one in the lane. Then start your three offensive players upcourt, either in a three-man weave or passing back and forth to simulate a fast break. When they approach the far end, you have a three-on-two situation. The offense must take the ball to the basket immediately.

When the defense retrieves the ball, either by rebounding or after a made basket, the two defenders run a fast break against the former offensive player who was closest to the offense's basket when the offense lost possession of the ball. The two other players remain on defense when the ball returns to that end of the court.

Press Offense

The press offense is less concerned with scoring than it is with simply getting the ball past midcourt before committing a ten-second violation (with the exception of women's college basketball, the offense has only ten seconds to get the ball past midcourt).

When taking the ball out of bounds in your backcourt against a full-court press, what do you need to know?

- **If you're in-bounding the ball after a made basket (either a field goal or a free throw), you are allowed to run the length of the baseline.** You are not allowed to do so after a violation, however, or after a ball has been knocked out of bounds.

  Quiz: You're in-bounding the ball after your opponent makes a basket, running the baseline, and your pass is deflected out of bounds. Your team retains possession, and again you in-bound from the baseline. Are you still allowed to run along the baseline? ***Answer:*** No.

- **The backboard is a blocker.** Be aware of the backboard, especially if you attempt to in-bound a pass to beyond half-court. If you're standing directly under the backboard, your pass may hit it.
- **The corner is a deadly place.** If you receive the inbounds pass, stay away from the corner. The defense can easily trap you with two players.
- **Screen and release.** Set a screen for a teammate and then cut to open space.
- **Come to meet the pass.** Don't wait for the pass to come to you. Be aggressive.

- **Don't pick up your dribble.** Once you have the ball and start to dribble, do not pick up the dribble (in other words, don't stop dribbling and hold the ball) until you know to whom you're going to pass the ball. If you're dribbling toward a trap, pull yourself back and *arc your dribble* — attempt to go around the trap. Or back up and look for an open teammate. Passing or dribbling backward in the backcourt is not a sin. Sometimes you have to take a step back to move ahead (see also *Philosophy For Dummies*).
- **Take the ball to the hole.** Too often, an offense becomes so obsessed with beating a full-court press that it stops working after the ball passes the midcourt line. If you've beaten the press and have a man advantage on the defense (that is, you beat them down the court and have more players there than the defense does), the situation is no different than a fast break. Unless your coach has ordered you not to shoot, take the ball to the hoop.

Breaking Half-Court Traps

Defenses run half-court traps for different reasons: They may be trailing late in the game and trying to force a turnover. In a recent Lakers-Rockets game, for example, Del Harris, the Los Angeles coach, ordered a half-court trap in the second quarter. Harris hoped that if he could awaken his team defensively, that liveliness would spread to the other end of the floor.

To beat the half-court trap, an offense must spread out, almost as if playing the four corners. Here are some other tips:

- **Ball fake prior to passing.** The defense is playing so overaggressively that they'll usually fall for the ball fake.
- **Bounce pass when the defender has his arms outstretched high.** A bounce pass is much harder to intercept and much easier to make.
- **Don't pick up your dribble.** You have less freedom to move against a half-court trap, because you can no longer venture into the backcourt. The defense has to guard only half as much space.
- **Always have someone flashing to the foul line.** In a half-court, the foul line is the epicenter. If you position one player in each of the four corners and the fifth as a rover, the free throw line is an open area. It offers the best combination for a short pass — if the player with the ball is trapped in a corner — with adequate spacing. The rover should move to the area vacated by the player who flashes to the foul line.

Chapter 7
Defense

In This Chapter

- Understanding the principles of sound defense
- Playing man-to-man defense
- Playing zone defense
- Trapping, pressing, and other fancy tricks

This is one of the oldest basketball bromides, but it's true: Good defensive players are good defensive players because they *want* to be. Playing defense is hard — I'm not going to kid you — and rarely is it glamorous. How many hoops posters have you ever seen of a guard crouched low, shuffle-stepping against the player with the ball? Or of a forward denying his man a pass on the wing? Of a center fronting her opponent in the low post?

But defense is literally half the game. And it is every bit as instrumental in winning — perhaps more so — as offense. The objective, remember, is not just to score but to outscore your opponent. The less your opponent scores, the less you need to. Here are two reasons why defense may be *more* important than offense:

- **Great defense begets instant offense.** Defensive plays, such as steals and blocked shots, often lead to easy fast-break baskets — for your team, that is.
- **Defense relies on attitude, not aptitude.** In some games, your jumpshot just isn't going to drop — even Michael Jordan has an occasional 7-of-25 shooting night. But good defense is as reliable as the tides, because its foundation is effort. You can count on this facet of your game every time you suit up.

So how do you play defense? You use your arms, legs, body, and mind (but no biting) in an attempt to make scoring difficult for your opponent. Blocking shots, stealing passes, and making opponents take low-percentage (difficult) shots are all part of a sound defense.

An old coach once said, "You play defense with three things — your head, your heart, and your feet." That's funny, considering how often coaches tell their players to keep their hands up on defense, but it's true. You play with your head because a good defender outsmarts his man. You play with your heart because a good defender outhustles his man. And you play with your feet because, as this chapter explains, defense is mostly about establishing position. You establish position with your feet, not your hands.

Playing with Your Head

In order to play defense with your head (and I mean your brain, not the thing that sits on top of your neck), you must know your opponent. Offensive players are creatures of habit. For example, a player may always dribble to his right or favor the jumpshot from the free throw line. Like bad poker players, these opponents can be "read." Be aware of your opponent's tendencies, and you'll play better defense.

But remember that defense is also a *team* concept. Because of screens and *double teams* (where two defenders guard one player), you'll *guard* (defend against; not to be confused with the position of guard) various players on the court. Good defenders know the strengths and weaknesses of at least a few players on the opposing team.

A smart defender's checklist:

- **Quickness:** Is your man quicker than you are? If so, give him enough room in front of you to take a full step — you want to be able to retreat quickly and reestablish your defensive position.
- **Range:** Is your man a better-than-average shooter? Just as important, *from how far away* is he a good shooter? When a marksman gets within his range, you must play him close.
- **Weaknesses:** Most offensive players — including you, when you're on the other end of the floor — have flaws in their game. Maybe the player you're guarding doesn't like to dribble to his left. If that's the case, move over to his right side, forcing him to go left. Or if he has little confidence in his 15-footer, dare him to beat you with it. Good defensive players always capitalize on their opponents' weaknesses.

Playing with Your Heart

In an article that appeared in *Sports Illustrated Presents* last year, All-Star guard Latrell Sprewell of the Golden State Warriors blamed his poor defensive season of 1994–95 on indifference. Sprewell, who had established a reputation as a tenacious defender the season before (his rookie year), admitted that the Warriors' trade of his best buddy, Chris Webber, affected his play. "I admit that my heart wasn't into it that season," said Sprewell, "and that's what defense mainly is — heart and dedication."

When Duke played my Notre Dame team at South Bend in 1987, I noticed that coach Mike Krzyzewski had his players perform a gesture that, though symbolic, acted as a reminder to play tough defense. After the Blue Devils made a basket and retreated past midcourt, each player crouched and slapped both hands against the hardwood. Bending that low requires extra effort, and maybe that was Coach K's point: Defense requires extra effort. (We won that game, however.)

Playing with Your Feet

The most important aspect of defense is making sure that your feet are doing the work to keep your body in balance. If you play too far up on the balls of your feet, you lean forward. That's bad. If you play on your heels, you lean backward. That's bad, too.

The *defensive stance,* as it's known in hoops, is the fundamental position for a defender to assume. Your feet are shoulder width apart. Your knees are bent, but your back is not; you move on the balls of your feet. Your arms are low — not hanging at your sides, but slightly outstretched — with your elbows bent and your palms upward, almost as if you're ready to catch a baby.

In-the-paint drill

Place three players in defensive stances in the free throw lane: one at the baseline, another in the middle of the key, and a third just below the free throw line. All of them face you, the coach, standing at the top of the key with the ball.

Why three players? Competition. If you just have one player, he won't try to beat anyone.

Blow the whistle and point the ball in one direction. All three players shuffle-step across the lane until they reach its end; then they shuffle-step (slide their feet swiftly sideways, never crossing their feet) to the other side of the lane and return. Run them back and forth for 15 to 30 seconds and then blow the whistle and have three more players step in. Speed is the objective.

Never cross your feet on defense. If the dribbler sees you do that, she's going to switch direction and blow right by you. When shuffling your feet, you must move as quickly as possible, but your feet should never come within a foot (as in 12 inches) of one another.

On-the-diagonal drill

The defender lines up at the right corner, facing midcourt. He shuffle-steps toward the right end of the free throw line, his left leg in front. At that point, he turns his hips and heads to the opposite corner of the lane, facing the baseline on a diagonal. Upon reaching that point, he swings his hips again so that his right leg is now the lead leg of the shuffle-step. The player shuffle-steps to where the sideline meets the free throw line extended. The goal here is not speed but rather form.

The width of your stance is the most important aspect in determining balance. Remember the shooting principle from Chapter 5? If you put both feet together and someone pushes your chest, you're going to fall over. The same principle applies to defense. Spread your feet the width of your shoulders, and you have better balance.

Man-to-Man Defense

Of the two types of team defense, man-to-man is the defense that purists respect — the all-natural-ingredients, no-preservatives defense. It is *Defense Unplugged,* if you will — the way the game was meant to be played. You defend one person, as does each of your teammates. Theoretically, if every player wins his individual battle, the defense prevents a basket from being scored.

You must remember one rule at all times when playing man-to-man: At any time on defense, four defenders are guarding players who do not have the ball, and the fifth is guarding the player who does.

- **If your man has the ball:** Stay between your man and the basket at all times. If your man has the ball, his objective is to penetrate closer to the basket for an easier shot. Your objective is to prevent that.
- **If your man does not have the ball:** Stay between your man and the ball at all times. Without the ball, he cannot score. Maintain that state of affairs by denying him the ball.

Simple, eh?

The three stages of an offensive player's possession

As a defender in a man-to-man defense, you must keep in mind the three stages of any offensive player's possession of the ball: the pre-dribble stage, the dribble stage, and the post-dribble stage. Then adjust your defensive technique accordingly.

Pre-dribble stage

When a player has just caught the ball, she is the most dangerous because she has the most options: She can pass, dribble, or shoot. Do the following as you guard a player who has just caught the ball but has not yet begun to dribble:

- **Assume your defensive stance** (unless you're defending a player in the post, which I discuss later in this chapter). You must stay low. Good defense should create a burning sensation in your thighs. But you must be able to move laterally quickly, too. My suggestion: Practice, and keep the following in mind.
- **Keep your eyes on her midsection.** You gain nothing as a defender (except maybe some toughness points with the fans) by looking into your opponent's eyes, at any of her limbs, or at the basketball itself. The offensive player uses her head, her limbs and feet, and the ball to *fake you out* — that is, to fool you into committing one way so that she can go the other. However, an offensive player's belly button is like her shadow: She can never shake it. The belly button cannot fake you out, so keep your eyes on it.
- **Know your opponent.** If she's quicker than you — this is no time for pride — back off a step so that she can't dribble past you. Then again, if she's a deadly outside shot, you have to guard her more closely. If she is both quicker than you *and* a great shooter . . . well, that's why some players are called unstoppable (check out Sheryl Swoopes, who scored a record 47 points for Texas Tech in the 1993 NCAA championship game against Ohio State).

In college ball (but not in the NBA), the player with the ball has five seconds to make, in the official's judgment, a positive move on offense. In other words, she can't just stand in place holding the ball for six seconds. Keep that in mind as you defend her. If she's pushing that five-second mark, look for her to make a move, either by dribbling or by passing.

Dribble stage

After receiving the ball, the player you're guarding may decide to dribble in an attempt to drive toward the basket. He can still pass or shoot off the dribble, but unless he is still dribbling in front of you, he is not the triple threat that he was before putting the ball on the floor. Play him closer.

The sideline or baseline is your best defender. Always try to force the dribbler toward the sideline if he's up top — or the baseline if he's dribbling from the wing or corner. If the dribbler beats you to the middle, he can pass in either direction. If he beats you along the sideline, you at least dictate where the pass must go.

Post-dribble stage

After the player picks up his dribble, he can only pass or shoot. At this point, he may move only his pivot foot, which he sets by moving his opposite foot. Play as close to him as possible without fouling him.

If your man attempts a shot, remember the principle of verticality. You may legally jump straight up with your arms straight over your head. Raise your hands straight up so that you can attempt to alter the shot's trajectory, as opposed to jumping toward your opponent with your hands extended at a 45-degree angle. The key to executing this move well is to close out tighter — that is, to get closer to your man *before* he shoots. That way, you're not leaping *out to* him but rather *up against* him.

The principle of verticality is especially important for the defender to keep in mind when guarding the post player (see the section "Playing post defense" later in this chapter) to keep in mind. Not only can you alter the shot's trajectory, but if the ref notices that you're leaping straight up with your arms straight up, he's far less likely to whistle you for a foul.

The first day of practice

If you want to make your point as a coach about the importance of defense, begin your first day of practice — in fact, begin *every* practice — with man-to-man defense drills. And don't give defense the perfunctory attention that you might to, say, mailing out thank-you letters. Emphasize defense; insist that players do every drill correctly.

Zigzag dribble drill

This should be your principal man-to-man drill — it drives home the fundamentals of good footwork. Run it at three speeds: walking, at half speed, and then at full speed.

Players pair off, with one player getting the ball. The player with the ball dribbles from baseline to baseline in a zigzag motion, reversing the dribble every few steps. (Make sure that he zigs before zagging; don't ever zag first.)

The defender's job is to assume a defensive stance, using the *shuffle-step* to head off the dribbler's intended direction and force him the other way. When the offensive player dribbles to the right, the defender "drops" his left foot backward and shuffles to the left. When the dribbler changes direction and moves to the left, the defender drops his right foot and shuffles right. (See Figure 7-1.) The defender does not try to steal the ball, and the dribbler does not try to blow past the defender. When the pair reach the far baseline, they switch roles and return.

After a walk-through of the zigzag, players should go at half speed. The defender's job is still to keep his man in front of him (between himself and

Figure 7-1: The zigzag dribble drill.

the basket) and to force a change in direction by shuffling his feet. Finally, the players run the drill at full speed. If the dribbler beats the defender — as often happens — the defender must turn and pursue the dribbler.

Few, if any, players can out-shuffle-step a player who's dribbling the ball at full speed. So if the dribbler beats the defender, the defender abandons his shuffle, turning and sprinting to cut him off — known as the *turn and go.* A defender sprinting all-out should be faster than a player dribbling. The defender's intent is to pick a spot upcourt to which he can beat the dribbler, sort of like heading him off at the pass. If he can do that, he can resume his defensive stance or shuffle.

Do not let the dribbler beat you to the middle; force him to the sideline instead. When you "force sideline," you give yourself defensive help because the sideline acts as a wall — the dribbler can't go beyond it. If you're going to overplay the dribbler in one direction, overplay to the middle.

Zigzag dribble drill, part II

Occasionally, the defender should keep both hands behind his back during the zigzag dribble drill; doing so compels him to focus on footwork. Although the defender's objective remains to prevent the dribbler from beating him, the defender will begin to appreciate the importance of having his body balanced.

Defense is TEAM defense

To play great team defense, each defender must know where the ball is at all times. Covering your man in a man-to-man defense is not enough. If you focus on your man alone, you'll soon be the victim of a screen (explained in Chapter 6). If you know where the ball is, on the other hand, you can surmise your man's next move. Will he cut toward the basket? Is he going to set a pick for a teammate? Anticipating his next move is half the battle.

The triangle principle of man-to-man defense

The triangle principle, shown in Figure 7-2, is simple: Imagine yourself as one point of a triangle, the other two points being the person you're guarding and the ball. Now use your peripheral vision to see both the man and the ball. You won't be able to look back and forth on the court. The moment you turn away from your man, if he's a smart player, he'll cut behind you and be wide open for an easy shot.

When you're guarding the player with the ball, you stay between that player and the basket. Your reason for living is to prevent the offensive player from penetrating to the basket. When you're guarding a player without the ball, on the other hand, you're playing both the ball and the person you're assigned to defend. Sound, solid defense gets back to peripheral vision: watching your man closely in a position from which you can also see the ball out of the corner of your eye.

Playing guard in a man-to-man defense

A guard who's defending the player *with* the ball should stay in a low defensive stance. Why? His man is more of a threat to drive to the basket than the players being guarded by a forward or center. Also, a guard's man

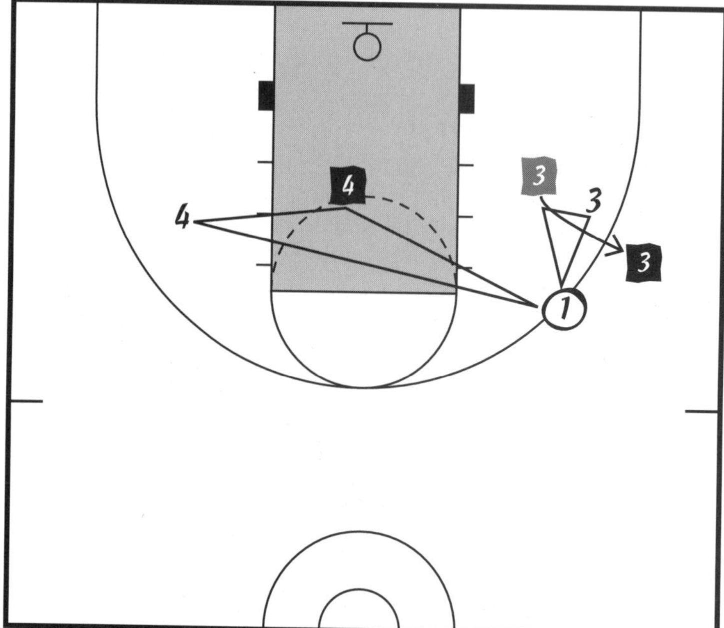

Figure 7-2: Triangle principle of man-to-man defense.

probably has the ball farther away from the basket than a center's or forward's would.

The defending guard has three big responsibilities:

- Don't let your man beat you on the dribble.
- Don't give up an uncontested three-pointer.
- Force the man away from the middle to one side of the floor.

A guard guarding a guard *without* the ball (known as the *off guard*) has two ways to play the situation. (Quite a mouthful, eh? Just think if one of them was a beat poet — that is, an avant-garde guard.)

- **Deny the passing lane:** The off guard often guards the opposition's best outside shooter, so he may choose a *closed* stance on defense. His lead foot is in the passing lane (the path via which the ball would travel to get to his man), and he may guard him closely and overplay the pass, knowing that his teammates will help him if his man goes back door, or cuts behind him to the hoop. (See Figure 7-3.)
- **Play help defense:** Here the guard uses an *open* stance, meaning that he is in position to react to the ball just as much as to react to his man. His foot is not in the passing lane. (See Figure 7-4.) You use this method if you don't consider your man to be a major outside scoring threat. You want to be in position to help out a teammate if necessary.

Figure 7-3: Denying the passing lane.

Figure 7-4: The weak-side guard: helping to the ball on penetration (left), and recovering to the player who receives the ball (right).

Rotation defense

Rotation defense is one of the best innovations of the past decade. In any discussion about why scoring is down, improved defense is usually mentioned, and rotation is at the forefront of this revolution. The idea behind rotation defense is to leave your man to help out the defender who got beat, with the understanding that one of your teammates will pick up the player you're guarding. The rule of rotation is to leave your man (when necessary) and find a player who's more likely to receive the next pass.

The Detroit Pistons teams of the late 1980s, who won two NBA titles under the guidance of Chuck Daly, were the first practitioners of this rotation defense, and they elevated it to an art. Blessed with athletic and eager defenders, such as Isiah Thomas, Joe Dumars, and Dennis Rodman, Detroit always seemed to have six men playing defense. Watch an NBA or college game today, and you'll see that almost every team plays this sophisticated defense.

Rotation defense is easier to understand if you see it happening. Take a look at Figure 7-5, where you have two guards (1 and 2) and two forwards (3 and 4). If the strongside guard (1) passes to the strongside forward (3), the weakside guard (D2) slides down to take the weakside forward (4), and the weakside forward (D4) goes over to help on 3. For the guard on top playing 1 (D1), the first thing is to take away the passing lane with a closed stance.

This is a difficult rotation for the D2 guard because he ends up defending a taller forward. Once the ball leaves the fingertips of the passer, the D2 guard must react defensively, even though he's not guarding the ball. Once the ball goes from guard to forward, the defender has to anticipate, cheating a little toward the baseline. He can do so because the ball is now two passes away from his man.

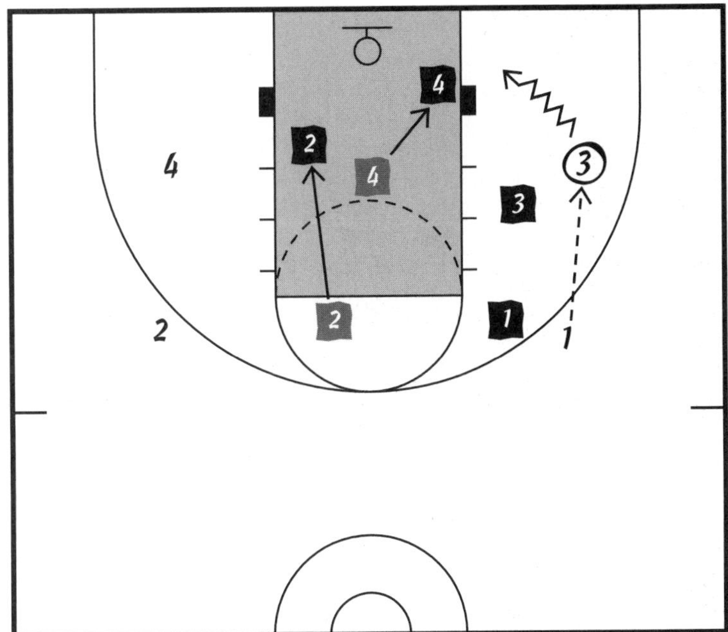

Figure 7-5: Rotation defense.

Shutout defense

When the ball handler picks up his dribble, both guards instantly switch to *shutout defense* mode, which means that they both face-guard the ball handler, denying him the pass or even much of a view of the court. In college ball, if the player who picks up his dribble does not pass the ball within five seconds, a turnover results.

The mission of shutout defense is to shut down all passing lanes, as shown in Figure 7-6. Because the player holding the ball is no longer a threat to do anything but pass, the defender guarding that player should swarm him like a narcotics official at a Phish concert.

Playing forward in a man-to-man defense

The responsibilities of a forward in a man-to-man "D" are fairly straightforward:

- **Defend the pass to the post player:** In this situation, you turn and open to steal the pass; or turn and face your man, reverse yourself (go behind him), and steal the pass or deflect the pass to the post on the back cut. You must either deflect the pass or steal the pass to the post player on a back cut to the basket. If you let the post player get the ball that close to the basket, the player will score nearly every time.

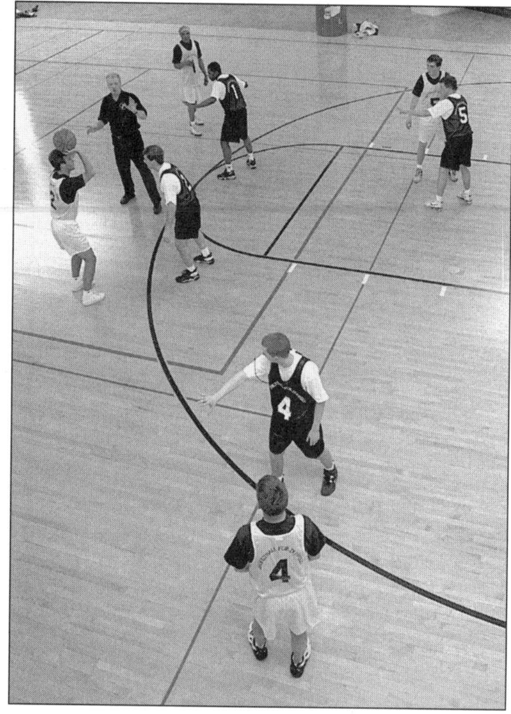

Figure 7-6: If the guard picks up the dribble, all defenders play shutout defense, denying all passing lanes.

- **Defend the flash pivot (cut) to the foul line:** As a power forward, you must close out your man with your lead foot. At the same time, try to keep that player in front of you so that the player can't back cut to the basket. When that player starts to make a move, let him cheat a little bit, commit to go to the foul line. Then you know where he's going.

Don't make the mistake of giving the forward you're guarding an option to go high or low after faking the opposite way. (You'd better not give him low, because he may dunk on you!) Be in a balanced defensive position when guarding a forward with the ball. (See Figure 7-7.)

When playing a forward one-on-one, apply the same principles as when playing guard on defense (as I mentioned earlier). Know the strengths and weaknesses of the shooter. If the forward is a good shooter, keep a hand up in his face; if he is not a threat to score, play it loose and let him shoot. Always remember, especially when defending a forward, to turn and box out (see Chapter 8) after he shoots — he's in a position to rebound.

When defending a player on the weakside of the court (opposite the side of the ball), a forward must be ready to slide over and help the other forward or center. Sometimes the other forward is beaten by his man. Or the center may need help on a double team (where two defenders guard a player) because he is physically overmatched.

Figure 7-7: The strongside forward (3) must help to the ball but also be ready to deny the flash pivot.

Watch when teams attempt to defend Shaquille O'Neal, who overpowers anyone who's not allergic to Kryptonite. ("Shaq," by the way, has a Superman tattoo on his right bicep.) The weakside forward almost always slides over to "seal off" Shaq — at least he gives it an honest try.

When the forward slides over, he leaves his man and yells, "Rotate!" Normally, the off guard slides over to take the forward's man because the forward on offense is now a more viable scoring threat than a guard who's positioned up top.

Playing center in a man-to-man defense

Centers need help — more than most of us, actually. The center is normally a team's tallest player; that's the main requirement for the job. Inherently, fewer centers are populating basketball teams than forwards or guards, and that means that a greater disparity in talent exists at the center position.

Gary Payton, guard of the Seattle SuperSonics, was named the NBA's Defensive Player of the Year for the 1995–96 season. Payton's nickname, "the Glove," refers to his ability to cover an opponent. But Payton is only 6'4". He can't be expected to defend even the worst center in the NBA, which is why the Sonics spent $35 million to acquire backup center 7'0" Jim McIlvaine. Seattle needed a body to put on Shaquille O'Neal of their Pacific Division rivals, the Los Angeles Lakers.

Having a combination of McIlvaine's size and Payton's talent in one person is rare. A good offensive center, such as the New York Knicks' Patrick Ewing or O'Neal, will destroy a McIlvaine in a one-on-one situation.

With that in mind, here's a defensive cheat sheet for centers:

- Do *not* react to the ball fake.
- Do not lean on the opposing center; instead, keep a hand or forearm on his back.
- Once your opponent commits to a move, beat him to the spot to which you anticipate he wants to go.
- Keep your arms straight up (not at 45 degrees) when contesting a shot.
- After a shot is released, box out.

If the center attempts to play in front of a physically dominant or taller center, the offense will often attempt a lob pass over the center's head. A forward needs to slide over from the weakside, or a guard needs to slide down from the elbow, to intercept the lob. This play often works because a good lob pass requires ultimate precision.

Double team the center

Most great centers (with the exception of players like Tim Duncan) are not great passers. When they are double teamed, they have trouble finding the open teammate. The center on defense usually double teams with a forward, and the other three defenders play against that center's four offensive outlets.

Double down off the passer

Another way to neutralize the post player is to *double down* (a guard leaves his man to double team a forward or center on the blocks). You see this all the time in the NBA. The player defending the entry passer follows the pass and collapses on the center, who finds himself with a big body on his back and a pesky guard or forward in front, swiping at the ball. (See Figure 7-8.) The offensive center's best bet is to return the pass to the player who fed him the ball.

Note: Doubling down can lead to a bonanza of three-pointers for the wing player left unattended. This is how John Starks of the Knicks, often left open when his opponents double down on teammate Patrick Ewing, puts food on the table. (When teams double down on Ewing, he simply throws the ball back out to Starks for a wide-open three-pointer.) You have to factor how dangerous a shooter that wing player is when considering the double down.

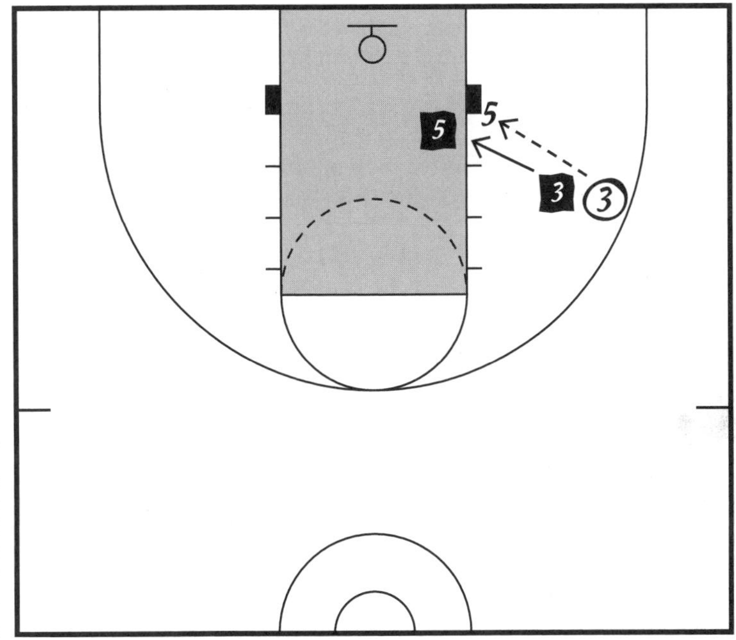

Figure 7-8: Doubling down on the post player.

As the player doubling down, don't lose sight of the offensive player who made the entry pass. Smart ones will slide to another spot when you leave them to double down. When you go to help, keep yourself in a triangle between your man and the ball. If your man cuts to the basket or to the weakside of the court, either follow him or yell, "Rotate!" so that your teammates help you out.

The shot block: The center's last-resort weapon

When all else fails for the center — when he has allowed his man to get the ball on the low post and a shot is imminent — he has one last line of defense: the shot block. Sure, guards and forwards are allowed to block shots, too, but almost without exception, a team's shot-block leader is its center.

There are smart shot blockers and there are not-so-smart shot blockers. The smart shot blocker merely deflects the ball, allowing himself or a teammate to gain possession of the ball. Bill Russell was a great example of a smart shot blocker. "Russ" would catch an opponent's shot in midair and toss it to a teammate to initiate a fast break. The unwise shot blocker tries to swipe the ball into the third row of the stands (while simultaneously bellowing some tough-guy line like "Not in my house!"). The crowd gets fired up, the defender bumps a teammate, and . . . the opponent retains possession of the ball.

Teach your players to block the basketball, but to keep it in bounds. There are no macho points in hoops. The idea is to get control of the ball.

Thriving on rejection

On December 12, 1991, the New Jersey Nets blocked an NBA-record 22 shots in a 121-81 blowout of the Denver Nuggets. Three different Nets — centers Sam Bowie and Chris Dudley and forward Derrick Coleman — said *Nyet* to Nugget shots at least four times. The irony of it all was that the Nugget center was 7'2" Dikembe "Mount" Mutombo, who has since become the first player in NBA history to lead the league in blocked shots for four consecutive seasons (1993–94 to 1996–97). Maybe Mutombo was taking notes that night.

Playing post defense

Offensive players *post up* a defender (face away from the basket and then turn and shoot) whom they think they outmuscle or are able to shoot over. Some post players just prefer playing with their backs to the basket. Most post players are centers, but guards occasionally play the post if they feel that doing so is to their advantage. Kevin Johnson, for example, who has played ten seasons with the Phoenix Suns, was a wiry 6'1" point guard who loved to post up defenders.

Post defense is different from perimeter defense because the player you're guarding has her back to you. Keep a hand — or better yet, a forearm — on the back of the offensive post player to give yourself a point of reference. Don't place your body against hers, though, because then she knows exactly how you're leaning — vital information for helping her spin around you to the basket.

When a player gets the ball in the post, her first option is to shoot. When she attempts her shot, don't leave your feet too soon. Post players often fake a shot to get the defender airborne so that she can either dribble around her defender or draw contact — and a foul. The best advice is to wait until the offensive player leaves her feet before you leave yours.

Defending the entry pass

The entry pass is *one pass away* — it's the pass that the ball handler intends to make to the player you're guarding. As the defender, you attempt to deny the passing lane (the lane through which the ball handler can pass the ball to the player you're guarding), but you must be aware that, if you overplay the passing lane, your man may slip by you in the other direction.

Deflections: The new stat in college basketball

Former Kentucky coach Rick Pitino headlines a growing list of coaches who believe that if the defense deflects 30 passes per half, they'll win. The thinking is not that deflections lead directly to turnovers, but rather that deflections are a good indicator of a team's defensive activity.

Each deflection also disrupts an offense's timing to some degree. Some teams even give an award to the player who has the most deflections over the course of the season. More often than not, the player with the most deflections at the end of the year is usually the player who is named the team's top defensive player. Deflections may never find their way into the official box score statistics (see Chapter 4), but you can bet that coaches understand their importance.

When defending one pass away, place your lead foot (the one closer to your man) forward and extend your corresponding arm, with your elbow bent. You want your hand — but not your foot — in the passing lane to deflect the bounce pass or chest pass.

Why your hand and not your foot in the passing lane? Two reasons:

- The pass will be aimed toward the player's chest, not the lower half of his body.
- By keeping your foot back, you minimize the chance of your opponent cutting behind you and receiving a back door pass.

An entry pass from, say, above the top of the key to the wing encompasses many of the defensive elements I've described. The defender guarding the dribbler is between the dribbler and the bucket. The defender who is one pass away is between his man and the ball. The one-pass-away defender must gauge his man's quickness. If his man is quicker, he shouldn't play him tightly for fear of being burned on the back door play. Another element to consider: Has the ball handler dribbled yet, or has he already picked up his dribble? If the answer is the latter, the one-pass-away defender can play his own man more tightly, knowing that the ball handler is eager to pass the ball.

Defenders often err by putting both their hand and their foot in the passing lane. A smart wing player will coax you into leaning forward and then *backcut* to the hoop (that is, escape through the dreaded back door) for a pass that leads to an easy lay-up.

Defending screens: To switch or not to switch?

To *switch* on defense means to exchange assignments with a teammate during a play. Switching occurs when two offensive players, one of whom may have the ball, come close to each other in order to force one of the defenders to become separated from the player he's guarding. The result is often a mismatch in favor of the offense. Say that 5'3" Muggsy Bogues has been screened. His teammate yells "Switch!" in order to help Muggsy out, but then Muggsy finds himself guarding the 7'6" Shawn Bradley.

How do you defend a screen? First of all, anticipate the screen before it occurs. It's like seeing the initial phase of mitosis and realizing that cell division is imminent. (Okay, this isn't the most vivid example, but you get the point.) Defenders are coached to call out — different coaches use different terms — to alert the teammate being screened. Then the two defenders involved have two options: Either of them may yell "Switch!" and exchange men (see Figure 7-9), or the defender being screened can try to fight through the screen and stay with his man.

Screens work because they create a moment of indecision for the defense. No single formula exists for defending them. Defenders must learn to work together well, to have a sense of what each one likes to do. The most important element of successfully defending screens: communication between the two defenders. The defense must talk.

Defending the pick and roll

A *pick and roll* is just a screen that's set for the player with the ball, as shown in Figure 7-10. The screener rolls off the screen, to the hoop, and the player with the ball passes to him. How do you defend it?

Say the offensive center drifts up from the post to screen for the guard who has the ball. The defensive center must help by stepping out, or *hedging,* on the dribbler — doing so slows down the dribbler and gives the dribbler's defender extra time to fight over the screen and stay with the dribbler. The defensive center, having halted the guard momentarily, recovers and slides down to defend the screener, who is rolling to the hoop. If the defensive center gets beaten on the roll, the weakside forward must be prepared to slide over to help.

Never go behind (around) a screen to find your man. Anytime you do so, whether or not your man has the ball, he'll have room and time enough to bury you with an open jumper. Always go *over* the screen, between the offensive players.

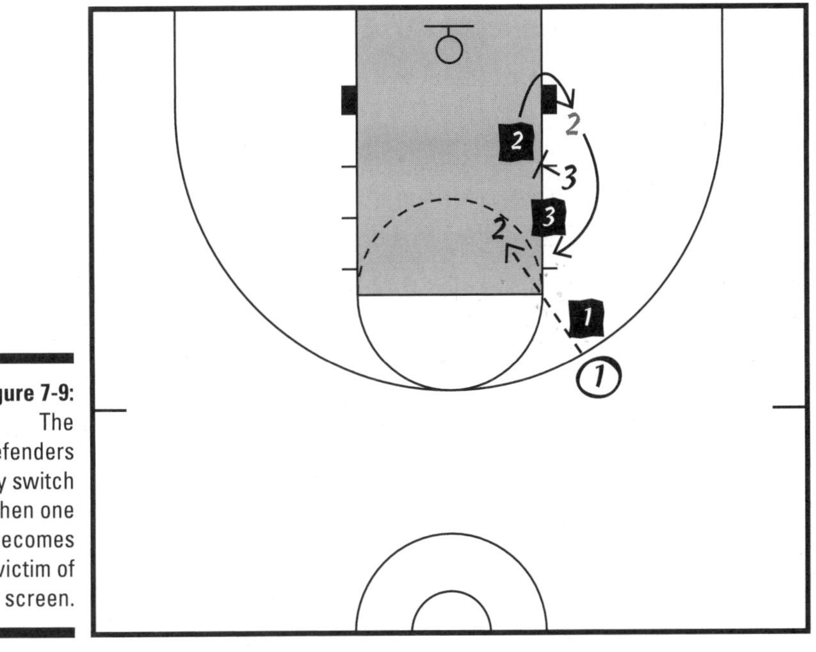

Figure 7-9: The defenders may switch when one becomes the victim of a screen.

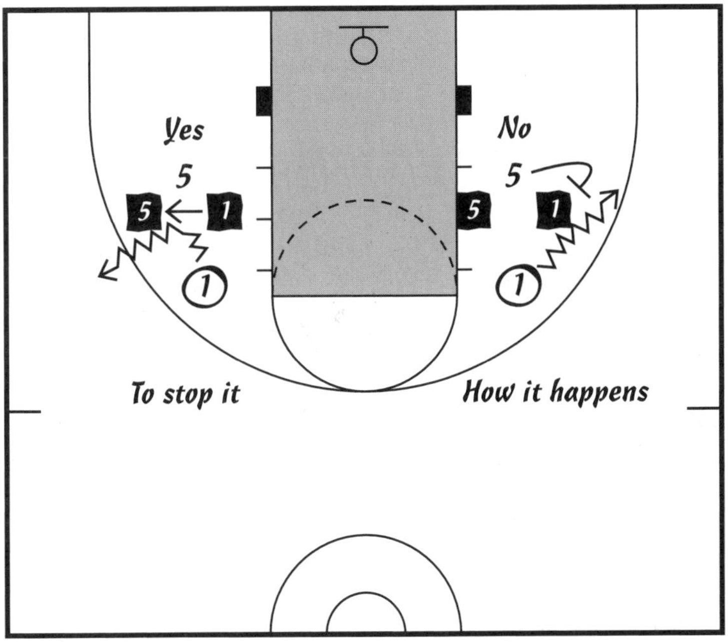

Yes

No

To stop it

How it happens

Figure 7-10: A pick and roll is a screen set for the player with the ball (1).

Digger's switching rule

If you switch and find yourself in a physical mismatch ("Mr. Bogues, meet Mr. Olajuwon"), *front* the player you're guarding (that is, get between him and the ball, still facing the ball). Play in front of him, and expect the cavalry (your teammates) to provide weakside help against the lob pass over your head. If you play behind him, you make it easier for the entry pass to arrive, and he can score easily over the top of you.

Here are some basic principles of switching on man-to-man defense:

- **Don't switch if you can effectively slide through the screen, using your teammate to help you recover.** The defender not being screened gives his teammate room to slide through the screen closer to the ball.
- **If a switch occurs, the screener is often the player left open.** Jump in front of him as soon as possible.
- **The defender of the screener should look to step in front of the player coming off the screen and draw a charging foul.**
- **Remember to communicate.** You must talk to each other to let each other know whether to switch and where the screen is coming from.

Switch on a pick and roll? Never. Step out and go over the top, or trap the ball handler. The reason that Karl Malone and John Stockton, the Fred and Ginger of the pick and roll, are so effective is that Stockton is nearly impossible to trap with two men. But if the ball handler isn't that skilled, the trap is a good, proactive defensive approach.

Always switch when a screen is set at the three-point line. Size is not the big factor out there; the shot is. Guards usually attempt threes, so if a forward is setting the pick, switching is to the defense's advantage: The shooting guard now faces a taller defender. If you are the guard who's switched to defending the forward, don't worry. A pick and roll from 23 feet away is harmless.

The Last Word on Man-to-Man

Eventually, despite all your defensive tenacity, the offense will get off a shot. *Box out!* Grab the rebound. Two seconds of lethargy can spoil 24 or 35 seconds of solid defense. The reward for well-played defense is offense, not more defense. (See Chapter 8 for more information about rebounding.)

And another thing — you can always foul. In theory, a player should never intentionally foul an opponent. But it happens all the time. You foul a player intentionally (making it look unintentional) under two circumstances:

Illegal defense

I could write an entire book entitled *The Illegal Defense For Dummies,* and I'm still not sure that you, or I, would understand the NBA's arcane illegal defense guidelines. The illegal defense rule has been continually amended so as to be nearly as long as the United States Constitution — and far less comprehensible. The intent was to inhibit the sophisticated matchup zones that teams such as the Lakers and Pistons used to their advantage in the late '80s.

Offenses exploit the rule by positioning their three weakest players outside the three-point arc above the foul line on one side of the court. With their two best players, offenses play a two-man game on the other half of the court. The defense must play them honestly, two-on-two, leaving six grossly overpaid spectators on the floor. When was the last time you saw an offensive player in the NBA move without the ball?

The illegal defense rule both punishes common sense and is bad for basketball. Three defenders do not need to be guarding three players in the same area, at least two of whom are usually positioned beyond their shooting range, anyway. Besides, everyone in the league plays a matchup zone. It's just a matter of whether the refs are in the mood to call it.

- The player has an otherwise uncontested basket, and you'd rather see him earn his two points on the free throw line.
- The player being fouled is Shaq (who's a notoriously poor free throw shooter).

Some of the best defenders in NBA history almost never fouled out. Center Moses Malone, for example, played 20 seasons and fouled out only five times. Wilt Chamberlain *never* fouled out in 1,205 games he played over 14 seasons. That statistic is as amazing as any of the other eye-popping numbers attributed to "Wilt the Stilt."

Zone Defense

The word *zone* is synonymous with *area.* In a *zone defense,* each defender covers an *area* as opposed to a player. When an offensive player moves from one area to another, the defensive player in the first area does not follow; she remains in her zone (area).

How do you know when a team is playing a zone? Watch an offensive player move around the court. If one defensive player does not shadow her, the defense is playing a zone.

Why play zone?

- The opponent is a poor outside shooting team. You can pack a zone defense into the lane, making it difficult for your opponents to pass the ball inside, thus forcing your opponents to take outside shots.
- Your team is slow afoot and will be beaten on defense by cuts and screens (explained in Chapter 6).
- One of your players is in foul trouble. The zone protects him from having to defend a player one-on-one and lessens his chances of fouling out of the game.
- Your zone takes your opponent out of their man-to-man offense.

For example, during a Notre Dame game against the University of Washington, we used a zone press (a full-court zone defense) to combat UW's Detlef Schrempf (who's now with the Seattle SuperSonics). Detlef liked to take the ball in the backcourt and go one-on-one against his man, and he became frustrated when he was unable to do that versus our press.

The NBA: A no-zone zone

Officially, the word *zone* is anathema in the NBA; playing a zone defense is illegal in that league. In fact, NBA members do not refer to a zone defense as a zone defense — they refer to it as an *illegal defense.*

Types of zone defenses

Zone defenses are usually named according to their configuration, starting from the farthest player upcourt (that is, away from the basket) to the baseline. Thus a 2-3 zone, the most common form of zone defense, features two players up (near the foul line) and three below (closer to the basket). Other zones you see include the 1-3-1 and the 1-2-2. If the numbers add up to a number other than five, you've got a problem.

2-3 zone

Most teams play a 2-3 zone (shown in Figure 7-11) as a means to defend against a potent offensive post player. The 2-3 allows more than one defender to surround that player at all times. What you surrender by playing a 2-3 zone is perimeter shooting (see Chapter 5 for details on this type of shooting).

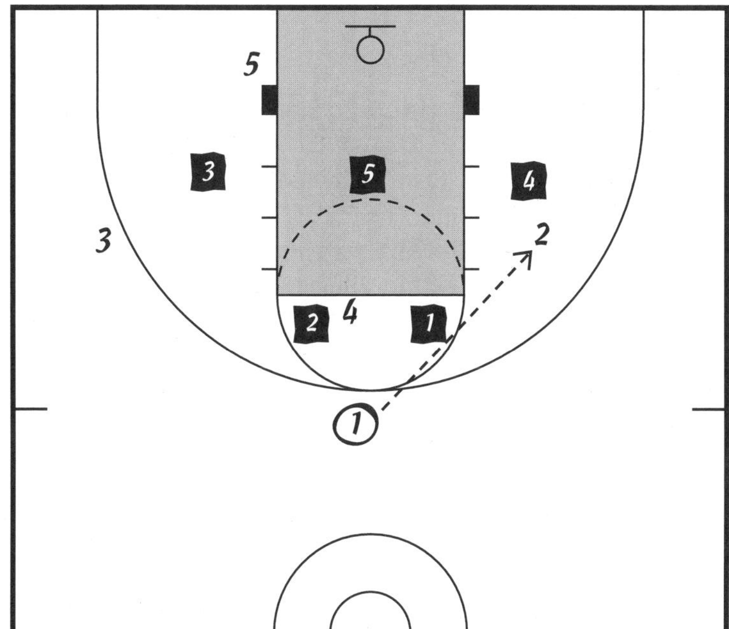

Figure 7-11: The 2-3 zone.

Guard responsibilities in 2-3 zone

The two guards in a 2-3 zone are responsible for covering the three perimeter players. "Wait a second," you may be saying, "I thought you said that defenders guard an *area* in a zone, not *people*!" That's correct. The two guards are responsible for the *area* that those three perimeter players inhabit — that is, the perimeter. If two of those three players converged in the lane, they'd no longer be the guards' responsibility (because they moved out of the perimeter).

Guards work hard in a zone, and guarding three perimeter players requires a lot of legwork. The guards must chase the ball within the perimeter, not giving up an uncontested three-pointer.

Here are some hints for guards playing a 2-3 zone:

- **When the ball is on the wing, send another player to guard the center in order to deny the pass to the center.**
- **Prevent dribble penetration.** The cardinal sin for guards playing a zone is to allow the ball handler to dribble between them, which is known as *splitting the zone.* Allowing the split forces other defenders to converge on the ball handler, leaving one (or more) opponents open for an easy shot.

Forward responsibilities in 2-3 zone

The forward must do the following in a 2-3 zone:

- **Defend the wing** until the guard arrives to help and then head toward the basket.
- **Defend the baseline.** Nobody with the ball should get around the forward on the baseline. The idea is to force the action back to the middle, where a teammate can help.
- **Guard the post player if he steps to the baseline.** If the center receives a pass on the baseline and has no shot, he'll be looking for the high post player, who will be cutting to the hoop. That's where the defensive center comes in, sealing off that route.

Center responsibilities in 2-3 zone

Centers have the following responsibilities in a 2-3 zone:

- **Defend the paint.** The center, in the middle of the back line of three defenders, is responsible for the post area.
- **Seal off drives.** If a guard splits the zone or a wing eludes the forward and *drives the baseline* (dribbles at full speed along the baseline to the basket), the center must step in to halt the penetration.
- **Rebound.** The center rarely has to worry about solo coverage in a zone. Even when defending the post, she has a teammate to help. Thus she needs to shoulder more of the rebounding burden.

Drills for the 2-3 zone

The hardest part about teaching zone defense is getting five players to move as one unit. Think of that elite U.S. Navy jet unit, the Blue Angels. All five jets fly in formation, aware of each other's movements. (Of course, the stakes for those guys are a little bit higher.)

To teach your five players to act as one, slowly take them through reacting to passes. Place three players on the offensive perimeter and have them pass the ball to one another, slowly at first. After each pass, show your defenders how they need to rotate. Then allow another pass, again waiting until your defense properly rotates before moving forward with the drill.

Next, add a fourth offensive player to run the baseline. He, too, can receive passes. After five to ten minutes of this, insert a post player. On all these passes, instruct the defense not to attempt steals. The job of the defense here is to react to the movement of the ball.

You've been waiting all chapter for me to say it. Here goes:

"HANDS UP ON DEFENSE!"

Arms up and out is the best way for a zone to shut down passing lanes. When you do the preceding drill, first keep your arms at your sides for a few minutes. Then spread your wings. See how much tougher it is to pass against a zone when ten hands are in the air?

1-3-1 zone

The 1-3-1 defense, shown in Figure 7-12, is designed to force the corner shot. Some teams give up the corner shot because it's a difficult shot to rebound offensively — the angle is harder. You're not going to get many easy offensive rebounds from corner shots.

If the opposing point guard is not much of a scoring or penetration threat, the 1-3-1 is also effective. If the point guard is able to dribble past the "1" defender up top, drawing one of the middle "3" to stop him, the zone will fail.

Matchup zone

Bill Green, the longtime successful coach at Marion High School in Marion, Indiana, was a master teacher of the matchup zone. Before the 1976–77 season, I invited him to South Bend to teach the matchup zone to my players. That season, we jumped out to a 7-0 record and beat top-ten teams Indiana, Maryland, and UCLA with the matchup zone. We finished at 22-7 before losing in the Sweet 16 in the NCAA tournament.

The matchup zone is a combination of the zone and man-to-man defense. Here are the assignments, at least the way I coach a matchup zone:

- The center defends the opposing center man-to-man.
- The point guard declares whom he will guard. His call dictates the three remaining defenders' jobs. The other guard, for example, takes the first player to the point guard's left. The small forward takes the other perimeter player, and the power forward covers the remaining player.

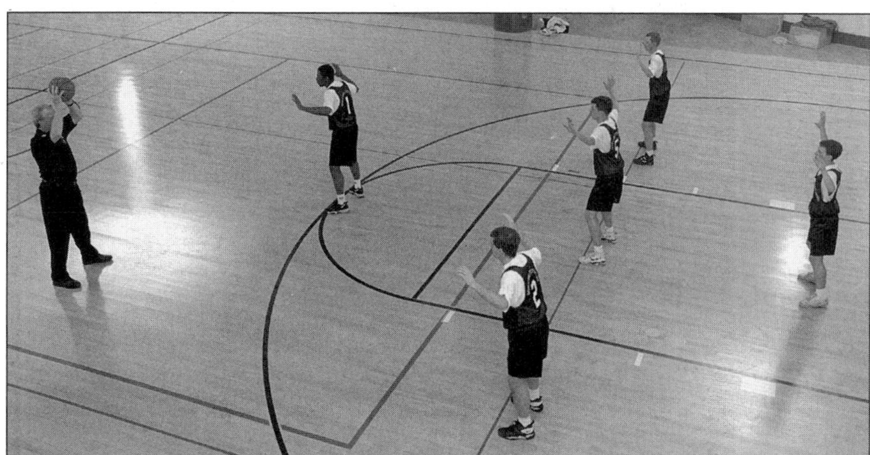

Figure 7-12: The 1-3-1 zone.

- The player guarding the ball can follow the pass, which obliges the other defensive players (but not the center) to rotate in that direction. Or the point guard can move opposite the pass, requiring everyone to rotate the opposite way.

Gadget defenses

Gadget defenses are not in any way similar to Gidget defenses. (If you're too young to remember who Gidget was, don't worry. It wasn't that funny, anyway.) They are short-term solutions used for unusual situations; they're rarely used throughout an entire game.

Box and one

A box and one is played when the opposition has one monstrous scorer, on whom they rely almost exclusively. In a box and one, you set up four defenders in a box around the three-second lane (a 2-2 zone, in effect). Your fifth player is deployed to cover — and by "cover," I mean that he should be able to tell you how many fillings that player has in his teeth — the opposition's go-to guy. (See Figure 7-13.) In other words, four people play zone, and the fifth chases the big scorer all over the court man-to-man.

Install your best defender in the "one" position in the box and one. If the opposing player is a dangerous enough scorer, you may want to start a non-starter if he's your best defensive stopper.

Keep in mind that the "one" is likely to get (a) in foul trouble and (b) very tired. Is he a valuable scorer for your team? If so, measure how important it is to sacrifice his offensive output — which suffers due to (a) and (b) above — to have him defend the opponent's dead-eye shooter.

The strangest box and one I ever saw

The strangest box and one I ever saw involved a 1991 game between Clemson and North Carolina State. The Tigers' 6'11" center, Dale Davis (now with the Indiana Pacers), was starring in his own highlight film against the Wolfpack. What was State left to do with its best defender being a 6-foot nothing guard named Chris Corchianni?

You must remember, State's coach was Jimmy Valvano, and there was nothing that Jimmy was afraid to try. So "Jimmy V." put Corchianni on Davis in a box and one. It worked. Corchianni held Davis scoreless for six or seven minutes, and North Carolina State rallied to win.

Then again, that story probably says more about the motivational skills of the late Jimmy V. than it does about the potency of the box and one.

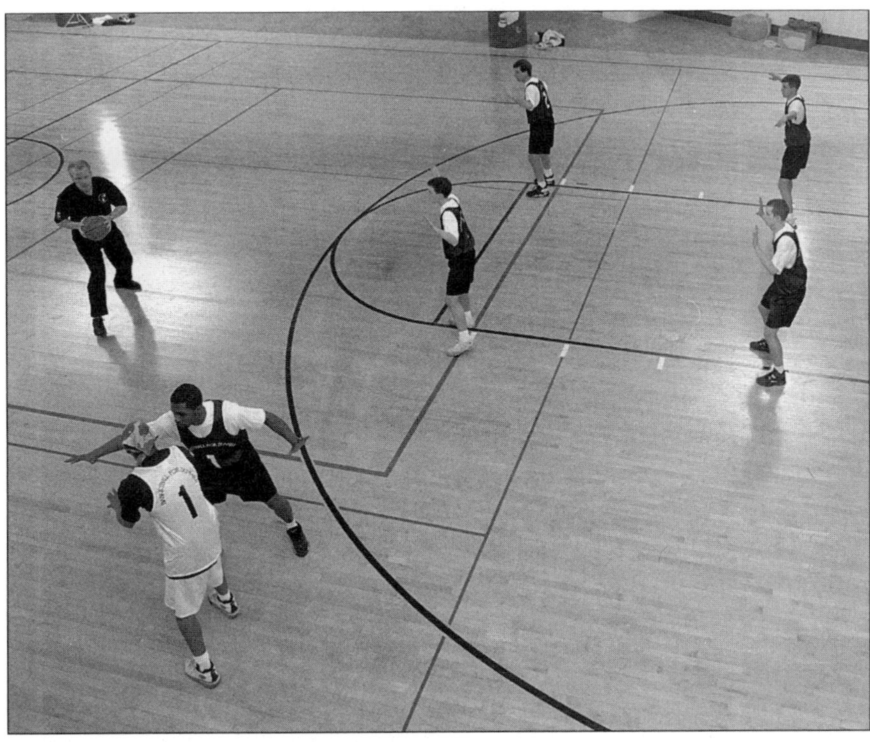

Figure 7-13: The box and one defense.

Triangle and two

In a triangle and two, three defenders (3, 4, and 5) play a zone in the paint — a guard up top, two big players down low — in the shape of a triangle, as Figure 7-14 shows. The two other defenders (1 and 2) have man-to-man assignments. The guard in the triangle plays just above the free throw line, and the two others position themselves along the blocks on the back line.

Beating the triangle and two

Yes, you're in the defense chapter, but this is the only place where I discuss the triangle and two, so I may as well tell you how to beat it. Follow these steps:

1. **Isolate the two players being guarded man-to-man on the same side of the court.**

   One of them should be handling the ball.

2. **Have a third player set a weakside screen against the guard on the triangle.**

   The player on the weakside wing should have an open jumper. As is the case with all zones, the best way to break a triangle and two is to bury your outside jumpshots.

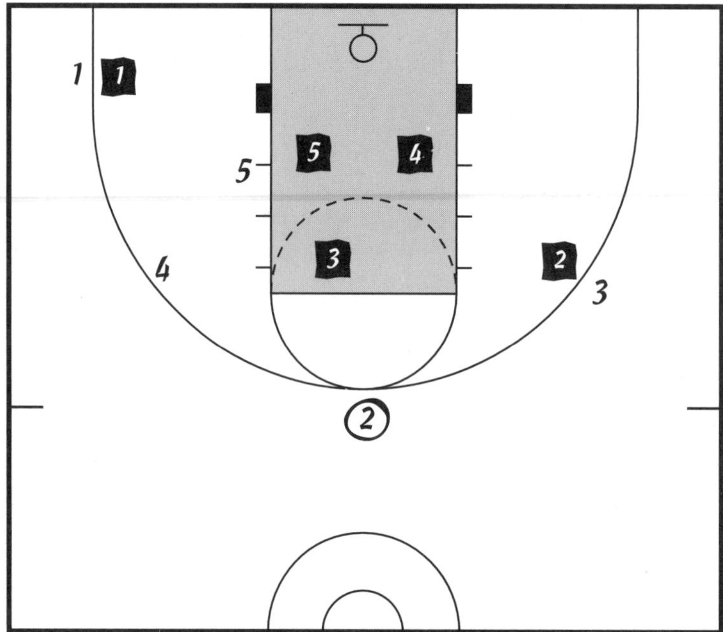

Figure 7-14: The triangle and two defense.

This defense is for a *short* period. Play it on a key possession to throw off the offense; the offense will not be prepared for it. Stay with this defense only until the offense figures out a way to beat it.

And that concludes our traipse through geometry. Don't worry; there's no rhombus and one or pentagon zone. At least not yet.

Meet the Press

Press is short for *pressure,* which is what a press defense is designed to inflict. A press (often called a *full-court press*) is an attacking defense employed in the backcourt, where the objective is not so much to defend against a basket as it is to force a turnover. Usually used after a made basket, the pressing team swarms all over the opponents in the backcourt; if the opponents successfully get the ball past half-court (called *breaking the press*), the pressing team usually falls back into their normal defense. The strategy of the press is to force the ball handler to make a decision before he wants to do so.

Why press?

- **Because the opponent has poor ball-handling ability.** A poor ball handler is anyone who makes turnovers; it's not necessarily a guy who cannot dribble behind his back.

- **Because you hope to disrupt the opponent's offensive rhythm.** The Cleveland Cavaliers are slow as molasses on offense. Other teams press them to speed up the game, but the Cavs are too smart to be pressed out of their game plan. They simply get the ball beyond midcourt and then use most of their allotted 24 seconds (the amount of time on the pro shot clock) unless they're granted an open lay-up.
- **Because you want to increase the tempo of the game.** When playing against a slow, methodical team, your offense may need a jump-start. By changing the game pace with a press, your offense is more likely to get steals and easy baskets, which helps their confidence.
- **Because your players believe in it.** Arkansas coach Nolan Richardson uses the term "40 Minutes of Hell" to describe what it's like to play his team. His players bought into the concept of pressing from start to finish — of turning the game into a war of attrition. If your players love to press and you have the bench depth to do it, pressing is a great way to play. Full-court pressure results in lots of turnovers and, hence, easy baskets. But it is also physically demanding and can tire players quickly.
- **Because it's something different.** Few hoops teams have the athletic ability and bench depth to press all game, hence most teams devote little practice time to breaking the press.

Figures 7-15 and 7-16 show two common press formations: the 2-2-1 full-court press and the 1-3-1 half-court press.

The trap press

The purpose of a press is to double team, or *trap,* a player, using the sideline as a third defender. The trap areas (shown in Figure 7-17) are as follows:

- The primary trap area is the spot where the in-bounds pass is received.
- The secondary trap area is between the foul lines and half-court on both sides of the midcourt line.
- The third trap area is deep in either corner in the frontcourt.

Three steps are involved in the trap press:

1. **Trap the ball.**

   After your opponent in-bounds the ball, trap the player who receives the pass. Two players attack him (not literally), forcing him toward the sideline. Don't give the player with the ball an opportunity to look for an open teammate; attack the ball immediately.

   What about the defender guarding the in-bounds pass? He should not leave his man to help trap until the player who received the pass begins to dribble. If the defender leaves his man, the player with the ball can simply toss it back to the player who in-bounded it.

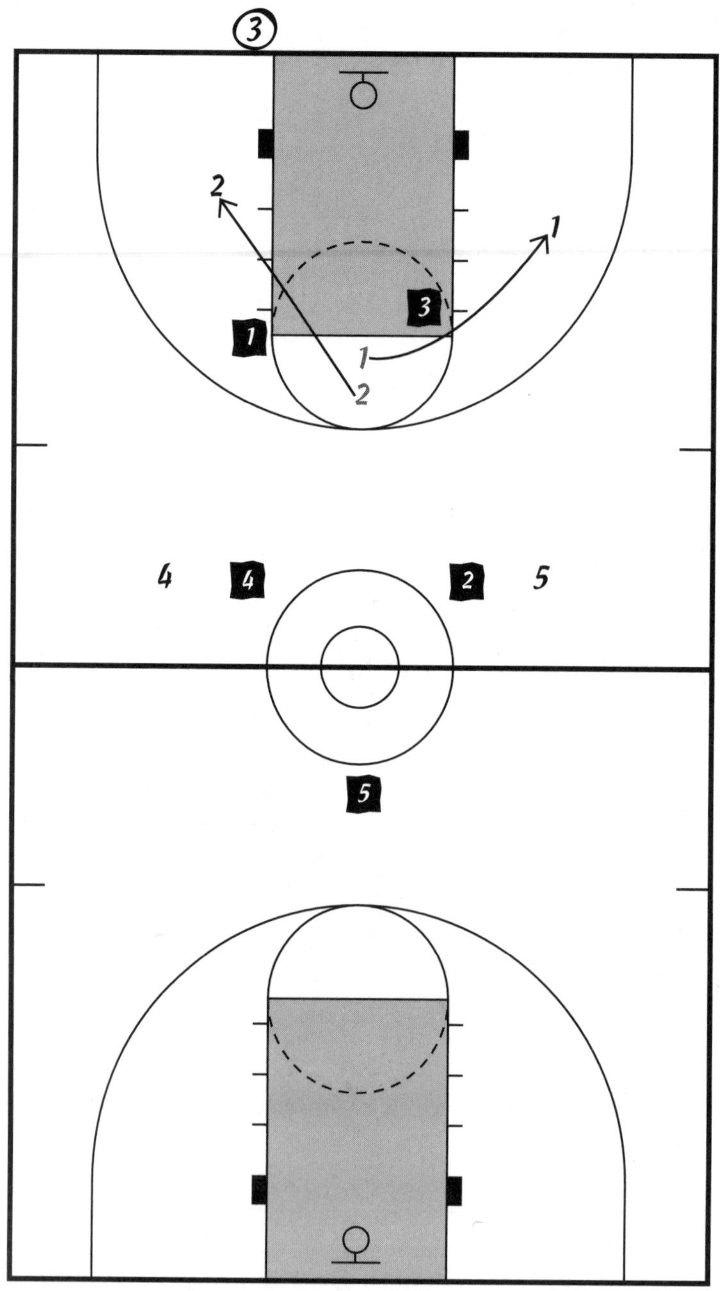

Figure 7-15: The 2-2-1 press: a common full-court press.

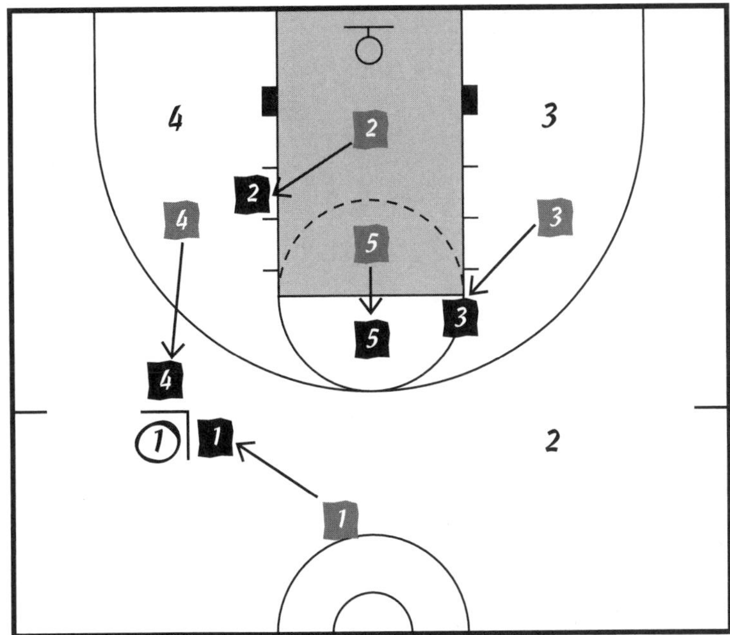

Figure 7-16: The 1-3-1 half-court press.

2. **Keep the player surrounded in the trap.**

   After the player with the ball puts the ball on the floor and begins her dribble, the defender in front of her must force her to the sideline. The in-bounds pass defender approaches from behind to effect the trap. If she picks up her dribble, converge on her and hound her.

   When she picks up her dribble, she should reach in for the ball with two hands. The player with the ball is holding it on the sides to make a pass. If you reach in, reach with one hand on top and the other on the bottom of the ball; don't try to slap the ball out, or the ref may whistle you for a foul. If the opportunity to put two hands on the ball — to either steal it or get a held-ball call — is not there, don't risk it. Better to try and force a five-second violation.

3. **Anticipate the desperation pass.**

   But do *not* foul the trapped player.

Teach all your defensive players every spot on the floor in the trap defense. When they're familiar with every spot, they get a feel for where everyone is supposed to be in this defensive alignment, and they know when to make the interception. The players have more confidence in what their teammates are doing, and you can sub each player in for anyone during a game.

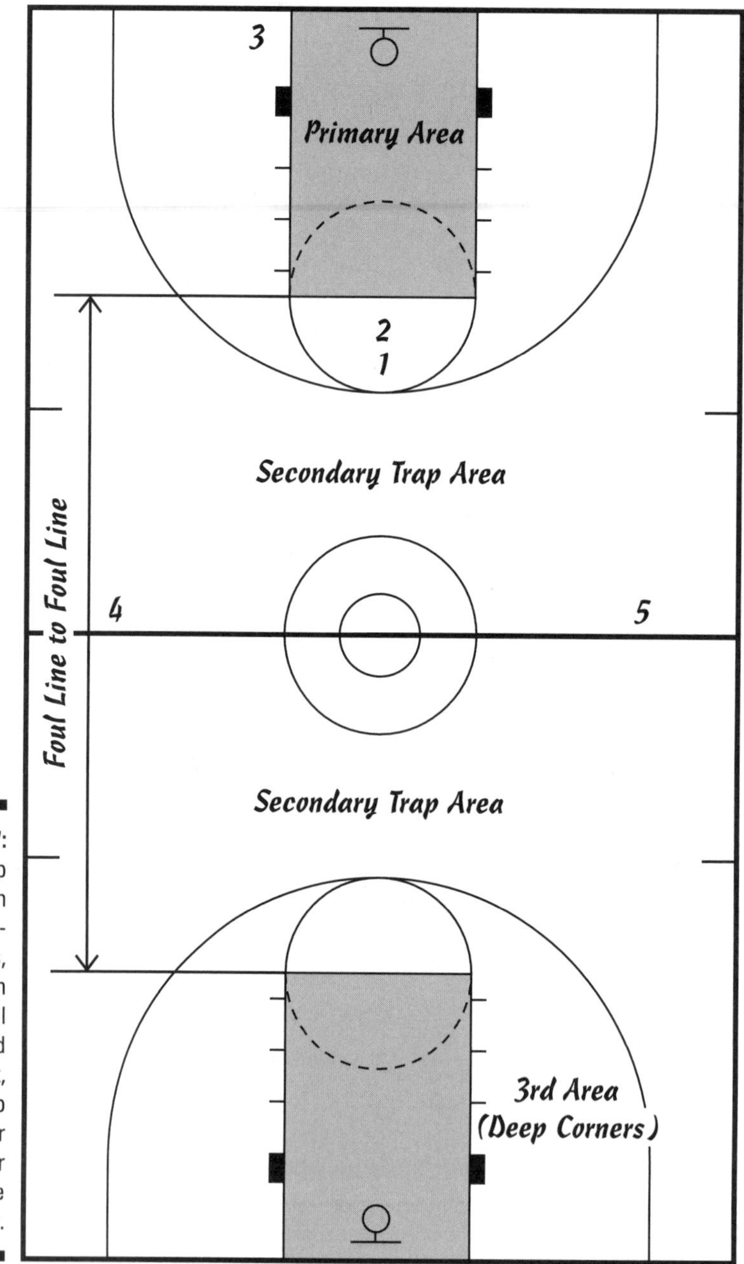

Figure 7-17: The trap areas: on the in-bounds, between the foul lines and midcourt, and deep in either corner in the frontcourt.

Defending the break

Every team would love to have tall, athletically gifted players, but in reality, most teams have to play at least one center in the press who's not as quick. If you're the deep man on defense — or one of the two — you're usually positioned at the foul line in the frontcourt. If no offensive player happens to be behind you, gamble. Move up to the top of the circle. Unless the offense tests you, tighten the press by moving up as far as their deepest player. But be careful: A desperate player trapped in the backcourt will throw the home-run ball (long pass) to a streaking teammate. Don't get beat deep.

If you're the center facing a 2-on-1 fast break, point out to your teammate who's recovering on defense where he should go. That way, you neutralize the 2-on-1 into an evenly balanced 2-on-2 situation.

Digger and presses

I first learned about presses in 1965–66 when I was coaching at St. Gabriel's High School. In the summer of 1965, I was working Bill Foster's basketball camp in the Poconos. John Wooden visited the camp that summer. His Bruins had won the NCAA title that year with a small, pressing team. The Wizard of Westwood enlightened us on the entire system.

When I first arrived at St. Gabriel's, the local folks told me that teams only pressed when they were behind in the fourth quarter. So I decided to do something different. We pressed for 32 minutes (the entire game) at St. Gabriel's and won a state championship.

When I arrived at Fordham, I too had a small team; not one of my players stood over 6'5". So my players pressed the entire game — 40 minutes of hell. That year, my only season at the Bronx school, Fordham's record was 26-3. Why did the press work so well that year? Yes, I had quick players. But those players believed in the press and the coach who was teaching it to them. That's half the battle.

Chapter 8
Rebounding

In This Chapter

- Offensive and defensive rebounding strategies
- Rebounding drills
- Great rebounders in basketball history

How valuable is rebounding? In 1956, Red Auerbach, the coach of the Boston Celtics, took aside his rookie center, Bill Russell, and gave him the following instructions: "Your game is to get me the ball. You get the ball and throw it up there for the shooters."

Then Auerbach, who understood that he was asking Russell to sacrifice individual stardom for the benefit of the team, dangled this carrot in front of his gifted player. Auerbach said, "We'll count rebounds as baskets for you."

Had the NBA bean counters conspired with Auerbach's scheme, Russell, on the strength of rebounds alone, would be the NBA's all-time career scoring leader with 43,240 points. Instead, the 6'11" center had to satisfy himself with leading the Celtics to 11 NBA championships, including nine in a row at one point, winning the league's Most Valuable Player (MVP) award five times, and retiring with 21,620 rebounds (second to Wilt Chamberlain of the Philadelphia Warriors, and later the Los Angeles Lakers, on the career list).

How valuable is rebounding? Consider that, with the exception of the exceptional Michael Jordan, only three players in NBA history have won the league's MVP award four or more times. They are Chamberlain (four times), Russell (five times), and Kareem Abdul-Jabbar (six times) of the Milwaukee Bucks and later the LA Lakers. Is it just a coincidence that Chamberlain, Russell, and Abdul-Jabbar are ranked one-two-three on the league's "Most Rebounds, Career" list? Or that the teams on which they played won 17 NBA titles? I don't think so.

Rebounding is hard work. Because many a rebound ricochets off the backboard, the phrases *clearing the boards* and *wiping the glass* — both *board* and *glass* refer to the backboard — have become slang for grabbing a rebound. Both terms infer blue-collar duties; the latter implies that a good rebounder, like good domestic help, does do windows.

Board-dom: A Glossary

Before I talk about rebounding techniques, I need to define a few terms:

- **Boxing out:** Establishing position between your opponent and the basket while a shot is in the air
- **Offensive rebound:** Gaining possession of a missed shot that either you or one of your teammates took
- **Defensive rebound:** Gaining possession of an opponent's missed shot

Rebounding: The Key to Victory

Kareem Abdul-Jabbar once said that if his team outrebounded the other team, his team would come out with a win. It really is that simple. Just as in baseball, where the team with fewer errors usually wins, in basketball winning teams outrebound their foes. Look at it this way: You have four ways to regain possession of the ball when playing defense:

- Your team rebounds a missed shot.
- Your team steals the ball.
- The offense turns the ball over via a violation. (See Chapter 3 for information about offensive violations.)
- The offense scores.

Certainly, your job as a defender is to prevent your opponent from scoring. Steals happen, as do offensive violations such as traveling, but steals are less common than missed shots. Hence the more rebounds you garner, the fewer shots your opponent can take, which means fewer opportunities for scoring. You're right, Kareem; winning a game *is* that simple.

Unlike scoring, rebounding involves all five players on the floor. For example, one player can theoretically outscore an opposing team. After all, only one player can shoot the ball on each possession down the floor. However, every player is a potential rebounder on each missed shot. Thus to outrebound the other team, each player must neutralize the player he's guarding, every time down the floor.

The Team Concept of Rebounding

As a player, you need to work individually, but rebounding is a team effort. Here's how the teamwork plays out on each end of the floor:

- **On defense:** All three front-line players (that is, the two forwards and the center) must act together as a wall underneath the basket. The guards must prevent the perimeter offensive players from swooping in, grabbing an offensive rebound, and making an easy bucket.
- **On offense:** If all five players crash the boards and no one remains at the top of the key, the defense will make you pay if they get the rebound. A defender, upon grabbing the rebound, will throw a quick pass — known as an *outlet pass* — to a teammate. In this situation, one of his teammates, probably a guard, will be streaking toward the basket with no one on your team in front of him. The "streaker" will convert this pass to an easy basket — what's known as a *breakaway.*

How do you prevent a breakaway? If you're out on top of the key when the shot is taken, your first obligation is to retreat on defense. If you're down low near the bucket, think of the ball that caroms off the rim as belonging to you and nobody else. If you're outrebounded, don't allow the rebounder to throw the outlet pass immediately. Get in his face with your arms extended skyward.

Rebounding Physics

Good rebounders understand shots and anticipate the outcome. For example, the longer the shot, the farther the miss bounces; that's simple physics. A longer shot has more velocity *and* a higher arc than a shot taken near the basket, so players most likely will have to rebound the ball farther from the hoop. With so many three-point shots being taken today, guards, who play on the perimeter, now have more rebounding opportunities than ever before.

Rims can be *hard* or *soft.* I'm not talking about the rims themselves; by hard or soft, I'm referring to how tightly the rim is affixed to the backboard. A rim that is tightly affixed has no give and is considered hard. A loosely affixed rim has plenty of give and is known to hoopsters as being soft (or generous). This varies from facility to facility. Tightly affixed rims not only result in errant shots that bounce farther away from the rim, but they also result in more missed shots.

Be sure to scout the rims of the facility in which you're going to play. You can do some rim scouting during pregame warm-ups. Watch the opposition shoot with two objectives in mind:

- To discover how hard the rims are.
- To observe which players, especially which guards, take low-arc shots, which bounce off the rim farther and faster.

Dayton Place

The University of Dayton had the hardest rims I ever encountered as a coach. On a court like that, it doesn't matter where the shot is taken; the ball comes off the rim long. My strategy was to have our front-line players box out a foot or two outside their normal perimeter when on defense. Rather than being 6 feet from the basket when boxing out, we'd go back to 7 or 8 feet, because the ball came out that long. Missed three-point shots used to bounce all the way back to the three-point line.

In 1973–74, Notre Dame arrived in Dayton with one of the top rebounding teams in the nation and a 24-1 record. Although we had played there a year earlier, I forgot to remind my players about the gym's hard rims. They outrebounded us, and we lost 97-82.

Defensive Rebounding

On defense, the perfect rebound hits the floor. *Uh oh, Digger's losing it.* No, really — think about it. As a defensive player, your job is to prevent the offensive player you're guarding from grabbing the rebound. You should think of your job that way rather than grabbing the rebound yourself. Now, imagine that the ball bounces off the rim and you're unable to grab it. As long as the player you're guarding fails to grab it as well, you've done your job.

If all five defenders are unable to grab the rebound, and each defender keeps the offensive player for whom she is responsible from getting the ball, too, the ball hits the floor. Theoretically, the ball rolls out of bounds, and the defense gets the ball. Perfect.

Don't misunderstand me: Players should go after the rebound. My point is that, defensively, your *top* priority is to keep your opponent from getting the rebound. If all five players do that, the ball hits the floor. In real life, that almost never happens, but then again, physics professors like to discuss frictionless surfaces. Humor me.

The key to defensive rebounding starts in pregame shooting practice. A great defensive rebounder watches how the other team shoots. Some shooters are *soft shooters* (they shoot with a high arc); others *shoot on the line* (with a low arc). Your job is to know the shooter, especially the player you're guarding. Here's what you can look for from either type of shooter:

- **High arc:** A missed shot may not bounce off the rim as far, but it may bounce off higher. The ball has a tendency to take a second bounce off the rim or backboard.
- **Low arc:** Fooore! This shot usually comes off as more of a line drive, and is less likely to take a second bounce off the rim. More important than the distance at which the ball travels is the speed. Your reflexes must be faster for this shot than for a high-arc shot.

Most shots taken from the perimeter travel in the air for *two seconds* from the moment the shooter releases the ball until it bounces off the rim or the backboard (or goes in). Two ticks: one-thousand-one, one-thousand-two. What should you be doing during these two seconds? Read on.

Find someone

Say your team is playing man-to-man defense. After the shot leaves the shooter's fingertips, your job is simple: Find the player you're guarding — hopefully she's nearby, or else you have other problems. If your team is in a *zone defense* — where each player guards an area instead of an opponent — locate the player near you who is moving toward the basket.

Everyone on defense should fight for a rebound with equal intensity. There are no "designated rebounders" on defense; rebounding is everyone's job.

Make contact

Rebounding is the most physical aspect of basketball. If you're squeamish about a little bumping and bruising, you won't become a good rebounder. But if you place getting the ball above personal safety, you may become a *great* rebounder.

There are two methods of making contact: the reverse method and the step in the path method.

The reverse method

By *reverse,* I mean that when you play defense, you always face the player you're guarding. However, after the ball is shot, the ball takes priority over your opponent: You must know where the ball is. But you don't want to lose your opponent, either, so you reverse yourself. Turn your body so that you're facing the hoop. Now your eyes can follow the path of the shot. (See Figure 8-1.)

Figure 8-1: The reverse method.

Use your backside — and by backside, I mean your rear end — to stay with your opponent. Put your body on her and use your butt for two purposes:

- To block out your opponent.
- To be aware of your opponent's movements.

The step-in-the-path method

You may find yourself away from the player you're guarding at the moment the shooter releases his shot (perhaps you were helping out on a double team or were simply out of position). Hence, when the shot is attempted, you may not be able to use the reverse method. Instead, you must anticipate your opponent's path to the basket to keep him from getting the rebound. Find the spot where you'll be able to intercept that player as he heads toward the basket — all this happens in a matter of a second — and race to that spot. (See Figure 8-2.)

Think of the player you're guarding as a missile en route to a target and pretend that you've been sent as an anti-attack missile. Your trajectory is not toward the target; rather, your aim is to intercept the missile *on its way* to the target.

Maintain contact

After you successfully box out an offensive player, never, ever lose physical contact with him until someone collects the rebound. The offensive player is attempting to elude you because you have the more advantageous position. When you lose contact, the offensive player's task becomes that much simpler.

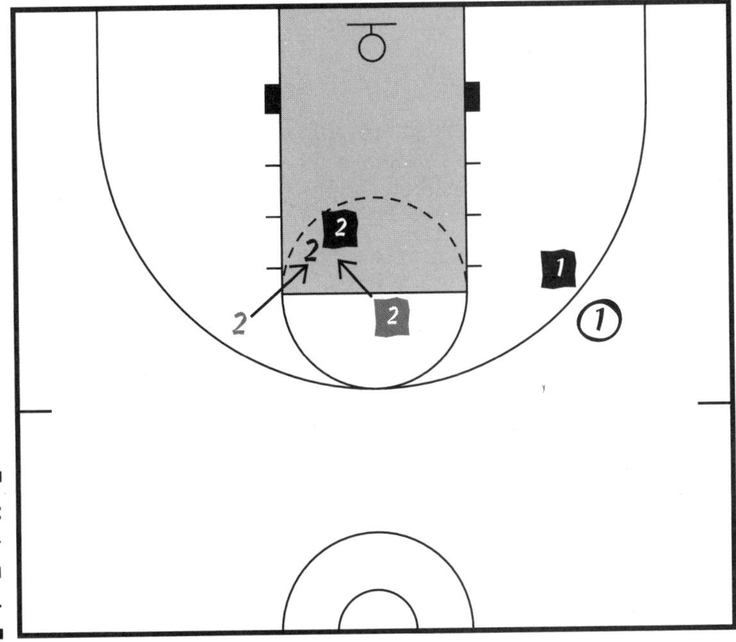

Figure 8-2: The step-in-the-path method.

You often hear coaches urging their players to "Box out!" — a phrase that condenses the first three rules (that is, find someone, make contact, and maintain contact). As with so many basketball skills, you must use the proper form for boxing out. Maintaining proper form is a matter of *leverage*.

Charles Barkley of the Houston Rockets has been one of the best rebounders in the NBA for more than a decade, despite the fact that he's only 6'6". His lower back problems hinder his jumping prowess, but he still managed to collect 33 rebounds in a single game in 1996 (ten rebounds per game is a respectable average). Why? Because nobody — not even Archimedes — understands leverage better than Sir Charles.

Try this experiment: Stand as erect as possible and have someone push you from behind. See how you move. Now bend your knees and stick out your derriere to establish a wider base. Keep your torso erect, but lean slightly forward. Have someone push you again. Notice that your wider base gives you more stability.

You want to crouch down and make yourself more horizontal when boxing out. Making yourself shorter to grab a rebound may seem paradoxical, but it isn't. Barkley has an airbag for a butt, and he uses it to his advantage. In essence, he uses his gluteus maximus to push the offensive player so far behind (no pun intended) that the opponent has no chance to get the rebound.

Your form: Keep your knees bent, butt out, and arms out and bent upward at a 90-degree angle. Your palms are facing the rim. Ideally, your butt is sitting on the offensive player's knees.

Think of it this way: You grab a rebound with your hands. Thus your hands should be as far *in front* of the player you're boxing out as possible. If he tries to jump over your back to grab the rebound, he'll be whistled for a foul. He may be taller than you and able to jump higher than you, but he can't jump *over* you.

The unpardonable sin of defensive rebounding is allowing the shooter to rebound her own shot. If you're guarding the shooter and attempt to block the shot, that's fine. But don't lose control of your body. Use the reverse method to box out the shooter, who must occupy herself with her follow-through before she can concentrate on rebounding.

Rebounding in a Zone Defense

When playing a zone defense, you're guarding an area rather than a player. You can't really box out an area. Therefore, in a zone, the emphasis is on *forming a three-defender triangle* around the basket, no matter what type of zone you're playing. The triangle protects the middle of the three-second lane and the two block areas from offensive interlopers. (See Figure 8-3.)

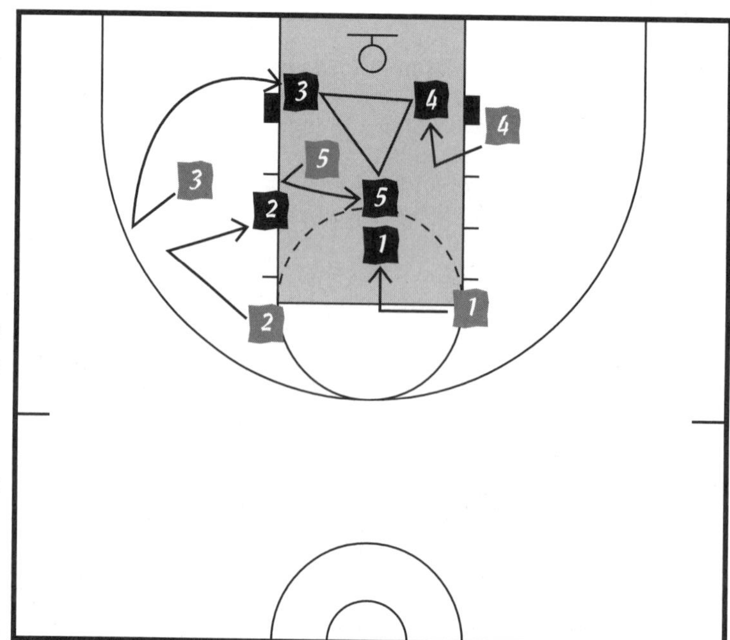

Figure 8-3: Forming a triangle around the basket when rebounding in a zone defense.

Even in a zone, though, you must find somebody to box out. You have an area to protect in that triangle, and someone will try to infiltrate. When that offensive player comes at you, box him out.

Offensive Rebounding

In the 1995 NCAA championship game, UCLA beat a favored Arkansas squad, the defending national champs, 89-78. Despite having a team composed of smaller players, the Bruins won the game because the players outrebounded the Razorbacks 50-31. UCLA hit the offensive boards especially hard, collecting 21 offensive rebounds that resulted in 27 points. If you're the coach of the losing team, those types of numbers can lead to ulcers.

A good offensive rebounder does four things:

- Anticipates where a miss will land.
- Looks for the quickest route to the ball.
- Avoids contact with the defender via quickness.
- Knows that he has two seconds to retrieve the ball after the shooter releases it.

The keys to defensive rebounding are positioning and leverage; the key to offensive rebounding is quickness.

Dennis Rodman: Chairman of the Boards

Will Dennis Rodman, a key player on four NBA championship teams (twice with the Detroit Pistons, twice with the Chicago Bulls) be voted into the Hall of Fame? Rodman has never been named to an All-Star team, and his shooting and dribbling skills are at best on par with those of a middling college player. On the other hand, "The Worm," as he's known, *has* led the NBA in rebounding for six consecutive years, and no one else can say that.

What about the 6'8" Rodman has made him the Chairman of the Boards this decade? First of all, he's a fabulous physical specimen, a stunning combination of quickness and strength, not to mention that he's blessed with disproportionately long arms. Rodman is also a *pogo-stick jumper* — he can leap two or three times in the time it takes most of his peers to leap once. That skill allows him to tap the ball to a place where he can get to it first.

Most rebounders try to go get the ball with two hands, which is a sound principle. But if you can only get close enough to tip the ball into a vacant area, and if you're quicker than your defender, go ahead and do it. When Rodman tips the ball into the corner, he's going to get it, because the Worm is quicker than his foes.

Always follow your shot. The moment a shot leaves your hands, you should prepare to rebound it. I'm not trying to instill pessimistic vibes here; it's just that you don't do your team much good just standing there admiring the ball in flight. As a shooter, you're often close to the rebound, and after a while, you'll be able to feel whether your shot is long or short or — hopefully — good.

Offensive rebounding is a mindset: When that ball is in the air, it's a free ball. If you're on offense, assume that every shot is a missed shot. Go get that rebound!

Free Throw Rebounding

The best advice is simple: Leave early. The rules stipulate that you may not move from your spot along the free throw lane until the ball leaves the shooter's fingers. Referees, however, are not vigilant about whistling this violation. Don't be obvious about it, but try to get a jump on your opponent.

Offensive free throw rebounding

You're at a disadvantage because the defense gets the two spots on the free throw lane that are closest to the basket. The next two spots, one on each side of the lane, are yours. Both teams continue to alternate. So the offensive team has to work even harder than normal to grab a rebound.

The back tap

A trick of the trade in offensive rebounding is the *back tap.* The idea here is that, because the shooting team will most likely be boxed out on a free throw, the chances of one of the interior rebounders grabbing the ball with two hands are minuscule. Better to try tapping the ball with one hand, volleyball-style, back toward the perimeter, where your teammates outnumber the defenders.

The defense ordinarily places four players on the line for a free throw, so if you can tap the ball past the free throw line, your chances of recovering it are great. And you're often looking at a wide-open three-pointer on top of that.

Crashing guards

If you're on offense, it's usually best to put two players on the free throw lane and have your other two nonshooters back near midcourt, ready to play defense. The defense often ignores those two players as potential rebounders of a missed free throw. After all, they're at least 10 feet behind the shooter.

Occasionally, then, you see one of those two players positioned near half-court time his advance so that he has a good running start just as the ball leaves the shooter's hands. (Picture two trapeze artists timing their midair rendezvous.) He flies through the lane, untouched, and soars in to grab the rebound and dunk it in one motion. Such a play pumps up an offense and utterly deflates a defense. Michael Jordan and the Philadelphia 76ers' Allen Iverson are two of the best at this.

The Hubie Brown play

Named for the well-traveled NBA coach who developed it, the Hubie Brown play, when diagrammed as in Figure 8-4, resembles the crisscrossed laces of a shoe (if you think of the tongue as the free throw lane). Remember, the defensive team gets the two positions nearest the basket (one on either side), the next two slots go to the offense, the next two to the defense, and so on.

On this play, one of the lower offensive rebounders (4) cuts straight across the lane and blocks out the defender occupying the lowest position (D5). The offensive rebounder's teammate on the opposite middle (5) moves into the lane to grab the rebound. The third offensive player in the lane (2), who is on the same side as the player who cut across, rolls down the lane.

By cutting across the lane, the low offensive player boxes out one player. The defender on the low offensive player's side usually follows him (because that defender thinks that his job is to box out that player). That leaves the other side open for the guard, who rolls down the lane to grab the rebound uncontested.

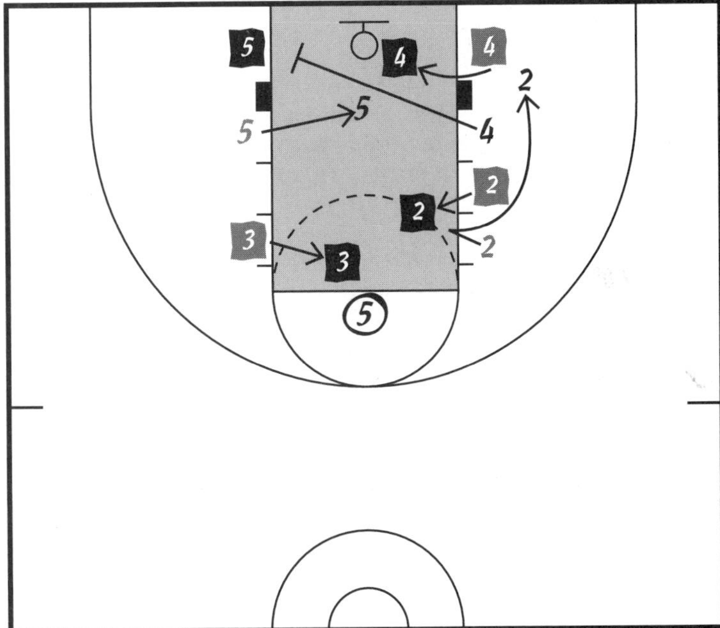

Figure 8-4: The Hubie Brown play.

Defensive free throw rebounding

You should never be outrebounded on a missed free throw when you're on defense. If you do the following, you probably won't be.

- **Squeeze the big man.** Whenever my team faced a team with a great rebounder, I placed three of my players on one side of the lane. The job of my two men on either side of that player was to pinch him (not literally, although I'm sure that rebounders have used that ploy); they didn't allow the rebounder into the lane. The third player was then free to grab the rebound.
- **Guard the crashing guards.** You almost always have two players not standing on the *blocks* — that is, along the free throw lane. Remind them that the players on the perimeter may crash the boards. To prevent this, if the guards inch up from the top-of-the-key area, the defensive players who are not standing along the free throw lane should guard the guards face to face.
- **Box out the shooter.** Always keep one player on the free throw line to box out the shooter. Whereas the shooter cannot leave the free throw line until the ball hits the rim, his opponent can move in to box him out the moment he shoots.

Allowing the free throw shooter to rebound his own miss is almost unforgivable. (As a coach, it's unbearable.)

Rebounding Drills

Rebounding does not avail itself to drills as well as other hoops skills, such as shooting or dribbling. First, you need someone to shoot the ball. *And* to miss it. Then you never know where the ball will go. The best rebounding drills are actually live scrimmages. That may be because rebounding is less about art than it is about feistiness.

As a coach, never be afraid to trade ideas. Remember drills — especially those you witness at clinics — write them down and include them in your repertoire. They'll be useful for years to come. And when another coach asks about one of your drills, be willing to share.

Keep rebounding simple. The most important notion to emphasize is the two seconds of work. I used to tell my players, "Your parents work a 40-hour week. I am asking you to work for two seconds." If you work hard on defense for 25 seconds and force the offense into taking a poor shot, only two seconds of lax play can cause all your work to go for naught: The offense gets the rebound and converts the miss into a bucket. If that happens, I don't want to hear it; you're on the bench.

Circle the wagons drill

Circle the wagons is a four-on-four drill. The four offensive players stand stationary outside the three-point arc, while the coach holds the ball. The four defensive players rotate in a square around the free throw lane. (See Figure 8-5.) As the defensive players move around the square, the coach shoots the ball. The defensive players much match up to an offensive player and box out. The offensive players can do whatever they want — push, grab, anything — to get the ball. The idea is to teach defensive rebounding. Have the defense get three straight rebounds. If they don't have them start over from zero or have them run sprints. Then have the offense and defense switch.

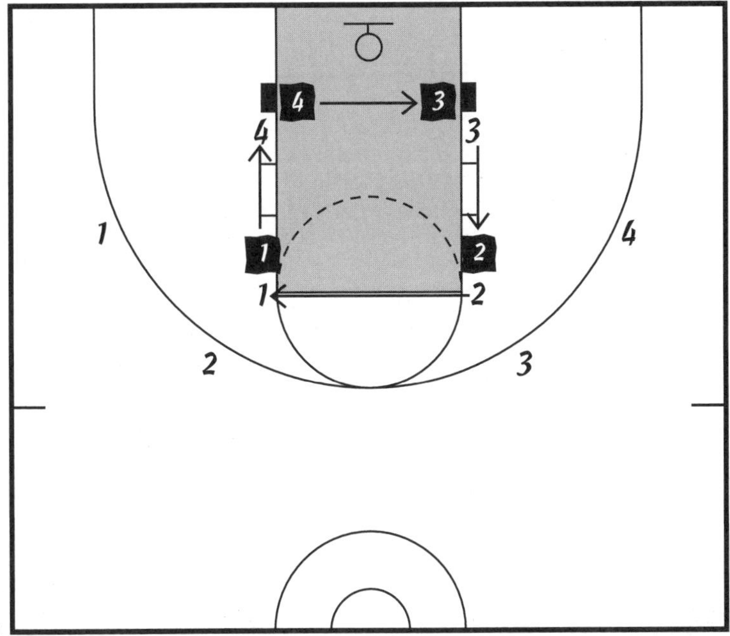

Figure 8-5: The circle the wagons drill.

One-on-one rebounding drill

As Figure 8-6 shows, the shooter (5) takes a perimeter jumpshot over a defender (2) in a one-on-one situation. You may have the shooter begin from either wing or the top of the key, and allow him no more than two dribbles in either direction. He cannot attempt to drive past the defender. The defender should have his hands up as the shooter takes the jumper. After the ball leaves the shooter's fingertips, the defender boxes out the shooter by making and maintaining contact. The rebounder must use all the principles in this drill: go right or left, step in the path, and reverse into the opponent. He should make contact, hold position, and look for the ball.

The bubble

In the 1970s, Notre Dame led the nation in rebounding three times and was ranked in the top ten nationally for a number of years. One reason we were so successful was the bubble.

During practice, especially in preseason, we used a rebounding drill in which we put a plastic bubble over the basket. The bubble prevented shots from going into the basket, so every shot required a rebound. Shot after shot had to be rebounded, which led to some fierce rebounding action.

If you choose to use the bubble with your team, never keep it on the hoop for a long period. Doing so depresses your players, who constantly take shots that have no prayer of going through the hoop. To solve this problem, have a coach or manager put up shots.

This is a fantastic drill for both offensive and defensive rebounding. The defender must hone his reverse method boxing out skills. Because this is a one-on-one situation, the shooter uses his speed to pursue the loose ball.

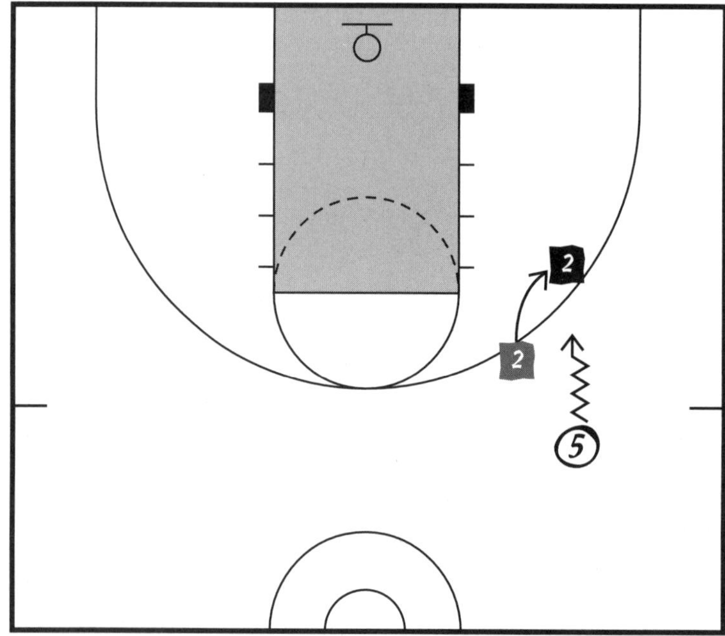

Figure 8-6: The one-on-one rebounding drill.

Two-on-two rebounding drill

This drill is designed for guards, though you can use it for any position. As Figure 8-7 shows, guard 1 has the ball on one wing, guarded by D1. (D1 and D2 represent the defensive guards, and 1 and 2 represent offensive guards in Figure 8-7.) Guard 2 is on the opposite wing, and her opponent, D2, plays off her, ready to help on 1. When 1 shoots the ball, D1 must box out the shooter, and D2 must step into the path of 2.

As in many drills, once players understand the parameters of the drill, they may have a tendency to cheat. D2 may not help out as much as she should, and her opponent, 2, may want to crash the boards preemptively. To counter this, allow Guards 1 and 2 the freedom to improvise. For example, 2 can go *back door* (see Chapter 6) if D2 is not paying attention to her, or 2 can receive a pass and shoot the ball herself. The only offensive maneuver you can disallow in this drill is a dribble-drive to the hoop by either offensive player.

On every one of these drills, the defender's hands are above her shoulders when she boxes out. She does not use her hands to grab her opponent, nor does she use her arms to block. Those moves are fouls of laziness. The defender uses her butt to do the work.

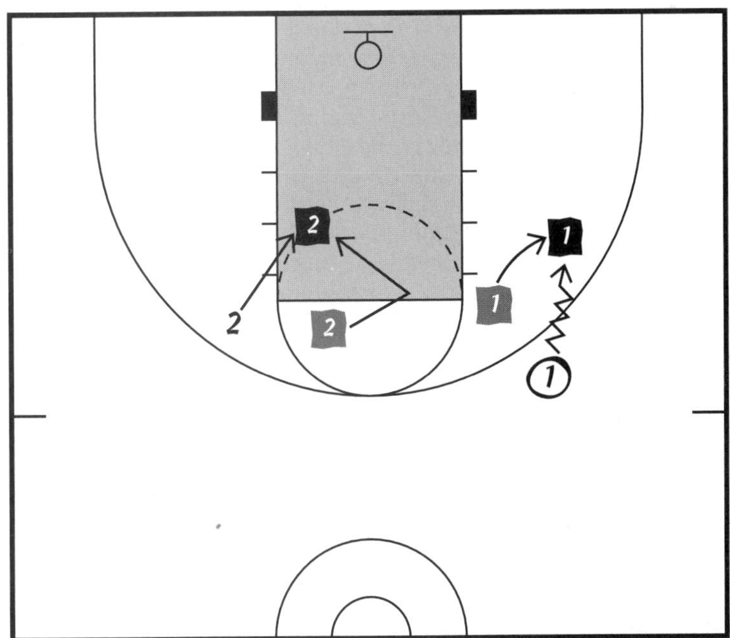

Figure 8-7: The two-on-two rebounding drill.

Manhattan drill

I learned this drill from Jack Powers, the former coach at Manhattan College, when I attended one of his clinics in the 1960s. This survival-of-the-fittest drill is useful in finding out which players are true scrappers.

Note: This drill may not be suitable for young kids.

Take three players and put them in the paint. The coach has the ball on the foul line and shoots. The three players vie for the rebound; whoever recovers it attempts to score. Allow the other two players to foul the rebounder, though not flagrantly — they should be physical. When a player makes a shot, the ball becomes live again the second it goes through the net. The first player to score three times gets to go out, and a new player joins the other two, who start again from zero.

This drill is great for teaching the conventional three-point play (the shooter is fouled: two points for the basket plus one free throw). You want players to become accustomed to being fouled and scoring on the same play. You want them to go up strong and expect contact.

As you may have concluded, this is a bear of a drill, stamina-wise. Nobody relaxes after a shot, even if it is made. I've seen players who were stuck in that drill for ten minutes look as if they'd just completed a triathlon. Hopefully, that fatigue motivates them to be a tad more feisty the next time through.

The Manhattan drill was instrumental in Adrian Dantley's rebounding prowess in college and later in the NBA. "A.D." was a virtuoso at this drill because he was so strong and combative. He simply jumped through people's arms whenever he followed a shot, and he never shied away from contact, realizing that the defender would be whistled for a foul. (A.D., not coincidentally, attempted and made more free throws than any player I ever coached.) By his junior year, he never stayed in this drill very long; nobody could stop him.

Board or bench?

With me as coach, you had a choice when it came to rebounding: two seconds of hard work or the bench. The number of points you scored didn't matter, because in the last minute of the game, boards (as well as free throw shooting) determine who wins.

So if a player didn't rebound — or worse, he didn't keep his opponent off the boards — I benched him. The conversation, always succinct, went something like this:

"Why did you come out?" I would ask.

"My man got a rebound."

"Good," I would say. "We're on the same page. So sit down and think about it. And let me know when you're ready to go back in."

Four-player full-court rebounding drill

Here's a drill that's guaranteed to get the heart pumping. Play four on four and run live (that is, pretend that it's a real game) as if it's a fast break. A coach shoots the ball, and play continues until the defense gets the rebound. Now the defense becomes the offense and runs the fast break. Play continues until the team playing defense gets the rebound or until the fast-break unit scores.

The idea is to maintain solid rebounding habits even when play becomes frenzied. Every player is put in both a defensive and an offensive rebounding position. When on offense, the goal is to get the rebound. When on defense, the goal, above getting the rebound, is to ensure that the player being guarded does not get the rebound. As a coach, stress to players the importance of these fundamentals in the transition game, when play tends to become sloppy.

Note: Why four on four instead of five on five? It leaves more space on the floor.

Outrebounding a Taller Player

You may do a great job of positioning, blocking out, and maintaining contact, but the other player still gets the rebound. Why? That person reaches over you and plucks the ball out of the sky before you can reach it. What can you do to prevent that? Go out to meet her; don't wait for her to come to you. (You neutralize the extra inches on a taller player by getting her away from the basket.) Use your butt. After you position yourself against her (using the reverse method), stick out your butt to force her to move backward. In what other sport does the gluteus maximus play such an important role?

Even though you're using your behind to hinder your opponent's movement — if you were using your hands, they'd whistle a foul against you — no referee will ever call a foul against your butt. Consider it your arsenal against a taller player. Her only chance is to jump over your back to grab the ball, which will earn her a whistle for a foul.

Great Rebounders to Emulate

Rebounding determines so much about the end result of a game. Rebounding is really the meat of this book to me, and what I believe in the most, because I really feel that if you control the boards, you can control the game when it counts.

Remember, you don't have to be 7 feet tall to be a great rebounder. Just look at Table 8-1, which lists the all-time leading rebounders in NBA history. Only three of the top ten players are 7 feet or taller; four are 6'9" or shorter. At George Washington University last year, for example, a guard named Shontay Rogers stood 5'4" and still grabbed 11 boards in one game.

Table 8-1 All-Time NBA Rebounding Leaders

Name	*Height*	*Rebounds*	*Years*	*Average*
Wilt Chamberlain	7'1"	23,924	14	21.9
Bill Russell	6'9"	21,620	13	22.5
Kareem Abdul-Jabbar	7'2"	17,440	20	11.2
Elvin Hayes	6'9"	16,279	16	12.5
Moses Malone	6'10"	16,166	20	12.3
Nate Thurmond	6'11"	14,464	14	15.0
Robert Parish	7'0"	14,626	20	9.3
Walt Bellamy	6'10"	14,241	14	13.7
Wes Unseld	6'7"	13,769	13	14.0
Jerry Lucas	6'8"	12,942	11	15.6

Individual rebounding superlatives

The NBA's best rebounding performances are

- **Most Rebounds, Season:** 2,149, Wilt Chamberlain, Philadelphia Warriors (1960–61)
- **Highest Average, Season:** 27.2, Wilt Chamberlain, Warriors (1960–61)
- **Most Rebounds, Game:** 55, Wilt Chamberlain, Warriors (November 24, 1960, versus Boston Celtics)
- **Most Rebounds, Half:** 32, Bill Russell, Boston Celtics (November 16, 1957, versus Philadelphia Warriors)
- **Most Rebounds, Quarter:** 18, Nate Thurmond, San Francisco Warriors (February 28, 1965, versus Baltimore Bullets)

The top college men rebounders are

- **Most Rebounds, Season:** 734, Walt Dukes, Seton Hall (1953)
- **Highest Average, Season:** 25.6, Charlie Slack, Marshall (1955)
- **Most Rebounds, Game:** 51, Bill Chambers, William & Mary (February 14, 1953, versus Virginia)
- **Most Rebounds, Career:** 2,201, Tom Gola, La Salle (1952–55)
- **Highest Average, Career:** 22.7, Artis Gilmore, Jacksonville (1969–71)

Among college women, the following players stand out above the rest in rebounding:

- **Most Rebounds, Season:** 534, Wanda Ford, Drake (1985)
- **Highest Average, Season:** 18.5, Rosina Pearson, Bethune-Cookman (1985)
- **Most Rebounds, Game:** 40, Deborah Temple, Delta State (February 14, 1983, versus University of Alabama-Birmingham)
- **Most Rebounds, Career:** 1,887, Wanda Ford, Drake (1983–86)
- **Highest Average, Career:** 16.1, Wanda Ford, Drake (1983–86)

You may notice that most individual rebounding records were set long ago. I have a few theories concerning this: Regarding the NBA, I subscribe to the Wilt Chamberlain theory, which states that Wilt the Stilt was the single most dominating presence the game has ever seen. As for college records, they're a minor mystery. You can argue that players are more concerned with their scoring average than their rebounding average, or maybe that there are fewer physical mismatches these days. Teams also took more shots 30 years ago, thus there were more missed shots, and more rebounds were available.

The greatest college rebounding teams

Since 1973, the NCAA Division I championship winner has been determined by *rebound margin* — that is, how many more rebounds per game a team averages than its opponent. Table 8-2 lists the top college rebounding teams, and Table 8-3 lists the coaches whose teams have topped the rebounding charts.

Table 8-2 College Teams with High Rebound Margins

School	*Margin*	*Season*
Men		
Manhattan	+18.5	1973
Alcorn State	+16.3	1978
Alcorn State	+15.4	1980
Alcorn State	+13.8	1979
Massachusetts	+13.8	1974
Women		
Louisiana Tech	+18.3	1990
Louisiana Tech	+18.2	1996
Old Dominion	+17.3	1983
Bethune-Cookman	+16.2	1985
Louisiana Tech	+16.2	1989

Table 8-3 NCAA Coaches with the Most National Rebounding Championships

Coach	*School*	*Number of Championships*
Digger Phelps	Notre Dame	4
James McDermott	Iona	3
Davey Whitney	Alcorn State	3
Jim Calhoun	Northeastern	3
Don Haskins	UTEP	2
Ken Trickey	Oral Roberts, Middle Tennessee State	2
Tom Davis	Iowa	2
John Thompson	Georgetown	2

On the rebound

Valentine's Day has been the single best day for both men and women on the rebound. On Valentine's Day, 1953, Bill Chambers of William & Mary set the single-game collegiate rebounding record, grabbing 51 in a win over Virginia. Thirty years later, on February 14, Deborah Temple of Delta State pulled down 40 boards in a win against the University of Alabama-Birmingham. Both records still stand.

Chapter 9

Moves, Plays, and Strategies

In This Chapter

- Moves for centers, forwards, guards, and three-point shooters
- Picking a last-second play
- Deciding whether to call a time-out with only seconds remaining
- Getting your team ready for a big game

In his first five NBA seasons, Los Angeles Laker Shaquille O'Neal made only one three-point field goal (in 14 attempts). The people who pay Shaq the gobs of money that he earns in a Laker uniform do not begrudge him his dearth of long-range shooting, however. And why should they? Among current NBA players, only Michael Jordan has a career scoring average higher than Shaq's 27 points per game.

The point is, Shaq's best spot on the floor to score is near the basket. Teammate Nick Van Exel, on the other hand, a spry 6'1" guard whose firing range inspires comparisons to NORAD, has made more than 600 treys in his four years in the league. Van Exel belongs outside the three-point arc.

The tale of Shaq and Nick is the NBA version of a lyric from the musical Showboat: "Fish gotta swim/birds gotta fly." You position your players on offense at the spots where they are most likely to score. This positioning is usually determined by the player's position (center, forward, or guard), which is almost always determined by height. I said *almost* always. Charles Barkley of the Houston Rockets stands a whisker below 6'6", and in the NBA, that height usually places you out on the wing as a guard. But Barkley loves to play with his back to the basket; he's a terrific post player. So he plays forward. Christian Laettner of the Atlanta Hawks is 6'11". When coaches have attempted to play him as a true center with his back to the basket, Laettner has floundered. When the Hawks wised up and moved Laettner to forward, where he was able to play *facing* the basket, he responded with his first All-Star season.

As a coach, you must know where your players like to be, keeping in mind that you must space the players well. You need shooters out on the perimeter and at least one player inside who can play with his back to the basket. The most productive offenses have an array of weapons in their arsenals.

Twin Towers

Sometimes two centers are better than one. In 1984, the Houston Rockets, who had drafted 7'4" center Ralph Sampson a year earlier, picked up Hakeem Olajuwon in the NBA draft. (Trivia buffs know that Michael Jordan was also available, but it's hard to fault a team for selecting "The Dream," as Olajuwon is known.) Suddenly, Houston's skyline looked remarkably different. The Twin Towers had arrived.

The duo of Olajuwon and Sampson was hardly the first such structure erected in the NBA. In 1963, the San Francisco Warriors had 7'1" Wilt Chamberlain and 6'11" Nate Thurmond. Four years later, Wilt "the Stilt" joined the Philadelphia 76ers and played with Lucious Jackson, another 6'11" center. That 1967 version of the 76ers won a league title and was voted the greatest NBA team of all time (that is, the previous 50 years).

Olajuwon and Sampson, like the Chamberlain duos, thrived because one player, although a natural center, moved to forward on offense. The Rockets made it to the NBA Finals — losing to Boston — in Olajuwon's rookie season.

Playing Center

Whether your center is a 7-foot pro, a 6-foot sixth grader, or, most likely, somewhere in between, she must discover three concepts in order to excel in the role of playing with her back to the basket. This section outlines these concepts.

Working to get open inside

A center on offense sets up along the free throw (or three-second) lane. She does not set up inside the lane itself, because remaining in there for three or more seconds is a violation causing the offense to lose the ball. The area where the center sets up is called the *post.* If she sets up near the basket, normally within 10 feet, she's in the *low post.* If she positions herself farther up the lane, even on the elbow or free throw line, she's in the *high post.* (Refer to Chapter 3 for an illustration of these areas.)

The low post is a tight space. "Getting open" doesn't translate to losing your defender so much as it does to knowing which side of the center the defender is favoring. Rarely does a defender play directly behind the center. Instead, the defender overcompensates to one side in hopes of batting away an *entry pass* — that is, a pass thrown to the center from the perimeter area.

If you are the center, use your body to know where the defender is. That way, when a pass is thrown to you, you can use your back, butt, and arm to keep the defender from deflecting the pass.

Breaking contact with the defender

Assume that the ball is on the wing and that you, the center, are looking for the entry pass. You must break contact with the defender to get open. You break contact with your defender as the ball leaves the fingertips of the passer. Use your elbows or butt to create space between you and your defender. With your body, create a wide base by spreading your legs and bending your knees. Because the entry pass is often a bounce pass, prepare to catch the ball as low as possible.

Moving without the ball

Perhaps the defender has chosen to front you — that is, to position himself between you and the ball rather than you and the basket — or, for some other reason, the player with the ball can't get it to you. *Do not become a statue.* When folks referred to Hakeem Olajuwon and Ralph Sampson as the Twin Towers, they never meant it literally. A post player should *never* remain in the same spot for more than three seconds. Move within the paint (the free throw lane).

Think of the free throw lane as a rectangle — after all, it is (unless you're playing outside the United States). You are positioned at one of the four corners. When something doesn't work, move to one of the other three corners. You can

- Slide to the other low post.
- Cross over to the opposite high post.
- Slide up to the high post (or down to the low post) on the same side.

Move, plant, wait a few seconds, and then move again. If you can, set a pick for a teammate when you move to a new spot — or if she can set one for you, even better. But stay in and around the paint. That's your turf as a center.

Most "big men" are never taught how to move without the ball. Too often, coaches just station a tall player in the low post and hope that he'll win a wrestling contest with his defender. Although the big man's movements without the ball are nothing more than simple cuts (usually never more than three steps per cut), coaches should school centers in making these cuts and not being lazy on offense.

John Wooden's eight things you can do on offense when you don't have the ball

John Wooden is the standard by which all college coaches are measured. Within a 12-year span (1964–75), his UCLA Bruins won ten NCAA championships. Here are eight tips from "The Wizard of Westwood" for what to do on offense when the ball is not in your hands:

1. Be ready to screen at the proper time if the play or the situation calls for it.
2. Set up your man to run him into a screen if the play or the situation calls for it.
3. Keep your defender so busy that he will not be in position to help out a teammate defensively.
4. Make your defensive man turn his eyes away from the ball at the proper time.
5. Constantly work to get open to provide an outlet pass for the player with the ball.
6. Constantly work to get open and to receive a pass where you will be a triple threat player with the ball. In other words, try to get the ball in position where you are a threat as a shooter, as a driver, or as a passer.
7. Be ready and in position to cover the proper territory as a rebounder or as a protector in case someone takes a shot.
8. Be thinking constantly, as your moves will probably be predicated on the moves of the player who has the ball or the player who just passed the ball.

Source: Jerry Krause, ed., *Coaching Basketball* (National Association of Basketball Coaches).

Moves for a Center

You've worked hard to have the ball passed to you; now what? Fortunately for centers, the first option is to shoot the ball. Hey, you're close to the bucket, so why not? The more shots you make, the more often your teammates will *feed* you (pass you the ball) in the future. This section outlines a few moves to help set you up to take shots.

A cardinal rule for big men with the ball: Do *not* dribble unless you absolutely, positively must. Your height is a disadvantage when you dribble. When you put the ball on the floor, you give smaller defenders an opportunity to steal it.

The drop step

When you receive the ball in the post, be sure to have both feet planted. This way, you can use either foot as your pivot foot. (***Note:*** If you're an NBA All-Star center, don't worry about this; the refs will never call traveling on you.) Remember, your back is to the basket.

Say that you're situated on the right side of the lane on the low block, and your left foot is near the baseline. With two hands, show the ball away and high from your shoulder, with your back to the basket and the defender. As you show the ball, drop step your left foot to hook your defender so that she can't get in defensive position to stop you. "Wait," you say. "If my foot is already planted, how can I drop it any farther?" Good question.

When I say "drop step," I mean move your left foot closer to the baseline and inward. Your right foot is your pivot foot; it stays planted. Your left foot can move. You're taking the step to your side and back, but because your back is already to the hoop, it's actually a step *to* the hoop. (See Figure 9-1.)

After you drop step, notice that you have effectively hooked the defender and are using your backside as a shield as you move toward the basket. Now swing your right foot around outside to the left and face the basket, hopefully close enough to execute a lay-up or dunk.

Establish position on the *low block* (the tiny square along the three-second lane close to the baseline, used for positioning rebounders on free throws) close enough to the basket so that you can shoot a lay-up after taking the drop step without having to dribble.

Figure 9-1: Executing the drop step: At left, hooking the defender, and at right, taking a step to the hoop.

Power move through the hoop

Sometimes you lose the battle of position and receive the entry pass farther from the hoop than you'd like. You can still drop step, but follow it with one power dribble. As you drop step, pull the ball with you — two hands on it — and then dribble. Use your inside shoulder to shield the ball from the defender.

Now you're closer to the basket. Actually, many post players like to put the ball on the floor to establish a rhythm as they go to the hole. Shawn Kemp of the Seattle SuperSonics, for example, is notorious for this. The danger is that you leave yourself open to pesky guards swiping at the ball from the outside.

Remember to finish up strong. You worked like a lion to get this shot so close to the hoop; don't become a lamb now. If you're able to dunk the ball, do so with two hands. If you can't, jump as high as possible — explode to the basket — and lay the ball off the glass at the top of your leap. No one takes it to the hole with more *oomph* than Shawn "Rain Man" Kemp. Emulate him.

The pull-up jumper

Suppose that the defender anticipates the drop step and is playing a step off you. In other words, he is not placing his body against yours but instead is playing a step closer to the basket than he normally would so that you cannot drive past him as easily. To keep the defender honest, burn him by squaring up right where you receive the pass and burying a quick jumper from 10 feet.

You catch the pass with your back to the basket, but I don't advise shooting it that way. You must turn and square the front of your torso to the hoop. But in which direction? If you make sure that your feet are planted when you catch the ball, you can use either foot as your pivot foot. Practice so that you're equally deft at pivoting off your left and right foot. If you are, the defender can't anticipate your move. Also practice faking the pivot one way and then going the other: Use your head to fake in one direction, and then go the opposite direction.

But I must warn you against too many fakes as a big man. Referees will be quick to whistle you for traveling, especially at levels below professional, and often they'll be right.

Most shooting fouls are called in the lane. As a post player, look to draw contact when you shoot. Don't be shy. If your defender makes sufficient contact, the referees will almost never call the foul on you. Be prepared to be fouled when you shoot the ball — and if you hear the whistle, *always* follow through on your shot. You may make the shot and earn a free throw for a three-point play.

No one is better at this than "Sir" Charles Barkley of the Houston Rockets. No matter where he is on the court when the whistle blows, he takes a shot. If he makes 1 shot out of 20, that's one more than if he didn't heave up that prayer.

The crossover move

Your back is to the basket and you've just received the entry pass. Using either pivot foot, turn 180 degrees so that you face the defender. If his hands are low, shoot the jumper immediately. If not, you can fake one direction and then go the other. I call this move a *crossover* because you start your pivot foot in one direction, but, once you make your move, it heads in the other.

For example, say you're on the right block and just turned to square up to (face) the defender. You decide to fake right and then go left (toward the center of the lane). To do so, step with your right foot to your right; the defender will react. As he does, take the next step with your *right* foot across the front of your body — dribble with your left hand to use your body as a shield against the defender — as you drive toward the middle of the lane.

The up-and-under move

For the up-and-under move, you *pump-fake* a shot — that is, you move your arms as if you're taking a shot but do not actually release the ball. This action brings the defender up into the air. You then drive around her — which is very embarrassing for the defender. Follow these steps:

1. **Catch the ball.**
2. **Pivot 180 degrees to face the defender.**
3. **Fake the ball upward with both hands — the quicker the fake, the more likely that she'll buy it.**
4. **The second the defender leaves her feet, drive past her.**

Hakeem Olajuwon's not-yet-patented-but-oughta-be "Dream Shake" move is the best up-and-under maneuver in the business.

Pass to the open player

If you catch the ball in the low post and find yourself double-teamed, do the math: One of your teammates is open. Pass the ball to that teammate. It's a great way to garner an assist — and make friends.

Note: Center Yinka Dare of the New Jersey Nets went his first two NBA seasons without earning one assist. Notice that people haven't put him on their All-Star ballots.

Moves for a Guard

Unlike a center, a guard usually already has the ball. Her forte is *beating her defender off the dribble* — that is, dribbling past her to drive to the basket for either a score or an assist.

Tips for going one-on-one:

- **Take the optimum spot: the top of the key.** From there, you can go either left or right. Great guards (and they are rare) are just as strong dribbling and shooting the lay-up with either hand. If you can go only to your right, starting from the top of the key loses its efficacy. The defender will cheat to that side.
- **Read the defender's hands.** If the defender's hands are low, pull up and shoot the jumper. Good guards practice the quick pull-up jumpshot from just inside the top of the key. The difference between a good shooting guard and a poor one: A good shooter jump-stops (both feet plant), gets her feet underneath her torso, and jumps straight upward, not forward. A poor shooting guard stops without curbing her momentum, forcing her to jump forward as opposed to straight upward. It's very difficult to have the proper balance to take a good shot this way.
- **Read the defender's quickness.** If you can drive by the defender, by all means do so. You can still pull up anytime and take the jumper, but if you can go all the way to the basket, you have an easier shot.

  Defenses do not surrender lay-ups to guards gladly. Expect some company — that is, a second defender — if you beat your man off the dribble. When this happens, be ready to dish a pass to your center underneath, who is now open when her defender comes over to stop you. Watch Kevin Johnson of the Phoenix Suns; he's a genius at the last-second dish.

The pick and roll

As a guard handling the ball through a pick and roll (see Chapter 6), you have three options:

- Pull up behind the pick, and shoot the jumper.
- Stutter your dribble. (To stutter your dribble, wait until the ball reaches its apex in the air off the dribble, and instead of bouncing it again, cradle it in your hand for the briefest of moments. It's really palming the ball, but Utah's John Stockton has been getting away with it for more than a decade.) Then drive past the pick either for a lay-up or to dish off when defensive help arrives.
- Pass to the screener. If the defender guarding the player who is screening for you leaves his man to cover you, pass the ball to your screener.

Setting screens for the shooting guard

A common way to set up a good shooting guard for an open shot is by sending her through a series of screens, first by a center and then by another guard.

The Indiana Pacers often free up Reggie Miller, their spindly three-point shooting ace, by sending him through three screens on one play. Miller sets up on a wing — say the left wing. The Pacers put two players (the coaches like to use 7'4" Rik Smits and 6'11" Dale Davis) in the low blocks, one on each side of the lane. On the opposite wing, another Pacer (say, forward Derrick McKey) is also ready to set a pick. Miller takes off from his wing position and runs along the baseline, through Smits's pick and then Davis's. If the defender is still with Miller, McKey moves down a step or two as Miller runs to the outside of McKey and then cuts up to receive the entry pass.

A Move for a Power Forward

For this move, called a screen for the screener, the power forward positions himself at the foul line. The center is on the low right block, facing the basket, and the shooting guard stands on the opposite low block (in this case, the left block).

The point guard takes the dribble entry to the left wing. The power forward moves down the right side of the lane to set a *downscreen* (where a player moves toward the basket to set a screen) for his center to come up. You may think that the center is going to shoot the jumper at the foul line, but instead, the shooting guard moves across the lane, from the left low block to the right, and screens for the power forward at the baseline. The screen set by the off guard is called a screen for the screener because the power forward sets the first screen. Now you can pass the ball to the power forward.

Moves for a Three-Point Shooter

The best three-point shots come when the defense is drawn to a penetrating player and the player standing out beyond the arc is temporarily forgotten. Here are two examples:

- **1993 NBA Finals, Phoenix Suns versus Chicago Bulls, Game 6:** The Suns led by two points and hoped to force a seventh game. Chicago had the ball with less than ten seconds remaining. The entire world figured that Michael Jordan or maybe Scottie Pippen would shoot. Jordan drove and then dished out to power forward Horace Grant along the baseline. The Phoenix defense, already having converged upon Jordan, rotated to stop Grant, who seamlessly spotted guard John Paxson just beyond the three-point circle near the top of the key. Swish! Game, series, championship!

- **1997 NCAA tournament, Providence versus Arizona, Southeast Regional final:** Late in the game, the Arizona Wildcats led by three. Providence stole the ball at half-court with about 15 seconds remaining. Had they been smart, Arizona would have focused on preventing a three-pointer. Instead, in the frenetic pace, Providence guard God Shammgod wisely drove the lane, drew three defenders to cover him, and then kicked the ball out to the corner (he didn't literally kick the ball; that's just what you say when you pass to a teammate who's open), where teammate Jamel Thomas stood just beyond the arc. Boom! Tie ballgame. Providence ended up losing in overtime, but Arizona never should have allowed that shot.

Other means of setting up a three-pointer include the following:

- **Screens:** The two most popular screens involve either
  - The center setting a pick by the top of the key for the dribbler
  - The wing man setting a pick on the wing for a player (like Reggie Miller coming up from the corner)

  The defense converges, and the player *skip passes* to the open player on the opposite wing. Why is it called a skip pass? Because getting the ball from one wing to the other normally requires two passes — the defense is between the two spots. So a skip pass earns its name because, if you execute it properly, you save yourself the extra pass — that is, you skip it.
- **Pass from the center:** A good passing center — like Patrick Ewing of the New York Knicks — sees the double team and spots the open player beyond the arc. Ewing's teammate John Starks owes his second and third vehicles to Ewing's ability to spot the open three-point shooter.

Last-Second Plays

You're sitting at home on the couch, feet up, potato chip bag within arm's reach. Ten seconds remain, and your favorite team has the ball and is down by a point. Okay, maybe your feet aren't up. Maybe you're leaning forward and gnawing your fingernails down to nubs.

At this moment, you probably don't envy your team's coach. You aren't bellyaching, "How can they pay a college coach that much money when a prof makes one-tenth of that?" If anything, you're glad that you don't have to think of what play to call. They couldn't pay you enough to take on that kind of pressure. You just hope that the coach can figure out a great play during the time-out.

Fact is, he drew up the play a long time ago. Coaches include last-second plays in their game plans for these very moments. This section describes some of my favorites.

Sideline out of bounds

The scene: Syracuse versus Georgia, 1996 NCAA tournament. Syracuse had the ball out of bounds on the side. Center John Wallace in-bounded near half-court on the right side of the basket. The Syracuse Orangemen had two players (call them 2 and 4) by the half-court line. These two players screened for each other: 4 ran away from Wallace to screen for 2, who ran toward Wallace. But Georgia was ready. The Bulldogs defenders switched the men they were guarding so as not to be beaten by the pick, and neither 2 nor 4 was open.

Player 1 was on the three-point arc on the right side, and Player 3 (Jesse Sapola) was on the foul line. Both players ran a diagonal screen. Sapola ran diagonally away from Wallace, fading toward the far corner, and his defender failed to follow him. Wallace threw a lob over the top; Sapola caught it and buried the jumper at the buzzer. The diagonal screen was a fantastic call by Jim Boeheim, and an even better execution by his players.

You have to practice these situations throughout the season because players have to be comfortable with their options in each situation. Having Sapola score was not the primary option on this last play. The primary option was to try to get the ball near the foul line for the jumpshot. But smartly, Wallace and Sapola read the defense, and Sapola saw that if he drifted away from the primary action, Wallace would be able to find him with the lob pass.

Length-of-the-court game-winning play

You have to be prepared for last-second plays, and preparation starts in preseason practice. At Notre Dame, we practiced our last-second play once a week, and we reviewed it at shoot-arounds just to refresh the players' minds. I doubt that any of the players really believed that we'd ever need this "emergency chute."

In 1989–90, I coached Notre Dame against Syracuse. In the final seconds of the game, Syracuse scored to take the lead. We called time-out. The last-second play we used was a play that we'd practiced during the fall. Our center, Keith Robinson, in-bounded the ball from the endline and threw it to half-court to LaPhonso Ellis, who had cut up from the foul line. Ellis threw the ball to Elmer Bennett at the top of the key, who hit the three-pointer that won the game. The key to the play's execution was having Keith and LaPhonso work on that in-bound pass in the preseason.

Digger's tips on last-second plays

In any season, at least a few games are going to be won or lost in the last ten seconds of the contest (this period is usually referred to as "last second"). In these tense moments, a team needs all the poise and maturity it can muster. One way to avoid epic — or so they will seem at the time — blunders is to be prepared. Remember these points:

- **Go to the basket.** It blows me away when a team, trailing by only one point, chooses to shoot an outside jumpshot in the final seconds. *Why?!?* The defensive team, leading by a point, has a tremendous fear of fouling. So take the ball inside. You get a closer shot, you have a chance of being fouled, and your chances of tipping in a missed shot are greater. If you take a jumper from the outside, on the other hand, the defense has an easier time boxing out your players and rebounding a missed shot.
- **Don't wait too long to shoot.** The score is tied, and you have the ball for the last shot. Most coaches advocate taking the shot with so little time remaining that, if the defense rebounds the ball, the defense won't have a chance to call time-out and take a shot.

But I disagree. Teams wait too long to start a possible game-winning play. Why wait until only seven seconds remain to begin your move to the basket? You should start with at least 11 ticks showing on the clock. Give yourself time for an offensive rebound or two. More important, give yourself enough time to take a good shot if the first option fails, which it often does in these situations. Too many teams force shots because the clock is running down.

To call time-out or not to call time-out: That is the question

Here's the scenario: You're down one with ten seconds left in the game, and your team just grabbed a defensive rebound. Do you take a time-out, or do you just let the players run the fast break and ad lib? If you call time-out, you can set up a play. But does the time-out help the defense more?

My gut reaction as a coach: Go to the hole. The offense knows where it's going, and the defense has to react. Basketball is a game of matchups, and a time-out before a last possession is to the defense's advantage. Plus, a coach can have her team play a matchup zone or some defense you haven't seen before, and your offense won't have an opportunity to react to it. With no time-out, the scene is too chaotic for your opponent to set up anything more than their most basic defense. You also run the risk of not getting the ball in bounds or committing a turnover.

In your last time-out in a close game, plan ahead. If you call time-out with 30 seconds or less remaining, set up what you will do on offense and defense if you need to pull out a last-second play.

Preparing for the Big Game

All conscientious coaches prepare to the best of their ability for each game. But every schedule includes games that loom just a little bit bigger than the rest. Whether it be your big rival, the number-one team in your conference or league, or the number-one team in the nation, those games require special preparation.

My Notre Dame players always knew which games were the big ones. As a coach, you don't want your players to look past lesser teams, but you do want them to be ready for the big games. At the college level, those contests determine your seed in the NCAA tournament, not to mention the morale of your squad.

Scout the opposition — and yourself

I usually watched three videotapes of the upcoming opponent and then met with my assistants to develop a game plan.

Sure, you need to know your enemy. But you also need to take an honest look at your own team. Doing that is just as important, if not more so, as preparing to face a particular opponent.

Notre Dame's last play against Virginia in 1981

If Notre Dame had waited until the last second or two to put up a shot against Virginia in 1981, we never would have won. We had the ball out of bounds under our own hoop, down one to a 26-0 team led by Ralph Sampson. Our defense had forced a turnover with ten seconds left, and we diagrammed a play for Kelly Tripucka, our top scorer, to take the last shot.

Tripucka was *stripped* on his shot attempt — that is to say, the defender knocked the ball out of Kelly's hands. Tracy Jackson picked up the ball and took a shot that was blocked into the corner, where Orlando Woolridge picked it up. Woolridge calmly lofted a 17-foot jumper to win the game. Had we stalled so that Kelly's shot was taken with, say, two seconds on the clock, we would have lost.

The point is, if the game is tied, it's wise to wait until the last two or three seconds to shoot the ball. That way, if you miss and the other team rebounds, they have no time to take a shot. However, if you're losing by one or two points, *do not* wait until those precious last few seconds to shoot. You want to give yourself the opportunity to grab an offensive rebound and take one more shot.

Before a big game during a Notre Dame season, we would pay an outside service to scout our team and identify the areas in which we needed work. On my own, I liked to review our last two or three losses (which hopefully required more long-term than short-term memory skills) and see what needed fixing. If we weren't getting the ball into the post, for example, I tried to figure out why.

Challenge the opposing team's star

A big game means a tough opponent, who probably has at least one outstanding player. That's why the team is a good team. In many ways, that's how they got to be a good team.

Look at the mindset of the opposing team, opposing coach, and opposing star; then decide whether you can challenge that star player. Doing so has its benefits: First, it tells your players that you have confidence that they can stop the star. Second, it often forces your opponent to find alternative options on offense, which can spell trouble at any level of play.

For example, in 1978, my Notre Dame squad beat Marquette because we placed our 6'7" forward, Bill Hanzlik, against Butch Lee, Marquette's All-America guard. Hanzlik was not naturally suited to defending a point guard, but he was the best defender we had. Plus, with his long arms and rangy style, he gave Lee fits. Hanzlik shut down Lee (who went 3-15 in field goal shooting), and Lee's Marquette teammates were unable to pick up the slack.

Figure out which matchups are in your favor

After you review the key matchups by player position, determine what areas you can exploit in the opponent's defense. In 1986–87, for example, when Notre Dame beat North Carolina, David Rivers was the key. The North Carolina guards weren't quick enough to stay with Rivers, so our players isolated him at the top of the key. David was able to penetrate and dish to Gary Voce, our center, who had the game of his life that afternoon.

Look at the history of the rivalry

Talking about revenge seems to be taboo in athletics today — at least publicly. Inside a locker room, however. . . . Well, coaches are a little less politically correct. Revenge is a great motivator.

Sometimes, the best thing a coach can say to players is nothing. In the 1987 game against North Carolina in South Bend, for example, I knew that junior David Rivers was ready. Two years earlier, as a frosh playing in his first NCAA tournament contest, Rivers had been stripped of the ball by North Carolina's Kenny Smith, who drove in for the winning bucket. Final score: 60-58.

I knew that I would not need to motivate Rivers for this game. Instead, I let his teammates feed off their leader's energy. Rivers indeed got his payback, and we even won by the same 60-58 score.

Of course, the thing about revenge is that after you exact it, you become a target once again. Six weeks later, Carolina beat us in the NCAA tournament to end our season.

Special drills for what they do best

Coaches sometimes incorporate special drills to prepare for particular players on the opposing team when preparing for a big game. For example:

- **Shoot over a broom:** Use this drill when a player on your opponent's team is extremely tall. For Virginia and 7'4" Ralph Sampson, we had a student manager hold a broom in the air and try to swat away shots. The idea was to acclimate our players to having to arch their shots a little higher. (Of course, if we'd had a 7'4" student manager, the broom would not have been necessary.)
- **Practice against six players:** When you're getting ready to play a quick-pressing team, have your five offensive players practice against six defenders. Clemson did this in 1997 while preparing to face Kentucky in their season opener. Rick Pitino's team had the best full-court press in the country. His Clemson counterpart, Rick Barnes, mindful of all the "It felt as if the Wildcats had six defenders on the court" quotes from previously vanquished foes, decided to prepare his team for such a feeling. Clemson won the game in overtime.

Preparing your team mentally

There are many stories about the intangible aspects of mental preparation. One of the best psychological ploys that I used at Notre Dame took place in 1974 when we practiced cutting down the nets the day *before* the UCLA game.

After a big win, such as a tournament championship, it's customary to cut down the nets: Players take two snips and keep a strand for themselves. I wanted our guys to look as if they knew what they were doing when the moment came the following day. Because I was less afraid of them being cocky than of them being timid, I felt that I had to do something to let them know that their coach truly believed that they could snap college basketball's longest winning streak ever. They may have believed that I was nuts, too, but I didn't care.

Years later, Gary Brokaw, who scored a game-high 25 points in the win, told me that cutting down the nets made the difference in our mental preparation for that game.

Note: If you're a high school or junior high coach, make sure that your school has another set of nets before attempting this ploy!

Lean on your support groups

Students are the base of any college or high school support group, and I never forgot that. When we beat San Francisco in 1977, for example, the Notre Dame students were the key. The Dons entered the contest 29-0 and ranked number one in the nation. On the eve of the game, we staged a pep rally (I love pep rallies), and I told the students to arrive half an hour before the game and start chanting "29 and 1." We told them that San Francisco was going to leave Notre Dame with an L.

This strategy seems brash now, but it created an atmosphere. The place was packed half an hour before warm-ups, and I have to think that the USF players were somewhat intimidated.

Notre Dame won that game 93-82. For the first and still only time in history, NBC named our student body Player of the Game — that's how impressive the students were that day.

Part III
The Fanfare of Basketball

"JUST HOW MUCH DO YOU THINK YOU CAN EMBARRASS ME? IF YOU THINK I'M GOING TO THE BASKETBALL GAME WITH YOU WEARING THOSE RIDICULOUS SOCKS, YOU'RE SADLY MISTAKEN!"

In this part . . .

You can be a fan without necessarily being a player. This part delves into the world of organized basketball. Find out about all the ways that you can enjoy the game — from playing pickup ball to following the Dream Team in the next Olympics.

This part is also your ticket to understanding the NCAA tournament. I tell you what March Madness is all about and give you tips for filling out that all-important NCAA tournament bracket.

Chapter 10

You Don't Need to Play to Be a Fan

In This Chapter

- Watching a game
- Listening to a game
- Following your team on the Internet

Behind the statement, "That Jordan dude is a decent shot," the title of this chapter may be the all-time understatement in roundball. No sport, not even football, is as widely and enthusiastically embraced by television as basketball. ESPN, ESPN2, TNT, TBS, NBC, ABC, and CBS all televise the game at either the college or pro level; CBS even televises a high school basketball all-star game. And I haven't even broached the topic of Direct TV.

A typical season runs from early November to — thanks to the creation of two new women's leagues, the ABL and the WNBA — the end of August. In that time frame, a typical viewer has access to more than 1,000 men's and women's games if she has Direct TV. Watching all 1,000 games would be impossible. (Then again, there is the miracle of videotaping.) But for some folks, 1,000 games is a fervent goal.

For the last four years, I've been a basketball studio analyst at ESPN. This job has rekindled my fandom for hoops. Also, because I'm paid not only to sit there and look spiffy but also to discuss what I see, I have honed my skills as a couch-potato connoisseur of the game. You can do it, too — as long as you promise not to take my job.

Following a Game on TV

You'll get a lot more out of watching a basketball game on TV — or even live — if you do more than watch the ball go into the hoop. This section gives some insider tips for catching the *real* action and increasing your enjoyment of the sport exponentially.

Anticipate the next pass

Try to think like the players. When you can anticipate the next pass, you are as near to the players as you can be from your living room. You're thinking like the players.

Where the player passes the ball depends on a few factors: what type of ball handler he is, which teammates are on the floor, what type of offense the team is running, and what type of defense the opposition is running. See, you have to know what's happening on the court.

Against a zone defense, for example, you cut (that is, move without the ball), but don't screen (or set picks). In man-to-man, you cut *and* screen. Watch for cutting and screening, and you can see what type of defense and offense are being played.

Pretend that you're the point guard. Analyze the defense and then make decisions about how you would react. Did the point guard on television act accordingly? Disregard this tip if you're watching old highlights of Magic Johnson. Nobody could predict what he was going to do with the ball.

Watch the action away from the ball

Don't be afraid to stray away from watching the ball. Watch the action away from the ball on the weak side (the side opposite the ball), or watch the post action. Of course, the television camera's eye is yours, and it usually follows the ball; but most views are taken from the side and give a decent half-court view of the proceedings.

Examples of what to look for: pushing and shoving underneath the hoop, weakside screens (which are picks that take place on the side of the court away from the ball), Pat Riley's Armani suit. All are entertaining sideshows to the main event.

By watching action away from the ball, you can answer your own questions as well as other viewers' questions. For example, if All-American Ron Mercer, who played for Kentucky and is now with the Celtics, is such a terrific shooter, why doesn't the defense do a better job of denying him the ball? Answer: Watch Mercer during an offensive possession. As a sophomore at the University of Kentucky (in 1996–97), nobody in the country was better than he was at using picks set by teammates to get an open shot. You can argue that Mercer earns his buckets not so much when he shoots the ball but when he leaves his defender behind a pick.

The inveterate hoops fan is one whose Last Channel button on the remote is used only if both ESPN and CBS are broadcasting college hoops simultaneously on a Saturday afternoon. This kind of fan can spot the alley-oop play before the pass is ever thrown. She follows the weakside and notices the backpick (a weakside pick that frees a player who's cutting toward the basket) being set upon the alley-ooper's defender.

During the 1997 Final Four, North Carolina's Vince Carter sprang for at least three first-half alley-oop dunks against Arizona. The hoops junkie was already yelling "Lob!" or "Alley-oop!" before Carter ever left his feet. She saw the screen being set up on the weakside.

Avoid Jordan vision

Watch the other players on the court besides the star. Michael Jordan is fun to watch, but don't keep your eyes on his #23 all the time. Many great players are in this game, and you may miss something. Focus on one player for five or six straight trips down the court, and you'll find out a lot about him. Does he hustle back on defense? Does he "take a series off" (that is, fail to hustle on a trip down the court) on defense once in a while?

Get Jordan vision

Whether it's Michael Jordan or the star of your local high school team, watch his every move in crunch time. Jordan scored 20 points in the fourth quarter alone during a 1997 playoff loss to the Miami Heat. Who was going to shoot the ball was not a secret. But how did he create open shots for himself?

Sometimes the star is not the team's best player, but the girl with the hot hand that evening. Keep an eye on her. Then during the next game, when she reverts to the form of a mere mortal, try to ascertain whether she's doing anything differently.

Follow stats

You can keep stats yourself, or you can rely on the television statisticians to follow more than the score. Some of the less discussed but fun stats to watch are offensive rebounding, points off turnovers, points in the paint, and bench scoring.

If you look at the 1997 national semifinal game between Arizona and North Carolina, you see that North Carolina won the rebound battle 52-48, and the offensive boards 22-17. Sounds like the Tar Heels have the edge in that aspect of the game. However, Arizona won the second-chance points — in other words, scoring off offensive rebounds — 15-11. So even though North Carolina had more offensive rebounds, Arizona had more points off offensive rebounds. So Arizona really had the advantage in that area.

Continuing with that game, North Carolina shot 31.1 percent from the field (meaning that 31.1 percent of their shots went through the hoop) and Arizona, 33.3. But take a look at three-point shooting: Arizona made 11-29 shots for 38 percent, and North Carolina made just 4-21 for 19 percent. So while the overall shooting was fairly even, three-point shooting showed a wide disparity and was the reason for Arizona's eight-point win.

Watch the officials

Officials can dictate the pace of the game. If they're whistle-happy, they can slow the pace. Neither team can find a rhythm when the officials are calling a foul on every possession. If an official makes a *grandstand call* (a call that draws attention to the official) by running into another official's area to make a call, this is a bad sign. If an official overrules another official, this may mean that the first official thinks he is bigger than the game. A good official does not take the game out of the players' hands; he controls the game without being noticed.

Officials can also take a team out of its offense or defense by calling a game too tight (whistles too many fouls) or too loose (seldom blows the whistle). Some teams play more physically than others.

If I were a coach saying this right after a game, I'd be fined; but an official may have a bias — conscious or subconscious — concerning who is supposed to win the game. An underdog fights this problem, especially on the road. In a close call, many times, the call favors the team that the official believes is supposed to be the better team. In the NBA, this call is known as *star treatment* or, more recently, *Jordan rules.* Finding an official who will call a sixth foul on Michael Jordan in the United Center is as easy as shaving with a spoon.

The best officials are the ones you don't know or don't remember. When an official does the extra little things on a call, a little extra body English, he draws too much attention to himself. That's bad. Conversely, officials must keep a game from getting out of hand. They can do so by communicating to the players and then, if need be, calling a technical foul or two.

What I Watch For

Having coached for as many years as I did, I may watch a basketball game differently than you do. For example, I still have to remind myself that no matter how much I scream at the TV, the refs can't eject me. That's a nice change. Here's what I look for:

Check out the defense of both teams. Whenever Bill Raftery of ESPN (or CBS, or the Sports Channel; the guy must sleep at the Continental Airlines Arena in New Jersey) broadcasts a game, he establishes the first defensive set from the opening tip. In his staccato voice, Raftery says something like, "Duke opens man-to-man."

As you sit there, ask yourself, "Are they playing man-to-man? Matchup zone? 2-3 zone?" The defense acts as a harbinger for what type of game it will be. If one team has a great one-on-one player and the opposition is playing man-to-man, you're in for a show. It also means the team playing man to-man defense against the team with the star is not afraid of that star player. Perhaps the team has a defensive stopper to contend with the great offensive player.

Who is controlling the offensive rebounding? The team that controls the boards (rebounds) usually controls the game. Keep an eye on which specific players are grabbing the boards, too. Look for tendencies. Are the guards getting the offensive rebounds? If so, that team is taking quite a few outside shots, because long shots have long rebounds.

Pay attention to tempo. The Minnesota Timberwolves grab a defensive rebound. Are the Timberwolves running, or are the players slowing down? The Timberwolves have young, quick Kevin Garnett and Stephon Marbury; the players better be hoofing it. But what if they aren't? Maybe the coach feels good about the Timberwolves' half-court matchups. Maybe Garnett is nursing a sore ankle. Maybe Minnesota is playing a team that's even better in transition. At this level of hoops — that is, games that are televised — coaches do not develop strategies on a whim.

Watch what happens after a time-out. Has the coach changed defenses or a specific man-to-man assignment? Is the offense running a set play for one particular player?

One sign of a good coach is that his team scores on its first possession after a time-out. The coach can see a flaw in the opponent's defense and can take advantage of the flaw with a special play that leads to a matchup and a score.

Are a lot of turnovers occurring early in a game? Is either team capitalizing on those turnovers? Those turnovers are in effect extra possessions. Forcing a turnover is one thing, but scoring off them is another. You have to score off turnovers to make them worthwhile.

Who's paying for the free throw shooting? Free throw shooting is usually contagious. If you shoot free throws well early in the game, you may gain confidence late in the game at crunch time. In the opposite direction, missed free throws earlier in the game (like so many variables in a basketball game) often foreshadow what will transpire at the end.

How is an injury influencing the game? Whether suffered prior to the game or during the contest, an injury to a key player can dramatically alter his team's style of play. The classic example is Game 6 of the 1980 NBA Finals, when Los Angeles Laker center Kareem Abdul-Jabbar had to sit out. Laker point guard Magic Johnson, a rookie, filled in for "the big fella" at center.

The entire offensive look of LA was altered, oddly enough, to its benefit. Magic, who played in the post, still dribbled a lot — and scored 42 points to lead the Lakers to the title and emblazon his name as a legend.

What halftime adjustments were made? The first five minutes of the second half often dictate the rest of the game. During that time frame, each coach wants to make adjustments to take control of the game or get back in the game — whatever the case may be. For example, if you are ahead by ten at the half, you want to withstand the first five minutes of the second half because the opposing coach is going to try out her adjustments. If you are behind by ten, you want to insert all your halftime adjustments in the first five minutes of the second half. You want to make the adjustments work early so that you can build your team's confidence.

Notice bench points and substitution patterns. A team that substitutes often tells the viewer one of the following:

- Our bench is deep.
- Our starters are not that much better than the bench.
- We plan on running a lot and hope to fatigue our opponent.

Observe what's happening and then deduce *why* it's happening, and soon you'll be the guru of your sports bar (if you should aspire to such lofty heights).

Bench points, like offensive rebounding, are not how you keep score in hoops, but they usually dictate who wins. When I had a good bench, I always felt that the job of my subbed players was to increase the lead (assuming we had it) by five to seven points. In 1977–78, the year Notre Dame went to the Final Four, our bench had three future NBA players: Bill Hanzlik, Bill Laimbeer, and Tracy Jackson. I knew that those three subs were going to be better than my opponent's subs. So I set goals for those subs to increase the lead when they were in the game for their four-minute interval. I charted the points like a plus-minus statistic in hockey. (See *Hockey For Dummies,* also published by IDG Books Worldwide, Inc.)

In a *plus-minus statistic,* you simply keep track of the score when certain players are in the game. For example, Jackson would have a +6 figure if our lead increased by six points for the period of time he was in the game. You can chart this statistic for each player.

Who went on a scoring run and why? A *run* occurs when one team outscores the other by a large margin in a certain period, such as a 12-2 run in the first four minutes of the second half. A run normally is the by-product of good defense by one team and turnovers by the other. Runs seem to be more dramatic and occur with greater frequency in the NCAA, perhaps because one team gets too tight and begins to worry about the run being made against it, which only exacerbates the situation. The same thing often happens with football in the Super Bowl.

Who will be tired down the stretch? Because of the plethora of TV and game time-outs (in the NCAA tournament games, each media time-out lasts $2^1/_2$ minutes) combined with players being better conditioned, player fatigue is not as large a factor at the end of a game as it once was. The best way to spot player fatigue is to watch for players grabbing their shorts on free throws.

Case in point: Tim Duncan was the best player in the nation in college basketball during the 1996–97 season, but time and again, he struggled from the foul line in the last few minutes of a game. Fatigue? Probably. He played more minutes than anyone at Wake Forest that year.

Who has the stars for the stretch run? Most coaches want to have the ball in the hands of their best players at the end of the game. Who are the clutch shooters? They aren't always the top players. If you know who those clutch players are, you can see some great matchups on game-winning situations. Half the fun of watching a close game is figuring out what a team will do with its last possession. The other half is seeing your team win.

Watch for the key matchups. Watching for the key matchups is probably more important in the pro game because those teams have to play man-to-man defense, or at least some derivation of it.

Whenever the Chicago Bulls meet the New York Knicks in the playoffs, for example, fans greatly anticipate Michael Jordan being matched up against John Starks. Watching this matchup is like watching a fistfight between two men with the Battle of Gettysburg raging behind them. Sometimes the matchup heavily impacts the outcome of the game.

What is the field goal percentage differential? It's halftime and the stats flash on your TV screen. Say that Villanova is shooting 16 percent better from the field than its opponent, Seton Hall, but Villanova has only a two-point lead. What does that tell you as a viewer?

Answer: Villanova is in trouble. Shooting usually evens out during the course of a game due to a coach's halftime adjustments. But Seton Hall is probably rebounding better or scoring more points off turnovers. The general rule: A team should have a lead equal to its field goal percentage differential. In other words, Villanova should be up 16 points, not 2.

Televising basketball

Believe it or not, in 1972, college basketball was only televised regionally. As for the NBA, you need only to travel back in time to 1981 to find an NBA championship game between the Boston Celtics and Houston Rockets that was not televised live. (CBS aired the game on tape delay after the local news.)

The NBA had a national television contract as far back as the 1960s, but most of those games were joined in progress because the stations left only a two-hour window on Sunday afternoon. The average NBA game lasted 2 hours and 10 minutes, so tipoff would be at 1:50 p.m. Eastern time. Ten minutes later, ABC would come on the air with the score something like 10-8.

TVS's Eddie Einhorn is responsible for the two crucial national broadcasts in college basketball history. In 1968, Houston upset UCLA in the first made-for-TV regular-season contest at the Astrodome, 71-69. Einhorn's TVS syndicated the game nationally, and the results proved to the networks that college hoops was a viable product. Televising college hoops may not seem revolutionary now, but consider that, at the time, even the NCAA semi-finals were not televised. When Houston and UCLA met in a Final Four semifinal for a rematch later that season, few people got to see the game. Six years later, the TVS cameras were in South Bend for Notre Dame's regular-season victory that ended UCLA's 88-game win streak.

Two years later (in 1975–76), NBC purchased rights to a national college basketball package on a weekly basis. Notre Dame, I'm proud to say, was the most televised team in that package.

Following a Game on the Radio

Sometimes radio is the only way to follow your team, especially when your team is playing on the road. Listening can be even more captivating than watching on TV, because your imagination replaces your eyes. And there's more suspense, too, because sound spreads the news with such alarming speed. A roar from the crowd, as well as an able announcer's inflection and trademark phrase, tells you whether the shot went in.

Good play-by-play announcers are descriptive and tell you what's happening; good analysts tell you why. The play-by-play person is information; the analyst is theory. The play-by-play person tells you how a player floats in for the dunk; the analyst tells you how the player got open for the dunk.

While a lot of people keep stats when watching a game on television, keeping stats is more appropriate when listening to a game on the radio. Your eyes are free to look down at the paper without missing anything, and you can become more involved with what's happening. You just can't see Dennis Rodman's tattoos.

Following Your Team on the Internet (a.k.a. "Cyberspace Jam")

The Internet is a great source of information about particular teams and even the sport itself. (See Appendix B for a list of hot online resources.) You can follow your team on the Internet in three ways:

- **Listen to Internet broadcasts.** Most college and pro teams broadcast their games on the Internet. So if you're a Minnesota Timberwolves fan and you're out of town, you can bring your computer and listen to the game over your laptop. To locate the Internet site, call the team's public relations (PR) department.

  Listening via the Internet is a perfect solution for the fan who doesn't want to pay a hefty sum to listen to the game over the phone and wants a more detailed and visual account of the game.

- **Look at in-game Internet reports.** More and more teams are becoming sophisticated with their Internet sites, including the use of photos. Some organizations have one person at their press table transcribe the play-by-play over the Internet, while other people shoot photos of the game and transmit them to the site. Duke University was one of the first schools to use photos over the Internet.

- **Download Internet releases.** Nearly every college and pro team — as well as the NBA and some college conferences — has an Internet site. Expect to find such items as team rosters, statistics, bios of top players, and coaches' notes available for the downloading. Teams usually update these facts on a game-by-game basis. So if you want to know who's starting, who's healthy, or who's leading the squad in steals to minutes played, head to cyberspace for the most up-to-date system. A few NBA teams even arrange an online session with one of their players on a weekly basis.

  More and more of the college teams (about 20 so far, including the Big East Conference) are contracting with University NetCasting of Carlsbad, California. University NetCasting establishes sites that provide information about all the sports for a particular school, putting the school's entire media information guide on the Internet. Thus the school's site is a source for historical information as well as up-to-date releases.

Listening via TRZ Sportsline

If you don't have a home computer or are out of town and still want to listen to your favorite team's games, check out TRZ Sportsline. This service out of Cleveland, Ohio, allows you to listen to games over the phone.

Over the last several years, TRZ has established a system whereby you can call a number (with credit card in hand), punch in a code, and listen to the broadcast of your team's game over the phone. A complete college game costs about $40; you'll pay about $48 for a pro game. To reach TRZ Sportsline, dial 800-846-4700.

Many alumni clubs of major colleges establish listening parties at households and split the cost. Just make the call with a phone that has a speaker unit so that everyone can hear the game.

Subscribing to Magazines and Other Publications

Every hoops junkie needs to read about the sport in addition to watching games on TV — what else are you going to do when no game is on? Here are my top publications for following hoops:

- ***USA Today:*** "The Nation's Newspaper" provides daily updates of scores and stats, along with features and commentaries.
- ***Sports Illustrated:*** A feature-oriented publication that provides insight into players, coaches, and teams. People read it for the features and in-depth reporting on issues bigger than simply the games.
- ***The Sporting News:*** Also has features, but it's more statistics-oriented than *Sports Illustrated.* More of a baseball publication in the off-season, but covers hoops from December through the NBA playoffs.
- **In-house publications:** Most teams, college and pro, produce a weekly publication during the season devoted to that team. For example, Kentucky has *CatsPaws,* which covers Kentucky athletics from cover to cover. The reporting in these publications is biased because most of them are owned by the school or franchise, but they're a good way to keep up with your team.
- ***Basketball Times:*** A weekly national publication during the season, and monthly in the off-season. Has the largest compilation of basketball-oriented columns in the country. This publication, produced by longtime basketball writer Larry Donald, is one of the best for keeping up with hot hoops topics.
- ***Basketball Weekly:*** A national weekly publication that provides the best mix of columns and statistics. Not as many columnists as *Basketball Times,* but *Basketball Weekly* provides you with conference standings, and — most important to the college basketball junkie — the game-by-game results of the top 200 college teams. This section is pivotal when following the national scene or when trying to fill out your NCAA tournament bracket (see Chapter 16).

- ***Blue Ribbon Basketball Yearbook:*** The most complete of the preseason college basketball yearbooks. A truly impressive and exhaustive effort year in and year out that will, if you really love college hoops, be dog-eared by mid-January. *Blue Ribbon* gives a neat one-page summary on every team, complete with roster, schedule, and outlook. This publication comes out late (usually December 1), so it won't whet your appetite in the preseason, but it can serve as an in-season bible.
- ***Street & Smith's:*** The longest-running preseason publication puts out issues for both college and pro hoops. It covers all the top teams and selections of All-America teams in high school, college, and pro and prints all the schedules for men's college basketball. You'll find an ever-improving women's basketball section about All-America players, and a section that rates a preseason top 20.
- ***Basketball Almanac, Publications International Ltd.:*** A yearly publication that's handy for the basketball fanatic. This publication provides a full-page bio with complete career stats on every veteran NBA player, a bio on the top NBA rookies, a two-page feature on each team, and the NBA schedule. For the college game, it offers a one-page outlook on the top 64 teams and a page summary of the top 100 players. It's also the only publication I've found with a short bio on everyone in the Basketball Hall of Fame.

And here are five basketball books that belong on your shelf:

- ***Heaven Is a Playground* (by Rick Telander):** This former *Sports Illustrated* senior writer spent a summer on the asphalt courts of New York City playing hoops, and introduces us to a nation within itself.
- ***Loose Balls* (by Terry Pluto):** The funniest book on the game ever written, *Loose Balls* is the story of the defunct American Basketball Association. This is the league that gave luminaries from Julius Erving to Bob Costas to *USA Today* TV columnist Rudy Martzke a start.
- ***Life on the Run* (by Bill Bradley):** An honest and thoughtful account of life in the NBA from the vantage point of one of the NBA's most literate veterans.
- ***A Season on the Brink* (by John Feinstein):** The author had complete access to Bob Knight and his Indiana University program for an entire season. The General will never make that mistake again. Interesting note: The Hoosiers lost in the first round of the NCAA tournament with Feinstein hanging around, but the following year they won it all.
- ***Basketball: Its Origins and Development* (by James Naismith):** The man who wrote the book on the game wrote a book on the game. A difficult book to find, but well worth seeking.

Watching Your Child Play

Although you may not be in shape to play, or you may not be a fan of a particular school or pro team, you can certainly be your own child's fan. This duty comes with being a good parent.

All politicians talk about creating good family values. What could be more basic than attending one of your child's games, or better yet, taking her to a local court to play the game with her yourself?

Don't relive your youthful dreams through your kids. Let them decide that they like the game, let them play for fun, and give them nothing but encouragement. Sure, that includes giving them some hints from mistakes you may have made when you played, but always remember that it's just a game.

Participating in Fantasy Leagues

You want to own your own basketball team, but you don't have millions of dollars to spend? No problem! These days, it's easy to be the owner and general manager of your own basketball franchise. Welcome to the world of fantasy basketball.

More and more fans are enjoying basketball by participating in fantasy (or *rotisserie*) leagues. These imaginary leagues are popping up all over the United States. Some have money or other prizes at stake, and others are simply a competition for pride.

Participating in a fantasy league can be an enjoyable way to watch basketball and to get more out of it. The competition can be both fun and challenging — and in some cases, profitable.

Setting up a fantasy league

To form a league, you can gather friends in your community, at the office, or in your college dorm. (They don't even have to be friends.) The size of the league can vary, but if you're putting together an NBA fantasy league, you don't want too large a league because there are only 29 teams from which you can choose players.

Many fantasy league teams resemble all-star teams. A good, challenging league forces its participants to do their homework and make intelligent picks — that is, you probably won't end up with Michael Jordan, Karl Malone, John Stockton, and Shaquille O'Neal on the same team.

There are a few ways to put together the team rosters. One way is *open bidding* (which is an auction of players), which usually involves a salary cap. For example, each participant may have a maximum of $200 to spend on a roster of 12 players. Of those 12 players, only ten are active in the competition at one time, with four forwards, four guards, and two centers. Again, this is just a simple example, and different leagues utilize different ideas.

Another way to put together a roster is to hold a *draft*. The league commissioner determines a draft order (by drawing numbers from a hat, for example), and then participants choose players in order for the first round. Usually, you flip-flop the draft order for the subsequent rounds. (There are usually 12 rounds total.)

You can also make up your own league rules in terms of transactions. Some leagues charge per move; others allow trades and roster changes free of charge. The more complex the league, the more likely you'll need a secretary or statistical service to handle the standings and moves.

Putting together your fantasy team

Prior to bidding or drafting, it's important to know the rules that clearly affect your strategy. For example, say that ten teams are competing, and that seven categories are being used to keep score — total points, total rebounds, field goal percentage, free throw percentage, assists, three-point field goal percentage, and steals. You want to pick players who are strong in those categories.

A league can use many different categories, including percentages and ratios. The scoring in this example would go from ten points for the leader in each category down to one point for the last-place team in the category. Then the total points from the seven categories would be added up to determine the standings.

It's important to try to get good players and good balance on your team. You don't want players who are good in one category but struggle in others. For example, a player like Dennis Rodman can help you in rebounding, but he'll hurt you in scoring. Some of the more valuable players are those who score in double figures and excel in other areas as well. It doesn't hurt to have a Michael Jordan, though sometimes people bid so much on stars that they get hurt with less money available in later rounds.

You also need to think about the player-allotment process when choosing your team. A straight draft involves some strategy. Bidding involves a *lot* of strategy — you may want to call out a big-name star to get high bidding. Saving money for the latter rounds could lead to bargains. A lot depends on the savvy of your competitors.

In preparing for the draft, stay on top of injuries and off-season transactions. A player who's traded may not have as great an impact on his new team. Also keep an eye on the top rookies and newcomers, as they can have value in the right situation. Keep track of players *during* the season as well, as potential trades in your league could affect the standings.

A number of good sources for basketball information are available, both prior to the draft and during the season. Preseason basketball magazines are usually available on the newsstands. ESPN SportsZone on the Internet, as well as www.nba.com, have updated information. Publications such as *The Sporting News* and *Basketball Times* can be helpful, too.

Announcer slang

Were I to attempt to review *all* the play-by-play and color announcers, I'd undoubtedly inadvertently omit someone worthy of mention, offend him, and lose my spot at a few celebrity golf tournaments. So I offer some of my favorite terms used by announcers today and from yesteryear. Collect 'em! Trade 'em!

- **"Stat Sheet Stuffer" (Clark Kellogg):** This term describes a player who has high figures in a number of areas. It is often used for a player who records a triple double.
- **"Diaper Dandy" (Dick Vitale):** My partner Dickie V. is the reigning king of hoops phraseology. "Diaper Dandy" has had as long a shelf-life as any of his creations. It refers to an outstanding freshman player.
- **"PTPer" (Vitale):** A "Prime-Time Player" is someone who comes through in the clutch. The ultimate PTPer in the NCAA tournament in 1997 was Arizona swingman Miles Simon, who seemed to make every big basket of the tournament.
- **"The Kiss" (Bill Raftery):** Bill Raftery, known as the "Governor" in broadcasting circles, has a slew of pet terms. "The Kiss" is his trademark; it occurs when a player banks in a shot — that is, "kisses" it off the glass. The genial Governor goes to this term so often that he even invented a euphemism for his euphemism, referring to "The Kiss" as "The Smooch."
- **"Yesssss! And it counts!" (Marv Albert):** Marv's signature phrase refers to an offensive player who scores and is fouled on the play. The shooter gets the basket and goes to the foul line to complete the three-point play.
- **"Popcorn Machine" (Chick Hearn):** Hearn has been broadcasting Laker games since 1961. In the '60s, he referred to Jerry West as putting the ball in the Popcorn Machine — a great visual. This means that West's jumper is falling through the hoop as easily as popcorn falls into the basin of a popcorn machine.
- **"In again, out again Finnegan" (Les Kiter):** One of the top college basketball broadcasters for the TVS network in the late 1960s was Les Kiter. Kiter had many unusual phrases, but this is one of my favorites. He used it to describe a shot that rattled around the rim a couple times and then fell out; it was in and out.

Chapter 11

Pickup Basketball

In This Chapter

- Playing by the rules
- Understanding the terms and customs
- Picking out the best pickup game facilities
- Playing shooting and pickup games

e got next!”

If you watched the NBA playoffs in 1997, that phrase — also the slogan for the fledgling Women's NBA (WNBA) — is permanently embedded in your memory. In the culture of pickup hoops, players use “We got next!” to let everyone know that their team has dibs on the following game.

Using “We got next!” was a clever move by the league during its period of incubation. Using a term that's familiar to pickup hoopsters nationwide, the WNBA got across its point that, as soon as the rest of the NBA completed its in-vain quest of denying Michael Jordan and the Chicago Bulls yet another championship, the women would be taking the court — almost as if the WNBA was letting the boys know that it was no charlatan. To borrow another pickup hoops phrase, the women were saying, “We got game.”

Pickup basketball — the term refers to games that are seemingly spontaneously generated anywhere a basketball hoop exists — may be the best example of the game's robust health. Unorganized and unscheduled, pickup games not only pop up everywhere, but their partisans adhere to a uniform code of rules, lingo, and even fashion (adroitly captured in the movie *White Men Can't Jump*).

No national governing body of pickup basketball exists, thank goodness. But you can visit any playground, gym, or driveway in the United States and say, “We got next!” or call “Winners!” (the team that wins retains possession of the ball) and be understood. That's the beauty of it: A society of hoops was born through the sheer passion that folks possess for the game.

The Traits of Pickup Basketball

Considering how loosely defined the society of pickup hoopsters is, the rules and characteristics of pickup games are surprisingly uniform (no pun intended). The following sections describe what you see and hear in a typical pickup game.

Gimme the ball!

No one ever remembers how many assists or rebounds she had after a pickup game; everyone wants to score. On the playground, the highest tribute for a player is to be told that she "has game" — or that she has the ability to play well and score.

As David Letterman might say, "And the number-one phrase you won't hear after a pickup basketball game: 'Boy, your defense was just outstanding today.'"

Pass — or shoot — the rock!

You won't find a shot clock in pickup hoops, but that doesn't mean that the game moves slowly. Holding on to the ball too long is a cardinal sin; players are there to play. Any team that makes more than five passes on one possession will find itself, at best, jeered and, at worst, pummeled by the guys on the sideline who have next.

Trash talk

The very title of Ronnie Shelton's film *White Men Can't Jump* is trash talk, which is an indelible part of pickup hoops. Your manhood — or womanhood — is on the line when you step onto the court. Talking trash is one way to gain an advantage.

Trash talk is not politically correct, but it does not need to be profane. The best trash talk is brash, puts down the opponent or exalts the speaker, and — most important — is funny.

The lane: No place for the faint of heart

So you think that the NBA is rough! If you attempt to dribble down into the three-second lane for a lay-up (or "take your game down the lane"), expect to be *hammered* (or fouled). In pickup hoops, nobody fouls out or shoots free throws. If someone fouls you, you just take the ball out again. Don't

Pithy Pippen

In Game 1 of the 1997 NBA Finals, the Utah Jazz and the Chicago Bulls were tied at 82 when Utah's Karl Malone was fouled with 9.2 seconds left. Only two weeks earlier, Malone, known as "The Mailman," had beaten out Chicago's Michael Jordan for the league's MVP award. On this Sunday evening in Chicago, Malone stepped to the line to shoot two free throws. All he had to do was make one of the two and the Jazz would take the lead and be in prime position to score a Game 1 upset. Malone missed the first shot. Before the ball was returned to him, Scottie Pippen of the Bulls approached Malone and whispered, "The Mailman doesn't deliver on Sundays." (His language may have been slightly more colorful than that.) Malone missed again, and seconds later, Jordan buried a jumper at the buzzer to win the game.

Even though NBA players compete for much more than respect, they still talk trash. That, to me, shows that, despite their wealth, they play because they love the game. Larry Bird and Michael Jordan, arguably the best players of the 1980s and '90s, respectively, are also two of the most notorious trash talkers in hoops lore.

expect the guys playing defense — and it doesn't matter whether they're your brothers or total strangers — to surrender an easy shot without *hacking* (that is, fouling) you.

Arguments

You won't find any refs in pickup basketball, either. Every matter, from who touched the ball last to what is the accurate score, is contended. ("We were up by two *before* that basket!") The lesson here: Pickup basketball does not so much *build* character as it does *reveal* it.

If you're watching instead of playing the game, be careful. Chances are that the players will appeal to you as a last resort in these situations. Knowing whether any known felons are playing is always a good idea. I tend to side with them when such disputes arise.

Don't expect to learn Dean Smith's offense

Rare is the pickup game in which players behave as a team. That's forgivable, because most of the time you don't even know who your teammates are until minutes before the game begins. You may see an occasional pick and roll or give and go, but that's about it.

Midnight Basketball

In Chicago, Gil Walker of the Chicago Housing Authority has used basketball to help reduce crime. Walker founded the Midnight Basketball program, wherein gyms open late on weekend nights so that kids can play hoops instead of hanging out on the streets. Walker's idea was that hoops is a religion, and it can instill some of the same benefits, such as creating friendships and building community.

Most of the teams that win in pickup basketball have two players who are used to working with each other, or a guard who is not preoccupied with scoring. Setting up teammates in pickup basketball is easy if that's your intention, because few teams switch on defense, and no one ever heard of the concept of weakside rotation. (See Chapter 7 for details about playing defense.)

Other pickup basketball customs and terms

Cherry picking: In a full-court game, *cherry picking* refers to the practice of not returning to the defensive end of the court or simply heading toward the offensive end of the court the moment your opponent takes a shot. In theory, your team will get the rebound and feed you, the cherry picker, for an easy lay-up.

Courtesy: During warm-ups, a shooter continues to shoot the ball until she misses. Unless the shot is a lay-up, she keeps the ball until she misses. Shooting a lay-up is the shooter's unspoken way of saying, "It's time for someone else to shoot."

Firsts: Without a referee, players must have a way to determine a jump ball situation. Unless someone brings an arrow to the court, players determine who gets the ball after a tie-up by yelling "Firsts." Whoever has the presence of mind to say "firsts" first gets possession.

Free-ins: When there's little out-of-bounds room, some games are played by the free-ins rule. According to this rule, defenders may neither intercept the in-bounds pass nor harass the inbounder. In a half-court game, the in-bounds pass must be above the foul line. Otherwise, teams would have a lob pass for a free lay-up.

Game: When the winning shot goes in the hoop, the winning team says, "Game," as in, "We just scored the game-winning point."

Hold court: *Hold court* refers to a team remaining in successive pickup games by virtue of consecutive victories.

Li'l help: If the ball rolls away toward another game, or goes off the court to a bystander, or rolls under a car, you ask someone for "li'l help" in retrieving the ball. (A funny scene in the movie *Stripes* involves this term. Bill Murray is playing basketball inside his upper-floor apartment. He spins, takes a shot, and the ball flies out the window and far down to the street below. Murray calmly walks over to the window and, without raising his voice, implores, "Li'l help.")

Out front: *Out front* (or *up top*) is the area, usually beyond the foul line or the three-point line (if there is one), where the ball is *checked* (handled by a defender) before being in-bounded in half-court play.

Run it back: *Run it back* is a request for an immediate rematch made by a pickup team that has just been beaten. However, if another team has already called for *nexts,* the request is denied. (See the section "We got next" later in this chapter.)

Shirts 'n' skins: Rarely do teams have uniforms in pickup basketball, so many games are played with one team wearing shirts and the other without shirts (skins). Obviously, if a game involves women, the team with the women on it becomes shirts. If women are on both teams . . . well, memorize who your teammates are.

Skunk: *Skunk* is a term for a game that ends in a shutout — 11-0, 15-0, 21-0 or whatever the point total goal was when the game started. A skunk game can also be called before a team reaches the final score. For example, a skunk game game to 15 will be called at 7-0.

Straight up: In most pickup games, you have to win by two baskets. *Straight up* games waive this rule. The first team to score the winning number of points — for example, 11 — wins. A winning score may be 11-10. You call "straight up" on nights when Mom is making lasagna and you absolutely do not want to be late for dinner.

Stretch it out: *Stretching it out* refers to a game that is changed from half-court to full-court. Normally, players stretch it out when a three-on-three game becomes a four-on-four game. Having four players on a team is normally considered enough to play a full-court game.

Want to run?: In pickup parlance, a game is also referred to as a *run.* If your team's got next (see the section "We got next" later in this chapter) but you find yourselves short one player, you can approach someone who is also waiting to play and ask, "Want to run?" He won't assume that you mean a 10K race.

Gentleman's Rules of Pickup Basketball

As I alluded to earlier in the chapter, there's no evidence of a Continental Congress of pickup basketball having ever convened. No latter-day Thomas Jefferson framed a Bill of Rights for the playground game. The customs and rules that have taken hold are the product of millions upon millions of pickup games having occurred, and players gradually conforming to the ideas that made the most sense. The following rules of pickup basketball are the ones that are the most universally accepted.

To 11, 15, or 21 by ones

The first team to score 11, 15, or 21 baskets wins. Each basket is worth one point in pickup games. If you have a lot of time, 21 is a satisfying run. If other players are waiting to play or if time is short, 15 or 11 is better. Sometimes games only go to 7. I don't know why these are the universally recognized numbers or why they're all odd numbers, but that's the way it is.

Winners

Also referred to as *possession, winners* applies only to a half-court pickup game. The team that scores retains possession of the basketball. I'm not sure how this rule started, but it forces a team to play defense. If you don't play defense in a game of possession, you never see the ball on offense.

This rule keeps the game entertaining. Say you're playing to 15 and are down 14-9. If you get the ball, you can "make a run" (or score a few baskets in a row) without ever having to surrender the ball to your opponent.

Gotta win by two

Unless you have to be home for dinner by 6:00 p.m., your pickup game probably won't have a time limit. What fun would that be? If the other team knows that you're going to be grounded if you're not home by 6:00 p.m., they can go into a stall with a one-bucket lead at 5:51 p.m. Maybe that's why the shot clock was invented: Someone had to be home for dinner.

Instead, you play so that you have to win by a margin of two baskets. If you're playing to 21 and the score is tied 20-20, for example, you must score two straight to win (if you trail 20-19, you need to score three in a row). This rule is fun because it allows for the possibility of a game that lasts into infinity — although, last time I checked, no such game was taking place. If you play a game that should end at 21 and it extends into a 37-35 classic, you and your buddies will be talking about it for at least a day or two.

Call your own fouls

By "call your own fouls," I don't mean to call a foul that you committed. Sometimes a player does that, but the gesture is so noble that it causes other players to wonder about that player's sanity. "Call your own fouls" means that you, and only you, call the foul when one is committed against you.

If you're fouled in the act of shooting, make sure to call "Foul" (sometimes you hear players say, "I got it," which is fine) *immediately.* Don't wait to see whether the ball is going to go in and then, if it misses, call the foul. You don't deserve the call if you do that.

Take it back

"Take it back" is an expression used in half-court pickup games. This rule states that when a change of possession occurs via a rebound or turnover, the team that gained possession of the ball must take the ball back to a certain point, usually to the top of the key or the foul line, before they can take a shot at the basket.

The rule acts as an orderly way for teams to switch from offense to defense in a half-court setting. With quick changes of possession, you need to have a rule that allows teams to identify themselves as offensive or defensive entities on a possession. Taking it back allows players to catch their breath, too. But in many a pickup game, you don't have to take the ball back on a turnover; you can take it straight to the hoop. This is the defense's reward for forcing the turnover.

Many outdoor pickup courts — and almost all gyms — now have a three-point shot line, which makes a terrific take-it-back barrier. The defense, having just grabbed the rebound, may take the ball back in any direction: the top of the key, the wing, or the corner. Now the team making the transition from offense to defense has to be more alert. In the past, you could relax a little because you knew that the ball had to be taken above the foul line. No more.

We got next

Say that ten players are playing five-on-five, and you and a buddy arrive. "We got next!" you call. What happens then, assuming that no one else shows up, is that the team who wins remains on the court. Three players from the losing team join you and your buddy to challenge the winners. How do you figure which three? Normally, a free throw contest determines that: The first three players to hit a free throw get to play.

A court in New York City's Upper West Side burgeons with players when the weather turns warm. Watching players keep track of who's got next on this court is like watching the stock exchange at the opening bell. That's why you have to call "next" loudly, and you can't be shy when your turn to play comes. When you do play, be sure to win — or you may have to sit for an hour or two before playing again.

Check

Check simulates what occurs in an official game. When a referee handles the ball before giving it to a team to in-bound and start play, he is "checking the play" — that is, allowing the defense a reasonable amount of time to prepare themselves. As I mentioned earlier, though, refs don't work pickup games. Who needs the grief?

So how do you check the ball? The defender guarding the player in-bounding the ball after a made basket (which he does from above the top of the key) calls "Check." The player with the ball tosses it to the defender, whose job it is to be sure that his teammates are ready. When he is satisfied that they are, he returns the ball to the offensive player. Now play begins.

No free throws

You won't find any free throws in most pickup basketball games. Players call their own fouls, but shooting free throws is out of the question. The team whose player has been fouled in-bounds the ball from the top of the key. (Remember to check the ball first.)

Looking for Good Pickup Facilities

Goldilocks would fit the character profile of a pickup hoops player by sheer finicky nature alone. Pickup players search and search for the perfect game (by game, I mean the site, not the contest itself) — and, having found it, they're loath to venture anywhere else. Try suggesting an alternative, and pickup players may enumerate any number of reasons why it's no good: "Cement's too slippery," "Rims are too soft," "No water fountain," "Too many old men."

As you search for your own Pickup Nirvana, read this section for a few things to keep on your checklist.

A good number of courts

You want a facility with a lot of courts so that you have a better chance of playing. If 20 players are waiting to play on one court, you may be waiting an hour between games if you lose.

Be aware that, while regulation courts in gyms are 94 feet long, most outdoor courts are shorter by at least 10 feet. If you're a college or high school player trying to get in shape during the off-season, keep this in mind.

A good variety of courts and games

The ideal facility has some half-court games plus a full-court game or two. It also has a sidecourt or two where you can shoot baskets to warm up before or cool down after you play.

Many players who are waiting their turn to play in a full-court game shoot at one basket when the action is on the opposite end of the court. Do so at your own peril. Nothing annoys a player more than when somebody who's not even playing interrupts his fast-break dunk.

When a pickup basketball facility has a lot of courts, it usually means that different levels of competition are played. Some facilities have A-game courts and B-game courts, or a college-level court and a high school-level court. This is another reason why facilities with a higher number of courts are usually better pickup spots.

When you start out, just hang out and observe the levels of competition to determine where you belong.

Even baskets with nylon nets and rectangular backboards

Many outdoor courts fall victim to bent rims. Everyone loves to dunk — or at least try to — and over the years, missed dunks equal bent rims. The ideal pickup court (and I don't think it's a lot to ask!) has straight rims that are 10 feet above the ground.

The perfect facility also has nylon nets. Playing without a net throws the full-court game off because a pure swish keeps on going and rolls far off the court, and you have to chase it as though it were an airball. You can't appreciate the net's purpose until you play a game without one. Nets also help the shooter's eye by giving depth perception.

How about backboards? Most pickup baskets have fan-shaped backboards, which are less expensive. But as a result, bankshots suffer — smaller backboards give you less room to work with.

Some outdoor courts have the preferable rectangular backboards, but they're made of screen material. This type of backboard doesn't give your shot a true bounce. The rims attached to screen backboards also tend to be loose. Such a rim is more forgiving — that is, more bad shots fall in because they don't ricochet far off the rim — which gives you a false sense of confidence in your shot. Better to not play on these rims and become a better shooter.

Lights

The perfect pickup facility has lights. (Obviously, I'm talking about outside facilities, because all gyms are lighted.) But an outside facility that has lights means hoops for an additional three hours in the summertime, or all night.

Because of the summer heat, night basketball produces some of the very best pickup hoops you can find. Along the New Jersey shore, I can personally attest, hoopsters are like mosquitoes: dormant all day long and then suddenly appearing in droves after the sun goes down. Of all the things teenagers could be doing while out at night in the summertime, I'd opt for them to be playing hoops.

An adjoining gym

The perfect pickup basketball facility has both an outside and an inside court. If you have both, you can play no matter what the weather conditions. During the summer, most players prefer to play outside, especially at dusk or at night. That gym is too hot in the summertime. Besides, if you live in a cold-weather area, you've been playing inside all winter. The change of scenery is welcome.

A water fountain

How far to the fountain? Is the water cold? Does it have barely any pressure, or does it shoot 5 feet in the air? Devoted pickup players know exactly where the water fountain is at their favorite spot and can discuss the virtues or drawbacks of the fountains at three courts in the area.

Courtside concerns

Can you leave your watch, boom box, or car keys lying near the court without fear of them being taken or smashed? Is there a pond, busy road, or street adjacent to the court — all of which present danger to a ball that flies out of bounds? Is there a parking lot close to the court? Is there a nice place for you to sit back and watch a game going on in front of you? These are dire quality-of-life issues, pickup hoops-wise.

A chain-link fence surrounding the court area is another good thing to look for. There are two distinct advantages to a fence:

Cameron hoops

Some of best summer pickup games in the Carolinas are played in Cameron Indoor Stadium. Most of the summer, the players for Duke, North Carolina, and North Carolina State (those three schools are just *25* miles apart) play pickup games in this legendary arena. Players from the past often come by and challenge the younger stars of each school. And on some weekends, the players from Wake Forest (just 40 miles away) drive over.

Duke should think about selling tickets to these pickup games. In the summer of 1993, you could see pickup games that were, in effect, matchups of the players that formed the preceding three NCAA championship teams.

- **You survive after running into a chain-link fence.** If you're chasing a loose ball out of bounds and ram into a chain-link fence, at least you live to tell about it. Not so with a concrete wall.
- **Errant passes go only so far.** Nothing kills a game's momentum like a bad pass that flies off the court and into oblivin. Remember, pickup games don't have ball boys.

Padding on the basket support

You should take into account two aspects of the basket support:

- **The pole should be padded.** Fast breaks in pickup games often send players careening into the pole as if they'd been tossed from a car wreck. You don't want the poles (or the players) *looking* as if they'd been tossed from a car wreck, too. Padding the support solves that problem.

  During the 1977 Bookstore Basketball Tournament at Notre Dame, Jeff Carpenter, one of Notre Dame's point guards, separated his shoulder when he crashed into a pole. This happened in April, so he was not in danger of missing any time with the varsity, but his injury underlined that the poles needed padding — not just for varsity players, but for everybody on campus. The next year, Jeff's team won the Bookstore Tournament, defeating a team in the semi-finals that featured football great Joe Montana.

- **The basketball support should be recessed from the endline of the court.** On a lot of courts, the basket supports are on the endline. The farther the support can be recessed, the better. When the pole is on the endline, you just don't have much room to maneuver around the baseline.

A level court

Not that you need to call a surveyor, but the court should be level enough so that your shot is consistent from all areas. Though each pickup court has its own character that gives players homecourt advantages that Boston Garden never afforded the Celtics, such as overhanging tree branches and so on, having a court with a level surface is best.

Of course, having a court with something like a sloping right side can work to your advantage when an out-of-towner comes to play. Chances are, getting used to that shot takes some time. But by and large, an unlevel court is not good for your all-around game.

North-south orientation (if outdoors)

The perfect court runs north and south. If you're playing on a court that runs east and west, you'll have trouble seeing the rim on your jumpshots during late-in-the-day games when you're shooting at the goal that faces the sun. If the court runs north and south, you don't face this problem late in the day, except on wing-to-wing passes.

Bathroom facilities

Most outdoor facilities don't have an outhouse or a substitute. That's where an adjoining indoor gym may come in handy. While you are probably going to become dehydrated and won't have many occasions to use the facility, it still serves as a place to change clothes after games.

No stage in the gym

Earlier in this chapter, I stated that the perfect pickup basketball facility is probably near a school gym, because you can move inside if the weather is inclement. But many schools, especially elementary schools, also use the gym for school plays and concerts. A stage at one end of the court could very well cause serious kidney damage or adversely affect your ability to carry on the family name should you run into it.

Proper ventilation in the gym

Air conditioning is not absolutely necessary in a gym, but if it's not air conditioned, the gym should have enough windows and doors to keep the place relatively habitable. Hey, people sweat in gyms. And they should. But you shouldn't have to play hoops in a sauna, either.

Pickup Shooting Games

The shooting games in this section are competitions that you can play instead of playing an actual game. You can play shooting games to kill time while you're waiting for one more player to arrive, or you can play if someone in your group doesn't have the stamina for a real game. Or you can play shooting games just for fun.

H-O-R-S-E

Ideal number of players: 3 to 5

H-O-R-S-E is a simple and popular game. Establish a shooting order; then start the game. When a player hits a shot, every succeeding player must match that shot (in style and court location) until someone misses. As the caller of the shot, you *are* allowed to call whether the shot must be a bankshot or whether it should swish through the net. Just make sure that you make the shot as you call it. (If you call "swish" and the shot goes in but fails to swish, you don't get credit for making the shot.) The player who misses is labeled with an H for the first miss, and the next player then introduces a new shot. If all the players make the shot, the player who began the round introduces a new shot.

On your second miss, you receive an O, and so on until you spell out H-O-R-S-E. The last player remaining after everyone else spells out the word wins. Remember, you receive a letter only after missing a shot following a made shot. If you're the first player shooting after a missed shot (or after everyone has made the shot that you introduced), you are not penalized.

Note: If one of the players in the game can dunk and another can't, you can establish a "No Dunk" rule.

Here are some tips that just may help you beat that longtime foe:

- When you're not following a made shot, take your favorite shots. As long as you control the shot, someone will eventually slip.
- On your own time, develop a gimmick shot or two.
- Develop your off hand. In other words, if you're normally right-handed, get comfortable with a left-handed shot and use it. Call "opposite hand" — that way, if a guy is a lefty, he has to shoot with his right.
- Know your opponents. What shot do they have trouble making when you play pickup basketball with them? If they can't shoot from the corner, for example, exploit that weakness.

Here are some trick shots that can help you win H-O-R-S-E games:

- Shoot a shot from the baseline behind the hoops — in other words, a shot that requires an attempt over the top of the backboard. This shot is easier than you think, as long as you give it a really high arc.
- Call a special shot on a basic shot. For example, a 5-foot jumpshot is more challenging if you shoot it with your eyes closed.
- Call "bank" and then hit a bankshot from the wing.
- Call "swish" or "nothing but net" from wherever you feel most confident.
- Call "off hand" and shoot with your weaker hand. Try this on a lay-up.
- Shoot a behind-the-head shot. Set up in the lane with your back to the basket. Lean back and shoot the ball over your head to the basket.
- Shoot a hook shot. Not many people practice the hook — and shooting it when you have H-O-R-S is a tough time to start.

21

Ideal number of players: 3

In 21, your free throw shooting, aggressiveness, and individual offensive talents are put to the test. Although the game is suited for three players, you can play with as few as two or as many as you like. Free throws are worth one point, and shots made during live action are worth two.

Play begins with a player shooting a free throw. The other players may stand wherever they please in preparation to rebound. If the free throw shooter makes the shot, he shoots again. If he misses, the ball is live and the player who gets the rebound attempts to score a basket. All the regular rules of the game apply, except that when the ball goes out of bounds, it goes to the player closest to the ball, even if he was the last one to touch it. And there are no fouls.

After a player scores during live play (two points), he goes to the free throw line and shoots free throws, up to three in a row, until he misses. If he makes three in a row (three points), he takes the ball out from the top of the key, and play is live again.

The winner is the first player who scores exactly 21 points. If you are at 20 and miss your free throw, your score is dumped back to 11 points, and you must start from there. You can find true free throw pressure in 21. When you get to 21 points, you have to hit a shot from the top of the key. If you miss, you go back to 13.

Around the World

Ideal number of players: 2 to 5

Players shoot from different designated spots in a semicircle around the basket. If you make a shot, you move to the next spot. If you miss, you choose either to *chance it* — that is, to take a second shot from the same spot — or to stay put until your turn comes up again. If you chance it and make the shot, you advance to the next spot and shoot again. If you miss, you must start from the very beginning.

The game is called Around the World because you circle the basket by moving from spot to spot. Here's the order of the designated spots (see Chapter 3 for an illustration of these spots):

- Lay-up from the right side (shot with right hand)
- Right corner
- Right wing
- Top of the key
- Foul line
- Left wing
- Left corner
- Lay-up from the left side (shot with left hand)

But that's not all. The players then must return in the opposite direction — that is, another left lay-up, then left corner, left wing, and so on. The last shot, the game winner, is a lay-up from the right side.

Depending on your age and/or skill level, move the orbit shots, such as those from the corners, wings, and top of the key, closer to the basket.

5-3-1

Ideal number of players: 2 to 4

This game is fun for kids under ten years old — and it teaches them addition as well. Five, three, and one are the point values of the three different shots that are taken in each turn. You begin your turn with a foul shot (worth five points). You take your second shot from wherever you grab the rebound of the free throw (three points). You take your final shot from wherever you wish (one point). The first player to reach a certain number — say, 50 — wins.

Two extra rules: If you make all three shots in one turn, you go again. If you miss all three shots in one turn, your score returns to zero.

Pickup Games

Pickup hoops games, even when they involve two teams playing offense and defense, are not carbon copies of the stuff you see on television. This section lists a couple of my favorite flavors of pickup basketball.

Three-on-three

Three-on-three is the most popular half-court game. It wears you out in a hurry.

Three-on-three is great because all the aspects of half-court basketball as played in a real game exist. The give-and-go, pick and roll, post play, weakside shooter, and backdoor play are all available to the offense. The defense can double team, but that leaves the third defender in a bind. Smart, experienced hoopsters love three-on-three because good passing and moving without the ball — two facets of deft offensive spacing — are at a premium. Plus, with all that room (four fewer players on the court), you have room to operate one-on-one. But you also have room to run an offense.

Three-on-three is so popular that many cities have leagues and tournaments devoted to it. The most famous three-on-three tournament is the Gus Macker League. This competition started on Gus Macker's driveway in Lowell, Michigan, in 1974 and has been held every year since (although games are no longer played on his driveway).

Bookstore Basketball

Bookstore Basketball is a campus-wide, five-on-five, single-elimination tournament that captivates the Notre Dame community each spring. Upwards of 700 teams compete in this full-court outdoor endeavor that has become as interwoven in campus life as football Saturdays are. The tourney's name was derived from the original site of the tourney, a pair of adjacent courts behind the campus bookstore. This tournament is unique because the field is open to anyone currently involved in the Notre Dame community in any manner.

Bookstore Basketball is full-court basketball with no subs during a game. Games are played to 21 baskets. Unlike most pickup games, team fouls are kept by an official scorer, and after the pool is whittled down to 64 teams, free throw shots are allowed after a team has ten fouls.

Because of the overwhelming number of games that must be played in a limited number of days, contests are played regardless of northern Indiana's mercurial weather conditions, and I do mean regardless. The 1975 championship game was played amid tornado warnings. And one year, one of the early rounds was contested in a snowstorm. So much snow was on the court that players couldn't dribble; they had to pass the ball up the court.

Chapter 12
High School Basketball

In This Chapter

- Where high school basketball is today
- What "Hoosier Hysteria" really means
- How high school hoops differs from college and pro hoops
- What kids, parents, and coaches can do to maximize the experience
- Why going "from the prom to the pros" is usually a bad decision

Here's all you need to know about how precocious the high school game has become: In March 1997, the publication *Basketball Weekly* printed a list of the five most likely pro prospects who were currently in *eighth grade.*

Want more? Consider these tidbits:

- Sneaker magnates Adidas, Nike, and Reebok compete for the loyalty of even midrange high school hoops hotbeds. In 1996, the Swoosh doled out $20,000 to St. Patrick's in Elizabeth, New Jersey, for lacing up with them.
- The McDonald's High School All-America game is televised nationally on network TV.
- In the spring of 1997, 6'9" Lamar Odom, arguably one of the two most coveted high school prospects in the nation, shocked hoops observers by *not* going directly to the NBA. He decided on prep school instead.

Recently, talented prep players such as Kevin Garnett (class of 1995) and Kobe Bryant (1996) jumped directly to the NBA. Their leaps, though not prudent, were profitable — and, for them, at least, turned out to be sound decisions. In February 1996, Garnett, then all of 20 years old, appeared in the NBA All-Star Game. Bryant, 18, scored 31 points in the Rookie Game. He also won the Slam Dunk Contest, something he had dreamed of doing. The success of Garnett and Bryant has paved the way for a wave of from-the-prom-to-the-pros NBA rookies into the next millennium.

Class wars

High schools come in various shapes and sizes. Some have so few students that they can't even field a hoops team, whereas others have upwards of 5,000 kids. To level the playing surface, high school athletic associations in each state create *classes* based on student population. In Arizona, for example, the largest schools are denoted AAAAA. The next-lower class is AAAA, and so on.

Schools compete against opponents in the same class, the theory being that a coach who can choose from among 2,000 students is likely to find a dozen talented players, whereas a coach who can choose from among 20 players is lucky just to fill his bench. It isn't that a one-room schoolhouse can't produce the next Larry Bird; it's just that bigger schools have a greater depth of talent. Small-school kids deserve a championship that they can realistically strive toward achieving.

As for the distaff side of the equation, no girls' high school basketball player has yet jumped directly to either of the existing two professional women's leagues. But the Oregon City (Oregon) High School girls' team, the country's top team in the mid-1990s, does have a sneaker contract with nearby shoe monolith Nike.

Where It's At

Where is the high school game the biggest? The answer depends on how you look at basketball:

- **It's a rural game.** In Ohio Valley states such as Indiana, Kentucky, and Ohio, basketball is a religion, and high school hoops is considered the first stage of enlightenment. Here, in agrarian regions that have no professional teams, towns equate their identities with their high school hoops programs. Drive down a country road in Indiana: Any town whose team has won the state title advertises it on the sign welcoming motorists.
- **It's a city game.** The crowds may not equal those that parade — literally, in half-mile-long processions of cars — to games in Indiana on Friday nights, but the quality of play in cities is outstanding. City kids are raised in asphalt jungles where baseball backstops and football goalposts are rare but where basketball courts are readily available. Plus, inherently more talent is in the city than in the country because the pool of players is larger.

- **It's a suburban game.** The 'burbs are home to private schools, which, unlike public schools, are allowed to court students — and in many cases, offer them scholarships — while providing an above-par secondary school education. Take a gander at the perennial nationally ranked high school programs, such as Oak Union Academy (Virginia), Mater Dei (California), and St. John's at Prospect Hall (Maryland), St. Anthony's (New Jersey), and you realize that private schools rule. The two most gifted male players of the 1997 senior class, Tracy McGrady and Lamar Odom, both transferred to private schools (Mount Zion Christian Academy in Durham, North Carolina, and Redemption Christian Academy of Troy, New York, respectively) as their prep basketball careers progressed.

Understanding Hoosier Hysteria

In 1978, Notre Dame played host to the semistate round (a Sweet 16 regional) of the Indiana high school basketball tournament. We issued more press credentials for those games than we had earlier in the year for our game against top-ranked Marquette. Why do Hoosiers love their high school hoops so much?

- **For a long time, it was the only game in town.** No pro franchise existed in Indiana before the ABA Indiana Pacers (now of the NBA) were formed in 1967. High school basketball was the Hoosier NBA franchise and NFL franchise. The Indy 500 takes place over the course of three hours. Hoosiers need something else to fill the sports-page void the other 8,757 hours of the year.
- **A basketball support system exists in Indiana homes.** The basketball tradition leads dads and moms to install hoops on the sides of barns or against garages. Youngsters learn the importance of basketball at a very early age.
- **Indiana college teams.** Indiana University, Purdue, Notre Dame, and so on have viable programs, further enhancing the basketball aura in the state. Kids in Indiana grow up wanting to play for these teams.
- **Hinkle Field House.** For years, Butler University's cavernous gym in northern Indianapolis — as seen in *Hoosiers* — was the site of the state's semifinals and finals. Every Hoosier hoopster dreamed of playing there. A few years back, the state finals were moved to the RCA Dome. Though upwards of 30,000 now attend, the charm of Hinkle cannot be matched. Progress is not always better.
- **Facilities are fantastic.** New Castle High School, for example, boasts the world's largest high school gym. The fieldhouse seats 9,325 people and always sells out. Some Indiana high schools have gyms whose seating capacity outnumbers the town's population.

Hoosiers

In the eyes of Indiana, where hoops is the state religion, all high school basketball players are equal. At least that was the faith until the 1997–98 school year. Up until that time, every high school, from tiny rural schools to Indianapolis school North Central, which squeezes more than 3,000 students inside its brick walls, competed in one postseason hoops tournament. Although this system may seem unfair to the uninitiated, almost everyone in the state — players included — loved it. After all, you can't tell a high school boy or girl that he or she is not good enough to compete with anyone. Dreams are made of such David-versus-Goliath matchups.

Witness the saga of Milan High School's victory in 1954. The tiny school — immortalized and given the pseudonym Hickory High in the 1986 film *Hoosiers* — won the state championship on a last-second shot by Bobby Plump, defeating a much larger school, Muncie Central, in the finals. Supporters of Indiana's classless hoops system (classes exist for all other sports in the state) always point to Milan when making an argument. Detractors always say, "Give us another example of a small school winning it all."

There is none. For that reason, in 1997, after years of debate, the Indiana High School Athletic Association (IHSAA) voted to adopt a class system and stage multiple tourneys based on enrollment, with four state champions instead of one. David may only slay other Davids, and Goliath, other giants. To me, adopting a class system is akin to shortening the Indianapolis 500!

Fortunately, the IHSAA amended its decision so that the four class state champs meet in a Final Four. Still, you have to wonder: If a tiny school such as Milan were to beat a giant like Ben Davis, who had already defeated the state's largest schools (and, ergo, the toughest competition) in the Final Four to claim its class title, might many people still consider Ben Davis the de facto state champ? We'll see.

My bet: After a few years and much public outcry, they'll return to the original format.

The film *Hoosiers* says it all. Gene Hackman, playing Hickory's new coach, visits the barber shop and is ambushed with strategy by well-intentioned, if not diplomatic, locals. (Boy, I can relate to that.) One of the locals says, "We think you should be playing this zone defense." Hackman says, "I don't like that zone defense. I'll play what I want."

That scene transports me back to Hazelton, Pennsylvania, circa 1964. I recall meeting with some people in town and telling them that I wanted to press more on defense, something different from what the team had been doing. I remember the resistance that I faced. So when I saw that scene in the movie, I cringed. Been there, Gene.

High School Confidential

Though high school players have dramatically bridged the gap between themselves and their collegiate brethren in terms of talent, the game itself is still quite different from the college or professional game. This section explains the technical differences between the high school game and the college and pro game.

Rules

High school rules differ from college and pro rules in the following ways:

- There is no shot clock (in some states).
- Game time is 32 minutes, divided into four 8-minute quarters or two 16-minute halves.
- The three-point line is at 19'9" (same as college).

Style of play

Not every boys' team can count on having a 6'8" center — or girls' team, a 6'3" center. But those that do exploit the mismatch. Thus, on average, expect to see more *perimeter play* — that is, outside shooting and guard-dominated offense — at the high school level, but watch as a coach who has one clearly superior player attempts to take advantage of that situation. Consider this: A slew of young men in Texas right now are still recovering from the trauma of having had to guard Shaquille O'Neal (who now goes 7'1", 300 pounds for the Los Angeles Lakers) in high school. They may still be nursing bruises.

Turnovers

More of 'em. Youth is directly proportional to mistakes. You know going into a high school game that you're likely to see more turnovers, but that's the case in any sport. Young players are still learning.

Room to grow

At no age do kids grow more dramatically and sporadically than in high school. You may stand 6'1" as a freshman and be the frosh team's center. You rule! But flash-forward three years. You're a senior and the yardstick now says that you measure . . . 6'1". I hope that you learned to dribble well, or you may not even make the team.

Getting started in coaching

In the fall of 1996, Mark Granger inherited a Brophy College Preparatory (Phoenix, Arizona) team that started no seniors and had not made it to the Arizona high school boys' Final Four since Granger himself had been the point guard there. Of course, that was only ten years earlier.

At age 28, Granger seemed an unlikely choice to be named head coach at the largest private school in the state. He had never been a head coach at the varsity level and had not played a lick of college basketball while a student at Notre Dame. Still, he must have learned something by watching me coach from the student section. Granger led the Broncos to an upset playoff win against the state's top-ranked team, Mountain View, and a berth in the Final Four before eventually losing. For his efforts, he was voted the Arizona Class 5A Coach of the Year.

Granger offers his tips for high school coaches:

- Surround yourself with good assistant coaches who are loyal, work hard, and know the game.
- Develop an basketball program that has continuity in its philosophy and style of play, providing developmental goals for all three levels (freshman, junior varsity, and varsity).
- Develop a sense of teamwork — stress that the players need to be friends both on and off the court.
- Display enthusiasm, integrity, and honesty in dealing with your players.
- Be adaptable in developing a style of play that draws on the strengths of your players.
- Focus on the fundamentals of the game and pay attention to detail.

Of course, the converse also applies. Who doesn't love the story of the 5'4" prawn who is cut her freshman year, and then grows a foot and becomes the star of the school by senior year? Got milk, anybody?

High school coaches must constantly assess growth. School lets out for the summer, and by the time everyone returns, he notices that a few of his players have deeper voices, driver's licenses, and much bigger feet. A player may grow himself right out of a position, from guard to forward or even center. Or, by failing to grow at all, he may have to move from center to forward, or in extreme circumstances, even guard. You can't do much about this. Don't hang upside down from the monkey bars — it won't help.

Ya gotta have heart

High school basketball games produce real tears. For nine out of ten high school hoopsters, this is it: No Division I scholarship, no sneaker deal, no rap video or MTV guest veejay slot. These kids are in it for all the right reasons: to be the best that they can be, to represent their school, and, okay, maybe to earn a letter jacket and impress their friends. The passion in their eyes — the joy and the sadness — is honest, unfettered emotion.

Off-the-rack coaching wardrobes

High school coaches don't earn six-figure salaries. More important, most of them don't care. Many a high school coach would make an outstanding college coach — the game's pretty much the same — but opt to remain at the high school level. They find high school coaching rewarding in ways that the IRS can't measure. Many coaches will tell you that they still have a significant effect on youngsters' lives. They love being vested with that responsibility. At the college level, it may be too late.

What Kids Can Do

The dream for many a boy or girl dies in high school. You've grown up with the Michael Jordan or Grant Hill poster(s) on your bedroom wall and dreamed of becoming them. Then, on some early autumn day, a coach posts a list of names outside a locker room — the kids who have survived the cuts to make the team, be it freshman, junior varsity, or varsity — and your name is not on it. That's tough to accept, especially at age 15.

Don't give up. Here are a few things you can do to prevent being cut or, if you are, rebound from your setback. Above all, remember this: Michael Jordan, His Airness, was cut from his high school team. You can learn two lessons from that: (1) Everyone can be humbled, and (2) coaches make mistakes.

- **Practice smart.** If you're alone and really want to improve, don't just shoot around at the basket killing time. Give yourself goals. Shoot 100 free throws each day, for example, and chart your progress. Or take shots from each of the positions on the court that I mention in Chapter 6, forbidding yourself to leave any spot until you make three shots in a row. Or practice the drills that I discuss in Part II of this book.
- **Play up to your competition.** Look for games against players who are better than you. Though your ego may need a boost, especially if you have been cut, playing against kids who are worse than you or at best, on your level, does you no benefit. Get into games with better, bigger, older players. Look to guard the best player at your position. And watch how quickly you improve.
- **Ask your coach what you can do.** Most high school coaches are glad to help. They may not be able to give you their own time, but if they see that your interest is earnest, they may give you some drills to do or at least let you know which skills you need to develop. Don't be too proud to ask for help.

Iowa girls' hoops

Six-on-six, they called it. At many a high school in Iowa, girls played a quite different brand of basketball. Each team put six players on the court at one time. Three of the players, the forwards, remained on one side of midcourt and played offense exclusively. Their three teammates , the guards, remained on the other side of this imaginary Maginot Line and played nothing but defense.

Iowa girls played basketball in this manner from 1898 to 1993. In 1925, the game was dropped out of fear that it was overshadowing the boys' game, but one year later, it was reinstated and mushroomed in popularity. The 1955 tournament final in Des Moines drew 15,333 spectators — still the largest audience ever to witness a girls' high school hoops contest.

The quirky rules extended beyond the midcourt barrier imposed upon the players. Forwards, upon receiving the ball, could hold it no more than three seconds before dribbling, passing, or shooting. If they dribbled, they were only allowed to dribble twice and then had to shoot or pass. After the defense recovered the ball, the players had to advance the ball to, but not beyond, midcourt, whereupon they passed it to one of their team's forwards.

One of the most bizarre oddities of the game revealed itself in the stat sheet. Because guards played defense exclusively, their scoring average year in and year out never wavered: 0.00.

Forwards, on the other hand, shared the ball with only two other players in a half-court that was decidedly less congested than a country road outside Ottumwah. In 1987, Lynne Lorenzen concluded her four-year career at tiny Ventura High with 6,736 points, or 3,069 more points than Pete Maravich scored at Louisiana State. Of course, after Lynn accepted a scholarship to Iowa State, she *did* have to learn how to play defense.

- **Attend summer basketball camps.** You may not be able to afford a camp such as the one that Michael Jordan held in the summer of 1997 in Las Vegas (one week, $15,000), but chances are your local high school or even nearby college holds camps that are more modestly priced. You can receive terrific instruction from coaches who are in a more relaxed frame of mind (the big game is *not* tomorrow). If you attend camp at your own school, you'll probably play against your competition to make the team next fall. Camp is an early chance to assess yourself and impress the coaches.

If you've already made the team:

- **Listen to your coach.**
- **Hustle.**
- **Be a team player.**

If that advice seems old-fashioned or trite coming from this gray-haired veteran, remember: You'll be amazed at how much grown-ups learn between the time you are 14 and 21 years old.

What Coaches Can Do

A high school coach can become the most unforgettable and instrumental figure in a young person's life. Or she can just punch the clock. Teenage kids, no matter how they may strut, are still very malleable people. The values you impart and the skills you teach can last a lifetime.

- **Dedicate yourself to improving your kids as people first and winning second.** Improve their skills; improve their self-discipline and even their character. A high school coach has the ability to do all that. Why do you think it's such a great job?
- **Be firm, fair, and consistent.** Establish rules from the first day of practice. Apprise your players that the rules stand, that the rules apply to everyone, and then enforce them. This is the only way to earn your players' respect.
- **Listen.** You don't have to be Joseph Stalin with a whistle. Teenagers are blossoming adults with many good ideas themselves. They want to be heard.

Morgan Wootten

The second most successful college coach in men's history is named Wooden. The most successful high school coach in basketball history is named Wootten. For the last 40 years, just nine years less than the NBA has been in existence, Morgan Wootten has been the coach at DeMatha High School in Hyattsville, Maryland. Wootten's teams have won more than 1,100 games, an all-time high school record.

Wootten's sterling career has been much more than simply long. He has coached his DeMatha squads to five mythical national championships, 30 conference championships, and 13 Washington, D.C., city titles. Twelve former players, including Adrian Dantley, the most talented player I ever coached at Notre Dame, have ascended to careers in the NBA. (Another of note is Danny Ferry of the Cleveland Cavaliers.) Wootten's most memorable on-court achievement occurred more than 30 years ago, in 1965, when DeMatha played Power Memorial of New York City. Power Memorial, led by gifted (and very, very tall) center Lew Alcindor (now Kareem Abdul-Jabbar), entered the game with a 71-game win streak. DeMatha, behind future Notre Dame stars Sid Catlett and Bob Whitmore, halted the storied streak.

But it may be the indefatigable Wootten's off-court achievements — he underwent a liver transplant in July 1996 and was back on the bench for the first game of the season — that his players most revere him for. Between 1961 and 1990, for three full decades, every single graduating senior who played for Wootten was offered a college athletic scholarship. A college education is the greatest victory any coach can give his players.

- **Make time.** Your worst player is willing to stay half an hour late to work on her free throw shooting? At worst, leave the gym open for her. At best, stay a few minutes and give her pointers. It's a little thing, but that girl won't forget it.
- **Be a role model.** You knew this was coming. But it's true. Don't do anything on or off the court that you wouldn't want your players to do. It's that simple.
- **Have fun.** Create an environment in which the kids, though they know to work hard, understand that this is still a game. Don't lose the kid in yourself.

What Parents Can Do

If you saw *Hoosiers,* you may recall that Dennis Hopper played the father of one of the team's better players. Hopper was no role model — he was the town drunk — but he did show a genuine interest in the team. After having a heart attack, he would not be stopped from listening to his boy's games on the radio while lying in his hospital bed. Here's what *you* can do as a parent:

- **Accept your kids for who they are.** If they don't make the team, be there to support them. If they're the last players on the bench, attend their games anyway. If they're the team's stars, don't ask them why they're not the best players in the city (or state, or whatever).
- **Attend your kids' games.** Attending their games means a lot to them even if they are at that stage when they are too cool to say so. Be supportive, but don't coach them or tell their coaches how to coach them — not even if you're a former Division I college coach.
- **Use the Dark Socks, Dark Suit theory.** This is for when you attend games or even practices. If you don't wear any socks with a dark suit, people notice. If you wear loud socks with a loud suit, that gets noticed, too — for all the wrong reasons. Show up and blend in: Be the dark socks. Cheer but don't jeer. Teens are more sensitive than seismographs. Remember, it's your son's or daughter's game, not yours.
- **Keep things in perspective.** Chances are that the next David Robinson or Rebecca Lobo does not live under your roof. Enjoy this time, but make sure that your kids hit the books.

High School All-America Teams

I see very few high school games in a year now that my livelihood no longer depends on it; my hands are usually full following the 307 Division I college teams as an analyst for ESPN. Many news services, such as *USA Today* and

Parade Magazine, follow the high school game, selecting All-America teams and/or ranking teams on a national basis.

Though these lists and rankings whet fans' appetites — sort of like seeing your favorite store's catalog a month before Christmas — understanding that high school stardom does not guarantee college success is important, nor is it a prerequisite. In 1974–75, a high school basketball player out of French Lick, Indiana, failed to make an All-State team in this supposedly hoops-enlightened state, never mind an All-America team. But Larry Bird went on to become one of the greatest all-around players in this history of the game and will be in the Hall of Fame in his first year of eligibility.

In contrast, not every high school All-American goes on to become a star in the pros. Only half of the 25 McDonald's All-Americans from 1988–89 went on to make it in the NBA. (See Table 12-1.) Only three — Kenny Anderson, Allen Houston, and Shaquille O'Neal — are considered starters on NBA teams today.

Table 12-1 McDonald's All-Americans 1988–89

Player	*Position*	*Hometown*	*NBA Team*	*Years in League*
Kenny Anderson	G	Queens, New York	Portland Trail Blazers*	6
Aaron Bain	F	Falls Church, Virginia	Did not make NBA	
Darryl Barnes	F	Brooklyn, New York	Did not make NBA	
Anthony Douglas	F	Memphis, Tennessee	Did not make NBA	
Doug Edwards	F	Miami, Florida	Atlanta Hawks	4
Jamal Faulkner	F	Middle Village, New York	Did not make NBA	
Shaun Golden	G	Greer, South Carolina	Did not make NBA	
Bobby Hurley	G	Jersey City, New Jersey	Sacramento Kings*	4
Jimmy Jackson	G	Toledo, Ohio	New Jersey Nets*	5
George Lynch	F	Falls Church, Virginia	Los Angeles Lakers*	4
Billy McCaffrey	G	Allentown, Pennsylvania	Did not make NBA	
Conrad McRae	F	Brooklyn, New York	Did not make NBA	
Michael Tate	F	Oxon Hill, Maryland	Did not make NBA	
Mitchell Butler	F	North Hollywood, California	Washington Bullets	4
Calvin Byrd	F	Alameda, California	Did not make NBA	
Deryl Cunningham	F	Westchester, Illinois	Did not make NBA	
Greg Graham	G	Indianapolis, Indiana	Seattle SuperSonics	2

(continued)

Table 12-1 *(continued)*

Player	*Position*	*Hometown*	*NBA Team*	*Years in League*
Pat Graham	F	New Albany, Indiana	Did not make NBA	
Allan Houston	G	Louisville, Kentucky	New York Knicks*	4
Tracy Murray	F	Glendora, California	Washington Bullets*	4
Shaquille O'Neal	C	San Antonio, Texas	Los Angeles Lakers*	5
James Robinson	G	Jackson, Mississippi	Did not make NBA	
Deon Thomas	G	Chicago, Illinois	Did not make NBA	
Jeff Webster	G	Midwest City, Oklahoma	Did not make NBA	
Matt Wenstrom	C	Houston, Texas	Boston Celtics	1

*denotes still active in NBA

Prominent NBA players from this class who were not chosen to McDonald's All-America team include the following:

- Shawn Bradley, Dallas Mavericks
- Ed O'Bannon, Dallas Mavericks
- Calbert Cheaney, Washington Wizards
- Sam Cassell, New Jersey Nets

From the Prom to the Pros

Going pro right out of high school is wrong 90 percent of the time. As far as I can see, Kobe Bryant is the only player to go pro from high school who had the grades to qualify academically. He had over 1100 on the SAT and a B+ average in high school. His father played in the NBA, so he knew what it was all about. But many of the others are going pro to escape from not qualifying. (See Table 12-2.)

Last year, Red McDavid from Palmetto High in Williamston, South Carolina, applied for the NBA draft. McDavid either accepted poor advice or had an unrealistic view of his talents. Yes, he averaged 26 points a game and was South Carolina's 2A Player of the Year, but he was not considered an elite recruit for college. McDavid was not drafted. Fortunately, he did not lose his college eligibility due to a 1995 rule that states that a youngster who applies for the NBA draft may still attend college provided that he does not sign with an agent or sign a pro contract.

Table 12-2 High School Players Who Went Straight to the NBA

Year	*Name*	*Hometown*	*NBA Team*	*Draft Position*
1996	Kobe Bryant	Philadelphia, Pennsylvania	Los Angeles Lakers	Round 1, Selection 13
1995	Kevin Garnett	Greenville, South Carolina	Minnesota Timberwolves	Round 1, Selection 5
1989	Sean Kemp	Elkhart, Indiana	Seattle SuperSonics	Round 1, Selection 17
1974	Moses Malone	Williamsburg, Virginia	Utah Jazz	Round 3, Selection 22
1975	Bill Willoughby	Englewood, New Jersey	Houston Rockets	Round 2, Selection 20
1996	Jermaine O'Neal	Columbia, South Carolina	Portland Trail Blazers	Round 1, Selection 17
1997	Tracy McGrady	Durham, North Carolina	Toronto Raptors	Round 1, Selection 9

This entire process seems like something from the theater of the absurd. Might the average age of incoming NBA rookies be 19 by the year 2000? It's possible. But keep in mind that the NBA, especially the one run by commissioner David Stern, is painstakingly image-conscious. Young players are likely to do immature things on and off the court (though many of the NBA's elder statesmen are just as incorrigible as any adolescent), and that's bad for business.

Most teams have programs in place to help their young players adapt to life in the NBA, which is unlike anything you or I will ever encounter. So far, there haven't been any major problems, such as arrests or on-court incidents, involving these young players. Give them credit. They are living inside a very closely monitored fishbowl. Very few people would fare as well in the same situation. That's why, if I were the parent or high school coach of a young player, even Kobe Bryant, I would dissuade him from turning pro out of high school. Players have just too much to gain from the college experience as a part of the maturing process.

U.S. high school records

Boys: Team

Most state championships: 23, Cheyenne Central, Wyoming

Most consecutive wins: 159, Passaic, New Jersey, 1919–25

Most points, game: 211, De Quincy Grand Avenue, Louisiana, January 29, 1964

Fewest points scored, game, both teams: Georgetown, Illinois (1) versus Homer, Illinois (0), 1930; Magnolia, Illinois (1) versus Granville Hopkins, Illinois (0), 1929; Drain, Oregon (1) versus Wilbur, Oregon (0)

**In 1929, Alliance (Ohio) High defeated rival Massillon 3-2 on Jim Battin's half-court desperation heave worth three points. Battin's shot was Alliance's only attempted field goal in the game.*

Boys: Individual

Most points scored, career: 6,702, Greg Procell, Noble Ebarb, Lousiana, 1967–70

Most points scored, game: 135, Danny Heater, Burnsville, West Virginia, January 26, 1960

Most consecutive free throws made: 126, Darly Moreau, New Orleans De La Salle, Lousiana, January 17, 1978, to January 9, 1979

Most rebounds, game: 55, Mark Garbacz, Oil City Venago Christian, Pennsylvania, February 20, 1970; Ryan Roberts, Downs Tri-Valley, Illinois, December 22, 1980

Most assists, game: 35, Andre Colbert, Lockport DeSalles, New York, February 19, 1987

Most steals, game: 17, Mark Anderson, Gonvick Gonvick-Trail, Minnesota, December 4, 1984

Most blocked shots, game: 20, Dan Hicks, Lindsay, California, 1975; Nate Holmstadt, Monticello, Minnesota, March 18, 1995

Boys: Coaching

Most wins all-time: 1,123, Robert Hughes, Ft. Worth (Texas) Dunbar, 1958–Present

Girls: Team

Most state championships: 14, Albuquerque Eldorado, New Mexico; Milwaukee Pius XI, Wisconsin

Most consecutive wins: 218, Baskin, Lousiana, 1947–53

Most points, game: 179, Riverside Poly, California, January 26, 1982

Girls: Individual

Most points scored, career: 4,506, Missy Thomas, Gibsland Gibsland-Coleman, Louisiana, 1992–95

Most points scored, game: 105, Cheryl Miller, Riverside Poly, California, January 26, 1982

Most rebounds, game: 54, Andrea Keehne, La Verne Calvary Baptist, California, February 7, 1995

Most assists, game: 38, Theresa Cross, Brea-Olinda, California, January 13, 1987

Most steals, game: 20, Angie Kisena, Redondo Beach Gateway Christian, California, 1993

Most blocked shots, game: 17, Chris Enger, Vista, California, 1987

Girls: Coaching

Most wins all-time: 1,217, Jim Smiddy, Charleston, Tennessee, and Cleveland Bradley Central, Tennessee, 1948–93 (1,217-206, 85.5 percent)

Chapter 13
College Basketball

In This Chapter

- NCAA, NAIA, NIT, and other strange acronyms
- Players, coaches, and other important people
- Preseason games, postseason tournaments, and all the games in between
- Perennial powerhouses in men's and women's college hoops
- The leap from college to pro ball

It is naive to say that while pro basketball is a business, college basketball is a game. College hoops is big business, after all. But the games are played and attended by some of the most vivacious, resilient, and just plain fun people I know: college students. The college game has character. Witness midnight basketball practice to kick off the preseason. Or Temple coach John Cheney's players rising before the sun for 5 a.m. practice sessions. Or the University of Texas-Arlington's Texas Hall, which is actually a theater for dramatic productions, and whose stage doubles as the team's court.

What Makes College Basketball Special?

The biggest difference between the pro game and the college game (besides the amount of income tax the players pay) may be the enthusiasm of the fans. Boisterous Utah Jazz supporters notwithstanding, the enthusiasm at the college level is derived from its amateur nature. For example, Duke students camp out for days in front of Cameron Indoor Stadium — and Blue Devils coach Mike Krzyzewski often comes out to greet them — in order to secure the best seats in the student section, which happen to be the best seats in the house.

In short, most everyone rooting for a college team has a real connection to it. Most of the fans rooting for a pro team just happen to live nearby.

Cinderella stories

In no other sport does the underdog role receive such attention as in the NCAA tourney. The underdog is known as Cinderella and the tourney as "The Big Dance"; by now every Cinderella reference this side of Disney has been used in a newspaper lead.

Look at the excitement that was generated by the three Cs in the 1997 tourney, for example. These types of games and teams get folks talking in the latter half of March:

- The University of Tennessee-Chattanooga, who limped to a 3-6 start during the season, upset both Georgia and Illinois to advance to the Sweet 16.
- The College of Charleston went 28-2 in the regular season and beat Maryland in the first round before succumbing to Arizona, the eventual champ.
- Coppin State became just the third number-15 seed to beat a number-2 seed when they upset a South Carolina team that had beaten defending champ Kentucky twice in the regular season.

The little man

Recent years have seen the rise of the shorter player in men's college basketball, and I think that this rise has contributed to the interest in the game. The NBA has some terrific little men in Tim Hardaway, Muggsy Bogues, and John Stockton, none of whom are taller than 6'1". But they are rarities. In college, the little man predominates, because with so many teams, there are only so many 7-footers to go around. In college, you see a lot more male players between 5'9" and 6'1".

The adoption of the three-point goal in 1986–87 has had much to do with the added dimension of the little man in the college game. If you are short but can hit the three-point shot with marksman's accuracy and don't mind playing defense, there may be a place for you.

Diversity in style of play

More than 300 Division I teams exist in both men's and women's college basketball, which amounts to 600 different coaches who have not and will never come to a consensus on how the game should be played. The NBA menu reads like a White Castle menu in that there's very little diversity (no matter which two teams are playing); college hoops is a smorgasbord.

When someone says Temple, you think matchup zone. When you hear Princeton, you think back door cuts to the basket. (If you have no idea what I'm talking about, see Chapters 7 and 8 and start watching these teams play.) Because college coaches can't depend on talent and/or depth year in and year out as NBA coaches can, and because fewer rules prohibit certain styles of play in college hoops (for example, zone defense is okay), college coaches are more likely to adopt a signature style of play.

During the 1996–97 season, for example, Oakland City University in Indiana led all of college basketball in three-point shooting with a 47.8 percent mark. Did that team have the best three-point shooters in the country, or was the three-point shot something that the coach stressed more than other coaches around the country? A little of both.

If you're new to the game, check out the NCAA statistics in the newspaper or on the Internet. Those stats tell you the high-scoring teams, the teams that shoot the most three-point goals, the teams that play great defense (based on field-goal-percentage defense, not scoring defense), the best shooting teams, and the best rebounding teams — in other words, the teams to watch this season. See Chapter 4 for details on reading stats.

The NCAA and Other Governing Bodies

The NCAA (National Collegiate Athletic Association) is the national governing body of college sports, including basketball. NCAA schools are divided into three levels for college basketball: Division I, Division II, and Division III. These levels (which are always referred to in Roman numerals) are loosely based on enrollment figures, but schools are allowed to decide at which level they compete.

Most schools are members of the same division for all sports, although some schools compete in Division I in some sports and Division II or III in others. For example, only 111 Division I football schools exist, but 307 play Division I men's basketball. Here's a simple reason for this: expenses. Providing full scholarships to 80 football players costs an athletic department — which must pay the university for those scholarships out of its budget — a lot of cash. Outfitting 80 or more football players (and then transporting them to away games) also costs a lot more money than dressing a dozen hoopsters. Shorts and tank tops are still relatively inexpensive.

NAIA

But, as they say on the game shows, that's not all. Yet another, smaller-school layer of intercollegiate sports exists: the National Association of Intercollegiate Athletics (NAIA), which represents some 480 member schools.

You may not have heard of NAIA schools such as Central Arkansas or Southeastern Oklahoma State, but you probably know all about their former stars, Scottie Pippen and Dennis Rodman, respectively. Every year, the NAIA hosts an outstanding men's tournament consisting of 32 teams in Kansas City. The tournament is played over a one-week period in late February or early March, with games running from 9:00 a.m. to 10:00 p.m.

Junior colleges

Junior colleges, two-year schools (of which there are roughly 550 nationally) unravel yet another layer of backboards and mortarboards. *Jucos,* as they are known, have become havens for student-athletes who have problems qualifying academically as freshmen for four-year schools. Many players who don't have a high enough SAT or ACT score after their senior year of high school attend junior college for two years before transferring to a four-year school.

Keith Smart, for example, the former Indiana point guard who hit the game-winning corner jumper for the Hoosiers' 1987 national championship win against Syracuse, launched his college career at a junior college.

Conference Structure

Conference affiliation within the NCAA structure forms the basic hierarchy of college basketball. A school aligns itself with other schools in a conference for a number of reasons. First, it provides the school with stability in scheduling year in and year out. It also creates amicable rivalries between schools, which amplify interest in the sport. Within Division I college basketball, there are 30 conferences, with an average of ten schools each.

Some conferences are divided into divisions:

- The Southeastern Conference (SEC), which includes such universities as Alabama, Florida, and Kentucky, split its 12 schools into two divisions, East and West.
- The Western Athletic Conference (WAC), whose members include Brigham Young and Utah, is the largest conference, dividing its 16 member schools into four divisions.
- Conference USA is less than a decade old but includes such hoops powers as Cincinnati. It has 12 teams in each of three divisions, appropriately titled Red, White, and Blue.

Dan Mara

A few years ago, John Walters, one of my co-authors, was researching a story on a man he believed to own the longest regular-season winning streak in college basketball history. Walters phoned the school, Mitchell College, and asked for the sports information director.

"This is he," said the male voice at the other end of the line.

"I'd like to talk to you about your women's basketball coach," said Walters.

"You've got him," said Dan Mara.

A boyish gent with a quick wit and a slow first step that got him cut from the only hoops team he ever tried out for, Mara is proof that you need not be a former player to be a successful coach. The evidence lies in the 237 consecutive regular-season wins that Mara's Lady Pequots compiled in the early 1990s. Mitchell, a junior college in New London, Connecticut, was not only Mara's place of employment but also his home for 22 years. He started out as a summer dorm director right after he graduated from college in 1976, then advanced up the ladder to sports information intern, then to women's assistant coach for six years, and finally to women's head coach in 1984.

No other winning streak comes close to Mitchell's. UCLA's 88-game winning streak is usually considered the Mount Everest of basketball, and granted, the Bruins won regular and postseason games. Although Mitchell never won a juco national title, its wins, many of which were earned against four-year schools, extended over a seven-year period.

Mara, now the athletic director at Teikyo Post University in Waterbury, Connecticut, was an eccentric coach. He always started five guards, for example. His Samoyed collie, Pep, always sat beside him at home games. And he challenged his players to score 25 points every ten minutes, a challenge facilitated by his employing a full-court zone press for the entire game.

College conferences: A lesson in geography?

Michael Jordan earned his degree in geography from North Carolina. But he never would have graduated had he used the conference structure of college basketball as a guide in his studies. Teams join conferences for many reasons (such as athletic prowess, similarity in enrollment, and budget), but apparently geography is not one of them. For example:

- Notre Dame is in the Big East for basketball, but I wouldn't call South Bend an Eastern city.
- Arizona and Arizona State are in the Pacific-10, even though theirs is a landlocked state.

Conference ratings

Conference ratings and affiliations are most important when it comes time to determine the field for the NCAA tournament. The selection committee seeks more teams from the top conferences. It's that simple.

The buzzword for this system of rating conference strength is *power ratings.* These ratings are established in nonconference games in November and December, with a few sprinkled in during January and February. If you beat a highly touted nonconference opponent, your power rating goes up. If you lose to a weak team, your rating goes down.

For example, the Atlantic 10 Conference has become a power conference in recent years. Look at some of the conference wins in 1996–97: Massachusetts defeated Boston College and Maryland. Temple defeated Cincinnati, Tulane, and Louisville. Xavier also beat the Cincinnati Bearcats when the Bearcats were ranked first in the country. These nonconference wins established the Atlantic 10 Conference as a top conference and were a major reason why five of the conference teams made it to the NCAA tournament.

Team Size

Most men's college teams have between 12 and 14 players on their rosters. Women's teams have up to 15 players. The difference is a result of athletic scholarships. Women's teams are allowed 15 scholarships at the Division I level, and men's teams, just 13 scholarships (because of a rule called Title IX that ensures an equal number of scholarships for male and female athletes).

Some players on a team may not earn athletic scholarships. They are known as *walk-ons* and usually become fan favorites because students identify better with them. Walk-ons rarely, if ever, play — some never even suit up for a game — but they are invaluable during practice sessions.

Coaches and Managers

Each Division I college team has a head coach, two full-time assistant coaches, and a part-time assistant coach. The head coach and two full-time assistants are allowed to recruit off-campus, but the part-time coach is not. She may be involved in all other areas of coaching — scouting, corresponding with recruits, on-floor coaching during practice and games, and so on.

The roles of the college coach

All coaches deal with the media, watch film, prepare for practice, prepare resumes for when they get canned, run practice, and coach games. But NBA coaches never have to worry about midnight practice or one of their players failing calculus. One *new* problem that NBA coaches face that college coaches have long had to deal with: underage players consuming alcohol.

Here are some additional responsibilities that college coaches have:

- **Monitoring academic performance of players:** Academic affairs are a constant concern for college coaches at all levels. Phil Jackson never has to worry whether Michael Jordan will be academically eligible to play for the Bulls, but Arizona coach Lute Olson had that problem during the 1996–97 season. Miles Simon, the only returning starter for his Arizona team, was ineligible for the first ten games. But he returned and led the Wildcats to the national championship.
- **Speaking to alumni groups:** Alumni can help a program, but they can create a negative climate as well. Most coaches (especially those who have had a mediocre season) make inroads with alumni during the offseason through various speaking engagements.

- **Speaking to campus groups:** As with alumni groups, coaches can increase their fan base by putting in effort with student groups. For example, I used to spend September and April speaking on campus in the lobby of various dorms at Notre Dame. I talked about everything, sometimes even basketball, in a question-and-answer format. If nothing else, getting involved with the students creates campus interest in the program.
- **Consulting with players:** College coaches often play the role of surrogate father to their players. College is often the first time these young people have lived away from home, and it's only natural that their coach becomes the strongest adult role model in their lives.
- **Promoting the team:** Most college athletic departments do not have the marketing budgets that NBA franchises do, so athletic departments often enlist coaches to lend an assist. Coaches may be asked to speak to local civic groups, serve as grand marshal at a parade, or make an appearance at the local mall. *Tip for reticent coaches:* The more you win, the less you will be asked to do.

The identity of a college basketball team is the school and the coaches. The players change at least every four years — and the headliners, the ones the average fan recognizes, often leave earlier than that. The NBA game, on the other hand, is about the players, not the coaches or the franchise. In fact, when I was a boy, I remember going to Madison Square Garden to see the New York Knicks play the Minneapolis Lakers. The sign on the marquee read, "Knicks face George Mikan tonight at 8:00 p.m." (Mikan was Minneapolis's star center.)

College coaching salaries

Based on the laws of supply and demand and what a school can make from its college basketball program, coaches' salaries at higher-profile schools are going over the backboard. Just look at the terms of the contracts of two coaches in the state of South Carolina, Clemson and the University of South Carolina (who have been well known for their support of *football* coaches in the past). Clemson's Rick Barnes recently signed a seven-year contract at $668,000 a year, while South Carolina's Eddie Fogler signed for about $600,000 a year.

Their base contracts are appreciably smaller ($138,000 for Barnes and $130,000 for Fogler), but they're guaranteed outside income from radio and TV contracts, shoe deals, and other sources. (So you can rest assured that most of the lucre of these big salaries does not emanate from your or your kids' tuition bills.) Still, both programs have shown a commitment to these coaches and to basketball.

Perhaps for this reason, college coaches enjoy greater job security than NBA coaches. The NBA job mortality rate among coaches is approximately 35 percent annually, whereas college coaches have an 18 percent pink slip rate (which I would hardly call "secure").

The little guys

Each team also has a group of student managers who do the thankless work that no one else would do without being paid. During games, managers perform a very important task: They sit on the bench dressed like the coaches to make it more difficult for the referees to tell who's making the profane comments from the bench.

Games

Each team, be it Division I, II, or III, or NAIA, plays between 27 and 40 games per year. The numbers vary due to postseason success in conference and then national tournaments (you win, you play again; you lose, you don't) and scheduling by each school's athletic director. Some tournaments at the Division I level (such as the preseason National Invitational Tournament, or NIT) don't count toward the maximum 26 regular-season games allowed by the NCAA.

The Division I men's record for victories in a season is 37, set by Duke in 1985–86 and UNLV in 1991–92. Ironically, neither team won the national championship in those seasons. On the women's side, Texas (1982), Louisiana Tech (also 1982), Tennessee (1989), and Connecticut (1995) are tied with

35 victories. All except the Lady Longhorns of Texas advanced to win the national championship, with UConn being the only team to do so undefeated.

Tournaments: The Ultimate Goal

Most schools qualify for their conference tournament, but qualification for the NCAA tournament, which decides the national champion, is determined by a selection process that a committee oversees. Some teams qualify automatically. For example, the champion of each of the 30 postseason conference tournaments recognized by the NCAA selection committee receives an automatic bid, even if the team has a losing record. The other 34 teams selected receive at-large bids, which in effect are invitations tendered to the best teams remaining from the pool of teams that did not win their conference tournament.

The National Invitation Tournament (NIT), which long ago held more prestige than the NCAA tourney, also stages a postseason 32-team affair for Division I men's teams that are not invited to the NCAAs. The NIT features some of the year's biggest under- and overachieving programs. The underachieving teams are those that arrived on the first day of practice in October with a mess of talent and played well below their potential. For them, the postseason NIT is a bitter pill to swallow. The overachieving teams are those that played far better than anyone (perhaps even they) expected. Their NIT invitation is most welcome.

All tournaments are *single-elimination,* which means that if you lose, you're out. You catch an opponent on an off-day, and you can pull off an upset that alums discuss for years. Just ask Princeton, who upset defending national champ UCLA in a first-round game in 1996. (See Chapter 16 for more information about the NCAA tournament.)

I don't see anything wrong with accommodating teams with losing records in the tournament as long as they win their conference tournament. Then again, when I was a coach, I would have been livid if a team such as Fairfield — who qualified for the 1997 tournament with an 11-18 record — had been invited ahead of Notre Dame if we were 18-11.

Polls

America has a compulsive need to rank things, seen everywhere from David Letterman's *Top Ten List* to Casey Kasem's *American Top 40* to teams in just about every intercollegiate sport. (Ever notice how, in *The Sound of Music,* Julie Andrews as an *Austrian* nun sings "My Favorite Things" without ranking them?)

Polls are more important in college football — they determine the national champ — but they play a role in college hoops as well. The polls are a barometer, a pulse rate for teams during the season, right up until the national champion is crowned. For both fans and players, polls heighten interest in games. A game between top-ranked Kansas and #3 Duke sounds more enticing than one between just Kansas and Duke (although either is Must See TV for a hoops junkie).

Each level of basketball has polls. At the Division I level, two polls exist: Associated Press, which is voted on by AP writers, and *USA Today,* which is a compilation of the opinions of college coaches. Each week, from early November until the end of the conference tournaments, these polls provide a ladder for teams to climb — and descend — as fans debate their accuracy.

All-America Teams

You hear less about individual statistics in college ball than you do in the pros, but more about which players deserve to be on an All-America team. Unlike the NBA, college basketball does not feature a common ground of opponents — nobody wants to play a 300-game schedule. And that means the quality of opponents on one team's schedule may differ greatly from another's. Thus one player's 28 points per game may mean less than another player's 20 due to the level of competition that he faces.

Various services and organizations choose All-America players. You don't have to be an American to win; All-America is just a term for an All-Star team. Unlike the NBA, no single All-America team exists. Any organization may choose an All-America team, and depending on its selection procedure, the honor may be tantamount to being elected to public office, or it may mean nothing at all. Most basketball All-America teams are five-person squads selected by people within an organization. Each organization picks a first and second team so it honors at least ten players.

For example, the Wooden Award All-America team is a ten-person team chosen by members of the Wooden Award Committee. The award is named after legendary coach John Wooden.

The Wooden committee also selects a male and a female player of the year. The Associated Press, which picks a first, second, and third team, bases its selections on votes cast by AP sportswriters nationwide.

Each organization has its own system. For women, the oldest All-America team and the one with the most credibility is the Kodak All-America team. It has credibility because the people on the committee know their college basketball and have followed the game for many years.

How the Game Has Changed Since 1975

The college game has undergone many changes since I was in the heart of my career at Notre Dame. Seeing the willingness among coaches and administrators to allow the game to evolve with the times is refreshing. Had our hoops forefathers not subscribed to this ideal, we'd still be using peach baskets.

The three-point goal

The three-point shot has welcomed the perimeter player back into the game and opened things up underneath the basket. But the line is too close to the basket. (See my suggestions for improving the game in the section "Hot Topics: Digger's Suggestions for Improving the College Game" later in this chapter.)

Midnight Madness

Practice for college basketball at the Division I level begins on the first Saturday after October 15. It used to begin on October 15, but the rule was changed so that students wouldn't sleep through their first-period classes.

Prior to the rule change, it had become increasingly chic for teams to stage their first practice of the season at the stroke of midnight on October 15. These Midnight Madness sessions are a celebration of hoops, parties disguised as a basketball practice that are open to all students. So the NCAA instituted the "Saturday after" rule in 1997 so that students would not be up so late on a school night. (Do you ever get the feeling that the people at the NCAA have never stepped foot on a college campus?)

What happens at a Midnight Madness session? Some schools have a scrimmage, go through lay-up lines, perform a few dunks, stage a shooting contest or two, and then sign autographs. Midnight Madness has become more effective as a public relations tool for the school than as a legitimate practice. Many programs — Kentucky, Kansas, and others — have sold out arenas for Midnight Madness.

Officially, any student at a university is eligible to try out for the team as long as he has not already exhausted his four years of eligibility. The reality is that full-time coaching staffs — not just one coach — devote hundreds, sometimes thousands, of hours to recruiting players and building their rosters.

Unofficial "workouts" occur nearly year-round for these dozen or so players to whom the coach has awarded scholarships. The chances of a student appearing out of the blue for the first day of practice and making the team are almost nil. When I was coaching, I would hold a separate tryout for walk-ons and invite a few of the best from that tryout to give it a shot. We always tried to keep at least one walk-on player on our roster. These kids work hard, and scholarship kids, seeing this determination up close, are less likely to take their lofty status for granted.

Digger wonders: Why can't a student show up at Midnight Madness and announce to the coach that he'd like to try out for the team? Technically, isn't the team open to any student? And wouldn't the first day of practice be the best day to begin your tryout? This I'd like to see.

The shot clock

In the 1982 ACC (Atlantic Coast Conference) conference tournament championship game, North Carolina defeated Virginia 47-45. Both teams had marvelous players (Sam Perkins, Michael Jordan, James Worthy, and Ralph Sampson), but the game was boring. Believe it: A game with Michael Jordan was boring. Neither team was in a hurry to shoot the ball, resulting in fewer offensive possessions. Fans don't pay to see dribbling; they pay to see baskets. Something had to be done. That game, shown on national TV, helped to create support for the introduction of a shot clock to speed up the game.

Three-guard offenses

The advent of the three-point shot, as well as the shot clock, in the 1980s put a greater emphasis on speed in the college game. Offensively, coaches seek players who can penetrate defenses via the dribble and then pass to open teammates outside the three-point arc. Defensively, they desire players who can cover more space on the floor, especially around that three-point line. When Providence recruited gifted point guard God Shammgod a few years ago, God acknowledged his omnipotence at that point. Said God, "I'm a creator (with the ball in my hands)."

Twenty-two years ago, I would not have espoused the three-guard offense. The shot clock and the three-point goal did not exist. Today, however, I'd prefer the three guards, or even two quick, talented guards (the backcourt) over a middling frontcourt (forwards plus center), even if the frontcourt included a 7-foot center. The speedy guards are more valuable in today's offenses.

Look at the teams in the men's Final Four in the 1997 tournament, for example. None of them had a dominating 7-footer. Wake Forest had Tim Duncan, the best big man in college basketball in many years, and they failed to advance past the second round. Who won the tournament? Arizona, the team with *perimeter players* (guards who position themselves around the three-point arc) Mike Bibby and Miles Simon.

The women's game is no different. Connecticut had the best center in the country, Kara Wolters; like Duncan, she was voted Player of the Year by a number of organizations. But Connecticut failed to reach the NCAA championship game. Tennessee, led by the best perimeter player in women's college basketball, Chamique Holdsclaw, claimed the title.

Pressing defenses

Teams press more now than they used to — a function of having so many small, quick players on the floor. Rick Pitino and his success as coach at the

University of Kentucky had as much to do with that as anything. When his team won the national title in 1996, he had all the talent in the world. In 1997, Pitino returned to the Final Four with a less-talented team, leading coaches to believe that Pitino's *system* made the difference.

A 64-team field

Twenty years ago, only 32 teams made it to the NCAA tournament. And women didn't even have a postseason national championship tourney sponsored by the NCAA. Obviously, quite a few more teams now begin their seasons with realistic dreams of qualifying for the NCAA tournament.

The legalized dunk

Dunking was illegal between 1967 and 1976. The dunk returned in 1976–77, and with it came excitement and more college games in highlight reels.

Players turning pro

Spencer Haywood was 20 when he turned pro in 1969 and signed with the American Basketball Association (ABA) out of the University of Detroit. Then the NBA adopted a Hardship Rule, whereby a junior could turn pro if he showed financial need. The real hardship, of course, would have been on the NBA had the rule not been born: The ABA would have stolen the NBA's future talent. But in 1975, no coach feared losing a freshman to the pros.

Today, any freshman who earns third-team All-America honors is practically a slam dunk to go pro. But this trend has not killed the game. For every Stephon Marbury who turns pro as a freshman, a Miles Simon is waiting to take the spotlight. The people who complain are the fans or coaches at schools that lose a great player after a freshman or sophomore year. But the overall good of the game has not suffered and won't suffer.

Players who leave early can cripple their programs momentarily, because team chemistry and consistency are lost. Look at Georgia Tech with Stephon Marbury. That team won the ACC regular season with Marbury, a freshman playing point guard, in 1995–96. The next year, Marbury turned pro, and Georgia Tech finished last in the ACC. Do you think that Georgia Tech would have been last if Marbury had stayed? Neither do I.

The nature of the game — 5 players on the court at the same time and just 12 on an active roster — means that one star player can make a tremendous difference. That's true in CYO (Catholic Youth Organization) ball as well as in the NBA Finals.

Parity

Coaches can no longer stockpile talent and groom it for a year or two. Kids want to play immediately these days, and if one coach can't make it happen for them, a coach in more dire straits can.

UCLA was the top program of the 1960s and early 1970s. Back then, freshmen were ineligible to play, so coaches could sign them to scholarships and still load up a team of 12 players composed of sophomores, juniors, and seniors. That rule allowed UCLA to sign players like Swen Nater, a backup center at Westwood who played ten NBA seasons. This sort of stockpiling wouldn't happen today; Nater would have transferred.

Television

In 1975, just a few games were on national TV. Today, with ESPN and all the other networks combining to broadcast more than 1,000 men's and women's games, exposure is at an all-time high.

Has college hoops become oversaturated on TV? I don't think so. Every game, no matter how unimportant from a national standpoint, generates local interest. When your favorite team travels to a hostile gym and pulls off an upset, chances are greater that you will attend the next home game.

True, ratings are down, but that's due to the increased volume of televised games. Viewership is less centralized. Besides, ratings fail to take into account sports bars and other places where folks watch sports. Those establishments have a few games on simultaneously as well.

Stricter national academic requirements

With the implementation of Proposition 48 and Proposition 42, which set minimum academic standards that all incoming freshmen must meet in order to play, many student-athletes have been lost to junior colleges. They either refuse to sit out for one year at a four-year school (they are prohibited from practicing *and* lose a year of athletic eligibility), or the school declines to accept them.

Hot Topics: Digger's Suggestions for Improving the College Game

As much as I love college basketball, there's always room for improvement. Here are my ideas for how we can make the game even better to play and to watch:

- **Return to the jump ball.** Referees are paid $500 a game to officiate. They ought to be able to throw a ball straight up in the air with two hands. The current alternating possession rule eliminates one of the game's most exciting plays and fails to reward the defense that forced the jump ball.
- **No calling time-out as you sail out of bounds.** This rule should be changed in *all* levels of basketball, not just college. If a player lands out of bounds, she is out of bounds. Being able to call time-out is like being saved by the bell in a prize fight. The rule should be that you must have both feet in bounds on the floor when you call a time-out.
- **Move the three-point line back.** The three-point line is too close. I say move the stripe back to the international distance of 20'6" and restore some balance to the game in terms of shot attempts from within the line versus those from beyond.

  The best shooting percentages in the history of the three-point goal in college basketball came in 1986–87, the first year the three-pointer was used. That is not a coincidence. Coaches were conservative in their use of the three-point goal at first; players attempted the shot only when they had a good look. I want to revert to those days.
- **Start your last-second shot before the last second.** Why do offenses wait until seven seconds remain to begin their last-second shot play? Most coaches worry about leaving time on the clock for the opposition to score. What happens, though, is that the offense rushes its play and takes a poor shot. Start with 11 seconds showing on the clock, I say.

  I would rather score and believe in my defense for three seconds than rush a shot, miss, and go into overtime. Whenever I see teams start with seven seconds left, I just yell, "Overtime!"
- **Allow TV replays in the last two minutes of a game.** Referees should have the option to view instant replays in the last two minutes of a game. We have the technology; why not use it and get the call right?

  Wake Forest played North Carolina State in 1997. NC State hit a three-point shot to win a game in overtime. But the replay showed that the shooter's foot was on the line, and the game should have gone into a second overtime.
- **When up by three in the final seconds, FOUL!** You're leading by three points with five seconds left, and the opposition has the ball. Why not foul the opposing team and put them on the line for two shots? Think about the percentages you're playing: your three-point defense versus another team making the first free throw, or missing the second one intentionally and getting the rebound and scoring. I'd rather put my money on boxing out and rebounding (see Chapter 8) than on giving up a three-point basket. Whenever I sit in the ESPN studios and watch this scenario unfold, I froth at the mouth and scream at the monitor. I even have our host, Chris Fowler, convinced by now.

NCAA Women's Basketball

Said John Wooden in *USA Today,* "To me, the best pure basketball I see today . . . is among the better women's teams."

In my first seven years at Notre Dame, we had no varsity women's basketball program. (But you should know that, in my first year there, we didn't even admit women.) The only competition of note for women on campus was the annual "Jocks versus Girls" pickup basketball game. Seeing Notre Dame's women's team go to the Final Four in 1997 reminded me of those games and how far Notre Dame women's basketball in particular and women's basketball in general has come in such a short time.

The smaller ball

In 1984–85, the NCAA adopted a smaller ball for women's college basketball. The women's ball is 1 inch smaller in circumference and $2^1/_2$ ounces lighter than the one used by men. This modification has had a great deal to do with the popularity of the women's game nationwide.

The NCAA thought that the smaller ball would increase scoring and shooting percentages, but that has not been the case; neither statistic has varied greatly. But what has happened is that ball handling has improved, teams are committing fewer turnovers, and the quality of play is much better.

The women's professional leagues are divided on the smaller ball issue. The WNBA uses the small basketball, but the ABL uses the big ball. All international basketball teams use the big ball.

Increased media attention

Another reason for the increase in women's basketball interest is media attention. Interest had been growing since the 1980s, but when the media in the East fell in love with the Connecticut women's team in 1995 and its magical 35-0 season, everyone took notice.

When Connecticut won the national championship to consummate only the second undefeated season in women's NCAA history, the media embraced Connecticut star Rebecca Lobo in particular. Lobo appeared on the *CBS Morning News* and *Late Night with David Letterman* and joined her teammates on *Live with Regis & Kathie Lee.*

Attendance at women's college games is also on the rise. The 1997 Final Four in Cincinnati, for example, sold out in four hours. The 1998 Final Four will use a lottery system to distribute tickets for the first time in women's history.

(Nearly) pure amateurism

In the last ten years, college basketball fans have become increasingly disgusted with the mercenary aspect of men's hoops. Players openly admit that they will remain at their schools only until they are assured of being selected early in the NBA draft (which translates into millions of dollars). They often base the choice of what school to attend on whether the coach can assure them that they will start as freshmen.

Then along comes the women's game. Until 1997, females had no hope of playing professionally on this continent after their college careers ended. The few women's pro leagues — such as the Women's Professional Basketball League (WBL) in 1978; the Liberty Basketball Association (1991), which clad its players in form-fitting unitards and folded after one game; and the Women's Basketball Association (1992) — that were launched never lasted long. The perception among fans, quite accurately, was that women were playing for the pure fun of it. Also, as men's hoops was making headlines off the court as much as on — NCAA recruiting and other violations, poor graduation rates, and an alarming upswing of felonious activity among players — women's basketball had real student-athletes in the forefront carrying the banner.

How many women's basketball programs have been on probation the last ten years? The number is appreciably lower than for Division I football and men's basketball. The question facing women's basketball in the next few years in light of the establishment of not one, but two, pro leagues is: Can they retain this pure amateurism image?

The top women players of all-time

You'll recognize a few of the names that follow because they currently star (or coach) in the WNBA. Those women whose names you don't recognize (unfortunately, few women's games were televised before this decade) were every bit as good. Here are my picks for the best women players in hoops history:

- **Carol Blazejowski, Montclair State, 1974–78:** "Blaze" still holds the women's career scoring average record with 31.7 points for four years and 38.6 points per game in 1977–78, her senior year. She was a three-time All-American and the first winner of the Wade Trophy, the Heisman Trophy of women's college basketball. She was inducted into the Naismith Basketball Hall of Fame in 1993.
- **Ann Donovan, Old Dominion, 1979–83:** The top player on two national championship teams and two Olympic gold medal teams. She is regarded as the first tall impact player in women's basketball. A three-time Kodak All-American and the 1983 National Player of the Year, Donovan is one of the few players in women's college history to shoot at least 60 percent from the field in four straight seasons.

- **Teresa Edwards, Georgia, 1982–86:** Edwards was a two-time Kodak All-American who had her jersey retired at Georgia — the first woman's basketball player to receive this honor. She is a three-time Olympian and was a member of the 1996 gold medal team.
- **Lusia Harris, Delta State, 1973–77:** Harris was the first female college player to be inducted into the Basketball Hall of Fame. She led Delta State to three straight national titles and was the MVP in all three tournaments; only Kareem Abdul-Jabbar earned as many MVB trophies in the national tournament. She averaged 26 points per game for her college career and shot over 60 percent from the field in all four years.
- **Lisa Leslie, Southern California, 1990–94:** The 1994 National Player of the Year, Leslie was a three-time All-American. She first burst onto the national scene when she scored 101 points in the first half of a high school game. (The other team walked off the court after that.)
- **Nancy Lieberman, Old Dominion, 1976–80:** Still very much involved in the game as a broadcaster and as a player in the WNBA, Lieberman elevated the sport to new heights with her ability to drive to the basket and score from anywhere on the court. She was a three-time Kodak All-American, captain of two national championship teams, and the 1980 National Player of the Year. Her nickname was "Lady Magic" because of her passing and all-around abilities.
- **Rebecca Lobo, Connecticut, 1991–95:** You could call Lobo the Arnold Palmer of women's college basketball; her charisma and engaging personality make her a great representative of the sport. She is perhaps the most recognized female athlete in the United States. This two-time All-American led Connecticut to the 1995 national championship and a 35-0 record. She was a National Player of the Year and was Phi Beta Kappa.
- **Ann Meyers, UCLA, 1974–78:** Meyers was inducted into the Naismith Hall of Fame in 1993. Her late husband, Don Drysdale, was also inducted into the Baseball Hall of Fame, the only married couple to be inducted into respective Halls of Fame. She was the first woman awarded an athletic scholarship to UCLA. An All-American, her UCLA team won the 1978 national championship. She is the only female to have signed a free agent contract with an NBA team (the Indiana Pacers in 1979), although she failed to make the team.
- **Cheryl Miller, Southern California, 1982–86:** Miller was a four-time All-American and three-time National Player of the Year, the only women's player in history with these honors. She led Southern Cal to the national championship twice and was named the player of the decade for women's college basketball by the United States Basketball Writers Association. She is a member of the Naismith Hall of Fame and continues her involvement in basketball as an announcer with television network TNT and as head coach of the Phoenix Mercury in the WNBA.
- **Sheryl Swoopes, Texas Tech, 1991–93:** Swoopes (as in "hoops") led Texas Tech to the 1993 national championship by scoring a finals-record 47 points. She was the National Player of the Year that season

and a two-time All-American. She was also a starter on the United States gold medal-winning 1996 Olympic team and currently plays for Houston in the WNBA.

- **Lynette Woodard, Kansas, 1977–81:** Woodard is the all-time leading scorer in the history of women's college basketball with 3,649 total points. She was a four-time All-American and a two-time Olympian in addition to winning the 1981 Wade Trophy. A role model for women athletes, she was the first female inducted into the GTA Academic Hall of Fame (1992).

Model women's basketball programs

Although the quality of play in women's basketball has improved dramatically across the board in the last decade, certain teams stand out as perennial powerhouses. This section talks about the "Female Finest Four."

Tennessee

The Lady Vols have dominated the women's game like no other program has dominated college hoops, men's or women's, in the last 15 years. Since the women's NCAA tourney was inaugurated in 1982, Tennessee has won five national titles (including the last two) and has played in ten Final Fours. Moreover, the Lady Vols have won at least 20 games in 21 consecutive seasons.

The reason: head coach Pat Summitt. Her career record of 625-143 through the 1996–97 season, and her age (44), argue well for her to eclipse Dean Smith's men's record for career wins. More impressive is the aptly named Summitt's 55-11 NCAA tournament record.

UConn

University of Connecticut (UConn) versus Tennessee has been a rivalry that has brought women's college basketball to the forefront. The Connecticut Huskies' victory over Tennessee in the 1995 regular season and then in the NCAA tournament brought Huskiemania to a new level and elevated the women's game to a plateau of national import to the average sports fan. In 1997, Tennessee returned the favor, eliminating an undefeated and #1 ranked Connecticut team from the NCAA tournament.

Connecticut women's basketball is one of the great stories in modern college athletics. A program that had an average of 500 fans per game six years ago now sells out every game.

Louisiana Tech

The Lady Techsters won the very first women's NCAA title in 1982 (and won their other title six years later). They own the longest win streak in Division I women's college hoops, winning 54 in a row from 1980 to 1982. Through the

1996–97 season, the Ruston, Louisiana school ranks number one in all-time winning percentage (.838) and number two in all-time wins (614) behind Tennessee. Coach Leon Barmore, who arrived in Ruston in 1982, is the winningest D-I women's head coach of all time, with a record of 397-63.

One of many reasons for Louisiana Tech's success is rebounding. In seven of the 17 seasons the NCAA has kept rebounding margin statistics, the Lady Techsters have been tops in the nation. In 1990, they grabbed an average of 18.3 more rebounds per game than their opponents, a Division I record for both men and women.

Stanford

Ever since head coach Tara VanDerveer planted herself on the Farm (the nickname for Stanford's bucolic campus), the Cardinal have risen straight to the top of the college game. The two-time national champions (1990 and 1992) have won no fewer than 20 games in each of the last ten seasons. An intense coach, VanDerveer is also a gifted recruiter who has produced four first-team All-Americans in the 1990s: Jennifer Azzi, Sonja Henning, Val Whiting, and Kate Starbird.

VanDerveer took a year's sabbatical in 1995–96 to coach the U.S. Women's Olympic team, arguably the best women's hoops team ever assembled. Without VanDerveer guiding them, the Cardinal still finished 29-3, but the coach did even better with her Olympic squad. The U.S. women went 50-0 in exhibition matches leading up to the Olympics in Atlanta, where they captured the gold medal.

NCAA Men's Elite Eight Programs: Today and for the Ages

A few college programs are nothing short of latter twentieth century American success stories; they are the McDonald's, Disney, or Microsoft of college hoops. Eight such giants stand out to me for meeting the following criteria: They rank among the winningest programs ever; they have distinct traditions replete with legends on the bench and in uniform; and they have not allowed the sport to pass them by.

Duke

Duke is the ninth winningest program in college basketball history. Coach Mike Krzyzewski's Blue Devils had the closest thing to a dynasty since UCLA went to seven Final Fours between 1986 and 1995. Duke's court, Cameron Indoor Stadium, may have the best aura and definitely has the best fans (the Cameron Crazies) in college hoops.

What have you done for me lately? Duke finished last in the ACC in 1995 (a year that "Coach K" missed with a back ailment), but that blip on the screen has been corrected. The Blue Devils were the ACC regular-season champs in 1997, and Coach K signed the top recruiting class in the nation for 1998.

Indiana

Indiana has the 14th winningest program in college basketball history and ranked among the top 12 programs in each of the last three decades. Coach Bob Knight, "The General," is the sport's most controversial figure, but he wins without ever bending the rules. The Hoosiers are the high priests in the state where hoops matters most to its disciples, and the 1976 team forged the last undefeated national title season the game witnessed.

What have you done for me lately? Indiana made the NCAA field in the last 11 consecutive years, including a trip to the Final Four in 1993 and an NCAA title in 1987.

Kansas

Kansas is the fifth winningest program in college basketball history and has a direct link to the game's genesis. Dr. James Naismith invented the game and then moved to Kansas, where he coached Phog Allen, one of the patriarchs of college coaching. Among Allen's pupils were Dean Smith, Division I's winningest coach, and Wilt Chamberlain, arguably basketball's most dominant player ever. The Jayhawks last won a national title in 1988 behind Player of the Year Danny Manning.

What have you done for me lately? Kansas is the winningest team in Division I this decade. With the exception of a Sweet 16 loss to Arizona, it was by far the top team in college basketball in 1997.

Kentucky

Even among this elite clique, the University of Kentucky stands out. The Wildcat program is the winningest in college hoops history (77 percent). And how's this for consistency: The Wildcats have ranked among the top ten winningest programs in each decade since the 1950s. No other school can claim that achievement.

What have you done for me lately? Kentucky played in the national title game in 1996 and 1997, winning the title in 1996. The Wildcats made a third Final Four appearance this decade and would have made a fourth were it not for Duke's miraculous win in the 1992 East Regional final.

Louisville

As with North Carolina, Kansas, Duke, Indiana, and Syracuse, Louisville's coach, Denny Crum, has been with the program for more than a decade. Crum is among the winningest coaches in history, a reason the Cardinals rank 12th in NCAA history in winning percentage. When you consider that Crum must recruit in the state where the University of Kentucky has long reigned, that feat is significant.

What have you done for me lately? Louisville advanced to the Final Eight of the NCAAs in 1997 before losing to North Carolina. This program went to the Sweet 16 four of the last five years.

North Carolina

While Kentucky has had four different coaches since the 1960s, North Carolina has had just one: Dean Smith. The winningest coach in Division I college basketball history gives this program unparalleled consistency. North Carolina is the second winningest program in college history on a percentage basis.

Year in and year out, North Carolina sends more players to the NBA than any other school: Charlie Scott, Walter Davis, James Worthy, Jerry Stackhouse, and that guy Michael Jordan, who enhances the reputation of the school in Chapel Hill each time he steps on the court, to name a few. Smith has succeeded because he molds such fantastic individual talents into a team. Folks often say of his relationship with Jordan, "Dean Smith is the only guy who could hold Michael Jordan to under 20 points a game."

What have you done for me lately? How about trips to the Final Four in each odd-numbered year in the 1990s, including a national championship in 1993?

Syracuse

Syracuse's inclusion in this list may surprise some fans; the Orangemen didn't even qualify for the NCAA tournament in 1997. But Jim Boeheim's team played in the championship in 1996 and is the seventh winningest program in college basketball history. Syracuse has ranked among the ten winningest programs in the country in the 1970s, 1980s, and 1990s, something only four other schools can claim.

What have you done for me lately? Prior to missing the 1997 NCAAs, Syracuse qualified for the Big Dance 13 times in the past 14 years, including championship game appearances in 1987 and 1996.

UCLA

UCLA is the fourth winningest program in college basketball history, but has the most national championships with 11. People talk about dynasties in sports, but UCLA sets the standard in college basketball with 7 consecutive NCAA championships between 1967 and 1973 and 10 in 12 years between 1964 and 1975. John Wooden, the Wizard of Westwood, won all 10 of those titles. He was fortunate to coach two of the best centers the sport has ever seen: Lew Alcindor (later Kareem Abdul-Jabbar) and Bill Walton.

What have you done for me lately? UCLA won the national championship in 1995, defeating defending champion Arkansas.

Does Great College Player = Great NBA Player?

Extrapolating whether great college players will become great pro players is akin to taking a junior high math test: The answer may be (A) >, (B) =, or (C) <.

- Patrick Ewing was a force in college and has never been less than a force in the NBA. Question: Ewing. Answer: (B) =.
- As good as Karl Malone was for Louisiana Tech, no one could have predicted that the 13th pick in the 1985 draft would become a league MVP and, in most experts' opinions, the greatest power forward the game has seen. Question: Malone. Answer: (A) >.

However, more often than not, great college players never meet the expectations placed upon them as pros. Players such as Corliss Williamson at Arkansas, Danny Manning at Kansas, and Scott May of Indiana, all of whom led their college teams to national titles, fall into the (C) < category. Here are a few reasons why the NBA treats college All-Americans so harshly:

- **Longer season, longer games:** The college schedule is basically a 30-game season, while the NBA is 10 exhibition games, 82 regular-season games, plus the playoffs. And sometimes getting up for the Tuesday nighter in Vancouver when you haven't seen your own bed in eight days is tough. Plus, NBA games are eight minutes longer. Rookies usually hit the wall in February and then either adjust or atrophy.
- **Size:** Some players are big enough to contend with the average player at their position in college, but the pro game can be drastically different. A 6'3" guard in college who is used to shooting over most of his opponents will find the average NBA guard taller — and stronger.

- **Quickness:** The NBA game is much faster paced. There's the 24-second clock, for starters. Then you have sophisticated defenses that swallow up most one-on-one juke specialists. Your crossover dribble that worked at State may not get you very far against someone who's guarded Michael Jordan and Grant Hill.
- **Bright lights, big cities:** Some players just have trouble adjusting to life in the real world. Players are coddled in some college programs, especially those who attend school close to home. If you live on campus at Notre Dame, for example, all male students have their laundry picked up at their dorm and washed for them. That's a little thing, but it contributes to the unrealistic security blanket that college provides. Plus, the media is much tougher on the pro game, and you suddenly gain many new friends who want you to be their good-time sugar daddy. You have to be mature to overcome the myriad temptations.

From BMOC to MIA: College stars who got lost in the NBA

Steve Alford, Indiana: Alford led Indiana to the national championship in 1987 with a 22.0 scoring average and a nation's best 53 percent accuracy from beyond the three-point stripe. Alford also converted 90 percent of his career free throws. A consensus first team All-American as a senior, he was the 26th pick of the 1987 draft. But in four seasons, first with the Dallas Mavericks and later with the Golden State Warriors, Alford started just three games. He never had the size or quickness to compete at the NBA level, but more important for the Hoosier-born and bred coach's son, he admits that he never had a taste for the NBA lifestyle. Alford is now a rising star in college coaching circles at Southwest Missouri State.

Keith Lee, Memphis State: Lee was a three-time All-American who was the 11th overall pick of the Chicago Bulls in the 1985 draft. He took Memphis State to the Final Four his senior year after scoring 20 points per game. A pure shooter as a 6'10" center and forward, he made 78 percent of his free throws. Lee lasted three years in the NBA and averaged just 6.1 points per game.

Lenny Rosenbluth, North Carolina: Rosenbluth led North Carolina to the 1957 national title and played a key role in the Tar Heels' upset of Wilt Chamberlain and Kansas. North Carolina went 32-0 behind Rosenbluth's 28 points per game that year. The sixth overall pick of the NBA by the Philadelphia Warriors, Rosenbluth played just two seasons in the NBA, averaging 4.2 points and shooting a lowly 21 percent from the field.

Nick Werkman, Seton Hall: Werkman was the leading scorer in the country in 1962–63 with a 29.5 average, and then finished second to Howard Komives in 1963–64 with a 33.2 scoring average. (I held him to 42 one night in 1963 while playing for Rider.) Nick averaged 32 points per game for his career, one of the top scoring averages in NCAA history, but he never played a game in the NBA after being drafted in the fifth round by the Boston Celtics.

Chapter 14

Professional Basketball

In This Chapter

- Checking out the organization of the NBA and other U.S. pro leagues
- Discovering the impact of the pro game's changing rules
- Watching famous moves by famous players
- Paying and coaching today's pro player

In 1996, pro basketball crossed the gender equity line, this time hopefully for good. The 1996 U.S. women's Olympic basketball team — featured on the cover of the *Sports Illustrated* Olympic preview issue — won the gold medal and, in doing so, proved dreamier to the American public than its male "Dream Team" counterpart. The wake of the women's triumph saw the launching of not one but two distaff pro leagues: the American Basketball League (ABL), which began play in November 1996, and the Women's NBA (WNBA), which started in June 1997. Boys on the side, indeed.

But the chromosomal XX Games explosion may not have been possible unless the NBA itself was in robust shape, which it was. In 1997, Michael Jordan and his Chicago Bulls culminated the two best seasons, in terms of wins (141), in league history and captured a second consecutive NBA championship. The 4-2 series win against the Utah Jazz was Chicago's fifth in seven years and fifth in a row with MJ playing a full season.

Who's to say whether the sisters will catch up to the brothers in terms of talent or popularity. Worth noting: The tallest player in the first NBA game in 1946 was George Nostrand of the Toronto Huskies, who stood 6'8". The tallest woman in the first WNBA game in 1997 was Zheng Haixai of the Los Angeles Sparks, also 6'8". When asked to name her two favorite players, Zheng said, "Jordan and myself."

Although more changes are likely as the newer leagues develop and the older leagues evolve, I want to introduce you to some of the elements of professional basketball that will stick around in one form or another. In this chapter, I talk about the organization of professional basketball in terms of conferences, divisions, and teams, and I discuss how the leagues schedule regular-season and playoff games. This chapter also explores the impact of changing the rules of the game, the moves and techniques of certain pros, and the special coaching that's required for a professional basketball team.

National Basketball Association (NBA)

There are 29 teams in the NBA, which is divided into two conferences, Eastern and Western. Within the Eastern Conference are the Atlantic Division and the Central Division. Within the Western Conference are the Midwest Division and the Pacific Division. As Table 14-1 shows, three divisions have seven teams each, and the Central Division has eight teams.

Table 14-1 NBA Conference Divisions and Teams

Eastern Conference	
Atlantic Division	***Central Division***
Boston Celtics	Atlanta Hawks
Miami Heat	Charlotte Hornets
New Jersey Nets	Chicago Bulls
New York Knicks	Cleveland Cavaliers
Orlando Magic	Detroit Pistons
Philadelphia 76ers	Indiana Pacers
Washington Wizards	Milwaukee Bucks
	Toronto Raptors

Western Conference	
Midwest Division	***Pacific Division***
Dallas Mavericks	Golden State Warriors
Denver Nuggets	Los Angeles Clippers
Houston Rockets	Los Angeles Lakers
Minnesota Timberwolves	Phoenix Suns
San Antonio Spurs	Portland Trail Blazers
Utah Jazz	Sacramento Kings
Vancouver Grizzlies	Seattle SuperSonics

Schedule

Since 1968, each NBA team has played an 82-game regular-season schedule. The teams play 41 games at home and 41 on the road — give or take a couple of international games early in the year. For example, two teams opened recent seasons with games in Japan, and a regular-season game is scheduled to be played in Mexico.

Each team plays four games (two home and two away) against every team in its conference, and two games (one home and one away) against every team in the other conference. For example, every team in the Midwest Division plays four games against each team in the Pacific Division, as well as four games against each other team in its own division.

But the Eastern Conference has an extra team in the Central Division. How do they solve the problem of an uneven number of teams? The NBA has proposed this creative, yet complicated-sounding, solution:

- Each team in the Atlantic Division plays four games (two home and two away) against six teams and three games against two teams in the Central Division.
- Each team in the Central Division plays four games against five teams and three games against two teams in the Atlantic Division.

Rosters

Each NBA team is allowed a maximum of 12 active players on its roster, which means that no more than 348 players suit up during the course of a season. A team can replace players due to injury, retirement, and/or players being waived (that is, *cut,* or in blue-collar terms, *laid off*) during the season.

A team must have at least eight eligible players dressed and able to play for a game. One special situation involving player eligibility: In the 1997 playoffs, a brawl involving the Miami Heat and the New York Knicks led to the suspension of five Knicks players. The league could not suspend all five players for the same game (12 – 5 = 7), so the league staggered the suspensions over a two-game period. Teams in need of a quick fix player-wise may sign a free agent to a ten-day contract to replace an injured or suspended list player. Teams can renew a player's ten-day contract but must waive or sign the player for the remainder of the season after the player has fulfilled two such contracts.

Teams may trade players until the trading deadline, which falls on the 16th Thursday of each season. Teams may resume trading at the end of the regular season, except that no playoff team may trade a player on its roster until that team is eliminated from the NBA playoffs.

Playoffs

Sixteen of the NBA's 29 teams qualify for the NBA playoffs, eight from each conference. The 16 teams are seeded one through eight within each conference. The league uses the following rules to determine how the teams are seeded:

- The division winner with the best record in each conference is ranked number one.
- The other division winner in that conference is ranked number two.

With these rules for seeding teams in the playoffs, the advantage goes to the team with the better record during the regular season, regardless of its standing in the division race.

I like this method of seeding teams for the playoffs because it puts more meaning into the regular season. When you consider that the NBA champ may play as many as 27 postseason games — one-third of the regular-season number — the regular season deserves as much meaning as you can give it.

The NBA Has Come a Long Way

In 1955, the NBA finals between Syracuse and Fort Wayne matched the two best teams in the league. They played the first two games in Syracuse and scheduled the third, fourth, and fifth games for Fort Wayne. However, the games were moved to Indianapolis because the America Bowling Congress had booked the War Memorial Coliseum, which was the home of the Fort Wayne team. It's hard to imagine a modern-day NBA team taking a back seat to a bowling tournament!

Stories like this one illustrate the plight of professional basketball in the early days. But proponents of the game have instituted rule changes that were designed to enliven the sport. The following sections describe some of these league-saving changes.

The shot clock: A rule that saved a league

On November 22, 1950, the Fort Wayne Pistons defeated the Minneapolis Lakers 19-18 in the lowest-scoring game in NBA history. Each team made four baskets. In the fourth quarter, Fort Wayne outscored Minneapolis by a score of 3-1. At this point in NBA history, games were plodding, brutish contests in which teams *stalled* (that is, held the ball and did not shoot), sometimes for many minutes at a time, late in the game. Fortunately, someone recognized that this molasses approach to playing the game was pretty *bor . . .* er, *not lively.*

Every NBA player owes a small percentage of his salary to Danny Biasone (not exactly a name that's on the tip of every NBA fan's tongue). In 1954, Biasone, the late owner of the Syracuse Nationals, invented the 24-second shot clock and altered the game of basketball forever — and for the better.

How did Biasone come up with his magic number? First, he determined that the average number of shots two teams take during a game is 120. He then divided the length of a game — 48 minutes or 2,880 seconds — by the average number of shots and came up with 24.

The 24-second shot clock rule debuted on October 30, 1954. During its first season, it produced dramatic results:

- In the debut game, the Rochester Royals defeated the Boston Celtics 98-95. That would have been the seventh highest scoring game of the previous season.
- The year the rule was instituted, NBA teams averaged 93.1 points per game. This average showed an increase of 13.6 points per game from the previous year.
- That season, the Celtics averaged more than 100 points per contest and became the first team in NBA history to do so.

Moving the three-point line back: The new league-saving rule

The NBA has been plagued by a scoring famine in recent years. The league has seen overall field goal percentage steadily decline from 49.2 percent in 1983–84 to a low of 44.7 percent during the 1996–97 season. Teams averaged 94.3 points per game in 1996–97, which is not much better than the 93.1 point average in the first year of the shot clock. More evidence of this scoring famine follows:

- In 1996–97, only the Utah Jazz shot above 50 percent from the field. The year before that, no teams did.
- In 1986–87, every team averaged at least 100 points per game. In 1996–97, only eight teams did.
- The Bulls beat the Jazz 84-82 in the first game of the 1997 NBA finals — the fewest points scored by a winner in the NBA finals since 1956. That record low lasted until Game 4, when Utah scored 78 points and still won by five.
- During the 1996–97 regular season, the Orlando Magic scored just 57 points in a loss to the Cleveland Cavaliers, the fewest points scored by a team since the shot clock was introduced. Houston scored a franchise-low 66 points in an 86-66 loss to Miami in December 1996.

Believing that this decline in scoring percentages is adversely affecting the quality of the game, the NBA is moving its three-point line farther from the goal during the 1997–98 season. For three seasons (1994–95 to 1996–97), the three-point line was 22 feet *from the basket.* Between 1979–80 and 1993–94, the line was 23'9" around the top of the key and 22 feet in the corners — which is where it will return.

At first, the logic seems perverse. Okay, the NBA wants to increase scoring and shooting percentages. So why move the line farther from the basket? Won't that make it even more difficult to hit three-pointers? Here are the good, better, and best theories:

- **Argument #1 (good): Players will look for better shots.** With the three-point arc extended by 21 inches, players will attempt fewer three-point shots, and teams will look inside more often for a higher-percentage shot. The players who do launch treys will be the long-range marksmen.
- **Argument #2 (better): Players will have more open floor space.** The extended arc opens up the floor by forcing the defense to cover more area. After all, who's going to attempt a three-point shot from a few feet beyond the arc? Offensive players come right up to the arc for such an attempt. Hence, the defensive radius, which doesn't extend beyond the three-point arc, will be forced to move farther out, giving the offense more room to operate within the arc. This changed offense/defense dynamic, and not a higher three-point shot percentage, may be the true impetus behind creating a bull market for scoring.
- **Argument #3 (best): History supports fewer three-point attempts.** In 1996–97, Utah had the best team field goal percentage and the second highest team scoring average. The Jazz also attempted the fewest three-point shots in the league — just ten per game — but were among the league leaders in three-point percentage.

Illegal defense: What is it?

Zone defense — the idea of defending an area instead of a person — is a no-no in the NBA. (See Chapter 7 to find out more about zone defenses.) The NBA disallows zone defense because *zone defense is the mortal enemy of high-scoring entertainment.* If teams were allowed to play a zone defense, the conventional wisdom goes, the game would be nothing but outside jump-shots. In fact, that trend is exactly what fans are seeing. Defenses, like mutant, more resistant strains of a malicious disease, are becoming more sophisticated and are obviating the existing rules.

Although you may not see a true zone defense — such as a 2-3 zone — in an NBA game, you do see double-teaming and trapping. There are provisions for it.

Why you and I can't be like Mike

You can break Jordan's greatness into two areas: the tangible, such as innate athletic ability and talent born of years of practice; and the intangible, such as the will to win.

Pure talent

At 6'6", 216 pounds, Michael Jordan is the perfect in-between height to drive defenders mad. As a guard, he's tall enough to shoot over nearly every opposing guard, and he's quick enough to drive by any taller forward who attempts to block his jumpshot.

Jordan can do just about everything in the game of basketball. He can shoot the outside shot, including three-point shots; he can post players up on the baseline; he can hit the pull-up shot; and he's the greatest creator of slashing and cutting to the basket that the game has seen since Julius Erving was in his prime.

What sets Jordan apart is his combination of offensive and defensive skills. In addition to his offensive talents, he is a perennial selection to the NBA All-Defensive team and was named the league's Defensive Player of the Year in 1988. He alters a game with his offense *and* his defense.

Pride and desire

Does anybody love to play the game more than Jordan does? Is anyone more competitive?

Think back to Game 5 of the 1997 NBA Finals, for example. Bedridden with the flu the day of the game and having slept very little the night before, Jordan appeared very ill as he went through his warm-ups for the contest in Salt Lake City.

But, playing at the Delta Center, the NBA's toughest arena to win in on the road (entering the contest, the Jazz had won 23 straight there), in a game Chicago absolutely could not afford to lose, Jordan scored a game-high 38 points, including a three-point goal that proved to be the game winner. Jordan gave one of the greatest performances under adverse physical conditions in the history of sport.

Jordan's accomplishments:

- Selected in 1996 as one of the 50 greatest players in NBA history.
- Is a member of five NBA World Championship teams.
- Named Most Valuable Player of the NBA four times (1988, 1991, 1992, and 1996).
- Named Most Valuable Player of the NBA Championship Series five times in five appearances.
- Has the highest playoff scoring average in NBA history, at 33.9 points per game.
- Holds the NBA playoff record for points in a game, with 63 points against the Boston Celtics on May 20, 1986.
- Named first team All-NBA nine times, 1987–93 and 1996–97.
- Holds the NBA record for most seasons leading the league in scoring: nine.
- Has participated in ten NBA All-Star games — nine as a starter.
- Is the fifth leading scorer in NBA history, with a 31.7 overall career scoring average.
- Has averaged at least 27 points per game in 11 of his 12 seasons.

A League of Signature Moves

In the way most singers have a signature song, great NBA players have identifying moves that are emulated on playgrounds all over the world. The NBA, after all, is a star-driven league. Here are a few of the best-known moves from a few of the best-known players.

Michael Jordan's fadeaway jumper

The fadeaway jumper is an almost unstoppable shot, one that "Air" didn't really develop until his return to the NBA in 1995. To prolong his career, Jordan avoids driving to the basket as a first option; the 6'6" guard instead relies on his fallaway shot. Jordan jumps away from the basket and usually extends one leg in front of him to put some room between himself and a defender. With his ability to seemingly hang in the air, Jordan rarely sees this shot blocked.

Hakeem Olajuwon's Dream Shake

Does any NBA center have better footwork than this former soccer player from Nigeria? The Dream Shake is a move whereby Olajuwon starts on the right or left side within 10 feet of the basket. He goes through a series of head and shoulder fakes (or "shakes") and spins into the middle of the lane for a baby jumper or a hook shot. What makes this move work is the threat that he may turn (or drop steps) to the baseline for a dunk or lay-up.

Shaquille O'Neal's Shaq Attack

This isn't an individual move as much as it is a philosophy. With his large, agile frame, O'Neal can overpower any opposing center. He is too quick and powerful. A law of physics applies here somewhere.

The basic move that Shaq uses from all areas of the court is the drop step (see "Moves for a Center" in Chapter 9), combined with an ability to drop a shoulder and gain an advantage. This combination usually leads to a power dunk. If Shaq ever gets as proficient from the left side as he is from the right and starts hitting 70 percent of his foul shots, it's all over.

Karl Malone's step-back jumper

This move is similar to Jordan's in its approach to creating a shot — except Jordan *jumps* backward, and Malone *steps* back before he shoots. Malone is effective at this because of his bulk; defenders have to guard against his ability to power by his defender. If you chart him during a game, with the exception of pick and roll plays (see Chapter 6), he probably shoots the step-back jumper when he's in a one-on-one situation four times as often as he drives to the hoop.

Grant Hill's between-the-legs hesitation move

Hill's signature move begins with a hesitation step — okay, he's palming the ball — followed by a between-the-legs dribble and a slithery drive in which he creates a seam for himself between two and sometimes three defenders.

When I coached, I frowned on my perimeter players dribbling through their legs, but for Grant Hill, I would make an exception. Hill puts the ball through his legs as he approaches his defender at a high rate of speed. (This is not easy — don't try it in your living room, or you'll break at least two lamps.) The secret to his success, though, is his ability to explode to the hoop from either side of the basket.

NBA Economics

Horace Grant was a power forward who felt appreciated on the court but not in his checkbook. Grant won three championships with the Chicago Bulls in the early 1990s — his deft pass to John Paxson, who nailed a three-pointer, iced the 1993 series against the Phoenix Suns. Then, to quote Cuba Gooding, Jr., in the movie *Jerry Maguire,* Grant said, "Show me the money!"

Grant departed from Chicago in 1994 to play for the Orlando Magic. Had he stayed put, Grant would sport two more championship rings and would have an indelible place in sports history. Instead, last year he earned $14 million, the second highest salary of any NBA player. What's worth more? You'd have to ask Grant.

Prior to the 1970s, players usually remained with the same team throughout their careers. They were drafted out of college, were given short-term deals (often only one year), and were afraid of losing their jobs. Today, pro basketball players are often drafted out of high school, are given long-term contracts, and can afford to lose their jobs because their sneaker-endorsement contracts are equal to the salary of a Fortune 500 CEO.

Players also have vagabond eyes. Because of the NBA salary cap, which places a limit on how much each team may pay its 12 players, the league's best players, upon fulfilling the terms of their contracts and becoming free agents, flock to the team that has the most money available under its salary cap.

The result is a bigger disparity between rich and poor than existed in medieval England. NBA teams today pay big bucks to their top two or three players — the marquee draws that fill an arena's seats — leaving little salary cap money available for the other players. You see teams with a couple guys making $5 million and four guys making the current minimum, $247,000.

Here are some facts about the NBA salary cap:

- The salary cap was $24.3 million per team for the 1996–97 season. It is increasing to $25.6 million in 1997–98.
- Exemptions allow a team to exceed the cap. For example, no limit is placed on how much a team may pay one of its own players in order to retain him if he enters free agent status. Michael Jordan, whom the Bulls paid $30 million for one season when he became a free agent in 1996–97, alone exceeded the standard salary cap of any NBA team. And most people will tell you that he's worth it.

The salary cap deals on a per-season basis. When you hear about players signing a $100 million contract, that contract is for multiple years. Then again, who knows what Jordan will command if he stays in shape and continues signing one-year contracts with the Bulls?

One for the money, two for the show: Player salaries and league rankings

According to Table 14-2, the Miami Heat got the most for their money in 1996–97. The Heat had the third best record in the NBA but spent the 25th most dollars on players' salaries, or a differential of 22 places between winning percentage rank and dollars spent. The Utah Jazz (second best winning percentage and 19th most money spent) and the Charlotte Hornets (ninth best record and 26th most money spent) tied for second with a differential of 17 places between win-loss rank and dollars spent rank.

Table 14-2 Who Got the Most for Their Money in 1996–97

$ Rank	*Team*	*Payroll in Millions*	*Wins-Losses*	*League Rank*
1	Chicago Bulls	$58.27	69-13	1
2	Orlando Magic	$45.11	45-37	12
3	Indiana Pacers	$40.93	39-43	17
4	Phoenix Suns	$36.03	40-42	15
5	Washington Bullets	$34.56	44-38	13
6	San Antonio Spurs	$33.27	20-62	27
7	Golden State Warriors	$30.58	30-52	21

$ Rank	Team	Payroll in Millions	Wins-Losses	League Rank
8	Seattle SuperSonics	$29.83	57-25	4
9	Sacramento Kings	$29.18	34-48	19
10	Los Angeles Lakers	$29.08	56-26	7
11	Detroit Pistons	$27.46	54-28	9
12	Los Angeles Clippers	$26.04	36-46	18
13	Boston Celtics	$25.99	15-67	28
14	New York Knicks	$25.93	57-25	4
15	Houston Rockets	$25.78	57-25	4
16	Atlanta Hawks	$25.38	56-26	7
17	New Jersey Nets	$25.32	26-56	23
18	Portland Trail Blazers	$25.15	49-33	11
19	Utah Jazz	$25.11	64-18	2
20	Denver Nuggets	$24.90	21-61	26
21	Philadelphia 76ers	$24.77	22-60	25
22	Dallas Mavericks	$24.70	24-58	24
23	Milwaukee Bucks	$24.46	33-49	20
24	Minnesota Timberwolves	$24.35	40-42	15
25	Miami Heat	$23.80	61-21	3
26	Charlotte Hornets	$22.43	54-28	9
27	Cleveland Cavaliers	$20.37	42-40	14
28	Toronto Raptors	$18.77	30-52	27
29	Vancouver Grizzlies	$18.64	14-68	29

Source: Payroll rolls from USA Today, *November 15, 1996.*

Has the NBA been profitable since the Larry Bird-Magic Johnson era took off in the 1980s? You can see by Table 14-3 that the average NBA salary has grown from $249,000 in 1983 to $2.2 million in 1996–97.

Table 14-3 NBA Salary History

Year	Teams	Cap in Millions	Average Salary
1982–83	23	no cap	$249,000
1983–84	23	$3.00	$260,000
1984–85	23	$3.60	$325,000

(continued)

Table 14-3 *(continued)*

Year	*Teams*	*Cap in Millions*	*Average Salary*
1985–86	23	$4.23	$375,000
1986–87	23	$4.93	$440,000
1987–88	23	$6.16	$510,000
1988–89	25	$7.23	$600,000
1989–90	27	$9.80	$750,000
1990–91	27	$11.87	$990,000
1991–92	27	$12.50	$1.04 million
1992–93	27	$14.00	$1.22 million
1993–94	27	$15.18	$1.32 million
1994–95	27	$15.96	$1.38 million
1995–96	29	$23.00	$1.82 million
1996–97	29	$24.30	$2.20 million

A fan's guide to NBA economics

According to a survey by the Chicago-based Team Marketing Report, the NBA's average ticket price for 1996–97 regular season games was $34.08, an increase of 8 percent over the $31.56 for the 1995–96 season.

Recent NBA finalists Portland, Chicago, New York, Houston, Orlando, Seattle, Phoenix, and the Los Angeles Lakers hold eight of the top nine spots in the ranking of average ticket prices. The Trail Blazers had the highest average ticket price in 1996–97, at $47.49.

This survey also calculated a Fan Cost Index (FCI), which estimated the cost for a family of four to buy four average price tickets, concessions, souvenirs, and parking at an NBA game. The league average for the 1996–97 season was $203.38, a 6.3 percent increase from the 1995–96 season.

Coaching in the NBA

Players are different today. Los Angeles Laker point guard Nick Van Exel refuses to enter games when his coach, Del Harris, tells him to. Utah Jazz forward Chris Morris irritated his coach, Jerry Sloan, so much that Sloan had security guards escort him from the bench in the midst of a contest. LA Lakers

Deal of the century

Although a merger between the two women's leagues is inevitable, it is doubtful that any ABL or WNBA owner will realize the deal of the century struck by the Spirits of St. Louis owners in 1976.

In 1976, the NBA, covetous of such talents as Julius Erving and George Gervin, agreed to merge with the American Basketball Association (ABA), which had been considered a pariah by the more established league throughout its ten years of existence. The NBA agreed to adopt four of the six existing ABA teams: the Denver Nuggets, the Indiana Pacers, the New Jersey Nets, and the San Antonio Spurs.

Two other ABA franchises — the Kentucky Colonels and the Spirits of St. Louis — were offered financial packages but were not permitted to enter the league. In exchange for agreeing not to contest the merger, the Spirits owners struck a deal that, at the time, did not seem too beneficial: They would collect one-seventh of the national television revenue from the four teams (Denver Nuggets, Indiana Pacers, New Jersey Nets, and San Antonio Spurs) that were taken into the NBA. Under the terms of the agreement, the NBA agreed that this deal would run in perpetuity — in other words, forever.

In the first year of the deal, the Spirits' owners split only $273,000. But the league soon became home to Magic Johnson and Larry Bird, and it began to prosper. To date, the owners have collected $46 million — with not a dollar spent on overhead.

The Colonels' owners, by the way, accepted a $3 million settlement. In retrospect, by investing in the NBA's future, the Spirits made a far wiser decision.

forward Cedric Ceballos went AWOL in the middle of the 1995–96 season to hang out on a boat at Lake Havasu, Arizona. The Lakers swiftly traded Ceballos to his former team, the Phoenix Suns. The following season, Ceballos threw a towel into the face of his coach, Danny Ainge, during a game in full view of the cameras. Ceballos was traded back to the Lakers where, next to Van Exel, he seems like a choirboy.

Note well: For all the problems that he causes, Ceballos can flat-out play. So he always lands on his feet. Welcome to the NBA Present, where the players run the league and the coaches do their best not to upset them. It's not a recipe for a winner — the best teams always have players who respect and do not challenge their coach's authority — but it's the way of the times.

In general — and you hear veteran players give voice to this opinion more than any other NBA observers — younger players do not appreciate the game. You see that appreciation for the game in players such as Michael Jordan and Charles Barkley — guys who hate to lose but, when they do lose, lose with class. Following the lead of Grant Hill and perhaps Kevin Garnett of the Minnesota Timberwolves, younger players hopefully will come around.

Women's Pro Hoops: ABL Versus WNBA

Women's basketball has exploded in popularity in the U.S. in recent years. And why not? Women play fundamentally sound hoops without — at least not yet — any of the 'tudes that mar the men's game. Moreover, 1997's NCAA semifinal between top-ranked Stanford and Old Dominion, an overtime affair won by ODU, was as exciting as any men's tourney contest.

But *two* pro leagues? I don't see how two leagues will survive. Just look at the NBA and the ABA in the 1960s and 1970s. Although the ABA survived for nine years, the league's demise leads me to believe that the best thing for the sport is to have one league with all the best players.

Women's leagues have been started in the past, but all have failed. The Women's Basketball League (WBL) lasted from 1979 to 1981, followed by the Women's American Basketball Association (WABA), which held out from October to December 1984. The National Women's Basketball Association (NWBA) was in existence from October 1986 to February 1987, but no games were played. Finally, the Liberty Basketball Association (LBA), which outfitted its players in Lycra unitards and set the rims 9'2" above the court, opened shop for two months in the winter of 1991 before folding.

The WNBA is sponsored by the NBA, and its marketing strength alone should be enough to crush any opponent. The NBA knows marketing. The WNBA also has NBC, ESPN, and Lifetime televising its games, and it has franchises in major markets, such as Los Angeles and New York.

The ABL, whose games are televised on the SportsChannel and BET, two small national cable companies, places its teams predominantly in smaller markets. What the ABL has going for it are higher salaries, a traditional winter season, and better players. Although the WNBA claims Rebecca Lobo, Lisa Leslie, and Sheryl Swoopes, it had just four of the 1996 U.S. Olympians in its inaugural season, as compared to the ABL's eight. Of the top 15 players in the college game in 1995, 10 signed with the ABL and 5 signed with the WNBA. Table 14-4 compares the ABL and the WNBA.

Table 14-4 A Comparison of the Two Women's Pro Leagues

Category	*ABL*	*WNBA*
Playing season	Mid-October to mid-March	June 21 to August 30
Length of season	5 months	2 months
Regular season games	40	28
Minimum salaries	$40,000	$15,000
Maximum salaries	$150,000	$50,000

Category	ABL	WNBA
Average salary	$80,000	Not available
U.S. Olympians	Teresa Edwards Jennifer Azzi Dawn Staley Kata Steding Nikki McCray Carla McGhee Venus Lacy Katrina McClain	Sheryl Swoopes Lisa Leslie Rebecca Lobo Ruthie Bolton-Holifield
Recent Associated Press College All-Americans	Saudia Roundtree Kara Wolters Jennifer Rizzoti Kate Starbird	Vickie Johnson Debra Williams Michi Atkins Wendy Palmer Clarisse Mechanguana Kim Williams Tina Thompson Kedra Holland-Corn Tamecka Dixon
Average attendance	3,536	9,669
Playing time	Four 10-minute quarters	Two 20-minute halves
Shot clock	25 seconds	30 seconds
Ball	Men's ball	Women's ball
Franchises	Seattle Reign Portland Power San Jose Lasers Colorado Xplosions Columbus Quest New England Blizzard Philadelphia Rage Atlanta Glory Long Beach Stingrays	Charlotte Sting Cleveland Rockers Houston Comets Los Angeles Sparks New York Liberty Phoenix Mercury Sacramento Monarchs Utah Starzz

Minor League Professional Basketball

If you don't want to play overseas and still aspire to an NBA career after or instead of college, there are two minor pro leagues stateside: the Continental Basketball Association (CBA) and the United States Basketball League (USBL). The former is a winter league whose season corresponds to the NBA's; the latter is a summer league.

The CBA is a step above the USBL. I cite the following statistic as proof: Since 1985, 323 players from the CBA have been called up to NBA rosters. In that same time span, 109 USBL players have earned spots on NBA rosters.

Both leagues serve a purpose: providing players with an avenue to work themselves into the NBA. Coaches, too. Before winning five championship rings as the Bulls' Zen coach, Phil Jackson drove the bus (literally and figuratively) for the CBA's Albany Patroons.

Continental Basketball Association (CBA)

Season: November 15 to March 15

Teams: Only 11 teams were in the CBA in 1996–97, the fewest since 1981–82

National Conference	***American Conference***
LaCrosse Bobcats	Connecticut Pride
Oklahoma City Cavalry	Florida Beachdogs
Omaha Racers	Fort Wayne Fury
Sioux Falls Skyforce	Grand Rapids Hoops
Yakima Sun Kings	Quad City Thunder
Rockford Lightning	

Games: 56 regular-season games, plus playoffs; eight teams make the playoffs

Motherhood and pro basketball

On top of the physical demands of the game and the mental stress of a hectic travel schedule, some women professional players have an added responsibility: motherhood.

The vast difference between the NBA and the WNBA became apparent before the latter league's launch ever occurred. Sheryl Swoopes, one of the three high-profile players marketed by the league, missed most of the first season because she was pregnant.

Swoopes's situation is not unique. Valerie Still, 35, had been retired for two years after playing 12 seasons in Europe. She then signed to play with the Columbus Quest of the ABL for the league's inaugural season. A few months before the season began, Still gave birth to a son, Aaron. At first, Still chose to bring Aaron on roadtrips with her, but by midseason, it became too much for one person to handle. Her husband, Rob Lock, said "I got next" regarding babysitting duty, and Aaron stayed home with Pop as Mom helped lead the Quest to the ABL title. In fact, she scored 14 points and grabbed 13 rebounds in the deciding game of the championship series with the Richmond Rage, a 77-64 Quest win. Mom was named MVP of the championship series.

Though both the CBA and the USBL have alumni in the NBA, the CBA is formally affiliated with the NBA. In December 1996, the CBA and NBA entered into a three-year agreement allowing the CBA to grow from a business standpoint by using some of the NBA's marketing resources. In return, NBA clubs have exclusive rights to call up an unlimited number of CBA players during the regular season and the playoffs.

The league has a unique way of determining its standings: Each game is based on a seven-point system. The winning team receives three points. For each quarter that a team wins, that team receives one point. So if you see some CBA standings in the newspaper, the column for points after the wins and losses does not mean points scored that season or in the last game. The column refers to standing points, which determine the order of finish.

The level of play in the CBA has improved in recent years. With NBA teams giving a high percentage of its payroll to three or four players, not as many guaranteed contracts are available as in the past. As a result, NBA hopefuls want to remain stateside in case an opening becomes available. More players are resisting the lucre of playing in Europe in exchange for a better chance of jumping to the NBA.

United States Basketball League (USBL)

Season: May 2 to June 25; playoffs end July 2. The early May to early July schedule of this league allows players who recently completed their college careers to get some professional experience before trying out for NBA teams, whose camps open in September.

Teams: Atlantic City Seagulls, Long Island Surf, Portland Wave, Connecticut Skyhawks, Westchester Kings, New Hampshire Thunder Loons, Philadelphia Power, Atlanta Trojans, Raleigh Cougars, Jacksonville Barracudas, Tampa Bay Windjammers, and Florida Sharks

Games: 25 regular-season games, plus playoffs

The USBL attempts to draw attention to itself by occasionally signing athletes whose first claim to fame did not come on the basketball court. For example:

- IBF Super-Middleweight Champion of the World **Roy Jones, Jr.**, plays for the Jacksonville Barracudas.
- Former Heisman Trophy winning quarterback **Charlie Ward,** now of the New York Knicks, is another former Barracuda.
- **Robert R. Kelly,** an R&B singer who gained fame from the *Space Jam* soundtrack, is with the Atlantic City Seagulls.
- **Simeon Rice,** a starting defensive end for the Arizona Cardinals of the NFL, played for the Philadelphia Power.

The Harlem Globetrotters

The Harlem Globetrotters, who have been around for 70 years, walk a fine line between pro basketball and pure Vaudeville. The Globetrotters may be the most famous basketball team this side of the Chicago Bulls and is one of the few teams, if not the only one, that lose less frequently.

The Globetrotters, America's Goodwill Ambassadors of basketball, play exhibition games around the world. The show is structured like a basketball game; however, the team plays by its own rules. The opponents on any given night are simply straight men for the team's antics. Players have been known to drop-kick half-court shots, hide the ball under their jerseys, or climb on each other's backs for lob dunks. But it is true family entertainment — and the greatest basketball show on earth.

Highlights in the history of this unique team include playing in front of the largest crowd ever to see a basketball game — 75,000 fans in 1951 in Berlin's Olympic Stadium. In 1954, the team played the first night event in the history of Wrigley Field; they brought in their own portable light system for a summer evening's exhibition. In the 1940s, the Globetrotters arrived in Peru while a Civil War raged. The Peruvians were so anxious to see the Globetrotters play that a cease-fire was declared for a few days until the team left town.

While the Globetrotters' play has been exhibition in style, other teams have developed strategies from it. The Globetrotters were the first team to use a fast-break offense, and they also developed the weave offenses you see some teams run today.

Three Globetrotters players stand out:

- Former guard **Marques Haynes** was a virtuoso of ballhandling. To this day, you still hear television announcers refer to a good dribbler as doing "a Marques Haynes imitation."
- **Goose Tatum** joined the team in 1942 and was a legendary comedian who brought many routines to the team's exhibition.
- **Meadowlark Lemon** joined the team in 1954 and was the "Clown Prince of Basketball," bringing unprecedented interest to the team.

Today, the Globetrotters are still going strong, playing a schedule of events that includes up to 20 games/performances a month.

Chapter 15

International Basketball

In This Chapter

- How basketball's popularity spread around the globe
- Following the NBA's influence on international hoops mania — and the influence of foreign players on the NBA
- Distinguishing American basketball from international basketball
- American influence on international basketball and vice versa
- Understanding why the world has caught up to the U.S. in hoops prowess
- Watching hoops around the world

According to a recent marketing survey by DMB&Bs Brain Waves regarding the popularity of sports worldwide, basketball ranked first among teenagers. Seventy-one percent of the teenagers polled worldwide participated in basketball. Soccer, which had a 67 percent participation rate, finished second.

In this chapter, I explore the synergy between American basketball and the international game. Pro leagues abroad, most notably in Europe, are a haven of modest wealth for American players who find themselves one rung below the NBA talent level. The NBA, on the flip side, has provided jobs for players from all over the world. The infusion of such talent will only accelerate as the children being raised in the homelands of these players — pioneers, really — are inspired to duplicate their feats.

How Hoops Took Over the World

Archeologists claim that the Mayans of Mexico played a crude form of basketball centuries ago. The game was crude not so much because the "basket" had no net but because members of the losing team were sometimes beheaded. Maybe that's why the game as then constituted never really took off.

In the last half-century, however, Naismith's invention has mushroomed into a vast empire. Basketball poles are planted in the ground all over the globe, their backboards and rims as stationary flags claiming yet another land as hoops territory. While it is not yet played extraterrestrially — despite what you may have seen in *Space Jam* — basketball's conquest will not be checked. This section explains how basketball took over the world.

Winning at the 1960 Olympics

The 1960 Olympics in Rome provided the initial spark for interest in basketball beyond American shores. The United States Olympic team, whose *backcourt* (that is, the duo of guards) was composed of Jerry West and Oscar Robertson, was one of the best squads ever assembled — the first "dream team," if you will.

That year, the U.S. won its Olympic contests by an *average* of 42.4 points (as compared to the 43.8 average margin posted by the 1992 Olympians, a.k.a. Dream Team I). The Rome Olympics were the first to be televised on a significant global scale, and as with the 1992 Dream Team, people were captivated by this club's excellence. Winning was a foregone conclusion; but you don't get to witness utter mastery in sports very often.

Losing at the 1972 Olympics

The 1972 Olympic final between the United States and the Soviet Union in Munich remains the most controversial international game ever played. That game ended an American streak of 36 years of international Olympic competition without a loss. Until then, making the U.S. Olympic squad was equivalent to earning a gold medal.

The controversy centered around the game's final three seconds. The Soviets trailed by one with three seconds left and had to in-bound the ball from under its own basket. A series of incredible misunderstandings between the officials, the timekeeper, and the coaches allowed the USSR three attempts at the last play. On the final try, Alexander Belov scored to give the USSR a 52-51 lead. The Americans, outraged by the officiating, refused to accept their silver medals.

Yugoslavia defeating the Soviets

At the 1976 Olympics, the Yugoslavs spoiled a much-anticipated Cold War rematch between the U.S. and the USSR by defeating the Soviets in the semifinal game. Everyone stateside wanted to see an American team coached by Dean Smith of North Carolina and led by Adrian Dantley of Notre Dame exact revenge on the Russians. But Yugoslavia's success (the U.S. beat them in the gold medal game with 30 points by Dantley) gave that country and others that were not considered "world powers" hope, and it stimulated worldwide interest in basketball.

Touring American college teams

In the 1970s, college teams began touring Europe; the NCAA adopted legislation that allowed college teams to play a foreign tour once every four years. Touring was a cultural exchange, hoops style, and everybody benefited. College teams were afforded a unique bonding experience, a chance to play against some truly hostile crowds, and a fantastic getaway. The Europeans were in essence taking a Berlitz course in basketball from the very best tutors around.

My trip with the Notre Dame team in 1979 was memorable. We traveled to Yugoslavia for a two-week tour in late May. The Yugoslavians at that time had just won the European Championships and, perhaps more impressive, had won 14 straight games against the previously indomitable Soviets. We beat the Yugoslavs on our first night in Belgrade, leaving the country in shock. Bill Hanzlik hit a shot to win at the buzzer. Judging by the reaction of the fans, you'd have thought that Archduke Ferdinand had been shot all over again and that World War I was about to be relived.

The NBA going global

The sun never sets on the league that includes the (Phoenix) Suns. The NBA has offices in Hong Kong, Tokyo, Melbourne, Geneva, London, and Paris. Each year, two teams travel to Japan to play back-to-back games against each other to open the regular season. Preseason schedules of recent vintage have included such far-flung destinations as Germany, Spain, France, Mexico, and Corvallis, Oregon.

Eventually, the league's international expansion, which technically began in 1995 when the Canadian metropolises of Toronto and Vancouver were awarded franchises, may extend overseas. Right now, the league's imperialistic fervor is all about marketing. If you can sell "Michael Jordan 23" jerseys in Venice Beach, California, why not sell them in Venice, Italy?

Toward that end, the league has operated locally but televised globally. Games during the 1996–97 season were telecast to 550 million households in 188 countries. Just think: Karl Malone reached more people in his MVP season than Karl Marx did in his lifetime. *Workers of the world, pick and roll.*

In addition to TV, the Internet has served the league of the (New Jersey) Nets well. About 35 percent of the hits that `www.nba.com` receives come from outside the U.S.

The great Drazen Petrovic

In 1980, I was teaching at a clinic in Sibenek and came upon what seemed to be a 16-year-old European Pete Maravich. This guy just shot and shot and shot and seemed to swish every attempt effortlessly. An interpreter told me, "That's Drazen Petrovic, the next great international player."

I knew from the first time that I saw Drazen shoot that I wanted him at Notre Dame. In the fall of 1984, Notre Dame played host to the Yugoslavian national team. After the game, Petrovic indicated that he'd be coming to Notre Dame as a student, not an opponent, the following fall. The media went nuts. I was ecstatic. David Rivers and Drazen Petrovic would have given us the best amateur backcourt in the world, never mind the NCAA. I had dreams of Rivers, a superb passer, setting up Petrovic for open shots.

Alas, Petrovic signed with a professional team in Spain, Real Madrid, which paid him something in the neighborhood of $350,000 a year — $350,000 more than I could pay him. I was heartbroken.

Petrovic did eventually cross the pond, playing five years in the NBA with the Portland Trail Blazers and New Jersey Nets. In the summer of 1994, however, he was tragically killed when his car skidded off rainy pavement on the German autobahn. He had been driving home to Yugoslavia from the European Championships.

Petrovic's death was a national tragedy. On the day of his burial in his hometown of Zagreb, more than 100,000 people gathered in the town square, and the whole country stopped fighting for one day to mourn a gifted basketball player's untimely death.

Dream Team I

The 1992 U.S. Olympic basketball team — the first American entry to be composed of professional players — took the game to new heights worldwide. The portal to such an ethereal assemblage of talent was opened three years earlier by FIBA (the International Federation for the Sport of Basketball), when a 56-13 vote allowed "open competition" in Olympic basketball. That score (56-13) was also the average margin at halftime of a typical Dream Team I game, or so it seemed.

Coach Chuck Daly's team was perhaps the most talented and famous group of athletes assembled in the history of sport. Of the dozen players who wore the red, white, and blue in Barcelona, ten have been named to the NBA's list of the 50 Greatest Players. The team averaged 117 points per game (in a 40-minute game), which is the equivalent of 140 points a game in an NBA game (which lasts 48 minutes).

Table 15-1 shows the roster, including each player's scoring average, for the best American-only team ever assembled.

Table 15-1 1992 Dream Team

Player	Position	NBA Team	Points Per Olympic Game
*Charles Barkley	F	Phoenix Suns	18.0
*Larry Bird	F	Boston Celtics	8.4
*Clyde Drexler	G	Portland Trail Blazers	10.5
*Patrick Ewing	C	New York Knicks	9.5
*Magic Johnson	G	LA Lakers	8.0
*Michael Jordan	G	Chicago Bulls	14.9
Christian Laettner	F	Duke University	4.8
*Karl Malone	F	Utah Jazz	13.0
Chris Mullin	F	Golden State Warriors	12.9
*Scottie Pippen	F	Chicago Bulls	9.0
*David Robinson	C	San Antonio Spurs	9.0
*John Stockton	G	Utah Jazz	2.9

** Named to NBA's list of 50 Greatest Players*

The NBA Goes International

The 1995–96 Chicago Bulls, a club that won an NBA-record 72 games in one regular season, was deservedly called the best basketball team in the world. They were also the best basketball team *of* the world.

Chicago's top eight players that year represent four countries and three continents. Center Bill Wennington is Canadian. Toni Kukoc, winner of the NBA's Sixth Man Award for the 1995–96 season, is Croatian. Center Luc Longley is Australian. Only Scottie Pippen, Michael Jordan, Dennis Rodman, Ron Harper, and Steve Kerr (who is American but was born in Lebanon) are Yankee Doodle Dandies.

Basketball's influence worldwide is seen every night in the NBA:

- Gheorge Muresan of the Washington Wizards, the league's tallest player, is from Romania.
- Dikembe Mutombo of the Atlanta Hawks, Defensive Player of the Year for 1997, is from Zaire.
- The All-NBA first and second-team centers, Hakeem Olajuwon of the Houston Rockets and Patrick Ewing of the New York Knicks, are from Nigeria and Jamaica, respectively.

International Players Infuse the U.S. College Ranks

International players have also made their mark — and three-pointers — at American colleges in terms of sheer volume. In 1984, the last time an all-amateur U.S. team won an Olympic gold medal, only 25 foreign-born players competed in NCAA Division I basketball. Just 12 years later, in 1996, six foreign-born hoopsters were taken in the first round of the NBA draft alone! The top NBA draft pick in 1997, Tim Duncan, is a native of the Virgin Islands. And the sleeper pick in 1997 (who went undrafted because of an international trade embargo, believe it or not) was a North Korean named Ri Myong Hun, who stands 7'9".

The world is gaining on the U.S., basketball-wise. Although that may be a bad thing for American nationalism, it's a great thing for the sport. For example, former Davidson head coach Bob McKillop suited up eight foreign players in eight years. Believe it or not, despite the distance, he found recruiting international players easier and less time-consuming than recruiting players domestically.

The infusion of international players, both male and female, into the U.S. college game will only continue to increase. With the stricter academic entrance requirements now set by the NCAA, the number of academically eligible players in the U.S. is shrinking. Meanwhile, the global popularity of NBA stars has accelerated the growth of the sport abroad. The talent gap between U.S. and international teams will continue to narrow with each Olympics.

It's a Different Game

The international game is not played exactly the same way as the American game. (Chapter 4 provides a complete list of rules for the American game.) During the Olympics, international rules, which are used everywhere but in the U.S., apply. Here's a list of the major differences between the American game and the international game:

- **The trapezoidal lane:** The international game uses a three-second lane that is trapezoidal instead of rectangular. (The wider end of the trapezoid is at the baseline.) Do foreigners simply have a greater affinity for trapezoids than Americans? No. The idea behind the trapezoid is that the lower an offensive post player sets up near the basket, the farther away she has to place herself from the basket — unless she wants to be whistled for a three-second lane violation. The trapezoid is actually a clever shape to use.

- **Three-point distance:** In the international game, the three-point distance is 20'6" — a tougher shot than college ball's 19'9", but easier than the NBA's 23'9".
- **The shot clock:** In international games, the shot clock is 30 seconds, skirting the middle between college (35) and the NBA (24).
- **The game period:** In international play, a game consists of two 20-minute halves — same as college, but shorter than the NBA's four 12-minute quarters.

Hoops Cultural Exchange: International Influence on the American Game

For years, Africans, Asians, and Europeans played the game without undue American influence. The game developed differently as players from those countries gave it their own flavor. Thus the international game has some glaring differences in style from the American game.

Offense, for example, rules. The French played better defense against Germany in World War II than you're likely to see them play in a European Championships outing. International games remind me of Arena Football: Whoever scores last usually wins. Position-wise, you'll notice that international big men are not excused from — in fact, they often relish — attempting three-point shots. They are by and large more deft at ball-handling and even passing than their American counterparts.

Watch an NBA or college game now. If you compared it to a game in the mid-1970s, for example, you'd see a few of the newfangled sights that I discuss in this section. All of these owe a little credit to the influence of international hoops, international players, and their ideas.

Outside shooting by big men

More and more frontcourt players in the NBA and on college teams are deft outside shooters. Big men abroad — as in wide *and* overseas — are not known to revel in banging elbows inside. As a result, 6'10" players such as Toni Kukoc shoot the three in international play (and now for the Bulls).

In 1991–92, center Christian Laettner, then a senior at Duke, led the NCAA in three-point shooting percentage. He is 6'9". Fifteen years ago, Laettner may have been yanked for taking such long-range shots rather than setting himself on offense in the traditional low-post position (along the three-second lane, near the baseline and under the basket).

Kresmir Cosic

Kresmir Cosic, a native of Zagreb, Yugoslavia, was the first foreign-born player to make an impact at the college level. Cosic was the star at Brigham Young University from 1970–73.

The first non-American All-American, Cosic led BYU in scoring in 1972 and 1973, averaging over 20 points each season; and at the end of the 1970s, he was named to the Western Athletic Conference's (WAC's) All-Decade team.

Cosic set BYU Cougar records for points, field goals, free throws, and rebounds and averaged 19.1 points per game for his career — also a school record. His style of play was revolutionary and had an effect on players worldwide. He was the prototype European player, a great passer — 196 assists over his last two years — and also a great outside shooter. Three-point goals were not allowed when he played, but trust me, he would have been a 40 percent three-point shooter. (See Chapter 4 for information about statistics.)

Skip passing

All commentators talk about skip passing when a team runs its offense. The *skip pass* is a wing-to-wing pass that skips one of the passes normally used — such as to the point guard at the top of the key — to get the ball to the other side of the court quickly.

The international style of play, where the three-point shot and zone defenses are the norm, features the skip pass (so that the offense can shoot three-pointers against a zone defense). The skip pass is an effective way to move the ball around the perimeter, because the defense can't move as fast as the ball. An open wing shot is usually the result.

Better passing

Though international players lack the reputation of being aggressive on the inside offensively, they do have the reputation for being outstanding passers. The American style of play features more one-on-one, "put your head down and go to the basket" action from the center; international centers are more pass-oriented. This fact may have something to do with soccer, a sport that most international hoopsters learn before they learn basketball. In soccer, you learn early that one-on-one play is an exercise in futility. Goals come more easily via efficient passing.

The three-point shot

The trey was a major contributor to the downfall of the United States in international competition in the mid-1980s. The U.S. lost international games in 1986 and 1987 and then in the 1988 Olympics. Not coincidentally, U.S. colleges did not adopt the three-point shot until 1987. (The NBA adopted it in 1979.) The three-point shot proved to be a great equalizer. I wonder if the NCAA would have adopted the shot if foreign teams had not been humbling college teams with such regularity during that era?

A more perimeter-oriented game

The trapezoid-shaped lane has made for a more perimeter-oriented game at the international level. Thus, when international frontcourt players come to the U.S., their perimeter skills are superior. They know how to play facing the basket (in other words, they can rely on more than just their pivot moves).

The myriad talents of such athletes as Hakeem Olajuwon of the Houston Rockets and Detlef Schrempf of the Seattle SuperSonics — players who don't try to out-bang the defender but rather out-finesse them — explain why both have lasted more than a decade in the NBA. Their success also explains why the NBA lures so many big men who were born overseas: They don't spend their entire childhood trying to dunk a basketball.

Penetrating with the dribble and then passing outside for the three-pointer

When a guard dribbles into the lane, she draws a crowd. Two and sometimes three defenders converge on her, making it difficult to attempt a shot. But what if the guard is acting as a decoy? What if the goal of her penetration is to draw the defenders her way, thus freeing up a teammate outside the three-point circle? All the guard must do is pass the ball to her teammate, who shoots an uncontested three. International players had this ploy down cold long before Americans began copying it.

A 1986 exhibition game between the Providence Friars and the former Soviet Union changed the face of basketball in this country. In that game, held at Providence, the Soviets used the offensive tactic of penetrating the lane with guards. When the defense collapsed upon the dribbler, the dribbler kicked the ball out to a teammate — usually on the wing — who'd find himself with an open three-pointer. Although the Friars won the game 91-88, the USSR shot 30 of its 46 shots from beyond the arc. If the Soviets had made more than just 7 of 30 treys, they probably would have won.

What an NBA attraction he could have been!

Oscar Schmidt is a legend of international play; he is the best player that South America has ever produced, and perhaps the most natural-born scorer never to have played in the NBA. The 6'8" Brazilian was the top scorer in four different Olympic Games and averaged 42.3 points per game at the 1988 Olympics in Seoul. Schmidt scored an Olympic record 55 points in one of those games, and he still has three of the top four scoring game totals in Olympic history.

Schmidt first became known in the United States in 1987 when he scored 46 points in Brazil's upset of the United States in the Pan American games. That game, which took place in Indianapolis, marked the dawn of U.S. realization that the world had caught up in terms of international amateur basketball.

A truly charismatic player, Schmidt is also a hero in Italy, where he was the Italian league's leading scorer for eight seasons. His jersey was retired by two different teams. In his prime, Oscar had the range and ability to dominate a game as a noncenter in a way that only Larry Bird and Michael Jordan have had.

At the time, driving close to the basket to find an open shot farther away was literally and figuratively a foreign concept in the U.S. But that's the influence of the three-pointer, which at the time was in its inaugural year in college play. Then-Providence coach Rick Pitino was smart enough to copy the ploy. The Friars led the nation in three-point shooting that year (with an average of 8.24 treys per game) and marched all the way to the Final Four.

Hoops Cultural Exchange: American Influence on the International Game

The game of basketball was invented in America; how's that for influence? So was McDonald's, which seems to be a daily staple of the international hoopster's diet. Here are a few more American traits that have rubbed off on international hoops.

Improved ball-handling

Between the 1936 and 1972 Olympics, Soviet guards had trouble handling pressure defense. Their coaches saw that they had to improve ball-handling to the level of American guards. In 1988, the Soviets won the gold because the Americans were not able to pressure them into committing turnovers.

Improved perimeter defense

For the longest time, international players never seemed to deny the pass to the wing or pressure outside shots. International players were rough when the ball was passed inside — that is, around the three-second lane — but they never devoted much effort to denying the initial penetration. Now, having been burned often enough by quicker American guards, they have begun playing tough defense outside.

Development of the inside game

Although the larger (because it's trapezoid-shaped) three-second lane makes it next to impossible for a center to set up close to the hoop, the lane can work to his advantage if he's quick. Shaquille O'Neal, for example, dominates in international play because he has more room to maneuver once he gets into the lane. Thus international players are going to have to become quicker on the inside to contend with him.

Team USA: Pros or college players?

Dream Team I was not only a shot in the arm for America's ego but also a serendipitous gathering of many of the best basketball players ever to lace up sneakers. Dream Team I was akin to Woodstock — the equivalent of Jimi Hendrix, Janis Joplin, The Who, and so on all on one stage. But the novelty should have remained just that: a novelty.

I think that the United States should return to composing Olympic teams exclusively of amateur players. The Dream Team concept is now more about marketing than it is about sportsmanship. The 1996 Olympics were a bore as far as men's basketball was concerned; the country was much more interested in the women's game. Who was on the cover of the Olympic Preview edition of *Sports Illustrated?* The women's team, with Lisa Leslie and Sheryl Swoopes.

Besides, if the move to pro players is really about America retaining its hoops dominance, it's a short-term fix headed for long-term trouble. Exposing foreign teams to America's very best players will accelerate the bridging of the gap in talent levels between the U.S. and the rest of the world. The U.S. gains nothing — except gold medals for players who are already worth their weight in gold — by sending pros to the court at the Olympics.

Why the Rest of the World Has Caught Up to the United States

The challenge to American dominance by foreign imports is not restricted to auto sales; basketball has witnessed international players close the gap on Americans in the last decade as well. That direction is only natural. The learning curve was steeper for players abroad — they were so far down that they had more room for dramatic improvement. Following are some factors that contributed to that improvement:

- **Television:** Even in Jamaica, where cricket and soccer are the sports of choice, satellite dishes have NBA games going every night. Kids imitate what they see.
- **Foreign imports:** Since 1986, when the Prop 48 rule increased the academic entrance requirements for freshmen in college basketball, foreign players have been gaining recognition as a talent source. By and large, international players are older, more mature, and ready to make an impact right away.
- **American exports:** Because the money was there early, more and more United States players who failed to make NBA rosters began emigrating to European leagues, especially in Italy, Greece, and Israel. The American players were exciting to watch, so the locals went to see them play and became more and more interested in the game. Not only that, but the locals began copying their American hoops heroes.

Hoops Around the World: Top Pro Leagues

This section takes a look at top pro leagues around the world.

- **England:** The basketball league of England has grown tremendously over the past few years. The league consists of 13 teams located throughout England. Two teams, the Exide London Towers and the Leopards, are located in London. The season runs from early September through early April. The playoffs culminate with the Budweiser Basketball Championships, scheduled for early May at Wembley Arena.
- **France:** The LNB *(Lique Nationale de Basket)* is one of Europe's promising and growing pro leagues. The season runs from October through late April and consists of teams throughout France. Pau-Orthez is the defending league champion. The playoff champion is assured a place in the McDonald's Championship, which is played in Paris in October.
- **Germany:** The Veltins Basketball Bundesliga consists of 14 teams; the season runs from October through April. TSV Bayer Leverkusen has been the perennial powerhouse of the German league, winning 14 championships.

Hot hoops spots on the rise

Europe had been almost synonymous with "international" in terms of basketball for a long time. Make no mistake, Europe is still the dominant hoops force abroad. No country outside Europe has ever received a medal at the Olympics, for example. But in the next millennium, a few other points on the globe figure to be heard from. Keep an eye on these countries:

- **The Philippines:** Basketball is now the most popular sport in the Philippines. In 1975, the Philippines Basketball Association (PBA) was organized as a professional league, and the PBA has been the highest-rated sports program on TV in that country for the last 22 years. The schedule begins in February and ends in December of each year. The legend of the league is Robert Jaworsk, who is still a player-coach at age 50.
- **China:** The most populous nation in the world has an eight-team league called the Chinese New Basketball Alliance (CNBA). This league is truly a learning opportunity for the Chinese. Each team in the league has one American coach and one or more Chinese coaches. The league limits each team to two foreign players on the court at one time. ("Foreign" almost always means "American.") Some former NBA players take advantage of the league's opportunities, including 37-year-old Mike McGee, a former Los Angeles Laker who played on two NBA championship teams.

- **Greece:** In Greece, unlike most of Europe, basketball outranks soccer in popularity. Over the years, Olympiakos and Panathinaikos have maintained a rivalry not seen in the Mediterranean since the tilts involving Greece and Troy. The 14-team league competes from late September to mid-May. In each of the last two years, Olympiakos Piraeus has earned the league title.
- **Israel:** Pro basketball is well represented in Israel, where the Israeli Club League has ten teams and is one of the world's best leagues. The Maccabi Tel Aviv team is the near-perennial champion, having won 37 titles since the league's birth in 1954, including 23 straight from 1970–92.
- **Italy:** LEGA A of Italy is one of European basketball's more formidable pro leagues. Cities throughout Italy are represented in the 14-team A League, which also has a B series league that is lower in stature. The LEGA A season runs from mid-September to May, when a champion is crowned.
- **Spain:** The ACB (the Association of Club Baloncesot) has a rich history of basketball. Eighteen teams are in the league, and the season runs from mid-September through May. Real Madrid and FC Barcelona, two clubs with a strong soccer rivalry, have an equally strong rivalry in basketball.

Major International Basketball Tournaments

FIBA (the International Federation for the Sport of Basketball) is basketball's international governing body. Currently, 201 national member federations belong to FIBA. (The acronym FIBA is derived from the French *Federation International de Basketball Amateur.* The word amateur was dropped in 1989, but the A remained. Who wants to belong to an organization named FIB?)

FIBA consists of five zones: Europe, Asia, the Americas, Africa, and Oceania. (Where is Oceania, you ask? Is this Kevin Costner's pickup basketball team from *Waterworld*? No, Oceania represents Australia and the islands of the South Pacific.) This section discusses major FIBA basketball tournaments played internationally.

The Olympic Games

Twelve countries compete in Olympic basketball every four years. The host country automatically qualifies, as does the winner of the most recent World Championship game (assuming that the winner is not the host country). Each of FIBA's five geographic zones receives one spot for the Olympics; the remaining five or six spots (depending on whether the host country qualifies anyway by winning the prior World Championships) are awarded to the top five or six finishers at the most recent World Championships.

The top international tournament in the world is held every four years as part of the Summer Olympic Games. Qualification for the games for both men and women is gained by the top 12 countries in the world, based upon success in prior Olympic competitions and other basketball tournaments, such as the World Championships.

Each region of the world (Africa, Asia, Pan America, Europe, and Oceania) is represented. Upon qualification, the 12 competing nations are divided into two 6-team pools. National teams compete against others within the same pool, and the top four teams in each pool qualify for the medal round. Teams that continue to win compete for gold, silver, and bronze medals. (The next Olympic competition will take place in Sydney, Australia, in September 2000.)

The United States men's team has dominated Olympic competition and has posted a 101-2 all-time record. Check out Table 15-2 for details.

Table 15-2 Past Olympic Medalists in Men's Basketball

Year	*Gold*	*Silver*	*Bronze*
1936	United States	Canada	Mexico
1948	United States	France	Brazil
1952	United States	Soviet Union	Uruguay
1956	United States	Soviet Union	Uruguay
1960	United States	Soviet Union	Brazil
1964	United States	Soviet Union	Brazil
1968	United States	Yugoslavia	Soviet Union
1972	Soviet Union	United States	Cuba
1976	United States	Yugoslavia	Soviet Union
1980	Yugoslavia	Italy	Soviet Union*
1984	United States	Spain	Yugoslavia
1988	Soviet Union	Yugoslavia	United States
1992	United States	Croatia	Lithuania
1996	United States	Yugoslavia	Lithuania

**The U.S. did not compete in the 1980 games in Russia because the entire U.S. Olympic contingent was participating in a boycott. Likewise, the Russians did not compete in 1984.*

The European Championships

The European Championships is perhaps the most prestigious basketball tournament held outside the United States. Europeans are rabid hoops fans, and future NBA stars such as Vlade Divac, Toni Kukoc, and the late Drazen Petrovic all distinguished themselves there. Sixteen teams compete, and five advance to the World Championships.

The Pan American Games

NBA players often take part in the World Championships and the Olympics, but not in the Pan American (Pan Am) Games, which are held every four years. Usually, the Pan American games are staged the year prior to the Olympics, though they have no bearing on who competes in the Olympics.

Some of the more memorable moments involving the United States and international hoops have been the province of the Pan Am Games. In Indianapolis in 1987, for example, Oskar Schmidt, one of the best long-range shooters any country has ever produced, led Brazil to an unbelievable 120-115 backyard upset of the United States. That game was a watershed moment in international hoops because a U.S. national team had never lost a game to a foreign team in the U.S. — in Indiana, America's holy land of hoops, no less. Schmidt scored 46 points. I woke up early the next day to see if the sun would rise. It did, but nothing is a given anymore after that loss.

The FIBA World Championship of Basketball

This major international tournament involves national teams from 16 countries throughout the world. The tournament has been held every four years since 1950 for men and since 1953 for women.

Like the Olympics, each region of the world is represented. Both the men's and the women's World Championship are staged every four years at a different site.

The tournament grew from 12 to 16 teams in 1990. National teams compete in two 8-team pools, with the top national teams advancing to medal rounds to compete for gold, silver, and bronze medals, while others compete for ninth through 16th place.

The McDonald's Championship

The McDonald's Championship, formerly known as the McDonald's Open, was established in 1987 by the NBA and the FIBA. The tournament was an annual event from 1987 to 1991. But in 1991, FIBA and the NBA decided to make this competition a biannual event to be held in odd-numbered years as a complement to the national team competitions of the Olympics and the World Championships.

The tournament grew from three teams to a four-team format from 1988 to 1991. It increased to six teams in 1993. Beginning with the 1995 McDonald's Championship, the NBA sends its reigning champion to the event to represent the league against the best teams from pro leagues around the globe.

Chapter 16

Filling Out Your NCAA Tournament Bracket

In This Chapter

- Following the NCAA tournament from Selection Sunday to the Final Four
- Finding sources of information about teams when making your picks
- Which factors are *really* important in picking winning teams

Beware the Ides of March Madness. Every March 15 (or around that date), a fever grips NCAA tournament betters that rivals the antics of the games themselves. Unlike the Super Bowl or a college football bowl game, the NCAA tournament seems to entice even the most disinterested fans because of its scope: 64 teams, 63 games, 18 days. Upsets are a given, so even the most knowledgeable college hoops fans are humbled by the vagaries of the tourney. In 1997, for example, three number-one seeds advanced to the Final Four, but the tourney was won by the fourth team, Arizona, who had finished fifth in their own conference.

Whether you have a satellite dish, follow each team's home page, read the *NCAA News* for stats, *and* know Dick Vitale's barber, or whether you're a 61-year-old secretary who last heard the term *Sweet Sixteen* while watching *The Patty Duke Show,* you have a chance to win your office (or dorm, or family) pool. Winning is both an art and a science, but the more science you have, the less art you need. I'm here to give you the science.

Following the Chronology of the NCAA Tournament

Selection Sunday: On either the second or the third Sunday in March, at 6:30 p.m. EST (eastern standard time), the tournament draw is announced. All 64 teams, along with where and whom each one will play in the opening round, is broadcast on television. (For the last 12 years or so, CBS has owned the rights to the tournament selection show, though in recent years, my ESPN colleagues and I have done a simultaneous telecast.)

At this time, someone in your office or dormitory or even family, who has already drawn up or photocopied a 64-team bracket, writes down all the matchups at a furious pace. Figure 16-1 shows a sample bracket.

If you aren't yet online and absolutely can't wait until Monday morning's paper, I suggest that you make writing down the teams a two-person job. Each regional has 16 teams. Designate one person to write down the first eight teams (four games) of each regional and a second person to pen the latter eight. Otherwise, you'll be so confused between Middle Tennessee State and Southwest Missouri State and University of North Carolina-Charlotte that you may just miss those easy names, like Duke.

Monday: Office pool sheets are distributed. Most pools do not require an entrant to return her sheet until just before the first game of the tourney, which usually begins at noon EST on Thursday.

Don't forget to make a copy of your picks for yourself to peruse during the tourney.

Thursday through Sunday: Bring the TV to work or call in sick. Do not answer the phone. In these 96 hours, 48 of the tourney's 63 games are played, leaving only 16 of the teams that began this odyssey.

Resources for Picking Your Teams Wisely

Before filling out your bracket, you can inform yourself by doing a little research. Fortunately, about as much literature pertaining to college hoops is published each season as literature pertaining to the Kennedy assassination. I draw that comparison as a reminder that no matter how much you read about either topic, you'll never solve the mystery.

Preseason magazines

Why read these magazines at the *end* of the season?

- They contain preseason rankings. If Iowa State was ranked number 25 in the preseason magazine you're reading and they are undefeated entering the tourney, you can deduce one of two things: (1) The Hawkeyes overachieved this season, or (2) the people who published that magazine don't know much about college hoops.

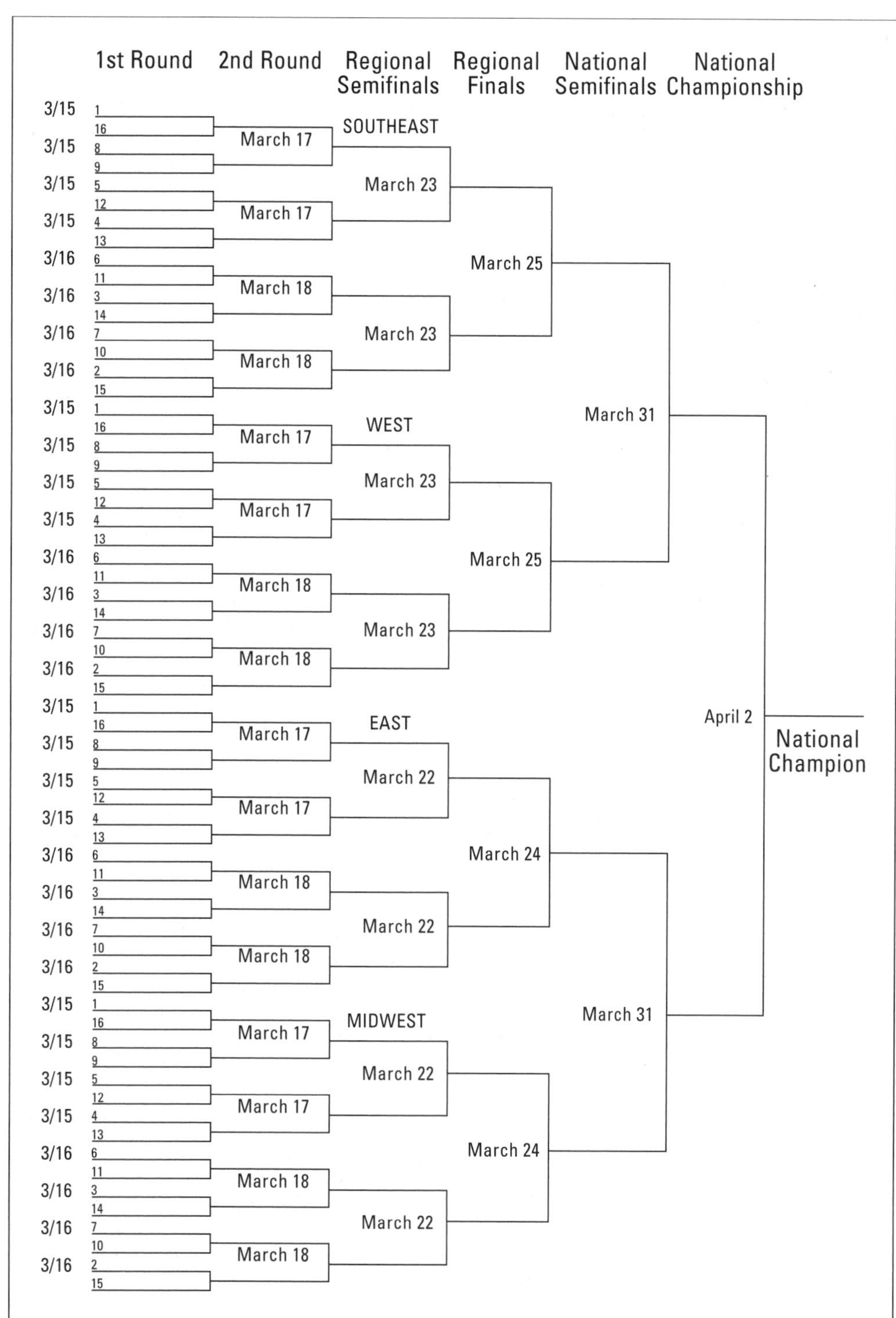

Figure 16-1: A sample championship bracket, minus actual teams.

Types of pools

The objective of any NCAA pool is the same: to correctly pick as many of the Final Four teams as possible. The most common type of pool is also the most mathematically complex. The entrant must pick the winner of each of the 63 games, all the way to the championship game. Point system pools — that is, how many points you receive for each winner correctly picked — vary. Check out the following three types:

- **Graduated point system:** A correct pick in the first round, which has 32 games, is worth 2 points. A second-round pick is worth 4 points, a Sweet 16 (Regional Semifinals) pick is worth 8, a Regional Final game is worth 16, a Final Four winner is worth 32, and correctly picking the champion is worth 50 points. This puts a premium on picking the Final Four teams correctly and does not penalize you for missing a few of the first-round upsets, which are almost inevitable.
- **One point for every game selected correctly:** Your maximum possible score is 63 points. Here, the drama tends to be at its peak during the early rounds, because 48 of the 63 games are played during the tournament's opening weekend.
- **NCAA auction:** You bid on each team in the tourney. Obviously, a top seed commands a higher price than a number-16 seed. Once you "buy" that team, it's yours for the tourney. After all the teams have been auctioned off, the auction fees go into a hat (or other safe place; I'm not married to the hat idea). The champion collects 40 percent of the pot, while the remaining 60 percent is divvied up equally among the "owners" of the other three Final Four teams.
- **Random draw:** The names of all 64 teams are placed in a hat (you may use a bowler or sombrero if you so choose, or even a box), and participants pick a name at random. If you want to choose more than once, you contribute double to the pot. The drawback of this game is that you can't use any of your hoops wisdom, accumulated over a season of watching games on TV. That's half the fun of playing.

- Many include rosters that give each player's year in school, which tells you something about whether a team has veteran leadership. As I explain later in this chapter, experience is an important factor in determining a team's potential in NCAA play.
- They can tip you off to a school's rigorous (or not-so-rigorous) schedule, especially if that school plays in a relatively anonymous conference. Then you can find out how the team fared against the competition.

  Take the College of Charleston, for example. John Kresse's team plays in a small conference, the Trans American Athletic Conference (TAAC). But during the 1996–97 season, Charleston defeated Stanford and Arizona State, and also played well in losses to Kentucky and Oklahoma State. After you realized that Charleston was no dog, you might have picked this team as a sleeper. (As it turned out, they upset the University of Maryland in the first round of the tournament.)

If you ask me, the best and most complete preseason magazine is *Blue Ribbon Magazine.* It comes out later than any other magazine, so it is the most up-to-date, and it offers a comprehensive analysis of every team. Many coaches use it as a starting base for scouting reports (that is, their research on teams that they play).

Other outstanding preseason publications:

- ***Sports Illustrated* preview issues:** Provide background on players, more stats now than in past years, and a starting lineup for top teams with classes, strengths, and weaknesses.
- ***Sporting News*:** Good lists of top players and accurate preseason rankings.
- ***Street & Smith's*:** The patriarch of college preseason annuals.

In-season publications

Following the game *during* the season is important, too, especially in December and early January when nonconference games are more common. *Sports Illustrated*, *Sporting News*, *Basketball Times*, and *Basketball Weekly* all do a solid job.

Basketball Weekly is the best publication to purchase come tourney time because it is the only source of game-by-game scores for every team. Game results are necessary data when analyzing how a team played at the end of the year, the strength of a team's schedule, and margin of victory.

Newspapers are also helpful. Among the best are *USA Today, The Atlanta Constitution, The Washington Post, The Boston Globe, The Chicago Tribune,* and *The Dallas Morning News.* Look for newspapers that have a national college basketball beat reporter; those weekly notes columns that cover the entire country will keep you informed come March.

But don't overload that most personal of computers, your brain. Too much info can only confuse you — and how much do you plan on spending on all these journals, anyway? Will your investment exceed the return you reap if you win the office pool?

USA Today tournament preview

This special section appears on the first day (always a Thursday) of the tourney and offers the most amount of info in the least amount of space. Do not lose it or lend it out. So far, *USA Today* is the only publication that lists every team's starting lineup, record, and recent developments (for example, an injury to a key player). The "Nation's Newspaper" does this for both the men's and the women's tournament.

Schools' Internet sites

Say that you attend Princeton and are only concerned about your team's first-round opponent. To zero in on that matchup, you can find both schools' releases and updated stats on the Internet.

Every school should have an Internet site by now. If you have problems finding an Internet site, call the school; they should be able to provide you with the address.

Selection Sunday shows on CBS and ESPN

At the present time, CBS and ESPN are the leading networks in college basketball coverage. They assess the game all winter, and by the time Selection Sunday arrives, they are eager (no, foaming at the mouth) to tell you about such obtuse matters as RPI (Rating Percentage Index) rankings or a school's record against teams in the Top 50 or a particular conference's power rating (how strong one conference's teams are versus another conference's).

I'm partial, but I think the ESPN selection show is better. By airtime, we've been doing nothing for the previous ten days but watching all the conference tournaments play out. We know who's hot. But I'm not asking you to form an allegiance. If you're a complete basketball junkie, tape one show while watching the other.

Factors to Consider When Filling Out Your Bracket

I present these factors without taking into consideration whether or not you have a gambling problem or how many times you can stomach hearing the term *Big Dance.*

Ratings

When you evaluate your bracket, consider these four major ratings:

- **RPI (Rating Percentage Index):** Computed by Jim Sukup in the basketball-crazy town of Carmel, Indiana. Although Jim won't share his secret formula for rating teams, I know that the RPI takes into account a team's strength of schedule and the strength of the schedules of that team's opponents. It also itemizes every team's record in the last ten games and every team's ranking against top 25, top 50, and top 100 ranked teams.

Note: The RPI used by the NCAA is a bit different from Sukup's RPI, but it's close.

To get the RPI report, contact Jim Sukup, Publisher and Editor, Collegiate Basketball News Company, P. O. Box 3032, Carmel, IN 46032; fax 317-848-7942. The subscription rate is $150 a year by mail or $220 a year by fax.

- **Jeff Sagarin index:** Published every Tuesday during the season in *USA Today* and updated daily on the *USA Today* World Wide Web site. This index also gives a number to each team's strength of schedule in addition to its rating.

  The major difference between the RPI index and the Jeff Sagarin index is that Sagarin's factors in a team's margin of victory and also weights a win based on whether it occurs at home, on the road, or at a neutral site. Curiously, Sagarin and Sukup live just 60 miles apart.

- **Associated Press (AP) poll:** A human analysis, the collective opinion of members of the media from around the country. There's nothing scientific about it. How accurate is the AP poll? Well, don't use it as a guide for picking the national champion. The top-ranked team in the final AP poll has gone on to win the national title just four times in the last 21 years. The four top-ranked teams in the final pretournament poll rarely advance to the Final Four (although usually at least one does). This may be the very reason behind the tourney's immense popularity, pool-wise.
- ***USA Today* poll:** Similar to the AP poll, except that the votes are cast by 60 head coaches nationwide. As with the AP poll, each voter picks the top 25 teams, with the number-one team receiving 25 points, the number-two team receiving 24 points, and so on down the line to the number-25 team, which receives one point. Then the numbers are added, with the highest score being ranked number one.

Which one is the best? Of the top 16 teams in each of the four final pretournament rankings/ratings from the 1995–96 season, 12 of both the AP and *USA Today*'s selections advanced to the Sweet 16; Sagarin had 11 of the teams and RPI had 10.

But when it came to picking the champion, RPI and Sagarin were the winners. They both had Kentucky as number-one entering the tournament, while AP and *USA Today* had the University of Massachusetts.

Then again, the fact that I use the 1996 season for my example indicates how much stock you should place in any of the four. I did not use 1997 because none of the four systems predicted (nor should they have been expected to) that Arizona would win it all.

Strength of schedule

The NCAA Tournament Selection Committee, those enlightened few who select the 64 teams, do not pick the field based solely upon each school's win-loss record. Neither should you. A wide range of opponents are in Division I — remember, more than 300 schools are in the lot — and you have to look at whether a school's record is artificially inflated with a slew of patsy opponents.

Take a look at the University of Texas, for example. Before 1996, the Longhorns played in the Southwest Conference, a better-than-average league. The coach, Tom Penders, schedules difficult, nonconference foes. In the eyes of the NCAA committee, losing a close game to North Carolina is better than defeating Southwest Texas State by 40. In 1996, Texas went one better and beat North Carolina. That win was a big lift toward their NCAA bid.

How do you examine schedules? You can get out that *Basketball Weekly* and see who the teams in question have played. Or get the Sagarin rating or RPI index and find the schedule ranking.

Familiarity exists within a conference. Playing in a tough conference, but playing a Ho-Ho-Ho December schedule (in other words, playing an easy early-season nonconference schedule) does not make a team tourney-tough.

Player experience

You can play in all the tough gyms in the nation against all the great teams with the nastiest, most obnoxious fans, but if you haven't been to the Big Dance — Eek! That term! — you haven't seen anything yet.

Consider South Carolina in 1997. The Gamecocks had a tremendous season, running up a 24-7 record. Coach Eddie Fogler's team won the SEC regular season and beat Kentucky twice, once at Kentucky on the Wildcats' Senior Night. (This is like drowning out Sinatra on a duet: It just doesn't happen.)

When South Carolina was given a number-2 seed against number-15 Coppin State, it looked like a lock for the Gamecocks. But South Carolina was making its first appearance in the tournament since 1989. Final score: Coppin State 78, South Carolina 65.

Coaching experience

Coaching in the Big Dance (I tried to warn you about that term) is a whole new experience. Few coaches are successful in their first tournament. In 1979, Bill Hodges took his Indiana State team to the Finals his first year, but he had Larry Bird playing for him.

Why is preparing a team for the NCAA tournament such a challenge?

- You often play a team that you've never played before and do not have much time to scout.
- You are probably going to a facility that is unfamiliar to your team.
- You are probably going to an area of the country that is unfamiliar to your team.

In general, the more experience a coach has in the tournament, the better his team's chances in the Big Dance. Dean Smith is the winningest NCAA tournament coach in history and has won a first-round game every year since 1980. He has taken teams to the tournament a record 23 straight seasons. (See Table 16-1 for a list of the winningest coaches.)

Table 16-1 Most NCAA Tournament Wins, Active Coaches

Coach	*School*	*NCAA Tournament Record*
Dean Smith	North Carolina	65-27
Denny Crum	Louisville	42-21
Bob Knight	Indiana	40-18
Mike Krzyzewski	Duke	40-11
Jerry Tarkanian	Fresno State	37-16
John Thompson	Georgetown	34-19
Lute Olson	Arizona	28-18
Eddie Sutton	Oklahoma State	27-18
Jim Boeheim	Syracuse	27-15
Nolan Richardson	Arkansas	24-11

Last year's NIT champ — forget it!

The National Invitation Tournament (NIT) is a 32-team tournament that runs concurrent with the NCAA tournament. The field is composed of the best 32 teams (in theory) that were not invited to the Big Da . . . you know. The winner is sometimes referred to as the 65th best team in the country.

In the 1970s, the theory was that you could pick the preceding year's NIT champion to go far in the NCAA tournament. In 1976, for example, Kentucky won the NIT and then advanced to the Elite Eight (the semifinal round) in the 1977 NCAA tournament before winning it all in 1978. But that was a different era. Back then, the NCAA field was half the current size (32 schools), and most student-athletes played for four years. The NIT had better teams and younger teams with promise.

Seven of the last eight NIT champions made the NCAA field the next year, but those seven teams had just a 5-7 record in the NCAA tournament. Only Virginia in 1993 advanced to the Sweet 16 the year after winning the NIT. The verdict? Don't put too much stake in a team's success in the prior year's NIT tournament.

Conference tourney success

Winning a conference tournament may be a harbinger of a team on a roll — but not always. Beware of teams that win their conference tournament in an upset or win the tournament for the first time in school history or for the first time in a number of years.

In the last 11 years, the NCAA champion won its conference tournament just twice (UNLV in 1990, Duke in 1992). Granted, four of those 11 are from the Big Ten or Pac-10, which don't have conference tournaments (although the Big Ten is holding its first conference tournament in 1998).

Often, a team is motivated (that is, the coach rips the players) by a failure to win its conference tournament. The practice time gained from an early exit from conference tournament play, for example, can be used to fix glaring problems. Pretournament time is probably the most time the team has had to simply devote to practice in three months.

Bottom-line fact: Since 1980, there have been 72 Final Four teams: Thirty-seven of them entered the tournament as conference champions, and 35 were chosen as at-large teams. Winning a conference tournament is a nice addition to the trophy case, but it is not a free pass to the Final Four.

Conference ratings

You can evaluate the toughness of a conference in two ways: *top-heavy* and *top-to-bottom.* Conferences that are top-heavy, or have four or five teams that stand out and have a top-20 ranking, usually do better in the NCAA tournament than conferences that are tough from top to bottom.

In a top-heavy conference, four or five softies are on the schedule. Play each of them twice a year, and that's eight to ten games during which you can catch a breather. The emotional strain is harder on the players than the physical strain. No coach can have her team at top intensity each game. Emotional lulls are inevitable, and a seasoned coach coincides her team's lulls with the easy games.

In a conference that's tough from top to bottom, teams often get burned out. Yes, they're battle-tested come March Madness — but they're shell-shocked, too. See Table 16-2 for a list of NCAA tournament records by conference.

Table 16-2 NCAA Tournament Records by Conference, 1985–97

Conference	Record	Percentage
ACC	139-68	.671
Big East	109-64	.630
SEC	93-57	.620
Big Ten	101-72	.584
Big Eight	78-56	.582
Pac-10	51-45	.531

Despite what happened in 1997, since 1985 the ACC has had the most upsets of number-one seeded teams (12), the most Sweet 16 appearances (40), the most regional finalists (22), and the most Final Four appearances (12). Also, since 1980, 17 of the 72 Final Four teams (nearly 25 percent) have come from the ACC.

Who's hot, who's not

Going with a team that has been playing its best basketball of the season in the last few weeks is easy to do, and it seems to make perfect sense. As I mention later in this chapter, a team doesn't have to have a six-game winning streak entering the tournament. However, having a six-game winning streak at some point in the season is important. Why six games? That's how many in a row you need to win to capture the NCAA title.

Who has the guards?

The most important position in the NCAA tournament is not center; having an experienced guard who can control the tempo of a game is more important. Even the great UCLA teams in the 1960s and '70s had great guards in addition to Kareem Abdul-Jabbar and Bill Walton. Someone had to get them the ball and control the flow of the game, after all.

You may remember early 1990s Duke center Christian Laettner. Not only was he the Blue Devils' on-court leader, but he also set a tournament career scoring record that still stands. But where would Duke have been without diminutive but scrappy point guard Bobby Hurley? The media recognized this in the 1992 tournament when it named *Hurley,* not Laettner, MVP.

When appraising a team's ability to go far in the tournament, research the guards. How far did Shaquille O'Neal's Louisiana State teams go in the tournament, for example? They never went past the Sweet 16 because they didn't have anyone to control the tempo.

Geography

The points of the NCAA compass do not correspond to yours or mine. The NCAA Regionals are divided into four geographic zones: East, West, Midwest, and Southeast, the directions North and South having been deemed irrelevant. Moreover, to promote a tourney in which each Regional is equally stringent in terms of competition, at least half the teams in any one Regional are not from that geographic region of the U.S.

Teams that must cross time zones and face teams that are playing in their own time zones are at a disadvantage. Some period of adjustment may be involved. Also take into account altitude adjustments that must be made when teams play in the Mountain Time Zone. If North Carolina goes to the West Regional and plays a game in Utah against Weber State, for example, the player must acclimate to the 4,700-foot elevation and corresponding thinner air.

Home-court advantage has been eliminated — sort of. In the 1980s, teams hosted the subregional (rounds one and two). The sites were picked before the season, and if a school that happened to be hosting a subregional was invited to the tourney, it made economic sense (for both the school and the tourney hoping to sell tickets) to have that school remain at home. But now, teams can't play at home in the NCAA tournament.

Another geographic factor is familiarity with an arena. Playing at a previously visited facility can be an advantage; you know the rims and the dead spots on the floor.

Season records: Stubbing your toe isn't all that bad

Don't be enticed into picking a school just because the team heads into the tourney undefeated or with only one loss. College basketball is not like college football: Losing once in a while is good. Sure, you want to be on a roll entering the tournament, but if you're undefeated or have just one loss heading into the tournament, the pressure rises.

Just look at 1996, when Texas Tech had just one loss entering the tournament. Tech failed to move beyond the Sweet 16. The rule continued in 1997, when Kansas, at 34-1, lost in the quarterfinal round to an Arizona team that had lost nine times during the regular season. *In the last 21 years, 15 teams entered the NCAA tournament with one or no losses, and none of them won the national championship.* The last team to go undefeated in the regular season and win the national championship was Indiana in 1975–76, a perfect 32-0. Why?

- **Too much pressure.** Teams start playing not to lose instead of playing to win.

- **Losing is good once in a while.** It allows you to take an honest look at where you need improvement. Coaches can preach what needs to be improved — but if the team didn't lose the preceding game, their preaching may not sink in.

If you're looking for an ideal number of losses, I suggest two. Three of the last six national champs entered the NCAA tournament with two losses: Kentucky in 1996, UCLA in 1995, and Duke in 1992.

The importance of seeding

Follow the seeds when you make your selections. Although you can't pick every game according to seeds, you'll be right more often than not. In fact, in 1997, the higher seed won 45 of 62 games (one game was a matchup of number-one seeds) — so the higher-seeded team won about 75 percent of the time. That's why it's the higher seed, after all. Give the NCAA tournament selection committee some credit; they work long and hard on seeding the teams.

Although every rule I mention in this chapter has its infrequent converse side, one rule, as applied to seeding, has never been broken: *A number-one seed has never lost in the first round.* Top seeds are a perfect 52-0 in the first round since the NCAA first started seeding teams for the 64-team tournament in 1984–85. You can take the number-two seed (49-3) to the bank for the first round most of the time as well.

The 8-seed versus 9-seed game is supposed to be even, and it has been since the NCAA started seeding teams in 1979. Since then, the number-8 seed has won 36, and the number-9 seed has won 36. Heads or tails on that one. The 7 versus 10 games have seen the number-7 seed win 47 times, compared to 25 for the number-10 seed. The 6 versus 11 games are just about the same; the number-6 seed has a 51-21 advantage. Table 16-3 spells all this out for you.

Table 16-3 Records of Seeds in Opening Rounds

Year	*1 vs. 16*	*2 vs. 15*	*3 vs. 14*	*4 vs. 13*	*5 vs. 12*	*6 vs. 11*	*7 vs. 10*	*8 vs. 9*	*Total*
1980	___	___	___	___	3-1	4-0	3-1	4-0	14-2
1981	___	___	___	___	4-0	3-1	2-2	2-2	11-5
1982	___	___	___	___	4-0	2-2	3-1	2-2	11-5
1983	___	___	___	___	3-1	2-2	2-2	3-1	10-6
1984	___	___	___	___	3-1	3-1	2-2	3-1	11-5
1985	4-0	4-0	4-0	3-1	3-1	2-2	4-0	2-2	26-6

(continued)

Table 16-3 (continued)

Year	1 vs. 16	2 vs. 15	3 vs. 14	4 vs. 13	5 vs. 12	6 vs. 11	7 vs. 10	8 vs. 9	Total
1986	4-0	4-0	3-1	4-0	3-1	3-1	3-1	3-1	27-5
1987	4-0	4-0	3-1	2-2	3-1	4-0	2-2	1-3	23-9
1988	4-0	4-0	3-1	3-1	4-0	3-1	3-1	3-1	27-5
1989	4-0	4-0	3-1	3-1	3-1	0-4	3-1	0-4	20-12
1990	4-0	4-0	3-1	4-0	2-2	3-1	3-1	2-2	25-7
1991	4-0	3-1	3-1	3-1	3-1	2-2	2-2	3-1	23-9
1992	4-0	4-0	3-1	3-1	3-1	4-0	2-2	1-3	24-8
1993	4-0	3-1	4-0	3-1	3-1	3-1	4-0	2-2	26-6
1994	4-0	4-0	4-0	4-0	2-2	3-1	2-2	0-4	23-9
1995	4-0	4-0	2-2	3-1	3-1	3-1	3-1	2-2	24-8
1996	4-0	4-0	4-0	3-1	2-2	3-1	2-2	1-3	23-9
1997	4-0	3-1	3-1	4-0	3-1	4-0	2-2	2-2	25-7
Totals	**52-0**	**49-3**	**42-10**	**42-10**	**54-18**	**51-21**	**47-25**	**36-36**	**373-125**

Since seeding began in 1979, riding the number-one seeds to the Final Four has not been wise; only 32 of the 76 Final Four teams have been number-one seeds. Only two years, 1993 and 1997, saw as many as three number-one seeds advance to the Final Four. Never have all four made it.

Sticking with the number-one seeds doesn't guarantee you four teams in your Final Four, but it *is* the way to go when picking the champion. A number-one seed has won the national championship five of the last six years (the exception being Arizona in 1997, when the other three finalists were number-one seeds). In the last 19 years, nine number-one seeds have won the national championship. That's almost a 50-50 shot.

Avoid picking the number-one seed in the Southeast Regional. The top seed in that Regional has *never* won the national championship, and has a combined record of 46-19. In fact, only two number-one seeds from the Southeast have ever advanced to the Final Four: Oklahoma (1988) and Kentucky (1993).

Matchups

After you take into account a team's seed and geography and whether its astrological signs bode well for this lunar phase, remember this: The games are played, and won, by players. You have to assess the matchups, especially when you're looking at star players.

Two years ago in the NCAA Elite Eight, Wake Forest, with sophomore center Tim Duncan and junior point guard Randolph Childress, were on a roll, having won the ACC tournament. When Wake Forest ran into Oklahoma State in the East Regional semifinal, Childress was not quite as effective.

Why? Tim Duncan had to go up against Bryant "Big Country" Reeves, a senior center who was big enough to contend with Duncan. Reeves outscored Duncan 15-12. Not a big margin, but the big key was Reeves' ability to joust with Duncan without giving up the outside shot to Childress, who had a great postseason heading into this game. Oklahoma State's perimeter players were able to limit Childress to 3 of 11 three-point shooting because they didn't have to help out on defense on Duncan (as a team without Reeves probably would have). The matchup favored OSU.

Physical teams

Bob Huggins, the coach at Cincinnati, told me that there really is a difference in the way the game is officiated in the NCAA tournament. The attitude among the refs is to let the teams decide for themselves on the court. So to go a long way in the NCAA, teams had better not rely totally on finesse. They'd better play some defense and rebound and scrap for every loose ball. Rebound margin (see Chapter 8 for more information) is a good indicator of a team's penchant for physical play.

Injuries and distractions

Late-season distractions, usually centering around an NCAA violation, arrest, or academic suspension, can have a devastating effect on a team. The 1995 Arizona team is an example. The Wildcats were the heavy favorite over Miami (of Ohio) in the first round. Star guard Damon Stoudamire's eligibility was in question, and it was not known until the day prior to the game whether he would be able to play. Miami won.

Be aware of who's out due to injury and who's coming back from injury, too. Everyone marveled at the run that Jim Valvano's North Carolina State team made in the 1983 NCAA tournament, for example. One of the factors in the run was Derrick Whittenberg's return after missing ten games at midseason with an ankle injury. He gave State an outside shooter with experience that made a difference in many tournament games that year.

Teams on a mission

Be aware of special motivating factors for teams. In 1995–96, for example, Pete Carrill was coaching Princeton in his final NCAA tournament. The result: an upset of defending national champion UCLA in the first round.

Two other recent examples of teams with causes are Loyola Marymount in 1990 and Villanova in 1985.

Marymount had just lost its star player Hank Gathers, who died on the court in the conference tournament just days prior to the start of the NCAA tournament. Marymount beat defending champion Michigan in the first round in one of the greatest team shooting performances in tournament history, and advanced to the Elite Eight before succumbing to eventual champ UNLV.

In 1985, Villanova dedicated their postseason to trainer Jake Nevin, who had served Villanova for more than 50 years. Nevin was confined to a wheelchair due to a bout with cancer, but was obviously a motivating factor in Villanova's drive to become the only number-eight seed in history to win it all.

The charismatic leader factor

Every NCAA tournament has a most valuable player, but some players hoist their team on their backs more than others. In recent years, Danny Manning of Kansas (1988), Glen Rice of Michigan (1989), and Miles Simon of Arizona (1997) carried their teams to the title on what often seemed like sheer willpower.

In 1996, John Wallace was the MVP of the tournament and took Syracuse to the final game (where the team lost to Kentucky). Each year, someone makes a run behind a great senior player who's motivated by the fact that this is his last go-round. Who will it be this year?

Live by the three, die by the three

Watch out for the teams that live and die by the three-point goal. If Texas is hot from three-point range, for example, they can beat anyone, but if Texas is off from the outside, they can lose to anyone. I know that statement contradicts the glowing remarks I make about their schedule, but if Texas shoots 5 of 30 against a good perimeter defensive team, Texas isn't going to win.

UNLV made the greatest run by a three-point shooting team in 1987. Anderson Hunt and company launched 25 threes per game and advanced to the Final Four. But this is a rarity.

Rick Pitino's Kentucky squads often lived and died by the three. In a regular-season outing at LSU in 1994, Kentucky erased a 31-point deficit, tying a college record, via the trey to defeat the Tigers, still licking their wounds. A year later in the round of eight, North Carolina eliminated Kentucky when UK shot just 6 of 37 from beyond the arc. Six of 37 is more than just awful shooting. North Carolina scouted the Wildcats well, and UK failed to adjust.

The lesson: Don't fall in love with a one-dimensional team.

The Rodney Dangerfield theory

In the last dozen years, the number-nine seed has beaten the number-eight seed 30 of 52 games. Does the number-nine seed coach have an advantage because he sells his players on their underdog role?

In games in which the lower seed is the lone representative from a small conference, you often see the same thing. The team is not only playing for pride, but for the pride of the entire league as well. "*I tell ya, the Sunbelt Conference gets no respect.*" Upset city, baby.

The Fantasticks theory: Try to remember that time in December

NCAA tournament games are almost always nonconference contests. The tournament committee works the schedule so that teams in the same conference do not meet until the Elite Eight at the earliest. So when you pick games, be aware of how a team played against its nonconference competition. Granted, a lot of games have been played since December, and teams can improve or get worse, but don't discount these contests.

Many schools use December as get-acquainted time. In this era, when so many players transfer in from junior colleges or leave school for the pros after only a year or two, a team's starting five may use the month of December simply to learn each other's names. North Carolina, for example, was like two different teams in 1997. At the end of January, Dean Smith's team was 3-5 in the ACC and looked as if it might not make the tournament. But the Tar Heels won their last eight conference games and advanced to the Final Four.

Uniform colors or team nicknames

Even if facts and figures bore you, and you'd rather read the NASDAQ ratings than the Sagarin ratings any day of the week, you may still want to enter the office pool. If so, you may want some basis on which to select your winners. Try school colors or mascots.

If you use the color method, go with blue first and then red. Ten of the last 14 NCAA champions, including the last three, had some shade of blue in their uniform. Teams with red or blue in their school colors have won 18 straight tournaments. (Sorry, Oregon State.) The last non-blue or -red team to win it all was Magic Johnson's Michigan State squad (which wore green) in 1979.

Charting it out

If you really want to attack this 8-seed versus 9-seed theory from an analytical standpoint, make a chart of the points that you feel are important to consider, with both teams at the top of the column. Put a check mark or an X next to the team with the advantage.

Take the 1996 West Regional game between Clemson and Georgia, an 8 versus 9 contest, as an example.

Category	*Clemson*	*Georgia*
Team experience		X
Coaching NCAA experience		X
Conference strength	X	
Schedule strength		X
Record, last 10 games	4-6	(7-3) X
Record versus Top 50 teams	(7-8) X	6-7
RPI ranking	40	(34) X
Sagarin ranking	34	(18) X
Seed	8 X	9
More physical team	X	
Rebounding		X
Senior guards		X
Common opponents	(2-3)	(2-2) X
Three-point shooting		X

As you can see, Georgia has ten Xs and Clemson has only four. So go with Georgia. (You would have been right, too. Georgia won the game 81-74 and would have gone to the Elite Eight had they not lost to Syracuse on a last-second play.)

As for mascots, go with animals. The mascot of the last five NCAA champions — Wildcats, Bruins, Razorbacks, and Tar Heels — has been an animal of some sort. The Duke Blue Devils (in 1992) were the last non-animal to claim the title.

Part IV
Coaching Teams and Yourself

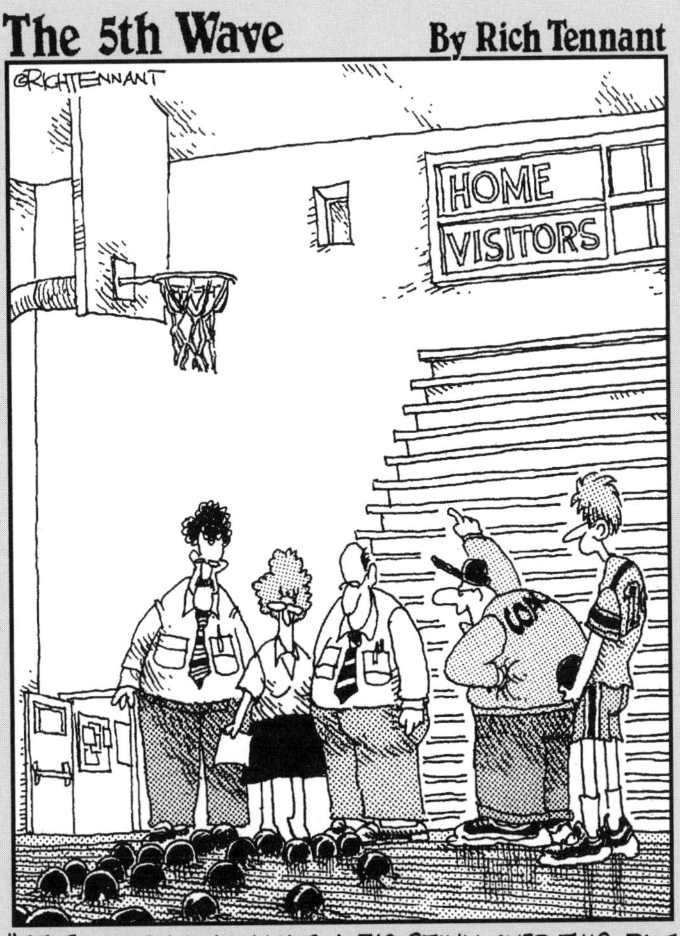

"IT FIGURES YOU'D MAKE A BIG STINK OVER THIS, BUT HAS ANYONE BOTHERED TO NOTICE HOW MANY MORE BASKETS WE'RE MAKING FROM THE THREE-POINT LINE SINCE WE STARTED PRACTICING WITH BOWLING BALLS?"

In this part . . .

This part speaks to all coaches and wannabe coaches out there — you know who you are. Whether you coach kids or adults, or you just want to improve your own game, you have to know yourself, your philosophy, and your motivation.

This part also gives you the latest scoop on conditioning, training, diet, and injury prevention. After all, having a great rebounder doesn't do you any good if he isn't fit to play. You have to protect your investments — and here I tell you how.

Chapter 17

Coaching Philosophy and Motivation

In This Chapter

- Developing your coaching philosophy
- Setting goals
- Stressing academics

A born basketball coach, a natural, is someone with an insatiable desire to explore the game. Obviously, you should love basketball and want to win. But successful coaches also explore themselves. Use the Socratic method. Who are you? What kind of coach do you want to be? Then again, the Greek philosopher was sentenced to death without ever having won a basketball game. So maybe there's a better way to explore yourself.

Searching for a better way — a good coach never stops doing this. There's no single tried-and-true manner in which to coach. Bobby Knight is a tempest in a red sweater; he's also a great coach. Dean Smith, the all-time winningest coach in Division I college hoops history, is milder than a Carolina spring day. Who's to say which coach's philosophy and motivational skills are more effective?

The best coaches are objective judges not only of talent but also of themselves. They analyze their strengths and weaknesses and do something about the latter. In this chapter, I survey a few different approaches to the game and unearth one or two universal truths of coaching.

Ten Simple Rules of Coaching

I guess if I had to further abbreviate this list of coaching rules, I'd mention just two, both dealing with survival:

1. **Don't listen to the critics.**
2. **Everyone's a critic.**

But because the editors have generously allowed me more space, here are ten credos that you'd do well to follow as a coach.

#1: Be yourself

All you have is your credibility; your players will see right through any of your attempts to be the next Rick Pitino or Tara VanDerveer. You may want to borrow an idea or two dozen from these great coaches (many of which they probably borrowed themselves), but season those ideas with your own personality. For example, Duke University coach Mike Krzyzewski played for Bob Knight at Army before he landed his present job. In comportment, the two men could not be more opposite. But Coach K doubtless has copied many of Knight's philosophies on defense and offense.

If you try to be someone you're not, your team will sense your insecurity. Who wants to follow a leader like that?

#2: Be a teacher; keep it simple

When you teach, whether it's hoops or history, you need to explain everything as simply and clearly as possible. Your limit as a coach is not how much your players can learn, but how much they can *retain.*

#3: Develop a philosophy

I'd stay away from nihilism, myself. Seriously, though, you must be consistent, and that stems from a belief in how you want to play the game. Do you want to press the entire game, à la the "40 Minutes of Hell" that Nolan Richardson has his Arkansas teams execute? Or do you believe that the triangle offense, which the Chicago Bulls alone run, is the best half-court offense?

One of the primary motivations to coach for anyone who loves the game should be the belief that you play this game a certain way. Then show your players how to demonstrate that style of play.

#4: Know your team

Sure, most uniforms have the player's last name on the back, but that's not what I mean. Know each player's strengths and weaknesses, as well as which players seem to have good chemistry with one another. Knowing your team goes a long way in influencing your coaching philosophy.

For example, say that you espouse the style of Paul Westhead, the former Loyola Marymount coach who believed in shooting three-pointers almost exclusively. However, none of your players can throw the ball into the ocean from the deck of the Pacific Princess. You may as well have Captain Stubing coach them — and play Gopher at point guard. Remember, your philosophy and your players' talents should not be incompatible.

#5: Know your opponent

If you want your team to be the *winning* team, you'll want to know more about your opponent. What does your opponent do well? What does your opponent do poorly? Your opponent has lost seven games — or is undefeated — this season: why? What is the common denominator in those losses or wins?

In 1981, Notre Dame faced the unbeaten Virginia Cavaliers, led by 7'4" Ralph Sampson. Watching films of the Cavaliers prior to the game, our coaches noticed that, when playing defense, Sampson did not like players going directly at him. For a guy that big, he had a silky game. We reminded our power forward, Orlando Woolridge, and our center, Joe Kleine, to take the ball directly at Sampson — never mind if he blocked the shot. Final score: Notre Dame 57, Virginia 56.

#6: Realize that everyone can play defense

Although anybody who watched the NBA in the mid-1970s may dispute this, offense is about talent, and defense is about desire and discipline. A coach never lets her players forget that there's no excuse for poor defense, and that *everyone* can rebound. (See Chapters 7 and 8 for defense and rebounding drills that you can run with your players.)

#7: Substitute wisely

Develop a pattern. Put your best players on the floor during the last four minutes of the first half and again during the last six minutes of the game. Do not oversub, or your players will fail to develop a rhythm with one another. This is not a square dance.

Often, coaches sit players too long due to foul trouble. If a player fouls out of the game (five fouls in college, six in the pros), he cannot return. Of course, he can't play if you sit him on the bench, either. If the game ends and your star sat for 15 minutes and had only three fouls, you don't receive any special reward. Better to have your best player foul out with three minutes left than to have him be a nonfactor the entire game.

#8: Give everyone a job description

Give your player a role, and she knows what facets of the game she needs to develop. Your point guard should be a terrific ball handler, a team leader, an accurate passer, and a skilled free throw shooter. Tell that to a player, and she'll stay after practice to work on her free throws. Keep her in the dark, however, and you leave her with nothing to focus on.

Also, don't be afraid to praise your players. (Do you ever get the feeling that the only film some coaches have seen is *Patton*?) Let every player, even the 12th player, know what her role is. In fact, be sure to praise the 12th player because her attitude is just as infectious, be it good or bad, as your star's.

#9: Figure out why you lost

This rule comes straight from the "Those who don't know history are doomed to repeat it" school of thought. Analyze the statistics sheet after a loss. In the 1995 NCAA championship game between Arkansas and UCLA, for example, the Razorbacks allowed 21 offensive rebounds that the Bruins converted into 27 second-chance points. Such a statistical shortfall provides a coach with something to devote his time to during a practice — that is, rebounding drills, and lots of 'em.

#10: Figure out why you won

What did you execute well in a win that you failed to do in your losses? Did a certain player perform better because you changed her role? Did you try a new defense? Did you push up the tempo or slow it down? This is another game inside the game, one of those minutiae of coaching that makes the job fun. The name of the game is improving your team.

Philosophy 101: I Diagram Plays, Therefore I Coach

A philosopher is someone who loves to learn. A coach should be a philosopher of hoops. You can never know all there is to know about the game — not even after reading this book. And in the end, your goal is to develop your *own* philosophy about coaching the game. Here are a few ways to discover who *you* want to be as a basketball coach:

- **Read the game.** Devour (not literally) textbooks, articles, and any written history that you can find about the game. You can also watch instructional videos — the '90s version of literature — made by successful coaches. Whoever is hot or has a unique theory will produce a video.
- **Watch the game.** Watch the game being played and listen to your heart. Are you a big fan of teams that trap on defense, like the University of Kentucky? Do you like the physical style of play that the New York Knicks have played for much of the '90s? Divorce yourself from any team allegiances and become a student of the game.
- **Talk the game.** Trade ideas with other coaches. Attend clinics, mingle, and expose yourself to different schools of thought. A coach should have a lot of mentors. In theory, you take the best from all your mentors and form your own philosophy.

When I was a volunteer assistant at Rider College, for example, I used to spend many hours with Tom Petroff, the school's baseball coach, watching him do eight different double-play drills with his shortstop and second baseman. Tom had broken down all the pivot moves into different drills. When I later devised my press drills for basketball, I borrowed ("borrow" is coachspeak for "steal") that theory of breaking down movements into drills.

Philosophy 201: Like the Universe — or NBA Salaries — a Philosophy May Expand Infinitely

Did you know that, in the early days of basketball, teams used to bring four players up on offense and leave one behind as a safety valve for defense? Then one coach had the bright idea to use five players on offense. This strategy worked, and suddenly every other coach followed suit. This changing process is called *evolution,* and it works quite nicely.

Seven seasons into my Division I coaching career, I discovered Bill Green and his matchup zone at Marion High School in Indiana. You might think a big-time college coach would feel silly asking a high school coach to be his tutor, but I was smart enough to know that you can get great ideas from coaches at any level, and I was willing to expand my philosophy and broaden my knowledge base. Notre Dame beat three top-ten teams in the first month of that 1976–77 season using Bill Green's matchup zone defense.

Philosophy 301: You Can't Grow Corn in the Desert

You have to win with what nature — or in my case, the recruiting trail — gives you. If you have a strong frontcourt-oriented team (big forwards and a big, dominant center), you don't play a fast-paced, fast-break game. Instead, walk the ball up the floor and play what is known as a *half-court game.* In 1985, when my best players were frontcourt men Tim Kempton, Ken Barlow, and Jim Dolan, we played a slowed-down half-court game.

Ten years earlier, however, my best three players at Notre Dame — Duck Williams, Bill Hanzlik, and Rich Branning — were primarily *swingmen* (players who combine the qualities of guards and forwards). We played an uptempo game, meaning that we attempted to run the fast break after every defensive rebound. We took advantage of our superiority in quickness rather than our size.

Both methods worked. Players, not styles, win ballgames. Smart coaches realize that.

Make a decision about what style of play your team will adopt first. For example, you may have a team filled with kids who will run through a brick wall for you but are such poor shooters that their shots would probably break the wall first — in other words, a team of hustlers but no stars. You decide that this team will have to win with defense.

Now sell your players on this philosophy. Be passionate. Make your enthusiasm and energy about who you are and what you stand for infectious to your players. No one follows a general into battle who's biting his nails.

One Big Job Equals Many Little Ones

You'll keep yourself, your assistant(s), and your players better focused if you break down a large unit into smaller units. For example, try breaking down a game into four-minute blocks and setting goals for each four-minute period. Or break down a practice into smaller increments so that your players can give themselves things to look forward to, such as a water break or a one-on-one drill. You can even break down the season into time blocks, setting goals for each block.

Breaking down a season

For clarity's sake, I'll use a typical season at Notre Dame as an illustration of breaking down a season into time blocks. If you really want to immerse yourself in the environment of a typical basketball season in South Bend, read this section inside a meat locker.

Preseason practice

Typically, we had six weeks to prepare for our season opener. From the first day of practice, my assistants and I organized each day into time blocks and established goals and objectives for each block.

- **Defense comes first.** At each practice, we taught defense before moving on to offense. We did this for the same reason that you don't wait until the end of dinner to serve vegetables: If you did, everyone would be too full to eat them. Also, players are at their most mentally focused during the first half of practice, so teaching defense then is better.
- **Be flexible on offense.** From day one, we taught each player how to play offense from every spot on the floor. There are no specialists in basketball below the pro level — at least there *shouldn't* be.

During the preseason, when games don't yet serve as a necessary distraction to practice, your players may begin to regard practice as drudgery. If this happens, work in four-day clips. In other words, work four straight days and then give your team a day off. Physically and mentally, your players need that day to recharge themselves.

No, you may not start scrimmaging yet . . .

Clip I (October 15–18): Teach the half-court man-to-man defense, passing, offense, rebounding, and fast break. Make sure that your players stretch well — the beginning of the season is the worst time for pulled muscle injuries — and begin conditioning.

Conditioning should change from practice to practice so that it doesn't get monotonous. For example, you may want to do sprints one day and touch-and-goes the next. Or put the clock up for ten minutes and say, "Go, back, go, forward." This change-of-direction conditioning drill simulates what players do in a game. Because a basketball game is a constant change of direction, this drill is a good way to condition. Anything you do in practice that closely simulates a game situation is a good thing.

Clip II (October 20–23): Expand the man-to-man defensive principles to full-court, which promotes aerobic conditioning. During the second half of practice — the offense half — run the motion offense.

Okay, now you may . . .

Clip III (October 25–29): Install the matchup zone and press defenses. Also teach new offenses. The players have been practicing for two weeks now and may be getting restless, so use the last hour of practice for scrimmaging.

A scrimmage always has a purpose. In these one-hour scrimmages at Notre Dame, we covered the three set offenses, three zone offenses, and four defenses that we had taught our players. We taped the scrimmages, too.

Clip IV (November 1–4): Get into zone offense and start preparing for big upcoming games. Then work on things that you want to cover, such as different zone offenses.

In 1982–83, for example, we had a game with Kentucky early in the season, so we began running Kentucky's offenses and defenses in practice during Clip IV. During the one-hour scrimmage at the end of the clip, we went over our man-to-man defense, our four zones defenses, and our four zone offenses. We also scrimmaged with Kentucky in mind, running their offense and defense.

Clip V (November 6–10): Finalize your strategies for upcoming opponents. Our first major opponent of the season was UCLA, so we reviewed UCLA's offenses and defenses. Finally, on the last day, we had a UCLA scrimmage. Our starting five and the first or second player off the bench scrimmaged against our other subs, who ran the offense and defense that we expected to see from UCLA.

Time-blocking your season

You can take your schedule and develop five time blocks. Say that you're playing 25 games — you have five blocks of five games. You can set up a big board in the locker room with all the time blocks on it, listing objectives in each block. Once your players see the breakdown of the schedule and the time blocks, they can see how important each game is.

Take a look in the first time block of five games and decide which teams you absolutely, positively cannot afford to lose to. I know, you never want to lose a game, but some losses are truly unacceptable. For example, when we used this same strategy at Notre Dame, we said, "We don't need a dumb loss against Valparaiso. We don't need to lose to Davidson because it may affect where we will be seeded in the NCAA tournament, making us a ten seed instead of an eight seed." (Your *seed* is your spot in the tourney bracket; the higher you're seeded, the less formidable your opponent, and vice versa.)

TEAM motivation

During my 20 seasons at Notre Dame, this slogan hung in our locker room:

To be successful:

- *We have to listen.*
- *We have to talk to each other.*
- *We have to concentrate on each situation.*

Those three things applied to everything we did as a team on and off the court. Players love motivational phrases or credos that help them to define who they are as players. My football counterpart at Notre Dame, used to hand out T-shirts to his players that read **"TEAM"** in big letters and then below, in smaller, less-bold letters, "me." It got the point across and was easy to remember.

Pregame Preparation: Prime Cram Time

Along the lines of the time-out theory that I discussed earlier in this chapter, the best time to reinforce your game plan is just before the game. Many times as a coach, I reviewed the entire game strategy with my players in the auxiliary gym at 7:00 p.m. for an 8:00 p.m. game. This review wasn't a practice, though.

For road games, many a coach uses the team's hotel ballroom as an impromptu basketball court, using masking tape to create free throw lanes and so on. A ballroom (or any big, open room) is a great place to make a run-through of your game plan on game day while retaining a little privacy.

Pregame Speeches

Pregame speeches are when coaches become evangelists trying to inspire their teams to victory. Are pregame speeches necessary? As long as the opposing coach is giving his team a pregame pep talk, you owe it to your team to do the same. But what makes a great pregame speech? If the speech is followed by a win, then in my book it's a great speech.

Some of what I thought were my greatest moments of rhetoric were followed by our worst losses ever. I delivered a terrific pregame speech before the Fordham game during my first year at Notre Dame. To top it off, I played the speech from the beginning of the film *Patton.* When the players burst from the locker room, we were ready to take on Fordham and the Third Reich. Or so I thought. We lost by 17 points.

Delivering a pregame speech is easy when you play a big game; coming up with a killer speech 28 or 30 times a year is another story. Sometimes it's a Tuesday in February and the players — and maybe even you — have your mind on something else. That's why, as a coach, you can't rely on the adrenaline rush of a mind-blowing pep talk to carry your team to victory. If you try to keep your players on an even keel, you'll find yourselves in better shape.

Halftime Talks: Know Your Players' Personalities

Why do coaches yell at halftime? Why do they throw things?

- Because they're losing and, hence, frustrated.
- Because they can't throw their players, who are bigger than they are.

Halftime is emote-time. Everyone has broken a sweat — including you — and, unlike war, you have a brief reprieve before you return to battle. Follow this plan of action in the locker room at halftime:

1. **Take a short break.**

   Let your players get a drink of water or use the bathroom. You can use this time to gather your thoughts, calm down, and discuss matters with your assistants, if you have any.

2. **Be a raging bull.**

   Okay, you don't have to be a maniac — again, be who you are — but this is the time to share your feelings. If you're going to criticize, criticize your team as a group first. With individual players, you have to have a feel for how they'll react to public "humiliation." Are their psyches tough? Will they use the second half to prove you wrong? Or are they sensitive souls who, because of a few harsh words from you, will lose all confidence?

3. **Form a strategy.**

   A quick and easy way to lose your players' respect is to chastise them for trailing the opponent and then not offering any solutions to fix the problem. Now that you have their attention, it's time to make adjustments.

   Players don't have a long memory span, especially during a game, so save the most important points for the end. For example, if you want your team to switch to a zone press defense with specific assignments for everyone, give your players this information at the *end* of halftime.

Finally, save a minute before you go out on the floor for a one-on-one conversation with your team leader. That conversation can be as productive as anything. Sometimes motivating your players through the most respected player on the team is best.

Just as you can break down your preseason or schedule into time blocks, you can do the same thing for an individual game. For example, say you find your team down by 16 at halftime. Give your players realistic goals toward which to work. "We gotta get the deficit under 10 points by the 12-minute mark of the second half," you say. "Then we need to cut their lead to 6 by the 5-minute mark."

If your team rallies ahead of schedule, don't try to stop them. But normally, you want to establish smaller goals in addition to the obvious "Win the game" quest.

Postgame Situations

After games, I never hid my feelings. The kids saw my sincerity, and I liked that. This is how I coached, and this is how I played. I'm a street fighter. I used to scream at Little League games as a kid. But that's my personality. I played to win, and I coached to win.

For example, we lost to DePaul in 1988 on a last-second shot when our center, Keith Robinson, failed to block out, and DePaul scored on an offensive rebound.

Sometimes external forces are with you

On a Sunday afternoon in January 1978, Notre Dame played host to a game versus Maryland — a crucial game for both teams. During that weekend, South Bend received 48 inches of snow in a 40-hour period. All roads were closed; the only ways to get to our on-campus arena were on foot or with cross-country skis. Virtually the only fans who attended the game were students.

We went into halftime with the score tied. Just before the opening tipoff of the second half, Jack Lloyd, our public address announcer, was handed a note saying that school had been canceled the following day. Mass euphoria broke out. The students went bonkers and stayed that way the rest of the game. We won by 15.

The lesson: If all else fails, announce "No school tomorrow."

When we entered the locker room, I threw everyone out — team managers, media, and the rest. Then I got hold of a tape of the game's final play and replayed it to the team six times. I ripped into Robinson for being so careless at such a crucial moment of the game.

As I mentioned previously, you have to know your players. Was Keith someone who could handle that type of verbal abuse? You bet. He didn't get beat for too many offensive rebounds the rest of the year.

Don't equate a player's size with his toughness. Keith Robinson was 6'11", but that didn't mean he could handle criticism any better than a 5'11" guard.

Here are some situations that warrant particular postgame speeches:

- **After an easy win:** You can't learn many things from an easy win, except perhaps misguided pride. Don't dwell on it too long. Congratulate your players on their effort, and while you have their attention, mention the chronic mistakes, such as turnovers, that they must address before the next game.
- **After a close win:** Celebrate a little, especially if your team was the underdog. Let your players know that they did a good job. Then, to guard against a false sense of security, emphasize that this game could easily have been a loss, and discuss the errors that you saw.
- **After a close loss:** As much as you may agonize over what happened in the final moments of a game, such as your center failing to block out an opponent for a rebound, you can't affix blame for a loss solely on that. It may be that your underdog team played way over their heads and gave a superior opponent a good scare. You want to acknowledge their efforts and tell them that they're capable of that high level of play each time they take the court.
- **After you are blown out:** Nothing is worse than a team that has lost its confidence. You need to be a cheerleader after a blowout, especially against a powerhouse opponent, building up your team's self-esteem. You may want to discuss with them why they think that they lost and what they need to do to improve. Communicate with your players. Otherwise, a blowout loss like this may haunt you for a long time.

Keeping Things in Perspective

Not only is there life after basketball; there is life before and during it, too. The best way to impart to your players the value of being well rounded is to be that way yourself.

While I coached at Notre Dame, we graduated all 56 players who remained at the school for four years. Obviously, the school and the types of student-athletes we took at Notre Dame were the most important aspects of that statistic, but you have to remember some things when keeping the academic side of life in proper perspective. I'd like to think that our 100 percent graduation rate had something to do with the example we set for our players. As focused as you can get as a coach, you have to keep the big picture in mind.

Some of the following ideas are easier for a college coach to adopt than other coaches. But a coach can be a teacher — and not just of hoops — at any level.

Encourage your kids to read

At the beginning of each season, Phil Jackson, the coach of the Chicago Bulls, gives each of his players a different book to read. He attempts to find a book that he thinks will carry special meaning for that particular player. Jackson does not *require* his players to read the book (although he hopes they will), but it's his small way of saying that something is going on outside the gym that his players ought to know about.

Post the front page, not the sports page, of a major paper in the locker room

One day, I asked a player what was happening in the world. He replied, "Congress is meeting in Washington this week." He was under the impression that Congress went to Washington one week, Seattle another, and Indianapolis the next, like a touring NBA team.

After that, I began posting the front page — not the sports page — of the *Chicago Tribune* in our locker room each day. Many times, I opened our team meetings by asking, "So what's going on in the world?" The players had to have read the headlines, at least.

Make road trips educational

If you have a three-hour bus trip coming up, encourage your players to crack open the books — especially on the outbound leg of the journey, when the mood is more subdued. After a game, most players have a hard time thinking about anything but the game. The rest of them probably just want to take a nap.

When we went to New York, for example, I always squeezed in a trip to Wall Street. Willie Fry, one of our former football players who worked for Merrill Lynch, gave the players a tour, and the players really listened to him. (At 6'5", 245 pounds, who wouldn't listen to him?) He took them right onto the floor of the stock exchange.

Almost every town you visit can teach you *something*. Try to make time for education. A lot of coaches are consumed in pregame preparation, but sometimes taking a side trip is the best thing for your players.

Cut class and you don't play

Education is more important than hoops. If you cut class when you played for me, you were in effect cutting the next game, because I wouldn't play you. One player was captain of the team his senior year when he cut class. I told him to tell the team before the game that he wouldn't be playing that night and why. He had to stand up in front of his peers and tell them that he'd let them down. Looking back, I'm sure he'd say that it would have been easier to attend the class than to do that.

Schedule individual meetings

Have individual meetings with each player in the spring and fall. Discuss their basketball objectives as well as their game-of-life objectives.

Communicate with the parents

When you talk with a player's parents, you gain a better understanding of that player and what motivates her. Also, parents can play the heavy for you. Often, one call to a parent about a player missing class is all it takes to set that player straight.

Remember Digger's discipline rule

I gave my kids three strikes before they were out. For example, I coached a player who never minded the team rules. On a road trip, he missed the bus to the airport; that was strike three. When we returned to South Bend, his father and I met. I told the player to keep his scholarship, but that he was finished that year — missing the bus was his third strike. Even if your team *really* needs the skills of the player who breaks the rules, you have to be consistent in your approach.

Chapter 18

Coaching Kids

In This Chapter

- Teaching kids of any age
- Dribbling, passing, and shooting fundamentals
- Playing defense
- Setting up a first-day practice

Look closely and you'll notice that nobody has to play right field in basketball and that everyone has a chance to touch the ball — even to score. In basketball, unlike baseball or football, there are no "cool" positions (quarterback), just as there are no crummy positions (substitute right fielder; *ouch!*).

What does this mean to someone coaching kids in basketball? It means that everyone should be involved in every drill, for every minute of practice. Basketball practice is not babysitting. Your center will dribble the ball less often than your point guard, but he'll still dribble occasionally. Teach your center how. Your point guard probably won't lead your team in rebounds, but you still need to teach him the proper way to do it. Get everyone involved: When I coached at Notre Dame (older kids, I know), I used to have my players practice cutting down the net to celebrate a victory. And *every* player took a snip out of that net.

If you want to coach kids in basketball, repeat after me: *Make it fun.* Leave the winning to Bulls coach Phil Jackson; your job is to be a teacher. Following are some common-sense tips to remember before you enter into the nuts and bolts of the job of coaching:

- **Everybody plays.** The development of the worst player on your team is more important than a win. I really believe that. If that child wants to be a basketball player — and if she's out there because she wants to be and not because her dad was the last player cut from the Stonybrook junior varsity team — you owe her a chance. Deliver unto each player *confidence,* not rejection.

- **Teach without teaching.** Your average kid attends school all day long. So when he arrives at basketball practice, go easy on the reminders that this is a classroom of a different sort. Some verbal instruction is necessary, but drills are excellent educators as well and are known to cure restlessness. Basketball is not boring. Don't you be, either.
- **Be a role model.** If you lose your cool on the court, how do you expect your kids to maintain theirs? Remember, nobody's getting fired for a loss here.
- **Remember that nobody's perfect — especially not that kid who just blew the lay-up.** Have a little patience. You watch ESPN or *The NBA on TNT,* and you're bound to be spoiled by the level of play you witness. Kids make mistakes, both mental and physical.

- **Keep it simple.** In a high school girls' game I once saw, one team had a one-point lead and the ball with less than a minute remaining. As the guard dribbled the ball upcourt, an assistant coach barked, "Sit on the ball!" That's basketball parlance for "Don't shoot the ball, because we want to run out the clock." This compliant hoopster, though, took him at his word: She literally sat on the ball. Whistle. Traveling violation. The other team was awarded the ball and made a last-second shot to win. You live, you learn.

It's Never Too Early

Boys and girls become attracted to basketball at a very early age — long before they become attracted to each other. Kids love to play with balls. They begin by rolling them and then bouncing them; then they learn to throw the ball at a target (a parent dozing on the couch, for example). A watershed day for any youngster is the first day she throws the ball at the basket, underhanded, and hits the rim. Soon after, the child finally makes a basket, and a lifelong love affair begins.

In the last 25 years or so, kids have been able to bond with basketballs at a much earlier age, because toy manufacturers have been creating basketballs and baskets that cater to kids. In 1970, Nerf introduced its line of sponge basketballs, footballs, and so on, which were an instant success. Parents love them because Nerf balls are too soft to break anything (had the Brady Bunch played with Nerf balls, Peter's errant football pass surely would never have broken Marcia's nose); kids love them because

- They can play indoors.
- The equipment is kid-sized and enables them to develop a feel for the game.

The Nerf ball: Foam in your home

One day in 1970, Reynolds Guyer and members of his staff at the toy company Winsor Concepts were playing around, as toy executives are wont to do, with a pile of gray foam rubber rocks. Guyer and his colleagues were developing a caveman-themed game, and the rocks were part of the apparatus. But then human nature came into play.

Before long, kids were throwing the foam rubber rocks — renamed Nerf balls — at miniature plastic hoops inside their caves all across America. In its first year of production, at a price of 99 cents per, the slightly larger than a softball (not to mention softer than a softball) Nerf sold 4 million units.

More than 100 million Nerf toys have been sold (42 different Nerf products are available today), mostly to children who want to emulate their idols: Chris Mullin of the Indiana Pacers, for example.

Growing up in Queens in the early 1970s, Mullin was fascinated by the gravity-defying feats of Julius Erving. "Dr. J," who played first in the ABA and later in the NBA, possessed large hands that easily palmed the ball when he soared to the basket. For a kid like Mullin, who was not a leaper, whose hands were too small, and who was confined indoors during the winter, the Nerf ball was a godsend.

Somewhere, right now, there's a kid who is probably doing his best foam-enhanced imitations of Mullin.

By the time kids are old enough to play organized basketball (usually when they're 8 to 10 years old), most of them have a deep-rooted knowledge of the fundamentals of the game — even if they don't yet realize it.

Kid-Sized Hoops

One of the most kid-friendly innovations is the 7-foot basket. You'll find 7-foot baskets at many grade schools across the country, and whoever thought of them is a genius.

The 7-foot basket can do more to curtail your child's poor shooting habits than a television ban on all Los Angeles Clipper games. Kids are little people. They do not have the strength, until they're at least 8 or 9, to shoot a basketball at a 10-foot basket with the proper technique. They'd have to be Bam Bam to toss the ball that high *and* finesse it at the same time. Hence they're likely to develop bad habits.

Besides, shooting a basketball well, like hitting a baseball or flirting, involves making eye contact, in this case with the front of the rim. Your wee hoopster shouldn't need a telescope.

Instead, teach her to shoot at a shorter basket. Not only will she enjoy it more — nobody likes to spend all afternoon chasing after misses — but she'll also develop a shot that she'll still be using when she's 15.

Here's a short list of other equipment that caters to kids:

- **Miniature basketballs:** A 5-year-old doesn't need an NBA regulation-sized ball (9 inches in diameter), but a tennis ball doesn't do him any good, either. Women's basketballs are slightly smaller than men's and are ideal for children to use. Sporting goods stores also sell smaller children's balls.
- **Kid clothes:** Forget what Spike Lee says. It's *not* the shoes; it's the kid in them who matters. If your child has the most expensive basketball shoes on the playground, he'd better have the best game. Otherwise, he's in for a lot of razzing from his peers. Your child doesn't need that kind of pressure. Besides, it's better that his friends admire his skills than his laundry.

Dribbling: Not from Your Mouth!

As a parent, you should put a basketball in your child's hands as early as possible. When a child drops a basketball, she notices that two things happen:

- Nobody scolds her.
- The ball bounces back up to meet her.

Maybe these reasons explain why dribbling is the first basketball skill, and maybe one of the first real coordination skills, that most kids acquire. Kids can never develop their dribbling skills too early. (Kids don't need much to dribble — just a ball and a hard surface.) Dribbling gives kids confidence to tackle other coordination-related skills (like tying their shoes), and for parents, measuring their progress is easy.

Use your fingertips, not your palms

How do you show a kid how to dribble? There's a little more to it than bouncing the ball. Dribble with your fingertips, not your palms, because your fingers exert more control. (See Figure 18-1.) Your palms should barely, if at all, come in contact with the basketball. In fact, a good test to see whether a child is learning to dribble correctly is to check his hands after he has been dribbling on the driveway or at the park. His fingertips should be dirty, and his palms should be clean.

Figure 18-1: Dribble with your fingertips, not your palms.

Keep the ball near you

Next, a child must learn to keep the ball near him. If you check out the great point guards, you'll see that the basketball looks like a yo-yo. Commentators say that the guard "has the ball on a string." The ball shouldn't wander. Keeping the ball from wandering becomes harder when you're moving, especially when you're moving fast. If the child is running and keeps losing control of the ball, have him slow down and dribble it. Once he gets used to a slower speed, he can shift into the next gear.

Don't watch the ball as you dribble

Once a kid is able to bounce the ball under control — using one hand only — she can work on a number of things. First, she needs to learn that she dribbles with her hands and not her eyes. Compare it to typing, for example. (Gee, how did I arrive at that analogy?) When you first learn, you have a tendency to peek at the keys to reassure yourself that you're tapping the correct letters. In order to improve as a typist, though, you must train yourself not to look at the keys. Give your hands a little credit. They know what they're supposed to do.

The same holds for dribbling. Kids, out of insecurity, want to guide the bounced ball back into their hand with their eyes. This need is only natural. But acting on it is a great way for the opponent to steal the ball. Instead, teach kids to look straight ahead when they dribble. In a game situation, they need their eyes to see which teammates are open, where the defenders are, and even whether there's an open path to the basket.

This drill, which I call the Vision Drill, is great for teaching kids not to watch the ball:

1. **Have the child dribble the ball in a stationary position.**
2. **Stand 5 to 10 feet away and hold up anywhere from one to five fingers. The child must tell you how many fingers you have raised.**

   Do this a few times, all the while having him continue to dribble. Move around him in a semicircle as you raise fingers. He must still face in the same direction but, of course, is allowed to rotate his neck or use peripheral vision.
3. **As the child becomes more adept, raise your hand higher over your head so that he has to lift his eyes even farther from the ground to see how many fingers you're holding up.**
4. **After the child masters these steps, have him attempt to dribble the ball five consecutive times with his eyes closed.**

Learn to dribble with both hands

To become a proficient dribbler, or *ball-handler,* a child should be able to dribble with either hand. Most kids get comfortable using one hand and never develop the other one. These kids are much easier to guard. If they are right-handed, for example, you overplay them to their right side. Next time you attend a kids' game, watch for this. A smart defender overplays the dribbler, and the dribbler keeps heading farther right until he's in Pat Buchanan's lap.

That dribbler simply needs to switch hands and change directions or — better yet — pass the ball. Instantly, he's twice as hard to guard.

This drill, called the Either-Hand Drill, is simple, really, and it can help kids develop their weak hand:

1. **Have the child dribble 25 times with her right hand and then 25 with her left in a stationary position.**

   (You can even combine this drill with the Vision Drill.)
2. **Have her dribble the length of the court with her right hand and do the return drill with her left.**

"Pistol" Pete Maravich

While "Pistol" Pete Maravich is duly known as the greatest scorer in college basketball history (see the scoring section in Chapter 3), he was equally renowned for his dazzling ball-handling abilities.

Pete's story began in Clemson, South Carolina. (Pete's dad, Press, was the head basketball coach at Clemson University between 1956 and 1962.) In this sedate Southern town, young Pete was known to the locals for being inseparable from his basketball. He dribbled the ball wherever he went. Even down to the grocery store to get Mom a bottle of milk, Pete dribbled the ball all the way, behind his back and between his legs, too. If the sidewalk was crowded, the pedestrians became defenders whom he had to weave his way through.

Saturday afternoons found 10-year-old Pete dribbling downtown to Clemson's lone movie theater. (It's still the only one in town.) He'd pay his 50 cents, dribble his way through the lobby and then be sure to find an aisle seat. After all dribbling during a movie is tough if there are seats on either side of you.

3. **Repeat each portion of the drill three times.**

The fact that a budding basketball player favors dribbling with one hand more than the other is almost inevitable. But it doesn't have to be that way. Advise your child to dribble with his weak hand when he is shooting baskets alone (Most kids won't allow themselves to look foolish in front of their pals.) Better yet, try this: Challenge your child to do everything left-handed (if he is right-handed) or right-handed (if he is left-handed) for a day: brushing teeth, opening doors, and so on. Make it a game.

Teaching Passing

The quickest kid on your team cannot outrun the ball. Passes are the most effective manner in which to attack a defense. How do you get this point across? On the first day of practice, stand on the baseline with your players. Tell them that anyone who can run to midcourt before you throw the ball to mid-court will start for the entire season. Up the ante. Give them a three-step head start before you throw the ball. Demonstrate. This should get the point across.

If you coach a kids' team, I recommend that you shower more praise on a great *assist* (a pass that leads directly to a basket) than on any shot. A player who can find the open man is invaluable; he gives his teammates easier shots and "demoralizes" the defense. You'll never see a bad team that passes well.

The three basic passes

Every novice should develop and incorporate three passes into his game:

- **Two-hand chest pass:** Hold the ball with both hands at chest level. Take a step toward the intended receiver and push your hands away from your chest. The *palms* of your hands should be facing each other and your thumbs should be pointing upward at the moment of release.

  The two-hand chest pass is effective because the ball is thrown with force, but by using two hands rather than one, accuracy is not surrendered.

- **Two-hand bounce pass:** Bounce passes are executed differently than chest passes: Although you hold the ball just as you do when making a chest pass, your thumbs should face inward when you release the ball. Bounce it hard. The ball should hit the floor about three-fourths of the way toward your target. (See Figure 18-2.)

  The bounce pass is very effective for two reasons. First, this pass is difficult to intercept because a defender must reach down to the floor to do so. Second, this pass is softer to receive, which allows your teammate a head start on his course of action. The bounce pass is a great, and horribly underemployed, offensive weapon.

- **Two-hand overhead pass:** Throwing with two hands over the head gives your pass more firmness and distance. *Two* hands control the ball. Teach this pass early. The finesse pass will come later in their game, after they get bigger and stronger. (See Figure 18-3.)

Figure 18-2: The two-hand bounce pass.

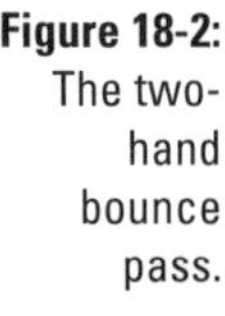

Figure 18-3: The two-hand overhead pass: Control the ball and step toward the target.

Always catch with two hands because of the control factor — just like the two-hand pass gives you more control. The one-hand catch is for Michael Jordan and David Robinson. Even with a smaller ball, a kid's hands are too small.

Of all the passes your players may eventually master, here's the best: the pass that their teammate catches. You don't get style points in hoops, just baskets.

Passing drills

A wall is a good stand-in for a parent or coach, and it helps kids develop strength because they have to get the ball to snap back at them. Have them practice the three basic passes against a wall. Have your players do 25 repetitions of each pass and practice catching the ball with *soft hands,* which means that the incoming pass should touch the receiver's first before she she cradles it in her palms.

If you're in a real practice, here are two drills for your team to execute:

- **Line Drill:** Break up your players into two lines. (See Figure 18-4.) Players at the front of each line stand facing each other, about 15 feet apart. (Put one line at center court, the other at the free throw line.) Have Player 1 pass the ball to Player 2. Player 1 moves to the end of Player 2's line. Player 2 passes the ball to Player 3 and then moves to the end of Players 1 and 3's line. When Player 1 and Player 2 return to the front of their respective lines, do a new pass.
- **Star Drill:** Break up players into five lines and put them in a star formation on the midcourt line. (See Figure 18-5.) Player 1 passes the ball to Player 2 and then moves to the end of Player 2's line. Player 2 passes the ball to Player 3 and moves to end of his line and so on. This is a fantastic drill for when your team first takes the court before a game. It gets everyone moving and involved. Most coaches seem to think that all of pregame should be devoted to shooting. Why? Emphasize the pass to your players, even in pregame drills.

No-dribble scrimmage

At the beginning of the season, when your players are begging you to let them scrimmage, say, "Okay, but neither team is allowed to dribble." Your players will hate this at first, but — kids being natural game players — they'll adjust.

By denying them the right to dribble — most kids' first instinct — you teach them the intellectual aspect of passing. Your players learn to look for the open teammate. More important, perhaps, they learn how to get open. When

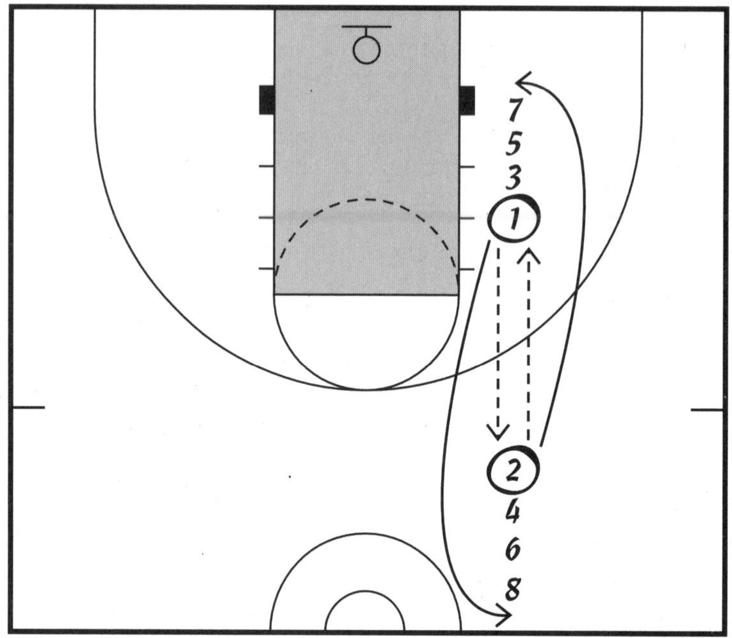

Figure 18-4: The Line Drill.

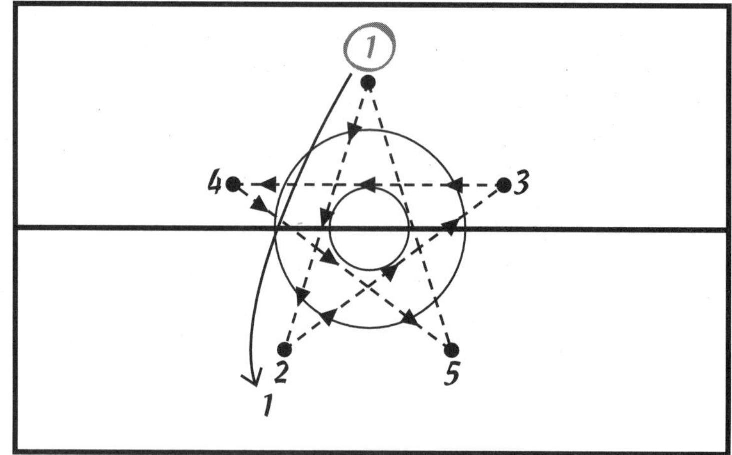

Figure 18-5: The Star Drill.

one kid dribbles the ball all day long, his four teammates tend to stand around. Eventually, your kids will recognize the fluid beauty of five players working in unison via passing.

At any point in the season when your players tend to lapse into overdribbling, reintroduce them to the no-dribble scrimmage. Watch how quickly they revert to passing.

Teaching Shooting

During a practice, you must use shooting drills efficiently. Make no mistake: Passing, ball-handling, and rebounding are important skills, but the game is determined by who makes the most baskets. Shooting is the *most important* basketball skill. (See Chapter 5 for more information.)

Lay-ups: You have to start somewhere

The first shot that any player should learn is the lay-up. A lay-up is the easiest shot to make besides a dunk, and what child can dunk the ball? (Yours can? Call me; I'd like to represent him!)

A *lay-up* is a shot taken when you are 2 feet away from the hoop. A lay-up is best taken from either the right or left of the basket and should always be shot off the backboard (so that the ball hits the backboard before going in the basket).

Lay-ups are almost always taken after *dribble penetration;* that is, the shooter is moving toward the basket with the ball. So a child must know the choreography of a lay-up. Take a lay-up from the right side, which is always easier for right-handers. (If you shoot the ball with the left hand from the right side, the rim becomes an obstacle.)

First, do a stationary lay-up to get your footwork down:

1. **Lift your right knee as you lift your right arm to release the ball.**

   The left foot remains on the ground. The left hand holds the ball in place and helps to guide it, but all the push emanates from the right hand.

2. **Push the ball toward a spot inside the square that is painted on the backboard.**

   To be more specific, the ball should hit a spot high within the square, a little closer to your side of the square. Don't put any spin on the ball; just lay it off the square softly. Unlike other shots, you do not shoot a lay-up exclusively with your fingers.

Then take a few steps back from the basket. Try dribbling the ball once and then stepping toward the basket for your lay-up. This time, because you are moving, you do not want to keep your left leg anchored to the floor. The right knee is still raised first, but you push off the floor with your left leg. In other words, you jump off your left foot for a right-handed lay-up. (See Figure 18-6.)

Reverse all the choreography for a left-handed lay-up. Lefties raise their left knee first and jump off their right foot.

Figure 18-6: Teaching a child to shoot a lay-up.

You can never begin too early to teach kids to shoot weakside lay-ups. In other words, a right-handed girl should be able to shoot a left-handed lay-up from the left side. A weakside lay-up can be frustrating at first, but all you need, as with most matters of physical coordination, is lots of repetition.

Jumpshots: The next step

You don't go straight from the lay-up to the three-pointer — though many hoops urchins seem to think so. You'll never have any trouble getting kids to practice shooting, but see that they do so wisely. Have them shoot within their range. Here are signs that a young shooter is attempting shots from beyond his range:

- His torso twists when he shoots the ball.
- He lifts the ball over one shoulder so that both hands are to one side of his head as he shoots.
- He emits an Olympic shot-putter's grunt upon releasing the ball.

Don't encourage this. Kids under 10 years of age should take shots from within 18 feet of the basket. Anything much farther than that is purely luck.

I explain the intricacies of shooting in Chapter 5, but these steps give the basics of a jumpshot:

1. **Stand with your feet parallel to one another.**
2. **Extend your shooting hand directly in front of you and then bend it 90 degrees upward at the elbow (so that your fingertips point toward the ceiling).**
3. **Cup your shooting hand so that the ball fits in it; use the other hand to hold the ball in position.**
4. **Bend your knees and then push up and release the ball.**

Shooting drills

Different players are likely to shoot from different areas of the court during the course of a game. Guards are likely to shoot many lay-ups on the fast break, as well as long-range jumpshots. Centers and forwards more often shoot closer to the basket, as well as from the baseline. Centers and forwards are also more likely to receive the ball with their back to the basket — guards rarely do — so they must be able to pivot and shoot.

Lay-up Drill

Have players stand in two lines. Each line begins midway between the free throw line and the sideline, one on each side of the court (see Figure 18-7).

1. **Player 1 on the right side dribbles the ball toward the hoop and shoots a lay-up.**
2. **Player 2 rebounds and bounce passes to Player 3, who also shoots a lay-up.**

Players go to opposite lines after shooting or rebounding. After a few repetitions, switch sides so that players shoot weakside lay-ups.

Digger Twist: Most fast-break lay-ups are taken on the heels of a bounce pass. This drill works well if Player 2 has the ball first and bounce passes upcourt to Player 1, who then shoots. Player 2 rebounds and returns the ball to his line. You can use two balls in this drill to keep things moving swiftly.

Perimeter Shooting Drill

Place players in line at five likely perimeter shooting spots on the floor. I suggest the two corners, the two wings, and just above the free throw line. (See Chapter 3 for an illustration of these spots.) Use five balls. Have the player at the right corner shoot, followed by the player at the right wing, and so on. Each player must rebound his shot, pass it back to the line from which he shot, and then move on to the next line (for example, right corner moves to right wing).

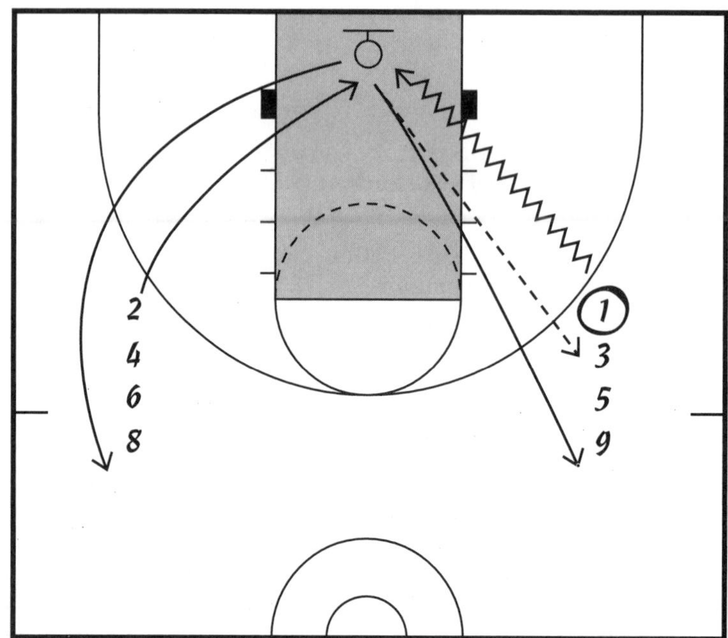

Figure 18-7: The Lay-up Drill.

Good shooting requires concentration and confidence. Setting team goals during shooting drills, therefore, is a good idea. For example, if you have 14 players on your team, tell them that if they make 14 lay-ups in a row during the lay-up drill, they will not have to run at the end of practice. Make the shots, even those taken in drills, mean something. Every shot in a game is important, after all.

Teaching Defense

As far as kids are concerned, playing defense is like eating vegetables: You have to do it, but nobody is enthusiastic about it. As a coach, however, you must be enthusiastic. Make defense a priority, or your kids never will. And remember: You need talent to score, but all you need is *desire* to keep a team from scoring, as Chapter 7 explains.

The first thing a kid should learn about defense is the *defensive stance*: knees slightly bent, hands out in front of you, palms up. Your body is balanced so that you're prepared to move in any direction: laterally, forward, or backward. When moving laterally, you shuffle your feet as quickly as possible. This is important: Your heels never touch when you're shuffling your feet (otherwise, you don't stay low to the ground), and you *never, ever* cross your feet. See Chapter 7 for basic defense drills.

Guarding the player with the ball

Here are the fundamentals for guarding a player with the ball:

- **Stay between the ball and the basket.** It sounds obvious, but I have to say it. This strategy is the fundamental tenet of any type of defense, whether you are defending Buckingham Palace or your basket: Stay between the enemy and his goal.
- **Keep your eyes on your opponent's stomach.** In some games, such as poker, eye contact is a good thing. Not in basketball. You don't figure out where the player with the ball wants to go by gazing into his eyes. But he must go where his stomach goes, so watch that.
- **Keep your hands out or up.** A bird seems much larger with its wings extended. So too does a defender become a greater nuisance with her hands out or up. If you keep your hands at your sides, you give your opponent larger passing lanes. You also invite her to shoot the ball.
- **Grow taller closer to the basket.** If you pick up a guard in the backcourt, you want to be low to the ground in your defensive stance. Why? Because you must be ready to change direction and even sprint. Your opponent is not going to shoot from the backcourt, so you don't need to be tall in order to block his shot. Conversely, the closer your opponent gets to the basket, the more likely he is to shoot and the less likely he is to dribble past you. Stand taller; be ready to pressure his shot.
- **Your goal: Make him pick up the dribble.** Once your opponent stops his dribble, he is a canoe without a paddle. Pressure him; create havoc.

Guarding a player without the ball

You must stay between the man and the ball, which requires split vision. Your body should face the player you're guarding, but your head should be on a swivel (let's hear it for vertebrae!). Keep one eye on the ball and the other on your man. Your objective is to deny the pass to your opponent. Keep your arm that is closer to the ball outstretched, ready to bat away an attempted pass.

Don't stand directly in front of your opponent. Remember, the goal is to prevent her from scoring, so cheat in toward the basket. For example, if she is on the right wing, your right (outside) foot should be even with her left (inside) foot. If she beats you up top, she only gets the ball. If she beats you underneath, she probably scores. Slipping behind your defender unnoticed and receiving a pass for an easy lay-up is what's known in hoops as a *back-door play,* and it's hard for a defense to look more foolish.

Bad habits to avoid

Fun and education are the primary goals when coaching kids. The latter will help kids to become the best basketball players they can be so that when the winning becomes important to them — and it will — they'll be well equipped to compete. Here are a few bad habits to remind them to avoid.

Avoid these habits on offense:

- Looking at the ball as you dribble it
- Shooting a lay-up without using the backboard square
- Favoring your strong side when dribbling
- Telegraphing your passes; that is, looking at the intended receiver of your pass for too long before you attempt to pass it
- Picking up your dribble before you know what you want to do next

Avoid these habits on defense:

- Watching a player's face instead of his gut
- Taking your eyes off the player you're guarding just because she does not have the ball
- Misjudging your speed (If the player you're guarding is quicker than you, don't play him so tight. He's not going to score from midcourt, anyway.)
- Watching the ball after it is shot instead of blocking out your opponent (When the shot goes up, screening off your opponent from the rebound is your sole objective.)

A word about zones

I don't believe in kids playing zone defense — teaching kids how to play zone detracts from their learning good fundamental defense. When I coached, teaching someone how to become a solid defensive player usually took two years, and this was for talented athletes, many of whom had come from exceptional high school programs. Stick with man-to-man.

Setting Up Your First Day of Practice

You never have a second chance to make a first impression. Watch Gene Hackman's portrayal of Coach Norman Dale in the film *Hoosiers.* In his first day on the job at Hickory High, a few of the team's best players challenge Coach Dale's authority. He stands up to them. They quit. The players who remain, Dale knows, respect him.

Your average 8-year-old is not that defiant. Still, all kids test your authority, even if they don't do so consciously. You earn their respect by being knowledgeable, organized, and fair. That's really all it takes.

Susan O'Malley, the 35-year-old president of the Washington Wizards, operates on this credo: *Plan your work — work your plan.* Before you switch on the lights to the gym, you should have the entire practice planned out and written down. Then adhere to your script, making allowances for unforeseen snags.

Following is a typical script for a one-hour practice. My tips:

- At the first practice and perhaps even the first few, stop and teach every drill first. Be patient and go slowly early. When a player does a drill incorrectly, show her how to do it properly. Most kids are eager to please; they just need guidance.
- The practice here is filled with fundamentals designed to enable you to assess the discrepancies in talent and experience of your players. As the season progresses, you can delve into more-advanced concepts, such as screens and full-court presses.

Five minutes of stretching

Kids are pretty limber folks. Jumping jacks get the heart rate going. Then take a smattering of the following (you can alternate at different practices): windmills, arm circles, toe touches, hurdler's stretches, groin stretches, and back stretches.

Twenty minutes of offense

Using the drills from this and other chapters in this book, break down this section of practice into five minutes of each of the following: dribbling, passing, lay-ups, and shooting.

Twenty minutes of defense

Begin with five minutes of full-court one-on-one drills. The first time through, perform this drill at half speed, with the players dribbling the ball and crossing over their dribble every few steps. The goal here is to train the defenders to shuffle their feet laterally while changing direction. They should not be attempting to make the steal. At the end of the court, no shot should be taken. The players switch positions and return downcourt. The second time through, you may run the drill at full speed, with the offensive player trying to beat the defender.

The second five minutes of defense can be devoted to one-on-one play from the foul line or wing. Let the players play, but stop play to make your points when you spot an error or a good play. Don't stop the action too often, however.

Devote the third five minutes to denying-the-pass drills. Set up an offensive player on a wing and another above the top of the key, with the latter in possession of the ball. Have a defender guard the wing man, who attempts to get open either by going back door or going up top. For the defender, this is like bullriding: He cannot deny the pass forever, but he must try to outdo the player before him.

Spend the final five minutes on blocking out for rebounds. Again, match an offender versus a defender. Let the offensive player shoot the ball; the defender must block him out.

Ten minutes of scrimmage

For the first day, I suggest the no-dribble scrimmage discussed earlier in this chapter. Establish early that you run the show. Don't be dour about it; sell it to the kids enthusiastically. This also shows the kids that scrimmage has a purpose and that it isn't just free play. After five minutes of no-dribble, switch to a regular scrimmage. Scrimmaging is a good way to find the real players, and it also keeps the troops from revolting.

Five minutes of conditioning

A basketball game is not an endurance run; it is a series of quick bursts. Condition your players likewise with sprints that emphasize change of direction. The "suicide drill" is among the most popular and sadistic drills: Players line up at the baseline and sprint to the near free throw line (extended across the width of the court), then run back to the baseline, then to halfcourt and back, then to the far free throw line and back, and finally to the far baseline and back. Three to five of these on the first day is a good start.

Coaching Kids' Leagues

Everybody should play, especially in 10-and-under leagues. For example, if you have 12 kids on your team, why not sub four players every three minutes? After all, what are the goals of youth leagues? First of all, fun. To be a part of a team and to play on it may be the most important thing in a kid's life at the moment. Second, you want the kids to develop their skills, which they don't do by sitting on the bench. Sure, everybody likes to win, but nobody likes to feel rejected.

When kids are that young, you have an obligation to be a positive force in their lives. Let them know that they belong. Let them have the opportunity to grow. *Let them play.*

Chapter 19

Getting into Basketball Shape

In This Chapter

- Getting yourself in shape to play
- Protecting your feet, ankles, and eyes
- Setting up a strength training and conditioning program
- Developing a stretching regimen
- Keeping your body hydrated and nourished

Strength, speed, agility, quickness, and explosiveness are assets that distinguish great basketball players from the ordinary ones, from pickup games to the pros. To build up those assets, you need to be in *basketball shape* — physically healthy, in good aerobic condition, well-muscled and strong, and, of course, injury-free. Basketball is predominantly a game of very short, intense bursts of energy, with only short rests in between (foul shots, time-outs, halftime, and so on). This chapter shows you how to get your body ready to handle those bursts — and how to keep it there.

You can get yourself in basketball shape through strength training and many other means that are as diverse as the members of your team or the players you compete against at your local gym. But the bottom line is that you want to stay healthy for the course of a season. With only 12 to 14 players on a team, time missed on the court due to injuries is pivotal. Injuries can make or break a team's season — or, in the case of a pickup player, her season of exercise.

Get a Physical Before You Get Physical

If you're serious about basketball — *serious* meaning that you want to play *real* games and not just shooting games like H-O-R-S-E or Around the World (see Chapter 11) — I recommend that you see a doctor for a physical.

Basketball is an affair of the heart, literally; it involves a lot of different kinds of running. Thus you need to know the state of affairs of your heart. Should every person over age 21 have an EKG (electrocardiogram) before lacing up their high-tops? No. But a visit to your physician before your season starts, whatever your level, is never a bad idea.

The heart is the most important area of the body to have checked before you play basketball. The nature of the game — endurance running, stop-start running, and jumping — puts stress on the heart. And basketball players, at least those who want to remain in the game, are never far from the action; only a referee's whistle allows them a chance to rest. So remember to stop by your doctor's office before you head for the court.

Why Get Fit?

Being in basketball shape, or being fit, brings you many advantages. This section describes the most important ones.

To prevent injuries

According to 1996 NCAA statistics, 6.5 percent of those who participated in basketball sustained injuries, while 7.5 percent of those who participated in football sustained injuries. That's right — only a 1 percent difference between a sport where players are *penalized* for contact and another where they're *rewarded* for it. Most people think of football as, at best, a collision sport and, at worst, a violent one. But as far as team trainers are concerned, injuries, though often different in nature, are just as likely to occur in basketball.

Because basketball is essentially a contact sport without pads, and injury is always a factor, you have to do what you can to make your body as strong as possible for the course of the season so that it's more resistant to injury.

Every sport sees certain chronic, nagging little injuries more often than others. This section talks about those Basketball Maladies and gives some horse-sense wisdom on preventing them. Obviously, I'm not a doctor, although a few of my former players have gone into the medical field. For anything more than a nettlesome injury, you should consult a physician.

- **Blisters:** The balls of the feet and the backs of the feet are the areas most prone to blisters. To help prevent blisters, I suggest wearing two pairs of socks, although the number of pairs you should wear depends on the thickness of the socks. A general rule: The right number and brand of socks are those that don't give you blisters. Just experiment until you find a combination that works for you.

How to tape an ankle

- The tape must be snug, but not loose enough so that it feels like an extra sock.
- The support should be strongest to protect against inward ankle sprains. Ninety-seven percent of all ankle sprains take place because the ankle turns inward (toward the other ankle).
- Tape the ankle when it is at a 90-degree angle to the floor.
- Use a prewrap between the ankle and the tape. With a prewrap, you can take a pair of scissors after the game and just cut off the tape and prewrap all at once — no painful pulling of ankle hairs.

- **Eye injuries:** A few years ago, a rash of eye injuries occurred, leading to the use of goggles by a lot of players. Horace Grant of the Orlando Magic was repeatedly poked in the eye when he was with the Chicago Bulls, so he has worn the goggles ever since. The result: no more eye problems.

  Several companies produce prescription goggles. If you wear glasses and play in a "physical" league, you may want to look into purchasing a pair. Goggles are the perfect answer for players who just can't get used to contact lenses.

- **Sprained ankles:** The feet (not the knees) are the most common area for basketball injuries. In hoops, the ankle is the Achilles heel. Finding the right kind of sneaker, as explained in Chapter 2, is important in preventing foot injuries.

  Players at the pro and college levels tape their ankles before every practice to keep them stable. In high school, taping depends on the school, the coach, and even the player. But taping is a terrific safety precaution, diminishing the chances of the ankle getting sprained, twisted, or broken. Consult a trainer for specifics on how to tape your ankles; doing it wrong can cause restricted blood flow and other problems.

- **Stress fractures:** Stress fractures are an increasing problem in basketball. The key to stress fractures is really the surface on which you play. If you play a lot of games on concrete, you're going to get shin splints and stress fractures, which result from constant pounding on a hard surface.

  Resting between games is a way to prevent stress fractures. That answer isn't very practical for college and high school players, but for pickup hoops players, rest can control the problem.

Put your players in a tub of ice water?

A form of prevention of torn muscles and stress fractures used by some coaches involves placing players in a tub of ice water (up to the chest) after practice or a game. (Ooh, that's cold!)

What does a tub of ice provide, besides chills? It reduces the amount of lactic acid that accumulates after a strenuous workout and that causes soreness, pulled muscles, and strains.

Coach Rick Barnes first used this chilly prevention technique at Providence in 1990–91 on star point guard Eric Murdock. Murdock was playing nearly 40 minutes a game, and Barnes felt that he could not afford to lose him. Barnes stopped short of bringing Murdock hot chicken soup every night, but he did prescribe the tub-of-ice treatment during hectic portions of the Friars' schedule.

Murdock's Mr. Freeze imitation worked. He played the entire season without injury and averaged 38 minutes per game. So if you're playing in a marathon basketball tournament some weekend, calm yourself down by jumping into a tub of ice water. Maybe there's something to those Gatorade showers that you see football coaches receive after a win. . . .

- **Torn ACLs:** You hear more and more about the torn anterior cruciate ligament (ACL) and the accompanying reconstructive surgery necessary to fix the problem. The ACL, which connects the femur (thigh bone) to the tibia (shin bone) in the center of the knee, most frequently is torn when the knee is twisted beyond its normal range of motion.

  How do you know if you have torn your ACL?

  - You hear a popping sound when the injury occurs.
  - You see swelling on top of your kneecap either immediately or within hours.
  - You feel that the knee cannot support your weight.
  - You cannot fully extend your leg.

  The rehabilitation period for a torn ACL or other knee injury can take a year, and it definitely takes dedication on the part of the athlete. If you injure your knee, see a doctor immediately!

To increase athletic performance

Getting fit also improves your speed, agility, and quickness, which enables you to jump higher, run faster, and be more explosive in the game of basketball. Being able to play for longer periods at maximum efficiency is the goal.

Have you hugged your Tiger today?

Toward the end of the 1996–97 season, Clemson's basketball team struggled, losing four of their last five games before the NCAA tournament. The day before Selection Sunday, the squad had a team meeting that helped to unite them as they headed into The Big Dance (also known as the NCAA tournament).

It occurred to strength coach Todd Wright that the team could enhance their togetherness during prepractice jogging exercises. He divided the squad in two, placed the two groups at either baseline, and then had them jog the length of the court. When the players met at midcourt, he told them to stop and hug each other. The players laughed, naturally, feeling awkward. But they did it.

Strange? Probably. But the hug sessions were a tangible reaffirmation of team unity. Did they help? Wright can't prove that they did, but Clemson did advance to the Sweet 16 for just the third time in school history.

Remember these points as you work to get in shape and improve your performance:

- **Strive for peak performance at tournament time.** You want to be strongest during tournament time (or at the climax of your season, whenever that happens to be), not during the off-season.
- **Make safe and efficient use of your workout time.** Strength training for basketball means being intense and efficient in your approach. Work in short bursts, reserving as much time as possible for playing and practicing the game itself.

To increase mental toughness, discipline, and team cohesiveness

Just when you think that you're out of gas, push yourself and your team further. College and pro strength coaches achieve this by making players responsible for each other in practice; if one doesn't work at a drill intensely enough, everyone does it again. It's important to stress that you are one team and depend on each other in everything you do, especially conditioning. Discipline is involved in all strength training sessions, whether you're alone or with a team.

Conditioning: Run on Your Own Before You Run with a Team

At a lot of the better pickup basketball courts, teams in need of a player or two will approach a stranger and ask, "You wanna run?" Translation: "Do you want to play with us?"

I like that phrase because it's accurate. Basketball players must be able to run, both in short bursts of speed and for long periods of time. So you need to do two types of running to get yourself physically ready to play the game:

- **Long-distance running:** No one is asking you to run the Boston Marathon. You should, however, be able to run a mile in eight or nine minutes if you are playing in an after-work or weekend league.

  You can't very well run long distances on grass or a basketball court, but the more of your running you can do on a surface that has some give to it (as opposed to cement or pavement), the better your chances of avoiding shin splints. You also reduce the stress on your knees by doing your running on softer surfaces.

  If you live in a cold weather area (like South Bend, Indiana), get a stair climber or stationary bike for your basement and use that in place of long-distance running. There's no sense getting sick from running outside, because that will keep you from playing altogether.

- **Short sprints:** You need to do long-distance running to build up endurance for the cardiovascular aspect of the game, but you also need to be in sprinting shape. I love to watch joggers pronounce that they must be in good basketball shape because they jog, say, 4 miles a day. A basketball court is just 94 feet long; you don't have time to establish a pace. Rather, basketball is a game of 25-yard sprints.

  As I say throughout this book, the best preparation for playing the game is to simulate the game. I don't know a single basketball coach who runs his team a mile after practice, but just about every coach runs his team through some sort of sprint workout, or a basketball drill that incorporates sprinting.

Always check with a physician before beginning an exercise routine.

Team Conditioning

If you coach a team that plays an official season — say, a high school or college team — you should take a different approach to conditioning in the preseason than during the season.

In the preseason, runs are of the same length, but give your team more recovery time. For example, in the first two weeks of practice, if it takes 10 seconds to run the length of the court and back, take 30 seconds to recover — a 3:1 ratio. In weeks three and four, shoot for a 2:1 ratio — so if it takes 10 seconds to run the length of the court and back, take 20 seconds to recover. Two weeks prior to the beginning of the season, move down to a 1:1 ratio. If the drill takes 10 seconds, take 10 seconds to recover.

Make your drills shorter but more intense as you get closer to the beginning of your season — that goes for conditioning and weight training as well. Start with drills that are in the 30-second range in the first two weeks of practice, and work your way down to shorter drills that are 10 to 15 seconds in length during game weeks.

Strength Training for Basketball

Strength training is a growing field in athletics. Twenty years ago, players were just starting to get into weight training as a serious aspect of preparing for a season. In the mid-1970s, Notre Dame was known for our strong frontcourt players (Bill Laimbeer, Dave Batton, Bruce Flowers) and our corresponding ability to rebound. We lifted weights, but our program was the equivalent of what most high schools do today.

More and more college and pro teams are hiring strength coaches to work with them on weight training. One of the top young strength coaches in the country is Clemson's Todd Wright, who helped me prepare this chapter. During the NCAA tournament last year, I stated on ESPN that Clemson could not stay with Minnesota in the West Regional semifinal because Minnesota was just too strong. Clemson and Todd Wright proved me wrong. Clemson was just as physically imposing as Minnesota. Clemson made the comeback in the second half, partly due to their conditioning, to send the game into two overtimes before Minnesota came away with the victory. Clemson's ability to stay with Minnesota physically, at all five positions and down to the tenth player on the team, was very impressive, and it shows how important this aspect of preparation is in today's game.

You don't need fancy equipment to establish a strength training program; you can exercise your entire body with a set of dumbbells. Why are dumbbells so great? You have to balance and control the weight, which helps in injury prevention. The strength you obtain by lifting dumbbells keeps your joints from getting into unnatural positions — even when someone inadvertently attempts to put them in unnatural positions.

One side of a person's body is always stronger than the other; you know, the right arm is always stronger than the left arm (or vice versa for lefties). That's called *bilateral deficit.* With dumbbells, you don't have the option to indulge that deficit. Your weaker arm has to get strong, because the dumbbell in your weaker hand weighs the same as the one in your stronger hand.

Other equipment that's useful in a strength training program:

- **A utility bench:** A utility bench tilts from zero (flat) to 90 degrees (upright); it may have five or six settings between zero and 90 for inclines. In other words, you can lay the bench flat or at an angle. You can do a million different exercises with a utility bench and a set of dumbbells, including shoulder presses, chest presses, upright rows, curls, French presses, pullovers, squats, lunges, and side laterals.
- **A barbell:** A barbell is a long, straight bar to whose ends you add weight. Exercises you can do with a barbell include bench presses, bendover rows, and standing shoulder presses.

Technique is very important when it comes to strength training. It's not the amount of weight you move, but how you move it that makes you stronger. Ego can play a big role in the strength room, but remember: Basketball players are not in the weight room to become weight lifters; they're there to become *better basketball players.*

Keys to efficient results from strength training:

- Raise and lower the weight through the muscles using full range of motion.
- Raise the weight in an explosive and powerful manner, allowing the muscles to raise the weight. Eliminate all arching, bouncing, throwing, and jerking movements while raising the weight.
- Lower the weight in a controlled manner, allowing the muscle to lower the weight. Do not drop the weight. The muscle that is used to lower the weight is the same muscle that raises the weight. As a guideline, allow three to four seconds to lower the weight.
- Be technique-conscious. Do not jeopardize safety for an inflated ego by lifting too much weight.
- Breathe while performing each exercise. Breathe out during the raising of the weight and breathe in during the lowering of the weight.
- Always have a spotter present when dealing with bench press equipment.

Strengthening the back

Next time you see highlights of Michael Jordan on one of his mystical drives to the basket, think about the back muscles he's using to make those contortions in mid-air. His signature jumpshot (he has a signature aspect of every phase of the game) is his fallaway jumper. He must have the strongest back muscles in the world, because it looks like he's jumping back at a 45-degree angle on that jumpshot.

Upper back

Basketball Benefits: You need a strong upper back so that you can make those fallaway jumpers like Michael Jordan does. On a more practical note, strong lats help keep your shoulders healthy. The *lats* (latissimus dorsi) are the largest muscle north of your waistline, so they help you in any pulling motion, like pulling a rebound away from your opponent when you're fighting for the ball.

Exercise:

- **One-Arm Dumbbell Row:** Stand to the right of the utility bench. Hold the dumbbell in your right hand with your palm facing in. Pull in your abdominals and bend forward from your hips so that your back is naturally arched and roughly parallel with the floor, and your knees are bent slightly. Place your left hand on top of the bench for support and let your right arm hang down.

  Pull your right arm up until your elbow is pointing to the ceiling and your hand brushes against your waist. Lower the weight slowly back down.

Lower back

Basketball Benefits: Think of the typical defensive stance that I discuss in Chapter 7. You are set with feet spread and in a semi-squat position, and you want to move laterally. The key to sustaining that position for a long period of time and with an ability to move quickly is the lower back. It has to be strong and durable to play defense, especially on the perimeter. Think of the muscles you use when you go after a loose ball, lean over to pick it up, and streak for the hoop. It is all in the lower back.

Exercises:

- **Dumbbell Straight Leg Deadlift:** Standing, slightly bend the knees. Lower the dumbbells by bending over. Keep the dumbbells close to your shins. With your head up and looking straight ahead, bend over until your back is parallel to the floor; don't look down. Keep your hips moving backward. (See Figure 19-1.)
- **Back Extension:** Using a flat surface, lie on your stomach facing the surface with your arms straight out in front of you. Keep your palms down and your legs straight behind you. Pull in your abs as if you were trying to create a small space between your stomach and the floor.

  Lift your right arm and left leg a couple of inches off the floor or bench and stretch out as much as you can. Hold this position for five seconds, lower your arm and leg, and then repeat the same move with your left arm and right leg.

Figure 19-1: The Dumbbell Straight Leg Deadlift.

Strengthening the chest

Basketball Benefits: The chest muscles are used predominantly in pushing. (Pushing? Oh, you mean gaining position underneath the basket!) How much pushing you get away with depends on the referee, but it would be nice to come to the gym with a chest the size of Karl Malone's — he doesn't seem to get pushed around much underneath the basket. Strengthening the chest is especially beneficial for players who battle for rebounds and make moves in that important 16-foot area called the *paint*. The closer you can maneuver, the easier the shot.

You need to remember some things when doing chest exercises. Here's some advice on the subject from Liz Neporent and Suzanne Schlosberg's *Weight Training For Dummies* (also published by IDG Books Worldwide, Inc.):

- Warm up with a light weight.
- Perform 8 to 15 repetitions per set, in general.
- Don't lock your elbows.
- Don't arch your back.
- Don't flatten your back unnaturally.
- Don't lift your shoulder blades off the bench or back rest.
- Don't stretch too far.

Exercises:

- **Bench Press:** Lie on the bench with your feet flat on the floor. Grip the barbell so that your arms are evenly spaced a few inches wider than shoulder width apart. Your upper arms should be slightly above parallel to the floor. Tuck your chin toward your chest and pull your abdominals tight.

  Lower the bar until your elbows are slightly below your shoulders. The bar should touch your chest. Press the bar back up. (See Figure 19-2.)

Figure 19-2: The Bench Press.

- **Dumbbell Chest Press:** Lie on the utility bench with a dumbbell in each hand and your feet flat on the floor. Push the dumbbells up so that your arms are directly over your shoulders and your palms face forward. Pull in your abdominals, but don't jam your back into the bench.

  Lower the dumbbells down and a little to the side until your elbows are slightly below your shoulders. Push the weights back up, taking care not to lock your elbows or allow your shoulder blades to rise off the bench.

- **Incline Chest Fly:** Incline the bench a few inches. Holding a dumbbell in each hand, lie on the bench with your feet flat on the floor. Press the weights directly above your chest, palms facing each other. Tuck your chin to your chest to align your neck with the rest of your spine and maintain your natural posture.

  Spreading your arms apart so that your elbows travel down and to the sides, lower the weights until your elbows are just below your shoulders. Maintaining a constant bend in your elbows, lift the dumbbells back up.

Strengthening the shoulders

Basketball Benefits: It's obvious that strong legs and abdominals are the key to jumping ability, but having powerful shoulders is also beneficial when underneath the basket. I used to have a player named Adrian Dantley who probably scored more old-fashioned three-point plays (see Chapter 3) than all my other players combined. He could get an offensive rebound and seemingly carry two players on his shoulders on his way back up to score the basket. It meant a foul and an extra point for the Irish.

Exercises:

- **Dumbbell Shrug:** Stand tall and hold a dumbbell in each hand, arms straight down, palms in front of your thighs and facing in. Pull in your abdominals, tuck your chin toward your chest, and keep your knees relaxed.

  Shrug your shoulders straight up toward your ears the same way you do if you don't know the answer to a question. Then slowly lower your shoulders to the starting position. (See Figure 19-3.)

Figure 19-3: The Dumbbell Shrug.

- **Dumbbell Front Raise:** Hold a dumbbell in each hand and stand tall with your feet as wide as your hips. Let your arms hang down at your sides, elbows relaxed and palms facing back. Pull in your abdominals and relax your knees.

Raise your right arm in front of you to shoulder height and then lower it back down. Then do the same with your left arm. Continue to alternate until you complete the set of eight to ten repetitions per arm.

Strengthening the arms

Basketball Benefits: Your arms and wrists are the parts of your body that come in the most contact with the ball. Your arms release your jumpshot, thus the strength of your arms affects your ability to score. Take a ball, go under a basket, and shoot the ball toward the hoop. It doesn't take much effort to make that shot. But as you get farther and farther from the basket, shooting takes more strength to get the ball to the rim. The more effort you must make, the less accurate you'll be. So if you want to be more accurate on that 20-foot shot (especially under duress), you need to have strong arms.

Strong arms (including wrists) can also help when it comes to long passes. If you can send the ball flying 75 feet at a time with accuracy to a waiting teammate (check John Stockton in the 1997 NBA Finals versus Chicago, for example), you're going to help your team.

Exercises:

- **Barbell Biceps Curl:** Hold the barbell with an underhand grip and your hands about shoulder width apart. Stand with your feet as wide as your hips and let your arms hang down so that the bar is in front of your thighs. Stand tall with your abdominals pulled in and knees relaxed.

  Bend your arms to curl the bar almost up to your shoulders, and then slowly lower the bar almost to the starting position. (See Figure 19-4.)

Figure 19-4: The Barbell Biceps Curl.

- **Dumbbell Biceps Curls:** Hold a dumbbell in each hand and stand with your feet as wide as your hips. Let your arms hang down at your sides with your palms facing in. Pull in your abdominals, stand tall, and keep your knees relaxed.

  Curl your right arm close to your shoulder, twisting your palm as you go so that it faces the front of your shoulder at the top of the movement. Slowly lower the dumbbell back down and then repeat with your left arm. (See Figure 19-5.)

- **French Press:** Standing, hold the dumbbell with both hands straight above your head. Pull in your abdominals, but make sure that your back is relaxed and arched naturally. Keeping your elbows slightly bent, lower the weight behind your head until the bottom of the dumbbell is directly behind your head. Pull the dumbbell back overhead, keeping the same slight bend in your elbows throughout the motion. (See Figure 19-6.)

- **Wrist Curl:** Hold a weight in your right hand with an underhand grip. Sit on the edge of the utility bench with your knees as wide as your hips. Lean forward and place your entire forearm on top of your thigh so that your hand hangs over the edge of your knee and your palm is up. Clasp your left palm over your wrist to hold it steady. Curl your wrist so that the dumbbell moves toward your forearm, and then lower the weight back down.

  Turn your palm down and again secure your wrist in place with your other hand. Bend your wrist up and raise the dumbbell to thigh height; then lower the weight back down.

Figure 19-5: The Dumbbell Biceps Curl.

Figure 19-6: The French Press.

Strengthening the abdominals

Basketball Benefits: Strong abdominals allow you to reach. Last time I checked, there was a lot of reaching in basketball. Reaching for the ball or to defend an opponent is a high percentage of the game. So when you're playing defense and you reach to knock the ball away from your opponent or reach a little farther for a rebound, you're using your abdominals.

Exercises: These exercises can be done anywhere. You don't need a dumbbell or barbell.

- **Abdominal Crunch:** Lie on your back with your knees bent and feet flat on the floor hip width apart. Place your hands behind your head so that your thumbs are behind your ears. Don't lace your fingers together. Hold your elbows out to the sides but rounded slightly. Tilt your chin slightly so that there are a few inches of space between your chin and your chest.

  Bend up and forward so that your head, neck, and shoulder blades lift off the floor. Hold for a moment at the top of the movement and then lower slowly back down.

- **Reverse Crunch:** Lie on your back with your legs up, knees slightly bent, and ankles crossed. Rest your arms on the floor beside you or behind your head. Rest your head on the floor, relax your shoulders, and pull in your abdominals.

  Lift your butt 1 or 2 inches off the floor so that your legs lift up and a few inches backward. Hold the position for a moment and then lower slowly.

- **Slide:** Remove your shoes. Lie on your back with knees bent, feet hip width apart, toes up, and heels digging into the floor. Rest your arms at your sides. Pull in your abdominals and gently push — but don't force — your back into the floor so that, to some extent, you flatten out the natural curve of the small of your back.

  Slowly slide your heels forward as you gradually straighten your legs; don't allow your abs to push upward or your back to pop off the floor. Continue straightening your legs until you can't keep your abs tight or your back on the floor, or until your legs are fully extended.

Strengthening the legs

Basketball Benefits: Finally, what many feel is the most important area for basketball: the legs. Leg strength is the basis for jumping and moving quickly. How does Michael Jordan jump so high and hang in the air (hence the nickname Air Jordan)? It has to be his incredible leg strength.

Exercises: These exercises work the glutes, quads, hamstrings, and calves.

- **Squat:** Hold a dumbbell in each hand or place your hands on your hips or on the tops of your thighs. Stand with your feet as wide as your hips and with your weight slightly back on your heels. Let your arms hang down at your sides.

  Sit back and down, as if you're sitting into a chair. Lower as far as you can without leaning your upper body more than a few inches forward. Don't lower any farther than the point at which your thighs are parallel to the floor, and don't allow your knees to shoot out in front of your toes.

- **Lunges:** Stand with your feet as wide as your hips and your weight back a little on your heels. Place your hands on your hips, pull in your abdominals, and stand tall.

  Lift your right toe slightly and, leading with your heel, step your right foot forward one stride, as if you were trying to step over a crack in the sidewalk. As your foot touches the floor, bend both knees until your right thigh is parallel to the floor and your left thigh is perpendicular to it. Your left heel will lift off the floor. (See variation in Figure 19-7.)

Figure 19-7: The One-Legged Squat is similar to the Lunge except the back toe rests on a block and the arms extend outward.

S-t-r-e-t-c-h-i-n-g Your Body

Before every workout, practice, or game, you must stretch. The following routine stretches the major areas of your body that you use most when playing basketball. The areas of concentration are the legs, lower back, groin, and feet.

Use this routine for stretching to get yourself ready to play, whether it be a pickup game in your driveway, a high school game, or a college game:

IT Band Stretch: Put your left foot forward so that the heel of your left foot is parallel to your right toe. Bend over and touch your left instep with both hands. Push your hip backwards. This stretches the back and hip area. Repeat the process with the right ankle. (See Figure 19-8.)

Figure 19-8: The IT Band Stretch.

The lower back is especially susceptible to injury in basketball because of the constant pounding and pressure applied in the jumping process. Remember Larry Bird lying on the court writhing in pain toward the end of his career? This due to constant lower back problems.

Remember, too, from *Weight Training For Dummies:* Always do back exercises slowly and carefully. If you race through your lower back stretching exercises, you may cause the very back problems you are trying to prevent.

Standing Groin Stretch: Spread your feet so that you feel a slight pull in your groin and hamstring muscles. Then bend over and put both palms on the floor. (See Figure 19-9.) This exercise stretches the groin and hamstring areas, which is important in any sport that requires sprinting.

Figure 19-9: The Standing Groin Stretch.

Side Lunge Stretch: Take same position as in the Standing Groin Stretch, but this time lean to the left and then to the right, alternately bending each knee. Keep your palms on the floor. (See Figure 19-10.) This stretches the *adductors,* or the inside leg muscles, which you use extensively when jumping for a rebound.

Figure 19-10: The Side Lunge Stretch.

Front Lunge Stretch: Kneel down with your right leg extended behind you. Put both your forearms on top of your left upper leg. Keep your chest perpendicular to the floor. (See Figure 19-11.) This exercise stretches the hip flexor of the back leg and the hamstring of the front leg.

Figure 19-11: The Front Lunge Stretch.

Seated Butterfly Groin Stretch: Sit on the floor and put your heels together in front of you. Grab your right ankle with your right hand and your left ankle with your left hand. Put light pressure on the knees and push forward slowly. (See Figure 19-12.) This also stretches the groin area. How many times have you seen a player miss a game because of a pulled groin muscle? This exercise decreases the chances of that injury occurring.

Figure 19-12: The Seated Butterfly Groin Stretch.

Hurdler Hamstring Stretch: Still seated, spread your legs at a 90-degree angle. With your left hand, reach out and touch your right toe. (See Figure 19-13.) Hold that position for 20 seconds. Then repeat the process with the right hand touching your left toe for 20 seconds. This exercise also helps the lower back in addition to the hamstring.

Figure 19-13: The Hurdler Hamstring Stretch.

Lower Back Crossover Stretch: Still seated, stretch your legs together straight out in front of you. Then take your right leg and put it over your left thigh, with you right knee pointing to the sky. Then rotate your upper body to the right so that your head is facing parallel to your left foot. (See Figure 19-14.) Hold this position for 20 seconds; then repeat the process by crossing your left leg over your right thigh. This exercise also strengthens the hamstrings and the upper back.

Figure 19-14: The Lower Back Crossover Stretch.

Lying Low Back Crossover Stretch: Lie down on your back. Take your right leg and move it to a position parallel to your left hip. Keeping your shoulders flat, grab your right foot with your left hand and hold for 20 seconds. (See Figure 19-15.) This also stretches the hip and hamstring. Repeat the process with the other leg.

Figure 19-15: The Lying Low Back Crossover Stretch.

Seated Quad Stretch: Sit on floor and put your right heel under your buttocks. Lean back and place your hands on the floor. Make sure that you don't lie all the way back — you want to protect your left knee. (See Figure 19-16.) Repeat the process for your left leg.

Lying Hamstring Low Back Stretch: Lie on your back and lift your left knee. Pull your knee toward your chest with your left hand below your knee. Hold this position for 20 seconds and then repeat with the right leg.

Standing Quad Stretch: Back on your feet, grab your right foot with your right hand and pull it behind your right leg. Your foot should be against your right buttocks. (See Figure 19-17.) This helps stretch the upper leg muscles on the front of your leg. Repeat with the left foot.

Saigon Squat: Standing with your feet a foot apart, squat down and put your hands together (in prayer position). Keep your heels flat and your chest up. (See Figure 19-18.) This is another exercise for the lower back and hamstring, in addition to the quad muscles.

Crossover IT Band Stretch: Lie on your back and lift your right leg in the air. Lock your hands under your right knee and bring your left foot over your right knee. (See Figure 19-19.) Repeat with the other leg.

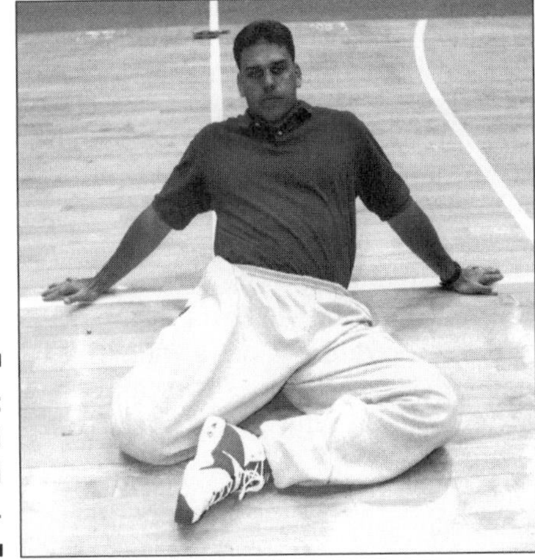

Figure 19-16: The Seated Quad Stretch.

Figure 19-17: The Standing Quad Stretch.

Figure 19-18: The Saigon Squat.

Figure 19-19: The Crossover IT Band Stretch.

Trunk Twists: Standing with your feet spread 2 feet apart, or to a natural distance. Twist your upper body left and right, holding your arms at chest level. (See Figure 19-20.) This adds to the flexibility of your upper body and hip flexors.

Tricep, Lat, and Posterior Deltoid Stretch: Standing, hold your left elbow and pull behind your head. (Your left elbow should be by your left ear, as shown in Figure 19-21.) Hold this position for about 20 seconds. Repeat the process with your right elbow.

Standing Calf Stretch: Stagger your feet (one in front of the other). Keep your heels flat on the floor and lean forward against a wall. (See Figure 19-22.) Repeat with the other foot forward. This stretches the calf muscle, obviously a key in running for long periods of time and in sprinting.

Figure 19-20: Trunk Twists.

Figure 19-21: The Tricep, Lat, and Posterior Deltoid Stretch.

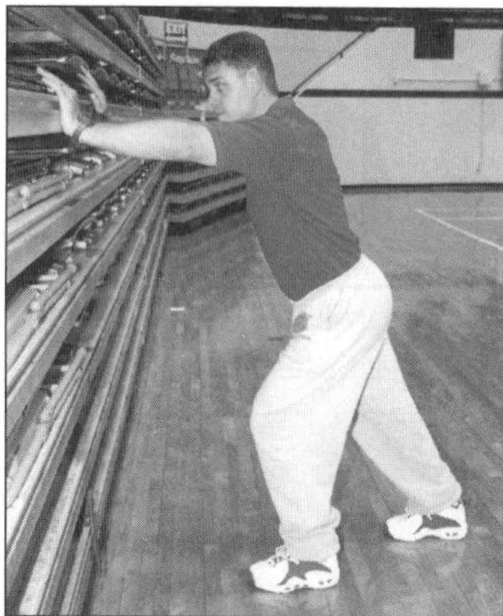

Figure 19-22: The Standing Calf Stretch.

Basics to remember in basketball strength training and conditioning

- Set your conditioning plan for an entire year. Keep your long-range goals in mind, with the aim to be at your strongest at the end of the year.
- Believe in the strength program. If you're the coach of a high school, AAU, or Little League team, you have to be sold on your strength program.
- Stick with the program. Just because you hit a little slump, don't give up.

  Late football coach Vince Lombardi said it best: "Fatigue makes cowards of us all." That's the bottom line. So the better conditioned you are, the tougher you are.
- Be organized in your approach to strength training.
- You don't need a million dollars worth of equipment to be effective. Get some dumbbells, barbells, and a utility bench.
- Keep the conditioning drills basketball-oriented, with short bursts of energy. Plan your workouts in 4-minute spans, just like the games.
- Do conditioning drills that involve a lot of change of direction, because that's basketball — learning to change direction quickly.
- If you have the funds, get a stationary bike for conditioning. A stationary bike cuts down on shin splints and stress fractures. Your body can take only so much pounding on the floor, and a bike solves that. It also allows weekend warriors to run inside when the weather is not so nice.

After you do these stretching exercises, do some walking and jogging. I like this active approach from the get-go because it elevates the core temperature of the body — you are at a lower risk for injury at the start of the workout, practice, or game because the body temperature is already elevated. During this routine, you stretch the body, but you also work on movements that help you with speed, agility, and quickness, so you accomplish three different things in the period that is usually the least productive.

Because you stretch for 10 to 15 minutes a day before a workout or practice, you're looking at almost an hour, an hour and 10 minutes a week (if you play every day) of working on movements that are directly related to speed, agility, quickness, and how you change direction on the floor, all of which are basic to basketball.

Nutrition: Fuel for the Body

Without a proper diet, you can never play up to your potential. Eating is a sensual pleasure — don't get me wrong. But it's also an essential part of the conditioning equation for every athlete.

To keep your body in basketball shape, strive to eat a balanced diet that's low in fat and that includes lots of fruits, vegetables, and whole grains. Multivitamin and mineral supplements are helpful, too. Though you consume most vitamins and minerals via your normal diet, supplements provide insurance against an intake shortage. See *Nutrition For Dummies* for the complete scoop on nutrition for athletes.

Selling athletes on nutrition

Todd Wright at Clemson uses the before-and-after method to inspire players to eat better. When an athlete arrives at the university, Wright takes a Polaroid photo of him right away. Every ten months, he takes another photo. The photos serve two purposes: Players can see for themselves the progress they have made, and Wright can use photos of athletes who have made dramatic improvements in their physique to motivate younger players.

Educate athletes about nutrition as soon as they come through the door. Most kids know the phone number of their pizza delivery guy as well as their own boyfriend's or girlfriend's. You must convince them that eating poorly is as detrimental to conditioning as skipping workouts.

Eating your pregame meal

Eat your pregame meal three to four hours prior to tip-off; your digestive system needs time to process what you have eaten. (Your mother probably told you that you had to wait only 30 minutes after eating before you went swimming, but your mom never had to guard Allen Iverson up and down the court for 40 minutes.)

For your pregame meal, you want to eat foods that provide maximum energy with minimal digestive difficulty. Certain foods are easier to digest than others. Good pregame meal items are high-carbohydrate sources, such as breads, pastas, cereals, and vegetables. Your body can convert those calories to energy instantly, relatively speaking, within those three to four hours.

Fatty foods remain in your digestive tract longer and make you feel sluggish. A double-bacon cheeseburger washed down with a milkshake is *not* the way to go.

Preventing dehydration

Not only do you need to eat the right foods to get in basketball shape, but you also need to drink lots of liquids. Basketball is a sweaty game, and the more you sweat, the more fluids your body loses. A common result?

Mangia, Walter!

When New York Knicks forward Walter McCarty played at the University of Kentucky, the 6'9" center's toughest foe was his high rate of metabolism. Kentucky's strength coach, Shaun Brown, once said that the Wildcats' 220-pound center needed to consume 8,000 calories a day just to maintain his weight.

Knowing that McCarty's chronic failure to add the adipose might reflect poorly on the job he was doing, Brown took no chances. For four years, he accompanied McCarty to almost every meal. Between meals, he loaded McCarty, who arrived in Lexington weighing just 173 pounds, with candy, sandwiches, and high-cal supplement drinks. By the time McCarty graduated, he still had no butt to speak of, but folks weren't flipping him their spare change, either. And best of all, Kentucky won a championship.

There's no **I** in team. But there is — and McCarty surely must know this — an **E**, an **A**, and a **T**.

Dehydration. Did you know that while your body is inadequately hydrated, you can lose up to 15 percent of your cognitive ability? Fatigued players are more prone to make mistakes; it's a scientific fact.

Dehydration, a severe deprivation of water in the body, causes your muscles to tighten up and eventually cramp. Basically, your muscles are short-circuiting. Your cells need water to perform their functions and rid themselves of *lactic acid,* a cellular waste material. When your muscle cells are deprived of water, the lactic acid excess initiates cramping, which is very painful but, thankfully, short-term.

Dehydration can occur in any aerobic sport (although bowling seems to be dehydration-free), but basketball is among the most widely plagued sports. In the 1997 NCAA championship game between Kentucky and Arizona, for example, Kentucky star Ron Mercer missed parts of the second half as a result of calf muscle spasms incited by dehydration. (Because of the leaping that occurs, the calf muscle is taxed more and thus is more prone to cramping.)

Do the following to help prevent dehydration:

- **Drink plenty of water.** Don't bloat yourself — you're not a camel — but drink prior to playing and during breaks in play. Gatorade and other sports drinks are also good because they replenish your cells with electrolytes and other minerals lost due to dehydration. Bring a water bottle with you to the gym or the park and fill it with water, Gatorade, or a similar product.
- **Watch your diet prior to the game.** Bananas, potatoes with meat, extra salt on your food, and oranges are good pregame menu items. These foods do not necessarily prevent dehydration, but they help lessen the effects of dehydration.

Part V

The Part of Tens

"WHAT DID I TELL YOU?! WHAT DID I TELL YOU?! YOU WANT TO BE LIKE DENNIS RODMAN?! THEN *EXPECT* TO GET YOUR NOSE RING CAUGHT IN THE NET!"

In this part . . .

Jump to this part if you need a quick breather. Here, you can join me on my reminiscent journey of games that changed the course of basketball history and the greatest NBA players of all time. Or find out the best arenas in which to watch basketball games.

In this part, I even clue you in to the types of things that coaches say on the sidelines. You don't have to read lips here — I tell it like it is.

Chapter 20

Ten Games That Changed the Course of Basketball History

So many games, so many stories. Literally thousands of basketball games occur each day, from the televised prime-time NBA Finals to a kid playing make-believe opponents on his driveway. Here are ten games that, in my opinion, have had the most resonance.

Springfield YMCA 5, Springfield Teachers 1

When: March 12, 1892

Where: Springfield YMCA (Springfield, Massachusetts)

What would a list of this nature be without including the first game? This game was played in front of 200 spectators and is considered to be the first public display of basketball.

The students won the game, but the most incredible note on the contest concerns the person who scored the only point for the teachers — none other than Amos Alonzo Stagg, the Hall of Fame college football coach of the era. According to the *Republican,* "The most conspicuous figure on the floor was Stagg, in the blue Yale uniform, who managed to have a hand in every scrimmage play. His football training hampered him, and he was perpetually making fouls by shoving the opponents."

Texas Western 72, Kentucky 65

When: 1966 NCAA championship game

Where: College Park, Maryland

Texas Western, now known as the University of Texas at El Paso (UTEP), became the first school to start five African-American players in an NCAA final. Meanwhile, Kentucky, the bastion of the old guard, started five white players, among them future NBA coach Pat Riley. Texas Western's win opened the gates for integration among American college teams, especially in the South. Just three years earlier, Babe McCarthy, the coach at Mississippi State, defied a school policy prohibiting the Bulldogs from playing integrated teams and snuck away in order to play Loyola (Illinois), which started a few black players, in a first-round tourney game. The complexion of the game never looked the same afterward.

Houston 71, UCLA 69

When: January 20, 1968

Where: Houston Astrodome (Houston, Texas)

This game foreshadowed the present-day Final Four: a domed stadium and a nationally televised, prime-time college basketball game. This was the first made-for-TV matchup that was marketed around the country (150 stations in 49 states). When these two teams met later that year in the Final Four, the rematch wasn't televised nationally.

Fortunately, the contest lived up to its billing, as Elvin Hayes scored 39 points and held Lew Alcindor (later Kareem Abdul-Jabbar) to 15 points and only 12 rebounds. Alcindor made just 4 of 18 shots from the field and was limited in his effectiveness by an eye injury that required him to wear a patch over his left eye. As if depth perception inside a dome wasn't already a problem — there were no floor seats, so it looked as if they were playing in the middle of a vast abyss. UCLA had entered that game on a 47-game winning streak.

North Carolina 54, Kansas 53 (Three Overtimes)

When: March 23, 1957

Where: Kansas City, Missouri

This is the only national championship game that ever went into triple overtime. This game is not in this chapter because it was a big upset, but rather because it was an exciting game for 55 minutes. North Carolina's Joe Quigg connected on a pair of free throws with six seconds left to score the winning points.

People remember this as a landmark game because North Carolina, who entered the game undefeated, beat Wilt Chamberlain, a dominant presence in basketball for many years. Chamberlain scored 23 points and had 14 rebounds in the game, but that contribution was not enough.

Adding to the drama was the fact that, in the national semifinal, North Carolina needed three overtimes to defeat Michigan State. Imagine winning two triple-overtime games to win the national championship on consecutive days!

Notre Dame 71, UCLA 70

When: January 19, 1974

Where: South Bend, Indiana

I'm obviously biased on this one, but when ESPN selected its ten greatest NCAA basketball games in history, this game was one of them. Beating a UCLA team that had won seven straight national championships and 88 straight games (surpassing the all-time national record by 28 games) was big enough.

As much as anything, the thrill was in the way we won. Imagine how UCLA must have felt when we called time-out with 3:22 left, trailing 70–59. Bill Walton had not lost at UCLA and never lost in high school. He had to think that this one was over.

We then scored the last 12 points to win the game — which created doubts in the UCLA dynasty. UCLA then lost two more regular-season games at Oregon and at Oregon State and then lost to North Carolina State in the national semifinals. The Notre Dame victory helped to crumble the UCLA empire and launch a new era of parity in college hoops.

Michigan State 75, Indiana State 64

When: March 26, 1979

Where: Salt Lake City, Utah

This remains the highest-rated college basketball game in television history. The attraction: Larry Bird of undefeated Indiana State against Magic Johnson of Michigan State. This matchup was the beginning of one of the great and amicable rivalries in the game.

Johnson won this matchup, scoring 24 points and grabbing 7 rebounds. Bird had 19 points and 13 rebounds, but shot just 7 of 21 from the field due to a hand injury.

This game turned the country on to college basketball. The future success of Bird and Johnson in the NBA only enhanced interest in the college game.

Soviet Union 51, United States 50

When: September 10, 1972

Where: Munich, West Germany

The United States' 63-game Olympic winning streak ended controversially when the Russians were allowed to make a final inbounds pass three times in the championship final. After the USA's Doug Collins had made two free-throws with three seconds left, the Americans led 50-49. International rules prohibited calling a time-out after a made free throw, but the Russian team's bench spilled onto the court after they in-bounded the ball. The referee called his own time-out to halt the chaos and allowed a second inbounds pass, this time with one second remaining. That inbounds pass was deflected out of bounds, and Team USA rejoiced in victory.

Or so they thought. An Olympic official — not a game official — ruled that the Soviets should have been given a chance to in-bound the ball with three seconds on the clock. On the third attempt, Aleksander Belov received a length-of-the-court pass between two United States players and made a game-winning lay-up.

That loss was the United States' first loss in Olympic play; *Sports Illustrated* called it "the greatest injustice in Olympic history." Adding insult to injury, USA coach Hank Iba had his wallet stolen (with $370 inside) during the frenzy immediately following the final buzzer. The members of the USA squad, protesting the outcome of the game, refused to accept their silver medals.

Soviet Union 82, United States 76

When: September 28, 1988

Where: Seoul, South Korea

This Soviet Union victory, an incontrovertible defeat of the USA's best collegians in the Olympic semifinal, helped to usher in the Dream Team. This long-awaited rematch between the two countries that had been involved in the highly controversial 1972 gold medal game (see the preceding section) and had not met in Olympic competition since, was a resounding slap in the face to American hoops zealots. If the 1988 U.S. Olympic team had won the gold medal, the U.S. probably would not have begun allowing NBA players in the Olympics.

The Soviet Union's Arvydas Sabonis, who would later play center for the Portland Trail Blazers, made the difference in the game. He got the best of David Robinson.

Connecticut 77, Tennessee 66

When: January 16, 1995

Where: Storrs, Connecticut

This was, excuse the expression, the debutante ballgame of women's hoops. Number-one Tennessee, 16-0, played against number-two Connecticut, 12-0. The game was televised nationally on ESPN and drew a sold-out, rowdy crowd to University of Connecticut's (UConn's) Storrs campus. The UConn Huskies went on to post a 35-0 record and beat Tennessee to win the national championship. But this regular-season game, played in the afternoon on Martin Luther King Day, ignited Huskiemania and has contributed to the increased interest in women's hoops in recent years.

New York Knicks 113, Los Angeles Lakers 99

When: May 8, 1970 (Game 7 of the 1970 NBA championships)

Where: New York, New York

Never has an NBA Game 7 been played on a bigger stage — Madison Square Garden may be basketball's most august — with more courage. Willis Reed, the New York Knicks' star center, had a thigh injury and could barely walk. Reed had missed Game 6 in Los Angeles, and Laker center Wilt Chamberlain toyed with New York's frontcourt (that is, its forwards and substitute center), scoring 45 points. Reed took a cortisone shot in the locker room and then limped out onto the floor near the end of the pregame warm-ups.

Reed made the game's first shot, a jumper from the elbow, and if a game ever ended with the score at 2-0, this was it. (He made only one other shot all night.) The Knicks rode Reed's leadership to its first world championship.

Often overlooked are the efforts of Knick guard Walt Frazier, whose 36 points and 19 assists marked one of the greatest performances ever by a guard at any level; and backup center Nate Bowman, who had to cover Chamberlain most of the evening.

This championship was the watershed moment at which New York officially made the transition from being a college hoops city to a pro hoops city. With the Big Apple decidedly in its corner, the NBA — whose headquarters are there — had fortified the most important media stronghold.

Los Angeles Lakers 123, Philadelphia 76ers 107

When: May 16, 1980 (Game 6 of the 1980 NBA championships)

Where: Philadelphia, Pennsylvania

Only a year earlier, Magic Johnson had mesmerized the college basketball realm. Then he bolted for the NBA with two years of eligibility remaining. Had he left too soon? Larry Bird, after all, would defeat him in the Rookie of the Year Award balloting.

Normally, the 6'9" Johnson moved from starting point guard to center when regular center Kareem Abdul-Jabbar had to miss some action with an injury. How did the rookie react to playing a new position on the road in the NBA Finals? Magic scored 42 points and put the title on ice. Magic's performance was comparable to Tiger Woods' win at the Masters golf tournament in 1997.

The NBA in the late 1970s had a serious image problem. The NBA style of play — as popularized by stars such as George Gervin, Bob McAdoo, and David Thompson — had evolved into one-on-one playground ball with little emphasis placed on teamwork. It was not a pretty game to watch, nor were any of the league's stars — with the exception of the Philadelphia 76ers' Julius Erving — particularly charismatic. The arrival of Bird and Magic put the NBA back on course. Suddenly, passing and teamwork were in vogue again. The game was fun to watch. If any one contest symbolizes this dramatic turnaround that may very well have saved the league, this is it.

Chapter 21

Ten NBA Greats

Whittling this list down to ten was impossible — I had to include 11 players. In 1996–97, the NBA, in honor of its 50th season, decided to pick its 50 greatest players. Even that list left off a few hallowed names, such as the Detroit Pistons' Joe Dumars and the Buffalo Braves' Bob McAdoo. This is a more elite club than the United States Senate — which, by the way, has its own in-house basketball court.

Kareem Abdul-Jabbar

Kareem Abdul-Jabbar is the league's all-time leader in points scored (38,387), ranking third in rebounds (17,440). He averaged 24.6 points per game for 18 seasons. He was the NBA MVP six times — more than any other player — and his team won the NBA championship six times. During his career, Kareem's sky hook was the single greatest offensive weapon in the game; defenders couldn't stop it.

Elgin Baylor

Elgin Baylor was the original hangtime player. Michael Jordan does some acrobatic moves, but Baylor invented that style of play. He was an 11-time All-Star and once scored 71 points in one game. When he retired, he was the number-three scorer in NBA history.

You hear a lot about the combos of Pippen and Jordan, or even Stockton and Malone. But if you ask me, I'd take Baylor and Jerry West any day.

Larry Bird

This three-time MVP led the Celtics to three NBA championships and was a ten-time All-NBA player. If you watched Larry Bird practice, you may have thought, "This guy isn't fast, and he doesn't have great jumping ability, but somehow he gets it done better than just about anyone else." Like Magic Johnson, Bird was outstanding in all phases of the game and was one of the smartest players ever to lace up sneakers. He could hit a three-pointer to beat you, or make a steal to beat you — whatever needed to be done.

Wilt Chamberlain

While Bill Russell was the greatest defensive force in NBA history, Wilt "the Stilt" Chamberlain must have been the greatest offensive force. The beauty is that Russell and Chamberlain played in the same era. Those were some battles!

Wilt's stats are mind-boggling: He scored over 4,000 points in one season, and 100 points in one game in 1962. Nobody has come within 28 points of the latter record. He averaged 50.4 points per game for the entire 1961–62 season and once had 55 rebounds in one game. Six years later, Wilt decided to show everyone that he was a great passer and led the league in assists. His durability was unmatched; he actually averaged over 48 minutes per game in 1962, and he never fouled out in 1,045 career games.

At a chiseled 7'1", Wilt was the most physically dominant force the game has ever seen. And yes, I know who Shaquille O'Neal is.

Bob Cousy

Bob Cousy was all-world, the original wizard with a basketball. The Celtics won nine NBA championships in a row from 1958 to 1966, but Boston never would have started that run of championships without Cousy. He was by far the most exciting player in the NBA in his early years; his over-the-head and behind-the-back passes set the standard for future guards. He was a 10-time All-NBA player and 13-time All-Star. Once, he won the NBA MVP award.

Julius Erving

Julius Erving is the only member of my Greatest NBA Players list whom I coached against in college . . . and defeated. In my only year at Fordham, we beat Erving and UMass — but that doesn't keep him off my team. "Dr. J" had as much influence on the game as anyone with his gravity-defying moves that graced the ABA and NBA for 16 years. After becoming one of only six players in NCAA history to average over 20 points and 20 rebounds per game for a college career, Erving became an 11-time NBA All-Star. In 1983, he led the Philadelphia 76ers to the NBA championship. Three times, he led the NBA in scoring, and he remains one of just three players in professional history to score over 30,000 points. Whereas kids growing up today have Michael Jordan to hold in high esteem, the players currently in the NBA owe much of their love of the game to Dr. J.

Magic Johnson

Earvin "Magic" Johnson was the game's greatest all-around player in the 1980s. Magic carved out an identity for his Lakers team, if not the entire city of Los Angeles, for an entire decade. LA in the '80s was Showtime — exciting, fast-paced, and glitzy — and Magic was the ringmaster. Magic had 138 career triple doubles, the most on record. He led the league in assists five times. He was the league MVP three times, was a nine-time first-team All-NBA player, and played on five NBA championship teams.

Magic was also first-team All-Charisma for 12 straight years. His smile and personality did as much to promote the game as anything. Along with Larry Bird of the Celtics, Magic returned two things to the league that had been missing for nearly a decade: a love of passing the ball, and a fierce desire to win that only Michael Jordan emulates today.

Michael Jordan

With a 32 points-per-game figure, Michael Jordan is the league's career scoring average leader; his playoff scoring average is even higher. Jordan has revolutionized the game, as Bill Russell did in his era, by playing above the rim. That is to say, he perfected the art of dunking and seemed to be immune to gravity. Ask yourself this: Before Michael came along, how many players in the NBA wore long shorts and black sneakers and shaved their heads? How many do now? Everyone, even NBA millionaires, wants to be like Mike.

Is Jordan the best player of all time? Arguing against him would be hard. I say this: He's the fiercest competitor of all time, and the one guy you want on your team when you're down by a few points with less than a minute remaining. The Bulls have played in five NBA Finals, all with Jordan; they are 5-0 in those series, which have not extended past a sixth game. And Jordan has five NBA Finals MVP awards somewhere in his overstuffed trophy case.

Nobody does it better. Or, as sportswriter John Feinstein said on television one day in June 1997, "There is no next Michael Jordan."

Oscar Robertson

Oscar Robertson's legend benefited from the statisticians who invented the *triple double* (hitting double figures in three statistical categories — for example, 14 points, 12 rebounds, and 11 assists). Because Magic Johnson was never known for his scoring as much as he was for his all-around sublime play, the public relations people at the Los Angeles Lakers (Magic's team) sought an innovative way to quantify his contributions. They arrived at the triple double — but in doing so, stumbled onto the fact that Oscar Robertson — like Magic, an oversized guard — had actually averaged a triple double over the course of a season more than 20 years earlier (1961).

"The Big O" played 14 years in the NBA and was a three-time MVP of the All-Star game. He averaged 26 points a game and dealt out almost 10,000 assists in his career, which included an NBA championship with the Milwaukee Bucs in 1972.

Bill Russell

Folks talk with amazement about Michael Jordan winning 5 NBA titles in 7 years. How about 11 titles in 13 years, including winning 8 years in a row (the final two seasons of which Russell was the player/coach)? This five-time NBA MVP revolutionized the game of basketball with his defense and rebounding; he's still the prototype center when it comes to defense. If you have a young center, show him films of Bill Russell and his ability to block shots and keep the ball in play.

Jerry West

Jerry West of the LA Lakers was Mr. Clutch; I'll never forget that three-quarter-court shot he made against the Knicks in the 1970 NBA Finals in Los Angeles. West had perfect form on his jumpshot — in fact, his form was used as the model for the NBA logo. He scored over 25,000 points and made the All-Star game every year he played. Only Michael Jordan, who has said that West is the one player from another era whom he'd relish facing, has a higher playoff scoring average.

Chapter 22

Ten Great Places to Watch a Game

You're a basketball junkie and want to take a tour of the United States and hit all the basketball hot spots. Where do you go? This chapter lists the ten most important stops.

Cameron Indoor Stadium, Duke University, Durham, North Carolina

Cameron Indoor stadium first opened on January 6, 1940; it used to be the home of the Sunday evening Perry Como radio show. The tones are less docile nowadays. Cameron is one of the great pits of college basketball because the Duke students surround the court on every side. They have their feet in the media's backs (their seats are *that* close to courtside, where the press sits), which I'm sure their fellow students on the court would say is an example of turnabout being fair play.

The student body, known as the Cameron Crazies, year in and year out have the most witty, creative, and acerbic cheers in the land. Example: When Steve Hale, a former North Carolina forward who had recovered from a collapsed lung, stepped to the line to shoot a free throw, the Crazies yelled, "In-Hale, Ex-Hale!" The cheers seem choreographed, yet you never can find a leader. They do something new on every opponent free throw, as if by sheer collective consciousness. Duke is the best school in the United States to play for in terms of home-court atmosphere.

America West Arena, Phoenix, Arizona

America West is the best of the new NBA arenas (others: the FleetCenter in Boston, the United Center in Chicago, and the Gund Arena in Cleveland, to name a few) that have been built in the last half-dozen years. Phoenix Suns players enjoy the Jacuzzi and big-screen TV in their locker room, plus a practice court and weight room adjacent to the main arena. There isn't a bad seat to be found, and there's also a terrific restaurant (the Copper Club) adjacent to the promenade.

Pauley Pavilion, UCLA, Los Angeles, California

In UCLA's heyday in the late 1960s and early '70s, Pauley Pavilion was probably the toughest place to play. The fact that Notre Dame won six times there did as much to help the school's image as a giant killer as beating those number-one teams. Plus, Pauley Pavilion is an on-campus facility in a pretty part of LA.

The Palestra, Philadelphia, Pennsylvania

The Palestra used to be the mecca of college basketball in Philadelphia. In the 1950s and '60s, everyone wanted to play here — the Big Five (Philadelphia city schools LaSalle, Penn, St. Joe's, Temple, and Villanova) was one of the hotbeds of basketball.

The Palestra has probably been the home of more college basketball games than any place in history. It holds close to 10,000, and the acoustics are something special; the atmosphere is electric. Built in 1927, the Palestra has done as much to promote the game of college basketball as any arena has. TV and gate-receipt concerns have caused most big games in the City of Brotherly Love to be moved to the larger and newly built Core States Center, but if you have a chance to catch a game at the Palestra (it still serves as Penn's home court), don't miss it.

Madison Square Garden, New York, New York

Billing itself as "The World's Most Famous Arena," Madison Square Garden always has a charged-up, big-city atmosphere. For more than 30 years, Marv Albert's voice made listening to a Knicks game on the radio as special as being at the Garden itself. If you do get tickets, bring binoculars so that you can scope out the celebs sitting courtside. Spike Lee and Woody Allen are easy to find. Extra points for locating John F. Kennedy, Jr.

Williams Arena, University of Minnesota, Minneapolis, Minnesota

The University of Minnesota's home arena is a pit, literally. The floor is raised; both benches and the media are below the court in a dugout area. But this place rocks. The Golden Gopher fans are loyal — hey, it's winter in Minneapolis-St. Paul, after all — and there's a sold-out crowd every night, no matter who's on the schedule.

I think that the raised floor is a big home-court advantage because of the Flat-Earth Complex. They may not admit to it, but you know that, in the back of their minds, all the players are wondering whether they're going to fall off the court, the way sailors used to fear sailing off the edge of the earth. Very distracting.

Rupp Arena, University of Kentucky, Lexington, Kentucky

Some of the big, new arenas have those airplane seats, and the fans get passive. (I won't name names — you know who you are.) But Rupp, the home court for the University of Kentucky, manages to seat more than 23,000 without losing its intimacy. Best of all, the Hyatt hotel is attached to it, which means that you can stroll straight from your pregame in-room tailgater to the game — no coat or parking pass needed.

Phog Allen Fieldhouse, University of Kansas, Lawrence, Kansas

"Rock-chalk, Jayhawk!" Besides an inimitable student cheer, Kansas's venerable home court boasts tradition, dating back to the inventor of the game, James Naismith, and perhaps the most dominant player in hoops history, Wilt Chamberlain. Dean Smith, the game's all-time winningest coach in Division I, also played for the Jayhawks.

I must confess that this arena holds a special place in my heart because Notre Dame beat DePaul in 1978 at Phog Allen Fieldhouse to go to the Final Four.

Gampel Pavilion, University of Connecticut, Storrs, Connecticut

Gampel Pavilion rocks for men's and women's games. A lot of schools schedule doubleheaders — but not at the University of Connecticut, where the men and women stand on their own. Basketball at UConn has taken off in the 1990s; both the men's and the women's games are a community event. Gampel is one of the cozy, new arenas, a veritable Camden Yards (the Baltimore Orioles' homey baseball stadium) of college hoops.

Delta Center, Salt Lake City, Utah

NBA arenas can be wonderful places to catch up on your reading, if you know what I mean. But not at the Delta Center, home to the NBA's loudest fans. Utah is known as Mormon country, but basketball is a religion there, too. You may have seen the evidence of the home-court advantage — the Jazz won 23 straight at one point — in the 1997 NBA Finals, when the Jazz went 10-1 and almost swept the Chicago Bulls three straight.

At the Delta Center, the fans are close to the action, especially the basket supports. Their double-digit (and sometimes triple-digit) decibel din can make those basket supports shake. Pregame intros for the Jazz players are the loudest and longest in basketball.

Chapter 23

Ten Things Said from the Sidelines

Ever wonder what coaches are saying to referees or players during a game? Suffice it to say that some of the language would make sailors blush. In this chapter, I hit you with some of the topics that coaches touch upon (and touch upon and touch upon) during the course of a game.

"Be consistent on both ends of the floor!"

The most coaches can ask from a referee is fairness; if the ref is making the same bad call at both ends, coaches can't complain too much. Of course, frustrated coaches have been known to utter such *bon mots* as "I can pay you twice as much as the opposing coach is!" to refs who evoke their ire.

"Switch!"

When playing teams that set a lot of good screens (see Chapter 6), defenses have to *switch* (a maneuver in which two players swap the players they're guarding — see Chapter 7) quite frequently. Of course, coaches usually bark "Switch!" too late for their players to adjust to what's happening.

"Box out!"

The defensive effort does not end when the opponent attempts a shot; it ends when the defense grabs the rebound. That's why coaches harp on their players to *box out,* or to keep the offensive players from getting at the ball after a missed shot. (See Chapter 8 for more information.)

"Don't pick up your dribble!"

When the player dribbling the ball stops dribbling but then doesn't pass or shoot immediately, he puts himself in a vulnerable position. Picking up your dribble allows the defense to pressure you as the player with the ball — you can no longer move — and that often leads to turnovers.

"Hand up in her face!"

Coaches frequently remind players on defense to put a hand up when the player they're guarding takes a shot.

"Come meet the pass!"

Players on the receiving end of a pass often wait passively for it instead of coming to meet it. Coaches want players to be aggressive and move toward the ball being passed to them — doing so greatly reduces the defense's chance to deflect or intercept it.

"Get back on defense!"

Players often need to be reminded to get back on defense — a smart player on the opposing team may streak to the other end of the court after an opponent's missed shot in hopes that the rebounder will throw her a long pass for an easy lay-up. Hustling back on defense after the opposing team has rebounded helps to prevent easy fast-break baskets.

"Pass the ball!"

This one is for youth league coaches. Youngsters commonly fail to spot an open teammate for two reasons: (1) They have not yet learned to dribble the ball without having to look at it, and (2) they simply love dribbling too much — they're the center of attention when they're dribbling. Young players need to learn the importance of passing the ball to the teammate who's open.

"Jump-stop and penetrate!"

Too many guards dribble wildy upcourt. When guards reach the foul line, they need to *jump-stop* — land with two feet — and either pass the ball or penetrate to the hoop. Nothing gives away a guard's inexperience like watching him careen out of control on a fast break and get called for a charge.

"Hey, Wilt, he's open!"

NBA standout Wilt Chamberlain averaged 50 points a game one season. You have to imagine that his four teammates stood around a lot that year, waiting for Wilt to pass them the ball. I don't know if Wilt's coach ever barked such a command — Wilt was an intimidating presence at nearly 7'1" and nearly 300 pounds — but the thought must have crossed his mind.

Appendix A

Glossary of Basketball Terms

airball: A shot that completely misses the basket, hitting only "air."

alley-oop: A designed play in which a player lobs the ball toward the basket and a teammate jumps up, catches the ball in midair, and usually dunks it.

alternating possession: The "we get the ball this time, you get it next time" rule in college and high school basketball only. In a held-ball situation, the lighted arrow on the scorer's table at midcourt points toward the team who gets possession of the ball.

assist: A statistic for which a player receives credit when he passes the ball to a teammate and the teammate then scores immediately. Thus the player who throws the pass "assists" in the scoring play.

backcourt: A team's *backcourt* consists of the defensive half of the court, including the opponent's basket and the in-bounds part of the backboard and the entire timeline. After the offensive team enters its frontcourt, it's a violation to return to the backcourt with the ball.

bankshot: A shot attempt that uses the backboard.

baseline (or endline): The line on each end of the court that separates in-bounds from out-of-bounds.

basket interference: Occurs when a player touches the ball when it's within an imaginary cylinder that extends from the basket ring all the way to the ceiling, or any part of the basket. An illegal act at all levels except international. See also *goaltending.*

block: Illegal personal contact by a defender that impedes an opponent's progress.

block out (or box out): Using the body to block or shield an opponent in order to gain better position to grab a rebound.

blocked shot: When a defensive player bats away or "blocks" an opponent's shot attempt.

board: Slang for "rebound." See also *rebound.*

bonus: A situation in high school and college games in which a team is awarded free throws after nonshooting fouls when the opposing team is over the foul limit.

bonus free throw: A second free throw that's awarded after a successful first free throw. In college ball, bonus free throws are awarded only after the team has committed seven fouls (any combination of personal, unsporting, and contact technical fouls) in a half. In college play, beginning with the tenth foul of a half, two free throws are awarded.

boundary lines: End lines and side lines of the court. The inside edges of these lines define the in-bounds and out-of-bounds areas.

box out: See *block out.*

breakaway: A situation in which a defensive player steals the ball and races toward his basket to score ahead of the defenders behind him. In the NBA, breakaways often produce spectacular, high-flying dunks.

brick: An especially ugly, misfired shot that clanks off the rim or backboard.

center: One of the player positions. Usually, but not always, the tallest player on the team. Scores from in close, blocks shots, and does the bulk of the team's rebounding.

charge: Illegal personal contact by an offensive player that involves pushing or moving into an opponent's torso. Charging is the single hardest call for a referee to make because the defensive player must be stationary or the call is a block.

cut: To quickly move from one spot on the floor to another in an effort to elude a defender and try to score.

defense: The team without the ball, who tries to prevent the offensive team from scoring.

double dribble: A violation in which a player dribbles with both hands simultaneously or picks up (stops) his dribble and then begins dribbling again.

dribble: To bat, push, or tap the basketball to the floor. A player holding the ball must remain stationary on her *pivot foot;* in order to move or advance with the ball, she must dribble. The dribble ends when the dribbler causes the ball to come to rest in one or both hands, the dribbler touches the ball with both hands simultaneously, or an opponent bats the ball away. Dribbling with both hands simultaneously is a violation (see *double dribble*), although you may alternate hands between dribbles.

dunk: To drive, force, or stuff the ball through the basket. One of the more exciting and athletic plays in the game.

endline: See *baseline.*

fast break: A play in which a defensive team rebounds the ball and quickly tries to advance the ball down the court ahead of its opponent — ideally, to score an easy basket.

field goal: A shot made from inside or outside the three-point arc with the clock running, worth two or three points, respectively.

flagrant foul: A personal foul that involves violent contact with an opponent. Such contact includes striking with the elbow, kicking, kneeing, and moving under a player who's in the air.

forward: One of the player positions. A team usually has two forwards. Forwards rebound, aid the center inside, and shoot the ball.

foul: See *personal foul* and *technical foul.*

foul out: To be disqualified by reaching the maximum number of fouls allowed per game: five in college and high school, or six in international play and the NBA.

foul trouble: A player who is close to fouling out (for example, a player has four fouls in a college game) is said to be in foul trouble.

free throw: An unhindered attempt to score one point by shooting a basket from behind the free throw line and within the free throw semicircle. Also known as a foul shot. The initial free throw is awarded when a player on the opposing team commits a foul.

frontcourt: The half of the court where the offensive team attempts to score. One team's frontcourt is the other's backcourt, and vice versa. A team must cross the midcourt line and enter its frontcourt within ten seconds after possession begins.

game clock: The clock that counts down the time remaining in the game. The clock runs down only while the ball is in play.

goaltending: A violation that involves touching the ball during a field goal attempt while the ball is in its downward flight and the entire ball is above the level of the hoop. The ball must have the possibility of entering the basket. Goaltending or basket interference is also called when the ball is touched within the imaginary cylinder that has the basket ring as its lower base and extends up to the ceiling. Basically, this violation prevents defensive players from leaping up to swat away shots right before they go into the basket.

guard: One of the player positions. A team usually has two guards. Guards usually are the primary ball handlers and are usually (but not always) the smallest players on the court. Also, to defend an offensive player.

hack: Slang for a foul, especially an overly aggressive one.

held ball (or jump ball): Occurs when a defender places her hands so firmly on the ball that both the offensive and defensive player can claim possession of it. A held ball results in a jump ball or alternating possession situation. Also, when a defensive player ties up a player in midair.

in-bounds pass: A method of putting the ball in play from out of bounds. The player with the ball has five seconds in which to in-bound it. The count starts when the official gives the player the ball and ends when the player releases the ball. On sideline in-bounds plays and baseline in-bounds plays after an opponent's violation, the in-bounder is subject to the laws of traveling. On in-bounds plays following a basket, the thrower may run — without bouncing the ball — along the length of the baseline.

intentional foul: A personal foul that's not a legitimate attempt to directly play the ball or a player. The fouled player shoots two free throws, and his team takes possession of the ball.

jump ball: A method of putting the ball into play by having an official toss it up between two opponents at midcourt. The jump ball begins when the ball leaves the officials hands. In pro hoops, jump balls are used to determine the outcome of all held-ball situations. At other levels, a jump ball is used only to start a game.

jumpshot: An aptly named shot where a player jumps in the air and shoots.

lane: The rectangular area, usually painted, directly in front of each basket, extending out to the free throw line. Also known as "the paint."

offense: The team in possession of the ball. Also refers to the plays a team executes while in possession of the ball.

one-and-one: A free throw situation in high school and college ball where a player shoots one free throw and is awarded another if the first is made. See also *bonus free throw.*

outlet pass: The first pass made after a defensive rebound, usually designed to trigger a fast break.

overtime: A five-minute session that is played when a game ends in a tie.

paint: See *lane.*

pass: Movement of the ball caused by a player throwing, batting, or deflecting the ball to another player.

personal foul: A violation, committed by an active player, that involves illegal contact with an opponent while the ball is live.

pick: A screen for the player with the ball. See also *screen*.

pivot foot: A player who is holding, and not dribbling, the basketball must keep one foot anchored to the ground. This foot is known as the pivot foot.

player control foul: In the men's game, a foul committed by the player who's in control of the ball. In the women's game, a foul committed by the player who is in control of the ball, or by an airborne shooter. Often called an offensive foul or a charge.

point guard: The primary ball handling guard. This player usually directs the offense. See also *guard*.

post: The general area outside the lane near the basket.

rebound: Retrieval of a missed shot, which may hit the court first.

screen: A legal action by an offensive player who, without initiating excessive contact or moving, delays or prevents an opponent from reaching the desired position.

shot: An attempt to throw the ball into the basket to score.

shot clock: A clock, separate from the game clock, that limits the amount of time the offense has to attempt a shot. For example, in men's college basketball, a team has 35 seconds to attempt a shot. If a shot is not taken in that time span, the ball is turned over to the opposing team. When the ball hits the basket or changes possession, the shot clock is reset.

sideline: The lengthwise boundary of the court.

strongside: The side of the court (right or left) where the ball is currently located. Not to be confused with frontcourt.

substitute: To send in one player for another during a stoppage of play.

technical foul: A foul by any active or nonactive player, coach, or team attendant that does not necessarily involve contact with an opponent. Technical fouls include unsportsmanlike conduct, acts of deceit, vulgarity, profanity, calling excessive time-outs, and hanging on the rim.

three-pointer: A shot made from outside the three-point arc, worth three points.

timeline: The line that splits the court in half; called the timeline because the offensive team must get the ball past half-court in ten seconds or less — failure to do so results in a violation (except in women's college basketball). Also known as the midcourt line or half-court.

time-out: Stoppage of play of a designated length. Either team may signal for a time-out when in possession of the ball. Time-outs are usually used to stop the clock or to discuss strategy.

tipoff: The start of a game. The ball is thrown in the air by the referee, and a player from each team tries to tip or bat the ball to a teammate.

travel: A violation that occurs when the player with the basketball moves his feet illegally. Common examples include running without dribbling (taking more than two steps), dragging the pivot foot from its original spot, or jumping in the air and landing without shooting or passing the ball.

trey: An oft-used slang term for a three-pointer.

turnover: On offense, to lose the ball to the defense without taking a shot. Examples include losing the ball out of bounds, violations such as traveling or double dribbling, or the defense intercepting an errant pass.

violation: An action that causes a team to lose possession of the ball, such as:

- **Throw-in violations:** Moving from the point of entry, tossing the throw-in over the backboard, carrying the ball onto the court without passing to a teammate, consuming more than five seconds from the time of receiving the ball from the official to the time of in-bounding the ball, throwing the ball so that it enters the basket prior to touching another player.
- **Traveling violations:** See *travel.*
- **Double dribbling violations:** See *double dribble.*
- **Three-second rule violation:** Remaining in your own team's free throw lane for three (or more) seconds.
- **Ten-second rule violation:** Taking ten (or more) seconds to advance the ball from the backcourt into the frontcourt.
- **Shot-clock violation:** Taking 35 (or more) seconds in men's college basketball, 30 seconds in women's college basketball, or 24 seconds in the NBA to attempt a shot.
- **Backcourt violation:** Bringing the ball into the backcourt after it enters the frontcourt.
- **Goaltending violation:** See *goaltending.*
- **Five-second rule violation:** Holding the ball in a closely guarded situation for five or more seconds.

weakside: The area of the court (right or left) opposite the side the ball is currently on.

wing: The area of the court on either side of the free throw line, outside the three-point arc.

Appendix B

The Essential Hoops Web Sites

espnet.sportszone.com: Where else to get fan polls and fast news and features on professional and college basketball than on ESPN SportsZone? Check out sportswriters and columnists such as Jeff Denberg.

griffith.dartmouth.edu/~douglas/superhoops.html: Douglas's SuperHoops program, designed much like the one the NBA stats crews use, lets you key in individual and team statistics while you watch a game. If you don't have a life, but do have a Mac, this one's for you.

www.ableague.com: The rebirth of women's professional basketball in the U.S. started here. This site carries information about all the teams, as well as a kids' club and a place to order gear.

www.bbhighway.com: Whatever you're looking for — instructional videos, books, even obscure items — it's all available here. This site also has great links for coaching clinics, a library, and chalk talks.

www.cbssportsline.com: Hard to beat the national lineup of writers and columnists — including Michael Jordan, who recently linked a ten-year deal with the network's online source of sports information.

www.cybersuperstores.com/ncaa/cover: NCAA and NBA videos of basketball championships, plus history videos of some of America's greatest teams and dynasties.

www.hoophall.com: This extremely well-organized site boasts offerings for the whole family, including a section on Hoops B.C. (that's Before the Clock for all you youngsters out there). With solid graphics, this site also has some of the best links collected in one place, with the major networks, tabloids, and team sites represented.

www.hoopshall.com: This site for the Indiana Basketball Hall of Fame has feature stories, plenty of history, and graphics as well as the lore that goes along with the state of legends.

www.hoopsnation.com: This group of guys fulfilled all basketball fans' dreams when they took a year to travel around the U.S. and play pickup games. This site chronicles their travels and serves as a diary and map of their favorite spots.

www.leaddogstats.com: Unless you are the lead dog, the view is always the same. . . . This site heralds itself as an amazing tool for basketball fans. Free downloads of stats so that you can track your fantasy team and compare your boneheaded McIllvanie-for-Olajuwon trade with your friends.

www.nando.net/sportserver/basketball/: Also known as The Basketball Server. This site offers information about NBA, WNBA, USBL, CBA, and NCAA basketball, as well as the PressBox Gang — links to a variety of articles about hoops and other sports.

www.nba.com: The official Mecca of basketball propaganda on all 29 NBA teams. This site includes RealAudio and video clips with both recent and historical pieces. Don't miss the coverage of the NBA playoffs with breakdowns of plays and action.

www.onhoops.com: A variety of essays, awards, opinions, and news items on the NBA from "Los Chucks." These guys really have it together and provide a cutting-edge perspective and humor in covering hoops. Readers can add their own writing samples to this eclectic collection.

www.opengym.com: Daily motivational messages and attitude adjustments that incorporate sport and sportsmanship. Post messages and congratulatory notes to friends and teammates in the Recess and Sidelines sections. Sign up for positive power-packed e-mails to get you through your season.

www.schick.com: Check out this site for information about the Super Hoops national 3-on-3 contest.

www.tsn.com or **www.sportingnews.com:** The site for *The Sporting News.* Get a daily dose of sarcasm with Fly and great coverage of both college and pro hoops.

www.usabasketball.com: This is the place to go for information about international basketball. From the Dream Team to the World University Games, this site provides bios, rules, schedules, and everything you need to know about the United States national teams and their opponents.

www.usatoday.com: A good source for news as it happens and national coverage of Olympic, pro, college, and elite high school programs. This is a must-visit site during March Madness.

www.wbasketballhof.com: The Women's Basketball Hall of Fame site is still growing. It features an online magazine with insightful and intriguing articles, as well as the Virtual Court and Booster Club. This site also has links to other sites devoted completely to women's basketball news.

www.wnba.com: Like the NBA site, boasts RealAudio and video clips for the eight Women's NBA teams and the players.

www.worldhoops.com: Fantasy hoops online, both college and pro. One of the most enjoyable games — give it a try!

Index

• Numbers •

• A •

• B •

(continued)

• E •

• G •

• N •

• p •

(continued)

• R •

• S •

• T •

• U •